Lands End to John O'Groats with a Bus Pass and a Dog

Lands End to John O'Groats with a Bus Pass and a Dog

Eric Newton

(and Archie)

authorHOUSE®

AuthorHouse™
1663 Liberty Drive
Bloomington, IN 47403
www.authorhouse.com
Phone: 1-800-839-8640

© 2011 by Eric Newton. All rights reserved.

No part of this book may be reproduced, stored in a retrieval system, or transmitted by any means without the written permission of the author.

First published by AuthorHouse   10/17/2011

ISBN: 978-1-4567-9675-4 (sc)
ISBN: 978-1-4567-9676-1 (ebk)

Printed in the United States of America

Any people depicted in stock imagery provided by Thinkstock are models, and such images are being used for illustrative purposes only.

Certain stock imagery © Thinkstock.

This book is printed on acid-free paper.

Because of the dynamic nature of the Internet, any web addresses or links contained in this book may have changed since publication and may no longer be valid. The views expressed in this work are solely those of the author and do not necessarily reflect the views of the publisher, and the publisher hereby disclaims any responsibility for them.

Contents

Acknowledgements ix
A Brief Resume..xi

PART 1. INTRODUCTION 1

Chapter 1: *THE IDEA* 2
Chapter 2: *ARCHIE*..5
Chapter 3: *THE BUS PASS HOLDER* 10
Chapter 4: *PLANNING THE JOURNEY*...............................15
Chapter 5: *WRITING THE BOOK* 21

PART 2. *ENGLAND—FROM LANDS END* 25

Chapter 1: *TRAVEL TO PENZANCE AND LANDS END—DAY 1* 26
Chapter 2: *PENZANCE TO NEWQUAY—DAY 2* 33
Chapter 3: *NEWQUAY TO TAUNTON—DAY 3* 44
Chapter 4: *TAUNTON TO SWINDON—DAY 4* 58
Chapter 5: *SWINDON TO NORTHAMPTON—DAY 5*..........72
Chapter 6: *NORTHAMPTON TO LINCOLN—DAY 6*...........92
Chapter 7: *LINCOLN TO SCARBOROUGH—DAY 7*.........125
Chapter 8: *SCARBOROUGH TO ALNWICK—DAY 8*........153
Chapter 9: *ALNWICK TO BERWICK—DAY 9* 185

PART 3. *SCOTLAND—TO JOHN O'GROATS* 207

Chapter 1: *PREPARTIONS AND TRAVEL UP TO BERWICK—DAY 10* 208
Chapter 2: *BERWICK-UPON-TWEED TO EDINBURGH—DAY 11.* 215
Chapter 3: *EDINBURGH TO DUNDEE—DAY 12.* 230

Chapter 4: *DUNDEE TO ABERDEEN—DAY 13.* 249
Chapter 5: *ABERDEEN TO INVERNESS—DAY 14* 264
Chapter 6: *INVERNESS TO JOHN O'GROATS AND THURSO—DAY 15.* 275
Chapter 7: *JOURNEY HOME—THURSO TO INVERNESS TO LINCOLN—BY TRAIN—DAYS 16 & 17* 292

PART 4. *SUMMARY AND FINAL THOUGHTS* 305

Chapter 1: *TRAVELS UP THROUGH ENGLAND* 306
Chapter 2: *TRAVELS UP SCOTLAND TO THE TOP* 321
Chapter 3: *SOME COMMENTS ON THE BUSES AND BUS STATIONS* 329
Chapter 4: *SOME COMMENTS ON MY "RANTS"* 333
Chapter 5: *FINAL THOUGHTS* 336

LIST OF RANTS 339

BUS JOURNEYS, TIMES AND MILEAGES 343

INDEX OF PLACES VISITED 349

Dedication

This book is dedicated to my Mother, who died in June 2009 aged 96 and who right up to her final days, gave me loving guidance, help and encouragement throughout my life. Thanks Mam.

WaterAid

All profits from the sale of this book are to be given to WaterAid, the charitable organisation set up in 1981 and supported by the UK water undertakings, water agencies and their staff together with many more.

WaterAid is an international non-governmental organisation focused exclusively on enabling the world's poorest communities to gain access to safe drinking water and sanitation. Approximately one billion people are without a clean drinking water supply and two billion people are without basic sanitation. A child dies every twenty seconds due to diarrhoeal diseases. Much time is spent on the collection of water and lost due to sickness and incapacitation that can be better used for education and other economic and social developments. The vision is a world where everyone has access to the basic human needs of clean drinking water and sanitation, which together with good hygiene, have a significant impact upon the reduction of illness and deaths.

Acknowledgements

In undertaking our bus journey, I am indeed grateful to the informative website titled "Public Transport Information" (www.carlberry.co.uk) that gives information of all the bus services from various destinations throughout Britain. This proved most useful during the planning stages of our trip. Also for the help and information obtained from the various Tourist Offices both in England and Scotland. The maps and information leaflets picked up were of great value. References in writing this book have also been made to a number of guide and reference books together with websites. I particular, I found the information supplied on the Wikipedia websites for the many places we visited and passed through of great help and am indebted to those who have contributed to the wealth of information contained on these web pages.

There are many people who have offered their help and advice to who I am grateful. In particular, I thank Sarah, a good friend who kindly proof read my initial draft, corrected much of my grammar and gave me encouragement to publish. My thanks also go to my daughter Jillian, who in addition to providing overnight accommodation when travelling through Somerset, as an author and illustrator of children's books, gave me much help and guidance. Thanks too to my brother-in-law Mike for the overnight accommodation at his home in Aberdeen. I must mention my son Keith, who first gave me the idea of undertaking this bus journey with my free bus pass and Archie my dog. There are a number of other people who have given me much encouragement in the writing this book, to all of whom I say thanks.

Without getting political, I suppose that I should also thank Gordon Brown, who as Chancellor at that time, did provide us "oldies" with free bus travel across the length and breadth of England, albeit with certain conditions applying. How long this free bus travel will last is another matter.

Finally my thanks to my wife Florence, who has put up and supported me and Archie in the preparation and undertaking of our bus trip and also in writing this book.

A Brief Resume

It was whilst talking with my son Keith that I mentioned that now that I had ceased working for a living, I was looking for something to do that would be different. With the introduction of "free bus passes" for the over 60's, it was he who suggested that I should travel from Lands End to John O'Groats using my bus pass. Also, so to be totally different, to take my dog Archie, a Jack Russell / cairn terrier cross, along with me. Sounded like a good idea especially as I enjoy travelling. So does Archie.

I was soon down to planning our bus journey from the most south westerly point of England to the most northerly in Scotland. My free bus pass was however valid for travel in England only and was restricted for use on local service buses, travelling in luxury by Intercity National Express was not allowed. In planning the route, I also tried to take in as many historic towns and cathedral cities as possible that would make our journey all that more interesting, taking time at each place to be able to walk around and explore. Having researched the possible local bus routes and timetables, together with suitable stopovers with dog-friendly accommodation, I eventually came up with a route that would take us on our twelve hundred plus mile journey north. Because of an impending knee operation, the trip was to be undertaken in two stages, Lands End to Berwick and then Berwick to John O'Groats with an eight month gap in between.

So it was in August 2008, Archie and I set out on the first stage of our epic bus journey from Lands End on a wet and windy afternoon. After a night's stay in Penzance, our journey across and up England took us through Truro, Newquay, Exeter, Taunton, Wells, Bath, Swindon, Oxford, Northampton, Leicester, Melton Mowbray and Grantham to my home city of Lincoln for a short break over the Bank Holiday weekend. Back on the bus, we then headed up the east coast via Hull, Scarborough, Middlesbrough, Durham and across the River Tyne into Newcastle where I was born and brought up. Finally our journey passed through Alnwick and along the North Northumbrian coastline to our destination at Berwick-upon-Tweed. Having successfully completed the first stage of our bus trip, it was back to Lincoln, this time using the railway.

Following my knee operation and the short winter days, it was in April 2009 that we took to the road again, or rather the bus. For our travels up Scotland, I would have to pay for my bus fare, my English bus pass not being eligible. Picking up where we left off the previous August, we set off from Berwick-upon-Tweed across the border and into Scotland. Calling in at Dunbar, we headed to Edinburgh for the first evening. Then it was over the Firth of Forth to Dunfermline, Glenrothes, Perth, Dundee and around the Angus coastline to Arbroath, Montrose and Aberdeen. Our route then cut across country to Banff and along the Moray coast to Elgin and Inverness. The final day of our journeyand possibly the most scenic, took us up the wild but beautiful coastline of Sutherland and Caithness passing through Dornoch and Wick before reaching our final destination at John O'Groats. At least the weather was much better than that when we set out the previous August and we were able to spend some time by the coast before proceeding west to Thurso, our overnight stay. Our train journey back the following day was equally as enjoyable passing through some magnificent countryside and crossing over the iconic Forth Railway Bridge.

The total mileage covered on our bus journey amounted to 1,230 miles, the direct route "as the crow flies" and as indicated by the sign posts at both Lands End and John O'Groats, being 874 miles. We did not rush our journey, taking time out to explore and enjoy many of the places we passed through. In total, we took the equivalent of thirteen days of bus travel to complete the whole trip up to John O'Groats. I know that a number of others have undertaken this bus journey using their "oldies" bus pass, some prior to myself. However, unless I am informed otherwise, I do believe that I am the first to complete the journey with a dog.

In writing up the story of our bus journey, I have included much historical information and points of interest concerning the cities, towns and villages that we passed through. Much of this information was unknown to myself before we set out and it makes you appreciate the wealth of archaeological, architectural and industrial heritage this Country has to offer. So too the wide variety of scenery across what is a relatively small island. Hopefully, it does not read too much like a travel log.

I have also included some of our experiences whilst travelling and of the people we met and encountered enroute. I mention in my book, that maybe because I am of a certain age, I have become a "grumpy old man" where certain things and the actions of some people, really do irritate and annoy me. Some of these annoyances that were observed and encountered on our trip, come out in the book, these I call "Rants" and are listed. When the revolution comes, these will be high on the agenda!

In writing this book, I have relived our bus journey traversing England from the most south-westerly tip up to the far north of Scotland. A number of places we passed by and called in at, I had not previously visited, which was a new experience. At many places we did not have sufficient time to fully explore but our brief call has wetted my appetite and given me a desire to revisit and spend more time looking around. Hopefully my accounts will have a similar affect on those reading my book to go out and explore this great Country of ours.

Eric Newton
February 2011

PART 1

INTRODUCTION

Chapter 1
The Idea

When I mentioned to a friend that I was about to write a book of my bus travels up the length of Britain with my dog, I was asked how I intended to begin my narrative. How about, it was suggested "Got on bus with dog". Why not indeed.

It all began with the then Chancellor of the Exchequer, Gordon Brown (soon to become Prime Minister), announced in his 2006 Budget address, that "from April 2008 at a cost of £250 million, for every pensioner and for disabled people (there would be) free off-peak national bus travel in every area of the country". He later added that this would exclude travel on the National Express bus services. At least for the likes of myself, there was something positive in that year's Budget even though we were being made to wait two years before being able to benefit.

For some years, we "oldies" had enjoyed the option of free bus travel on the local bus routes, but this area of free travel would be much more expansive. However, it subsequently turned out that the definition of "country" was for the likes of me living in Lincoln, for England only. This came as a bit of a disappointment as the inference in the Budget speech implied it was to be for the whole of the United Kingdom, or at least Great Britain. Perhaps the Chancellor had recalculated his sums and realised the potential costs. It was perhaps fortunate, that he did not see the "credit crunch" coming later in 2008.

At the time of the Chancellor's budget address, it was thought that the country-wide bus passes were to be for one year only, that is for pensioners in England and Wales. The Scots, it seems, had enjoyed free bus travel throughout Scotland for some time with those in Northern Ireland being able to travel throughout the length and breadth of the whole island of Ireland, this including the Republic. Another example of the English losing out, although it did subsequently turn out that the country-wide passes would go on into 2010 at least. However, with the huge national deficit following the credit crunch and the bank bail-outs of 2008/09, there were rumours that would be a review of this free "perk", although thankfully, this as yet has not materialised.

Nevertheless, as a pensioner myself and the possessor of an existing local bus pass for "senior citizens" (how I dislike that term), I looked forward to receiving my new country-wide, or rather England-wide, bus pass for use on and after 1st April 2008.

I have mentioned that like many others, I already had a bus pass that I could use for travel throughout the County of Lincolnshire. I well remember going down to the Council Offices when applying for my free bus pass and having my photograph taken, where I was instructed to sit before this contraption that would both take my photograph and prepare an encapsulated card with my name and photo on it. With aging and creaky knees, I lowered myself into the chair still wincing, when a blinding flash shot across my profile. No opportunity for gathering one's composure or getting comfortable, no chance to brush one's hair (not that I have much) and no option of a second shot. With an expiry date on the card of 2010, it seemed that I would have to live with this photo, which I can only liken to a convicted prisoner entering jail for a long term. However, with the announcement that new country-wide bus passes were to be issued, I had hoped for a second chance for a photo-shot. But no, the existing photos were to be reused on the new passes, the expiry date not being until 2013!!

Living in the Cathedral City of Lincoln, I had over the past years, made much use of my bus pass since passing the magical age of 65. Being retired and not tied down in having to report in at the office anymore during weekdays, I would on a fine day during the summer months, catch the Lincolnshire Road Car bus to Skegness or Cleethorpes. The ten o'clock bus from Lincoln, would be packed with pensioners. On the top deck of the bus, there would be a sing-a-along with an accordion player at the front and the driver calling the numbers for bingo for those sitting below—if only!! Nothing like a trip to the seaside on a fine day, especially when travelling was free, being able to paddle in the sea and enjoy the obligatory bag of fish and chips and ice cream. Some of the best fish and chips in the country are prepared and sold at Cleethorpes, the fishing port of Grimsby being next door.

Now we have a small dog called Archie. He is a cross between a Jack Russell and a Cairn Terrier—more about him and how we came to acquire him later. Like most dogs of his type, he requires plenty of exercise and he also likes splashing about in water. So, on my trips to the seaside, he always comes with me. From the top deck of the bus, he enjoys the journeys, taking in the countryside views and the goings on in the villages as we pass through. The only trouble is that whilst I go free, I have to pay for him—50 pence!!—each way!! Scandalous!!

It was over a pint of beer with my son, Keith, when we were talking about doing something different, that he suggested "why not travel the length of the Country from Lands End to John O'Groats using your bus pass and why not take Archie with you?" At the time, this was laughed off as a joke, but later, I gave it some serious thought. Why not indeed? It would be a bit of a challenge. Archie enjoys travelling whether it be by car or bus and it would certainly be something different. Some may think that it is a bit sad to have to resort to travelling the length of the Country by service bus to find a challenge, but that is what it turned out to be.

Gordon Brown's Budget Statement about free national bus travel, as it later turned out, had certain provisos. Firstly, it seemed that this was to be for one year only, commencing April 2008 although this was subsequently found not to be the case. Secondly, it applied only to local service buses and not to the National Express buses. Thirdly, it could not be used before 9.30 am on weekdays. Finally, it only applied to the "country" in which you resided, in my case England. So, instead of free travel from Lands End to John O'Groats, it would be only from Lands End to Berwick-upon-Tweed and using off-peak local bus services only. Nevertheless, it still turned out to be 740 miles of free travel on our bus trip from Lands End.

Chapter 2
Archie

Next, may I introduce you to Archie, our eight year old terrier cross. Archie arrived on this Earth following an impromptu liaison between my wife's sister's Cairn terrier Bramble, and a Jack Russell bitch called Pippa, on the sea front at Gosport, Hants.

My sister-in-law was walking along the seafront one day exercising Bramble, when she briefly stopped to chat with the owner of the Jack Russell, both dogs being on their leads. On walking away, she released Bramble off his lead who immediately made a "U" turn, heading straight back in a bee-line, to the female Jack.

It transpired that Pippa's owner was not too bothered as they had been trying to mate their pedigree dog for some time without success. However, soon the two dogs were locked together and being unsuccessful in trying to separate them, they had to be thrown into the sea to be parted. My sister-in-law was mortified by the whole proceedings and Bramble was literally "in the dog house". Not so with my brother-in-law when he returned home from work, who exclaimed "that's my boy". The upshot of the liaison on Gosport beach, was that on the 31st August 2000, Pippa delivered five pups, one dog and four bitches.

Pippa's owners kept in touch and kindly invited us around to see the five puppies. It just so happened that we were returning from a holiday abroad and were in Gosport at the time. So we went to see the five puppies—a fatal move. We previously had had cats but not dogs and were not necessarily looking to acquire a new pet. However, we were bowled over on seeing these five delightful little creatures and it was Archie, the single male dog, who choose us, nestling up against the feet of my wife, Florence. With the kind agreement of Pippa's owners, he was ours. As all five pups were still being weaned, it would be a few weeks before we were able to collect him and this resulted in another visit down to Gosport.

After a fair amount of deliberation, we both had agreed on the name of Archie, for no obvious reasons but because it sounded OK and was a bit different. Soon we were back in Gosport to collect Archie. The car journey back to Lincoln was some 220 miles and to our amazement and relief, young Archie made the trip without a murmur. Our life was to change a lot. With our children now all adults and having "flown the nest", we now had a new addition to our household.

From an early age, Archie has always been a lively dog though he has never been deliberately destructive. Whilst still a puppy, he was taken to training / obedience classes which were organised by a local professional dog trainer. Here he learnt a number a basic commands and discipline. He soon picked up certain words in English, of which some, like "cat" need to be spelt C-A-T rather than said out loud. Whenever we are about to go out, he is always there expecting to come with us. If he is to remain, he is told "Sorry Archie, but you're looking after the house" at which point he turns about, tail between his legs and slowly but reluctantly returns to his favourite beanbag in the corner of the lounge. When we return, he is there waiting for us at the door.

He is a good catcher of tennis balls when thrown up in the air, leaping up to catch them in his mouth after the first bounce. Also, he has good reactions in catching his night-time gravy bones treats when tossed to him. I feel that he would do well in the cricket field. He has a good sense of smell, always able to find his ball in dense undergrowth and often coming out of the thicket with other dogs' lost balls that he has found. It is a while since we have had to buy him any new balls to play with. He has his favourite toys, especially those that make a noise, although I have taken the squeaking widget out of most of them because of the continuous irritating noise he inflicts upon us, especially in the evening when watching television. He enjoys a bit of "rough and tumble" but has never spoilt or damaged any carpets, furnishings or other household items. We are very fortunate in that respect. This is not to say that he has not caused me any trouble.

It was whilst he was still a puppy, yet to reach his first birthday, that I was walking him one summer's evening in Hartsholme Country Park in Lincoln, which was once the grounds of a stately home. Forming part of the grounds is a large artificial lake that in the late 1800's, acted as a reservoir, providing a drinking water supply to the City of Lincoln. Along the downstream side of the lake is a long (not particular high) embankment with a brick wall and protruding piers, this being on the water face of the old dam. The top of this wall is approximately three feet above the footpath running along the top of the bank and nearly five feet down to the water on the other side. Now Archie liked to walk along the top of this wall and around the piers. I normally had him on the lead, but foolishly, this day he was not. To my anguish, on this particular summer's evening, he spied a ball floating in the water below and before I could catch him, he had jumped in off the top of the wall into the water below.

Now Archie is a good swimmer and enjoys the water, but the problem was that with the vertical five feet of brick wall, he could not get out. He was beginning to panic, clawing away at the face of the brick wall. I could not reach him from the top of the wall and left any longer, he would surely drown. So there was nothing else for it. Off came my shoes, socks and trousers and in I jumped, not knowing the depth of the water. Fortunately, there was an accumulation of tree branches that had built up over the years against the old dam wall and the depth of water only came up to my middle. I should mention at this point, that it was a quiet evening with no one else around. I grabbed hold of Archie and in my annoyance, threw him up and over the top of the brick wall back onto the path. It was at this point that I realised that I now had a problem. Although I could reach the top of the brick wall, there were no handholds to assist me to pull myself out. I then remembered that at the mid point of the embankment, there was an overflow that formed a low point where I could climb out. The only problem was that I had to work my way some distance along the wall and around two protruding brick piers to get to this point of escape.

I was treading barefooted on submerged tree branches along the wall with Archie barking at me from the top of the wall, when I suddenly realised, that my wallet, mobile telephone and car keys were in my trousers that I had hastily cast aside on the footpath. It was then with some urgency that I made my way along to the overflow point. Nearing my escape point and with Archie still barking, a voice from above said "Are you alright down there?" It was a fellow dog walker, mildly amused at my situation and offering his help. My mind was still focused on whether my trousers were untouched, so my response was "Thanks, I am nearly there, but can you see my trousers lying further along the footpath" Thankfully, they were and it was with some relief that I clambered out of the lake and retrieved my personal belongings intact. It was an uncomfortable drive home, wet, shirtless and trouserless, but at least Archie was still with us. Needless to say, whenever I walk him along that embankment, he is now always on his lead.

Another occasion when he caused me trouble was during the following winter months when I had taken him to another local Country Park at Whisby, just to the south of Lincoln. This had recently been developed and landscaped, with the aid of an EU grant, from a number of disused gravel pits. There are a number of walks around the various lakes that are very popular with bird watchers. For most of the walks, dogs need to be kept on the lead, but for one route, dogs are allowed off their leads. As soon as we get onto this walk, off comes his lead and away he goes, like a "bat out-of-hell" making a bee-line for the water, where without stopping, he jumps straight in for swim.

On this particular day in January, the temperatures were below freezing with a layer of ice covering the surface of the lake. Because of the bushes screening the lake, I had not realised this before releasing Archie off his lead. Instead of jumping into the water, Archie found himself skating about over the ice. He was quite enjoying himself, until through the thin ice layer he went. Here he was in another predicament, as he was unable to climb out of the hole in the ice he had broken through.

Fortunately, he was not too far out from the edge of the lake and there happened to be an overhanging bush. So again, off came my shoes, socks and trousers and with the aid of the overhanging bush, I was able to break the ice with my heel to make a passage for him to swim out. Another close call. It was with some embarrassment that I was met by three other dog walkers when climbing out of the lake. They seemed to find the situation amusing, me with no trousers on in sub-zero temperatures!

Being a terrier, he instinctively chases the squirrels (grey only in our area) when off the lead, especially at the local country parks where there are squirrels in abundance and considered as pests. As soon as he sees a squirrel, he is off like a shot, barking as he chases his prey. With all his barking, he will never catch one as with all the advanced warning, they are off up a nearby tree to seek refuge. It always reminds me of police cars speeding to crime scenes with their sirens blaring, giving similar advanced warning to criminals that they are on their way.

Perhaps because of his early initiation to long distance car travel, he is never any problem in the car when we have a long journey to make. On one occasion, Archie and I had to join my wife Florence in Northern Ireland, who had taken the car with her a few days earlier. Being unable to take him on a flight, we had to travel by train to Stranraer and then by ferry to Belfast. The train journey from Lincoln via Doncaster, Edinburgh, Glasgow to Stranraer was fine with Archie, settling down and enjoying the views. However for the sea crossing, he was confined to a special dog cage for the hour and a half crossing. This he did not enjoy and was very pleased to be released when we reached port in Belfast.

Archie generally gets on alright with most other dogs, although he does object when some start sniffing his hind-quarters, which I feel is quite understandable. My daughter's dog Bob (a collie) and step-daughter's dog Huey (another Jack Russell), are perhaps his best friends which he wrestles with and chases. There are also a number of other dogs belonging to friends with which he enjoys playing. However, now being middle aged, he is perhaps not as boisterous that he once was and maybe less tolerant. Nevertheless, he is still very active and is always ready when it is time for his walks. I put this down partly to him being regularly exercised.

Being a cross between a Jack Russell and Cairn terrier, the markings and traits of both breeds can be seen in Archie. He is about the size of a Cairn but his head and muzzle are the shape of a Jack Russell. He has a fairly thick russet-brown coat with the protruding velvety black ears of a Cairn. He also has a relatively long bushy tail that sticks up in the air and is untypical of either breed. His temperament is certainly similar to that of a Jack, always sniffing different scents and chasing squirrels, rabbits, and any other similar animal that moves, including cats given the opportunity.

He has been described by passers-by as an "Alsatian with his legs sawn-off" and compared to the puppet "Basil Brush". I suppose that with his russet-brown coat and long bushy tail, there are some close resemblances to that of a fox, although his legs are much shorter. Perhaps we should have called him "Basil", although calling out his name at the park might have been a bit embarrassing, especially for my wife, who may have been thought to have taken over the role of Sybil Fawlty.

All in all, he is fairly obedient and well behaved and compared to the problems experienced by others, I guess that we are fortunate insomuch as he causes us little bother.

Chapter 3

The Bus Pass Holder

I have been putting off writing this chapter to the very end. What does one write about oneself? (sounds very Victorian). Well, let us start off with some of the basics. My apologies in advance if this turns out to be a mini autobiography—you can always skip this Chapter if you wish.

I am a white Caucasian male born and bred in the North-East of England and for the past forty plus years, have lived in the cathedral City of Lincoln. You will have already gathered that I am retired and over the age of 65. Born close to the banks of the Tyne, I still classify myself as being a "Geordie" although my accent has since been diluted, albeit folk still recognise me as being from the North-East.

I am old enough to still remember the war years, hearing enemy aircraft flying overhead, ration books and the victory celebrations. I had a relatively happy childhood, playing with my friends on the local bombsites and when the war was over, on the nearby beaches and sea cliffs. I guess that we were quite inventive and to some degree adventurous in those days in some of the games we played and activities we got up to. Most would be a big "no no" these days because of health and safety issues, but we never experienced any serious injuries, only a few cuts and bruises.

We were living in the village of Cullercoats that is sandwiched between Tynemouth and Whitley Bay on the North East coast. The old fishing village has its own harbour and sandy bay protected by two piers (good for diving from) and backed by sandstone cliffs (good for climbing). At that time, the village had its own small fishing fleet, with the fishermens' cobbles (boats) hauled up onto the backshore. The village also had its own RNLI off-shore lifeboat, which was manned by the local fishermen. One thing that we were not short of in those days was fresh fish. For seamen and radio operators in particular, Cullercoats was best known for it maritime radio broadcasting station, that sadly is no-more. Over the years the village has greatly expanded, resulting now in a continuous housing belt along this part of the coastal strip.

On leaving school with a bunch of GEC "O" passes that I had struggled to obtain, it was by chance that I found myself entering the world of civil engineering with a firm of engineering consultants based in Newcastle. This followed on from advice and introductions made by a close friend of the family, to whom I shall be ever grateful. Despite the fact that the whole of my immediate family were involved in shipbuilding, it seemed at that time, I was heading for a career in banking. "Don't go into engineering lad" I remember my Grandfather saying, he being a foreman in the shipyards and who had experienced the hard times of the 1930's. I have always thought that at some time during their lifetime, everyone of us has at least one lucky break. I always consider this introduction by our family friend towards a career in civil engineering, was mine.

Most of my work was centred around the shipyards on Tyneside with the building of new drydocks, quays, fabrication sheds, etc, so I suppose that I was in a way carrying on in the family tradition. In 1961, I changed tracks and obtained employment with the local Water Board. It was also the year I got married. Life was good, although we had little spare cash to spend on life's luxuries. Soon I started to get itchy feet and was applying for other jobs, both at home and further afield. As a result, I was offered a post working on a major water supply scheme in Grimsby, Lincolnshire. So in late 1964, we moved, lock stock and barrel down to Grimsby, or rather Cleethorpes, which is next door.

The general impression of Lincolnshire is of boring flat fenlands, especially to those who have not visited the County. To my surprise on our arrival, there were the rolling hills of the Lincolnshire Wolds and some pleasant sandy beaches along the coast. At that time during the 1960's, the area around Grimsby was experiencing an economic boom, with new businesses being set up and the petro-chemical industries along the South Humber Bank expanding. The work that I was to be employed on was to provide new piped water supplies to these new and expanding industries. The fishing industry was also still vibrant and provided much work in the area. This of course was before the Cod Wars and the imposition of the EU Fishing Quotas. Coming from the North East, I had never seen so much cash in circulation. We soon settled into our new home in Cleethorpes and found the local people most welcoming and friendly. I have many happy memories of the three years we lived in Grimsby and still treasure the friendships that were made there.

The project upon which I had been employed, was soon coming to an end. So it was back to looking at the "situations vacant" columns. Work was becoming less plentiful for civil engineers in the late 1960's, so it was by good fortune that I found employment in 1967 with the then Water Board in Lincoln, later to become part of Anglian Water. Having planned to be there for only three to four years before moving on again, we have remained in Lincoln ever since.

At that time, there were a large number of engineering, forge and fabrication works in Lincoln, manufacturing large diesel engines, cranes, excavators, boilers, crankshafts, land drainage pumps, mining equipment, braking equipment, cast iron fittings, belt drives and a number of other engineering products. The first tank was designed and manufactured in Lincoln for use in the First World War. Sadly most of these engineering industries have now long gone, along with such names as Ruston and Hornsby, Ruston Bucyrus, Robey, Gywnne, Clayton, etc.

With major reorganisations at work, I was never sure where I would be next or if I would still have a job. I was perhaps fortunate in that I was kept in employment and that my work permitted me to continue to live in Lincoln. This was a blessing inasmuch that it caused minimal disruption to my family. By this time, we had three children, two boys (Ian and Keith) and a girl (Jillian) who were all at school. The work was interesting and challenging involving the design and construction of major water supply projects throughout Lincolnshire. The camaraderieship within the engineering office was great and I look back to realise that I was so fortunate in having such a great bunch of workmates around me.

However, my career was also soon to change. About every third year, my employer kept introducing so-called efficiency measures, resulting in reorganisations and staff cuts. By 1995, I had had enough and volunteered for early retirement. Although I enjoyed the engineering aspects of my work, the bureaucracy and administration that came with the management side of my job, was getting me down. The following year, I left my full-time employment with the Water Company and became my own free agent.

Being still in my late 50's, I wasn't quite yet ready to pack away my slide-rule and get out my slippers. Within a week, I found myself employed on a part-time basis, with a firm of Danish consultants, working primarily in Eastern European countries of the former Soviet Union and the Balkans. No more bureaucracy and unnecessary admin, just plain engineering that I had been trained to do and enjoyed. With the advent of computers and the internet, I was able to undertake most of my work from home, with overseas visits of two to three weeks at any one time to the towns and cities where I was advising on water supply matters.

My employment with the Danish consultant was dependant upon available work, which at first involved more than half of my time. Over the years, the workload has gradually reduced so that today, I am now fully retired, which suits me fine. The past twelve years have been an enjoyable experience, working in places that I would not otherwise have visited and meeting and working with people of different nationalities. Even in my late years, it has broadened my views of the world and some of its problems, especially in Russia itself and the Balkans.

Whilst both at and since leaving school, I have enjoyed participating in the game of rugby football, both on and off the field. On leaving school, I joined my local club in the North-East and on moving to Grimsby and then to Lincoln, joined the rugby clubs there too. In addition to providing some activity away from work, I have established many long-lasting friendships through playing rugby. As well as trotting out onto the pitch most Saturdays, a number of us managed to get tickets and were able to attend some of the England international games, home and away. This was during the 1970's and 80's when attending international matches was affordable and good fun. To this day, I still enjoy a pint with some of my old rugby-playing mates, reminiscing and talking of past encounters. Perhaps Will Carling, the former England skipper had the right phrase for us, when he used the term "old f**ts".

During my earlier years, I was involved with the Boy Scout movement and managed to become a Queen Scout, one of the very first in 1953 (they were previously Kings Scouts). Scouting introduced me to the outside life and in particular, to walking the fells and climbing mountains, especially in the Lake District and Scotland. I managed to introduce both of my sons when they were in their teens to the outdoor life and was able to spend a week away each year with them, either fell walking or walking one of Britain's long distance footpaths.

I became very familiar with the Lakeland Fells, have visited all 127 summits over 2,000 feet. So it was too with the mountains of North Wales and the Highlands of Scotland. During the 1990's, my sights started to focus further afield with trekking holidays to the Nepalese Himalayas, Patagonian Andes and Mounts Kenya and Kilimanjaro in East Africa. Kilimanjaro at 19,331 feet above sea level, is the highest that I have been. With my youngest son Keith, we have managed a few peaks in the Alps, Pyrenees and the High Tatras of Slovakia. Now with two new knees (which I put down to years of abuse in playing rugby and climbing mountains), my days on the fells are much reduced although the memories are very much still alive. I still have an ambition to climb one last Munro (a 3,000 foot Scottish peak) before they assign me to a wheelchair. Maybe with some assistance, I might make it.

Faced with little now to do to stimulate my "grey matter", I have decided to go back to college and undertake a course of studies in geo-sciences with the Open University. Studying is interesting and challenging but taking the exams is a different matter. However, so far so good. Embarking on my bus journey with Archie and writing this book has also provided a challenge and occupied much of my spare time. That and taking Archie for his daily exercises and trying to catch up with the many jobs that need doing around the house, keep me busy. It is a just as well that I am now not working. It's an old cliché but "I really don't know how I found time to go to work".

Chapter 4
Planning The Journey

The original plan, was to travel from Land's End to John O'Groats in one go thinking that I would be able to use my bus pass for the complete journey, as intimated in Gordon Brown's 2008 Budget speech. However, with the realisation that free bus travel was to be restricted to England only, some rethinking was necessary. Should I terminate my journey at the Scottish Border at Berwick, or should I continue north through Scotland to John O'Groats as originally planned, albeit I should have to pay my way north of the Border.

It didn't require a serious deliberation to decide to go the whole way, as for a start, the title of the book would have to be "Lands End to Berwick-upon-Tweed with a Bus Pass and a Dog". I think you will agree, that it does not have the same impact. I did think that there may be some travel concessions for "oldies" like myself in Scotland, but being English, perhaps this was wishful thinking and too much to be expected from the Scots.

The first task in planning my trip, was to decide upon the route we were to take across England and up Scotland. My route across England would have to pass through Lincoln of course so that I would be able to pick up some clean clothes and also take advantage of a free night's accommodation—also to report in. My daughter Jill lived in North Somerset, near Taunton, so to take advantage again of free accommodation, Taunton too would need to be included. I had in mind to take in as many historic towns and cities as were possible, so again this in part influenced the route especially across England.

I needed to consult the timetables of the service buses and find out the available bus routes across the Country. Here the internet came in useful, being able to access the appropriate web-sites and click on the routes available. I had in mind to travel through Plymouth on leaving Penzance in the south-west, but was very surprised to find that there were no service bus connections between the two towns. On "trawling through the net", the only way that I could get out of Cornwall without resorting to the National Express buses, was via Newquay via Launceston to Exeter. I also would have liked to have included York in my travels, but again found a lack of bus services that would take us north of York to Teeside. With calling in at Lincoln, the alternative route was obvious, that being over the Humber Bridge to Hull and up the east coast via Scarborough.

So, after studying the alternatives and attempting to make our journey as interesting as possible, I settled on a route across England from Lands End via Penzance, Truro, Newquay, Exeter, Taunton, Wells, Bath, Swindon, Oxford, Northampton, Leicester, Grantham, Lincoln, Hull, Scarborough, Middlesborough, Durham, Newcastle and Alnwick, finishing up at Berwick-upon-Tweed.

Up Scotland, the route from Berwick seemed obvious, following the east coast virtually all the way through Edinburgh, Dundee, Aberdeen and Inverness to the top at John O'Groats. My Brother-in-law Mike had a house in Aberdeen, so again there was an offer of accommodation for the night.

The next task was to decide where we should stop both en-route and overnight. As mentioned previously, there would be three locations where free accommodation was available, so that was a starter. Also, I had to take into account Archie would require exercising and that it would unfair to keep him on the bus for too long a period. I tried to avoid more than two hours travel on any one bus journey, but where this was difficult, had a maximum of three hours. It turned out that there would be two journeys of three hours duration, one of which was unavoidable. This was from Newquay to Exeter with only three buses a day, although we did have a long stop at Okehampton that gave us a five minute opportunity to stretch our legs. The other was from Montrose to Aberdeen a journey that with hindsight, should have been broken at Stonehaven, but time did not allow.

The timing of the buses was also crucial so to allow us time to explore the places of interest and catch our next connection. I did not want our journey to be rushed as firstly, Archie needed exercising and secondly, I wanted time to explore the towns and cities we were passing through, some of which I had never been to before.

With the above parameters in place, I finally fixed our overnight stays starting in Penzance, then Newquay, Taunton, Swindon, Northampton, Lincoln, Scarborough and Alnwick for the first stage of our journey across England. For the next stage, we would start off by staying in Berwick, then Edinburgh, Dundee, Aberdeen, Inverness and finally Thurso, just along the coast from John O'Groats.

The stopping off points could remain flexible but we could take in Truro, Exeter, Wells, Bath, Oxford, Melton Mowbray, Grantham, Bridlington, Durham and Newcastle on the way across England to Berwick. The Scottish section would take in Dunbar, Dunfermline, Perth, Arbroath, Montrose, Banff, Elgin, Dornoch and Wick before we reached John O'Groats in the far north.

Our route looked as if it was settled and finalised, meeting most of the objectives that I had set out. The next task was to arrange overnight accommodation, bearing in mind that I had a dog with me and understandably, not too many hoteliers accepted dogs. On the English leg of my trip, I decided to pre-book accommodation at Penzance and Newquay only for the journey up to Lincoln, as there might be some hiccups on my travel plans as we progressed. I was equipped with the telephone numbers of the various Tourist Information Offices and could arrange accommodation for the night with the use of my mobile phone. This proved not as simple as I had envisaged, especially as I was looking for somewhere that would accept dogs. As a result for subsequent stops from Lincoln northwards, including Scotland, I pre-booked our overnight accommodation before leaving home.

Pre-booking accommodation wasn't really too much of a problem, even for my England trip which was undertaken during August. The assistance given by the various Tourist Information Offices was excellent and I thank them very much for their help in guiding me to the right places. My trip up Scotland was to be undertaken some eight months later in April of the following year. By this time, I had been "surfing the net" and found an excellent web-site that identified not only availability and price, but also dog-friendly hotels and B&Bs, with booking being on-line.

Besides fixing a time and date to travel, the only other task was how to get to Lands End and back from John O'Groats, or rather Thurso. Also as I was to break my journey at Berwick, the arrangements had to include travel from and later back up to the border Town. The obvious answer was by using the train. It so happens that there was a direct train service from Sheffield (approximately a hour's car ride from Lincoln) to Penzance although the time taken was more than seven hours. However, it turned out that we had need to visit my wife's relations in Gosport (Archie's birthplace) in August 2008. Accordingly, I took the opportunity to travel to Penzance to start our trip by catching the west-coast train at Salisbury and changing at Exeter. Coming back from Berwick was relatively easy, using the main east-coast line and changing at Doncaster for Lincoln.

For the Scottish part of our trip, travelling back up to Berwick didn't present a problem, but getting back from Thurso was a long journey, albeit a very scenic one. With Archie in tow, it was too much to try to attempt in one day, so an overnight stop on the way back would be necessary. This was to be in Inverness, which allowed us time in Thurso and also to enjoy the scenic rail trip down the north-east coast of Scotland. The following day, the train journey from Inverness to Lincoln was achievable in one day, calling in at Perth, Edinburgh, Newcastle, Doncaster and Retford, some five stops in all but sufficient to take in some air and for Archie to "cock his leg". I had obtained a Senior Railcard for a modest sum that was valid for 12 months. This I was able to use on both my trips and which entitled me to a 33% discount on normal fares, which resulted in an appreciable saving. I was also able to make further savings on my Scottish rail journeys by booking on-line using the internet. It subsequently turned out that the cost of travelling by rail in Scotland worked out to be a third of that by bus, with no concessions being given by the bus companies. Who said that it was cheaper to travel by bus?

My final decision was when to travel. I had already decided to undertake our trip in two stages, breaking our journey just south of the English / Scottish border at Berwick-upon-Tweed.

I had had more than 12 months to plan my bus journey and had originally scheduled the English leg of my trip during June 2008, this being before the school holidays and the month of the long days. However, this plan was subsequently "knocked on the head" due to unforeseen family circumstances and commitments. July was out as I was undertaking an Open University course in geology that had its Summer School during that month. Later in the month of July, I was scheduled to go into hospital for my second knee replacement operation, the first having been undertaken the previous year. So on the face of it, August and September would also be out. It was looking like October at the earliest although the short days and indifferent weather at that time of year would be make the trip less enjoyable. Also I might not have fully recovered from my knee operation. March 2009 was also a possibility, but again, the short days were not good. We would also be away all February for a family wedding in Australia that we were combining with a trip to New Zealand. To embark on this epic cross country bus trip after being away "down under" for four weeks, did not sound like a good idea. It was looking as though I would have to defer my trip until later in 2009. At first, I thought that I might miss out on the free country-wide travel perk across England, but it was later confirmed that this was to be extended into subsequent years. So it was looking like both stages of our trip were going to take place during the following year in 2009.

My knee operation was scheduled for Friday, the 30th July. Reporting in and prepared to be wheeled into the operating theatre, dressed in my hospital gown and with a big black arrow marked on the upper part of my leg indicating the correct knee, I was informed that, due to sickness, there was insufficient qualified theatre staff available that day. I was to return home when another date would be fixed. After psyching myself up for the operation, it was, to say the least, a bit of an anticlimax. However, every cloud has a silver lining.

My operation was to be deferred for 6 weeks to the beginning of September. This would allow time to do our planned bus trip from Land's End to Berwick-upon-Tweed during August. The section northwards to John O'Groats would have to wait until 2009, although this would have no bearing on my free bus travel. As mentioned previously, we had need to visit relations down on the south coast of England during August, so this seemed to present a good time to commence my trip by first taking the train to Penzance. The start date was Sunday 17th August 2008, which besides the train journey to Penzance, included the short trip there and back to Lands End. Five days were taken to reach Lincoln, where we had a five night stop so to avoid the Bank Holiday weekend. We then continued on up to Berwick, arriving on the 30th August, with bus travel taking two and a half days. Allowing for say half a day travelling to Lands End on Day One, the total time taken up on our bus journey between Lands End and Berwick, across and up England, worked out to be eight days.

Stage Two of our bus trip was to be sometime in 2009. So as not allow too long a gap between the two stages, I subsequently decided to go for the second phase of our journey from Berwick to John O'Groats commencing on a Saturday in April 2009. Eight months had elapsed since my knee operation and although not fully fit, it was working well enough for me to travel without a stick. The first day was taken up by travelling to Berwick, so our actual bus journey up through Scotland commenced the following day on Sunday 26th April 2009. Our trip up to the top northerly coast took five days, reaching John O' Groats on Thursday 30th April 2009.

So when asked how long did it take for us to travel from Lands End to John O'Groats by bus, the answer is "thirteen days", which excludes the time getting to and from the starting and finishing points. It could of course have been done over a shorter period but firstly, I had to consider Archie and not subject him to long continuous journeys on the bus. Secondly, I wanted to explore the places that we were to visit and not just to rush through without stopping. I feel our bus journey was all the more pleasurable for this.

Chapter 5
Writing The Book

My initial task was to set out how the book was to be presented. Not having written a book before, it seemed to me that it should be in four parts, the first being the "Introduction", followed by the first stage of my trip from "Lands End to Berwick-upon-Tweed", then the second stage between "Berwick-upon-Tweed to John O'Groats". The final part would be a "Summary and Final Thoughts" to conclude our experiences and the book. Having been used to writing report studies over the years associated with my work, I have included some appendices at the end, which give the details of my travels and places visited. A selection of photographs are also included.

The big mistake that I made was not to write the English section of our journey immediately after completing it and whilst I could still remember the details. With other commitments, not least my OU exams, this was put off until later—a fatal error. It was not until I arrived home from the second stage of our trip up Scotland, that I started to "put pen to paper" or rather to get out my laptop. Because this section of our journey was recent and still fresh in my memory, I began on this part of my narrative first—another mistake and an indication of my lack of experience "in this field". Although I have tried to avoid it, the reader may notice that there maybe more detail of the second stage of our travels in Scotland than when travelling through England. My apologies if this appears so.

I also decided that I should write the book in the "plural" using the words "we, us and ours" rather than "I, me and mine". After all, there were two of us travelling and Archie being an intelligent little dog, needs to be included, especially as the book is partly about him. In one "doggie" book that I read recently, it was written as if by the dog itself using the words "I" and "me" with the owner being referred to only as "the Man". Perhaps the author got his priorities right, but I will not follow the same example.

The next was to decide the "tense" I was to use in my writings. Initially, I felt it would read best if I used the "immediate past tense" when writing up our travels. However, it became apparent that this would not work in all places and I have decided to adopt the "present tense" as if I was writing the book as we were travelling. For the final Part, the Summary, I have adopted the past tense for what I hope are obvious reasons. I am sure there are places where I may have got this wrong, but please bear with me.

Being retired and of a "certain age", I still have some problems in coming to terms with the new metric units of measurement and weights. Even whilst working, I was constantly converting measurements back into the old Imperial equivalents, which I could at least, visualise. I am also against anything that comes out of the EU and take exception to being forced to use the continental system of weights and measures. So throughout this book, all references to measurements and weights are in the good old-fashioned Imperial units of feet and inches, miles, acres and pounds weight. I make no apology for this. For those of you young enough to have brought up with only the Metric system and for those of you who have forgotten the workings of the old Imperial units of measurement, the following may serve as a useful conversation guide.

12 inches = 1 foot = 0.305 metres
3 feet = 1 yard = 0.914 metres
1 mile = 1,760 yards = 5,280 feet = 1.609 kilometres
1 acre = 4,840 square yards = 0.405 hectares
1 ton = 20 hundredweight (cwt) = 1.016 tonne
1 pounds weight (lbs) = 0.454 kilograms

I hope that this helps, but you may need to get out your calculator.

I have also used the "twenty-four hour clock" when giving times of the buses, etc, without in most cases, the numbers being followed by the word "hours". As a result, the reference to "am" and "pm" have been avoided so to avoid any misunderstanding.

When writing this book, I have attempted to include a brief history of the villages, towns and cities which we visited and passed through on our travels, together with points and places of interest associated with each location. It may be that the book reads a bit like a travel guide across England and up through Scotland, but I make no apologies for this. One of the pleasures in making this journey was to take in the history, traditions and heritage of our Country. For a relatively small island such as ours, there is a great wealth. I have also attempted to bring out the joy in admiring the varied scenery from the gently rolling hills and pastures of

England to the mountains and rugged coastlines of Scotland. Hopefully, by the time you have read through this book (if you make it to the end), the reader will have picked up some tit-bits of useless information that may well come in handy when playing Trivial Pursuit or taking part in a pub quiz. You may even be tempted to visit some of the places and enjoy the sights yourself, if in the area.

Much of the detailed information included in the book has been gleaned from pamphlets and other literature picked up at the many Tourist Information Offices that I called in at and my thanks for all the help and assistance that the staff gave me at these offices. Also from various guide books and in particular from the Wikipedia web-sites on the internet that contain a wealth of information on each village, town and city visited. Here I would mention that the populations given against the cities, towns and villages visited, have for the most part, been taken from the Wikipedia web-sites in which the numbers given are generally from the 2001 census. Since that time there have been significant increases in the population levels at some places visited, so my apologies for any inaccuracies. Finally, much information was obtained by observation and using my own eyes to read the many information boards, wall plaques, notices, etc, that are displayed. My digital camera came in useful in recording much of this information.

It is probably because that I am now retired and of a certain age that I find many things in life today objectionable. I know that you should not make comparisons with the past, but I do feel that today, we have lost many of our "old fashion values". Common courtesies and consideration for others seem to be alien to a number of people these days. It may be that these folk are in the minority but they do stand out. For sure, behavioural patterns and discipline have changed, in my view for the worse. It probably reflects the fact that society today is wealthier than it was say four or five decades ago, with people being more independent and less reliant on family and friends. But just to say "hello, good morning" to passers-by is not a big deal—obviously not in a busy high street. I could go on, but won't for the time being at least. I sound like one of those "Grumpy Old Men" on the TV show, which I probably am.

However, the reason why I raise all this is to forewarn the reader that throughout this book, I have included a number of what I call "Rants". During the course of my travels, I encountered a number of incidents and experiences that irritated and annoyed me greatly. Many were due to just simple lack of consideration for others. Some you may think trivial and wonder what I am on about. Hopefully for most, you will agree with me. My rantings have been numbered and listed at the end of this book. When the "Revolution" comes, most will be near the top of "the Agenda".

I must also mention that our bus trip was undertaken during 2008 / 2009 and since that time, there will have been changes that may make some of this text seem out-of-date, especially so by the time this book is written and published. So in reading through my narrative, try to imagine that you are back in the year 2009 and ignore subsequent happenings and changes.

To conclude this section of the book, I would hope that I have given the reader a background of how our bus trip came about and of Archie and myself. You may by now, have some idea of the type of person who has written this book and may wish to go no further. Hopefully you will continue and enjoy the experiences that both Archie and myself enjoyed on our bus trip, complete with bus pass, up the length of Britain from Lands End to John O'Groats.

PART 2

ENGLAND—from LANDS END

Chapter 1

Travel To Penzance And Lands End—Day 1

Sunday 17th August 2008

I have already made mention of the planning and travel arrangements that were required to be made before we embarked upon our bus trip across and up England in particular. The English section of our trip was to be split into two stages, with a prolonged stop of a few days at home in Lincoln. With my bus route and timetables sorted together including the locations of my overnight stops, all that was needed was to arrange overnight accommodation together with the travel arrangements to our start point at Penzance.

For the first stage of our trip up to Lincoln, I had decided to book in advance overnight accommodation in Penzance and Newquay, so to avoid the need to search for a B&B on the day. With the help of the local Travel Information Offices, a selection of suitable B&Bs was obtained over the phone that would accept pets and dogs in particular. After a few further telephone calls, accommodation was found and booked, the proprietors of both B&Bs seeming very pleasant and welcoming, happy to have Archie staying. I did mention that he was a small well-behaved dog and would not cause any trouble. I would of course say that although I know it is true. However, I did have to give an undertaking that any damage caused would have to be repaid. Fair enough, confident in that I knew that there would not be a problem, or so I hoped.

Packing my rucksack presented a bit of a challenge as I was conscious of not wanting to carry too much weight on my back when walking about town between trips. Whilst the knee that I had replaced the previous year was more-or-less working alright, my other knee was giving me some pain. This was to be replaced immediately I returned home from the English section of our bus journey. After a few attempts to get the weight right by packing and repacking both my kit and Archie's needs that included his food and treats, I managed to get the weight down to about 25 pounds in weight. This with my problem knees, I considered manageable. At least by calling in at home in Lincoln, I could unload my soiled clothes for clean ones. One essential piece of kit was my telescopic walking pole that I used when fell walking. This was to prove invaluable, especially when walking down-hill with a loaded rucksack on my back.

The next step was to fix our travel arrangements to Penzance, our first overnight stop and nearest railway station for Lands End. As mentioned earlier, we had a need to visit relations on the south coast during mid August in 2008. This would provide a good opportunity to travel onto Penzance to commence our bus trip, by catching the west coast train at Salisbury. The result would be a train ride of less than five hours in total rather than the seven hour plus journey from Sheffield.

The big day has arrived and off we set, with my wife, Florence, driving us both from where we are staying at Gosport (Archie's birthplace) to Salisbury Railway Station so to catch the 09.45 west coast train, changing first at Exeter. Being a Sunday morning, the road is quiet and progress good until we reach Salisbury itself where the traffic is moving slowly. Fortunately, we are alright for time and following the old British Rail rail-station signs around the ring-road, we arrive at the rail station without any problems. Here we are dropped off well before our train is due in, allowing us time to buy our tickets. For August, the weather is not good, it being a cold and cloudy day.

Saying farewell to my wife and with Archie giving her a big lick, we wait for our train to Exeter to arrive. Right on time, the First Great Western train glides into the station. On we get without having reserved any seats in advance. However, the train is only half full, so we soon find somewhere to sit with Archie settling down in the window seat. Off the train speeds, calling in at Gillingham, Yeovil, Axeminster and all stations west before reaching Exeter St. David's at 11.30.

We have a fifteen minute wait at Exeter, long enough for a brief walk for Archie to the end of the station platform and back. At 11.47, the Penzance train arrives. There are more passengers on the Penzance train, mainly young families on their way for holidays by the seaside. Fortunately, we are able to find a window seat on the left-hand side, the best side of the train for the views as we travel along the Cornish coast.

We depart Exeter, stopping at Newton Abbot, Plymouth and then across the Royal Albert Bridge that spans the River Tamar at Saltash. The bridge was designed for the Great Western Railway Company by that eminent civil engineer, Isambard Kingdom Brunel. The bridge design is of two spans, comprised of large twin lozenge-shaped wrought-iron trusses, each spanning 455 feet between the high masonry piers 100 feet above river level. Sadly Brunel was too ill to attend the opening in 1859, with his death coming shortly afterwards.

On we travel into Cornwall, calling in at Liskeard with the rail-track following the edge of the sea under the high red sandstone cliffs just before reaching St Austell. Archie is preoccupied looking out of the train window as we pass alongside the sea coast, wishing he could get out for a romp on the beach and splash in the water. There will be many opportunities for him to do this in the days to come. Next stop is Truro, then Redruth before reaching our destination at Penzance. The time is 15.00 and as we leave the shelter of the rail station, the weather outside is dreadful, it being cold, wet and windy.

From the railway station, we make our way up Market Jew Street through the central shopping area of the Town and past Sir Humphry Davy's statue, to our accommodation that I had booked for the night at the Con Amore Guest House in Morrab Road. Being August and so far west, we have at least another five hours of light left before darkness falls. So the decision is made to visit Lands End this evening, leaving more time to spend at Newquay tomorrow. Dumping my rucksack at the B&B, we head back into the town towards the bus station.

The No.300 First Group open-top double-decker bus operates during the summer months between Penzance and Lands End, for the benefit of tourists. It would indeed have been an enjoyable experience to be able to sit on the open top deck admiring the Cornish scenery as we travelled on our 55 minute journey to Lands End from Penzance. But today with the driving rain and strong winds, it is not to be. We have instead to be content in looking out of the rain-speckled windows on the lower deck, admiring the countryside we were passing through. A family with three young children all kitted out in wet gear, are also travelling on the bus looking very fed up with the bad weather. I do feel sorry for them.

I omitted to mention that on getting on the bus with Archie and showing my "oldies" bus pass, I was informed by the driver that whilst I could travel free of charge, there would be a charge of 60 pence for Archie—What!! It however turned out that his ticket could be used on other First Group buses during the same day, so at least I would not have to pay for him on the return journey back from Lands End. Nevertheless, if I have to pay for him on our journey all the way north up to John O'Groats, it was going to cost me a fortune! I subsequently learnt that this charge applied to travel on First Group buses in Cornwall only—big relief. It was nevertheless, the first time that I had used my bus pass outside my home area, so at least there is some relief that our travel plans would not be hampered.

Out of Penzance Town and onto the B3315, the bus passes the signs to Newlyn and then to Mousehole, before coming to the small hamlet of Sheffield, not a bit like the place of its namesake in West Yorkshire. The rain is easing as we travel along the narrow, twisty lanes with the overhanging trees catching the top of the bus. Driving a bus along these narrow leafy lanes must be difficult and our driver is doing well—I only hope that he does not meet any traffic coming in the opposite direction. The bus continues through the villages of Lamorna, St Buryan, Treen before deviating off down the "Valley Road" and into the pretty little village of **Porthcurno**. Also known as "PK" the village was once an important location for Britain's telecommunications systems. At this spot on the remote south-west coast of Cornwall, most of the submarine telephone cables that at one time, connected Britain with the countries of the former British Empire and the rest of the world came ashore. The telegraph station was first established in the 1870's where the staff of the cable office handled communications from up to fourteen cables connected to different parts of the world. Here at Porthcurno, there was once a large manned station and engineering college, but these no longer exist. Many of the old submarine cables are now replaced with the newer fibre optic cables that have a much greater capacity and which are connected direct to the country's national telecommunication system. However, the Telegraph Museum in the village still preserves the telecommunication heritage of Porthcurno. On the coast close-to Porthcurno, is the world famous open-air Minack Theatre, which is built into the sea-cliffs with a superb backdrop across Porthcurno Bay. Hopefully when the theatrical company is performing, their audiences normally enjoy better weather than the likes of today.

As we travel back out of Porthcurno via the Valley Road, the bus rejoins the B3315, calling in at Polygigga before arriving at the visitors' car park and tourists' complex at Lands End itself. The weather is not good but at least the rain has relented a little.

Lands End (Penn an Wlas)—Cornwall

We have about two hours to spend at Lands End on this cold windy evening in August, before the last bus arrives for the return journey back to Penzance. At this time of the day and with few visitors around, most of the facilities at the Visitors' Centre are closed, including the shops. Clad in my waterproofs, we brave the weather and head into the strong wind for the actual headland known as "Lands End". It isn't so bad for Archie, with his thick coat and with the wind whistling over his head although he doesn't look too happy.

Located on the Penwith Peninsula, Lands End is not the most southerly or westerly point on the British mainland. Lizard Point further east along the Cornish coast, is the most southerly, with Ardnamurchan in Scotland, the most westerly. However, projecting into the Atlantic, it is the most extreme point on the British mainland and the furthest from John O'Groats in the far north in Scotland.

We make our way down to the well-known and much photographed white painted signpost where we have our photo taken by another visitor braving the weather. At least it would be proof that we had been to Lands End. John O'Groats was shown as 874 miles away, presumably "as the crow flies" with the Scilly Isles 38 miles to the west and New York some 3,147 miles directly across the Atlantic. The 300 yards to reach the actual headland will for this particular evening, be far enough.

Battling our way against the strong headwind, we make our way along the coastal footpath with the seas crashing against the cliffs below. The Longships Lighthouse and reef is visible in the rain some one and a half miles offshore. Not a place to be if you don't enjoyed being lonely. We reach the rocky headland that is Lands End itself with only the open waters of the Altlantic Ocean separating us from the continent of America, over 3,000 miles to the west. At the headland, is the whitewashed "First and Last House" that is usually open to serve refreshments, though not today when we are here. The footpath is fenced off so to restrict access to the edge of the cliffs, but the views along the cliff-tops towards Cape Cornwall and out to sea to the Longships Lighthouse, are well worth the effort. While admiring the views, a couple who are walking part of the Coastal Footpath from St Ives, reach us. They are from Germany and were not put off by the bad weather, enjoying the wild scenery of the Cornish coastline. At least they have had the wind on their backs.

After a few words of pleasantries, we set off back along the cliff footpath to the Visitors Complex. At last, the rain has stopped. Lands End and the Visitors' Centre are owned by a private company, although there is a public right-of-way along the coastline. At the Visitors' Complex, there are souvenir shops, exhibitions, film theatre, hotel, restaurant, bar, café together with the "Penwith House Temperance Hotel est. 1860". Cornwall has a strong Methodist tradition where the drinking of alcohol was frowned upon by the church, especially during the 19th century. It is no longer a temperance hotel with the house now used as a gift shop. Also at the Complex, secured on dry land, is the fishing trawler *Confide* PZ741 alongside a RNLI lifeboat that can be clambered over by visitors.

The time being well after 18.00, we are in need of refreshment. I am carrying Archie's dinner in my rucksack, pre-packed by my wife in plastic bags, one for each day. The restaurant is still serving food, but it is against the hygiene rules to take Archie inside—fair enough. However it means that having ordered my meal and bought a pint of beer, I had to sit outside in the cold and the wind. At least the rain has stopped falling and having found a table that was sheltered, it isn't too bad. At least I am able to enjoy the views and fresh air!

Soon it would be time for the last bus to leave for Penzance. Not wishing for us to be stranded, I made sure that we are in plenty of time to be at the bus stop. First we have to walk around the "stone circle" by the entrance that consists of eight standing stones that seem to have been erected during more recent time—20th/21st century?

* * * * * * *

It has started to rain again, so we are quite thankful when our bus arrives to take us back to Penzance. The bus takes the same route back as it came, but still it is an interesting journey. It is a great pity that we have been unable to sit on the upper open deck of the bus. We arrive back in Penzance at 20.15, which on a fine night in August, would still have been warm with plenty of daylight left. Not this night, so we make our way back to our B&B in Morrab Road for a cup of tea and to watch some television. The final episode of Ewen McGregor and Charlie Boardman's round-the-world motor bike journey "The Long Way Round" is on—a bit different to my bus trip with Archie to John O'Groats, although they did have a support team with them.

Today, we have at least made a start on our trip with the visit to Lands End. It was a pity about the weather, but it could have been worse. We have done a lot of travelling with five hours on the train and nearly two hours on the bus to and from Lands End. I am not too sure if Archie has enjoyed himself today, there being no real opportunity to allow him off the lead and onto the beach. It must have been at bit frustrating for him watching it all pass by from the train window. However, tomorrow there will be plenty of opportunities for him at Newquay to romp about on the beach and splash in the sea. At least our B&B at the Con Amore Guest House is comfortable and warm.

Chapter 2
Penzance To Newquay—Day 2

Monday 18th August 2008

Up early to give Archie his early morning exercise, I enjoy a good fried breakfast, thanks to Keith and Carol, which will see me through most of the day. Having packed our kit, off we set to have a quick look-around Penzance before we catch our next bus. The weather is still wet and windy with grey skies above—what has happened to all this "global warming"?

Penzance—Cornwall—population 20,300

The Town and former borough of Penzance (first royal charter 1512) is the most south—westerly town in the whole of the U.K. Overlooking Mounts Bay with its sheltered port and harbour, the Town once had a large fishing fleet. This was supported by the dry dock built during the 19thC together with former engineering facilities nearby in the Town. Although a few fishing boats remain, the harbour is now primarily a marina for yachts and other pleasure craft.

The Town came into prominence when the Great Western Railway constructed the railway line into Penzance, with the *Cornish Rivera Express* making the journey from London in some seven hours, since reduced to five and a half hours. Penzance is of course the "end of the line" with passengers arriving to take the sea air but also to travel on by the ferryboat, to the Isles of Scilly. Today, The *Scillonian III* still ferries passengers on the three hour sea crossing to the Scilly Isles—weather permitting. These days, there is of course the alternative option of flying direct.

Like a number of other Cornish towns, there was a strong tradition in tin and copper mining. The under-sea / submarine tin mine at Wheal Wherry which closed during the mid 19th century is nearby and in the Town itself, there was a large tin smelter during the 19th century. All traces of tin mining and processing are now in the past. The Town's name was perhaps immortalised in Gilbert and Sullivan's operetta, *The Pirates of Penzance*, from which the local rugby club took their name, The Penzance and Newlyn Pirates RFC. The club have since moved their headquarters and ground to Camborne and changed their name to The Cornish Pirates RFC.

Penzance is today well known as a beach resort with its warm temperate climate (but not today) and sub-tropical gardens. It is through the sub-tropical Morrab Botanical Gardens that we first walk, admiring the variety of trees and shrubs and well laid out flower borders. The old traditional iron bandstand is still there, but I wonder if any bands still play there these days. Back onto Morrab Road, we walk up to the Penlee Gardens with its sub-tropical plants and tennis courts. Both botanical gardens host a variety of sub-tropical shrubs and trees and are a pleasure to walk around.

Back we walk up to the Market Place to the Victorian Market House with its granite façade facing down Market Jew Street. Above the main street itself at any elevated level, is the Terrace and its line of small shops. Sir Humphry Davy (1778-1829) scientist, inventor of the miners' safety lamp, lived in Penzance, his statue standing just outside Market House and facing down Market Jew Street, where he was born.

We walk down Chapel Street, passed the Egyptian House to the 1930's art-deco open air bathing pool that juts out over Battery Rocks towards the sea. It looks in good condition and is apparently still well used during the summer months when the weather is fine. The promenade stretches away to the west above the beach towards the picturesque fishing villages and harbours of Newlyn and Mousehole (pronounced *Mauzel*), neither of which we have time to explore. Newlyn in particular is well known to surveyors and map-users, inasmuch as the Ordnance Survey uses mean sea-level here as a datum for levels and heights throughout the whole of Britain, with ground levels and spot heights throughout the Country being referred to as "x" feet above "Ordnance Datum Newlyn".

Turning back-over, we head to the harbour and along the wall of the south pier with the prominent island of **St Michael's Mount,** a granite extrusion being clearly visible to the east rising above the waters of Mounts Bay. Being the smaller counterpart to Mont Saint Michel in Normandy, France, there have been monastic buildings and a castle on the Mount since the 12th century. Accessible at low tide from Marazion on the mainland, the Castle has for some time been the residence of the St Aubyn family. Below the Castle is the harbour surrounded by the houses and cottages of the small village. There is evidently a railway that runs underground from the harbour up to the Castle, but because of its steep incline, it is not available for public use.

The Inner Harbour at Penzance is nearly full with a number of fishing boats tied up to the quayside. It would seem that the Outer Harbour is now used mainly for pleasure craft. We continue along the harbour front across the swing bridge that provides access to the large 19thC dry-dock on the other side of the road to the harbour. The dry-dock is no longer in use and is now kept flooded. On we walk past the Old Lifeboat Station towards the bus station. Light rain is falling although the wind is not as strong as it was the previous day. On the placards for the Western Morning News outside a newspaper shop, it reads "Weather Warning for West Tourism"—looks like this weather is going to continue for a few days yet.

* * * * * * *

On reaching the bus station, we wait for the bus to arrive for our next destination, which is Truro. Whilst waiting at the bus stand, there are two open topped double-decker buses loading passengers for their trip to Lands End. I only hope that they experience better weather than we did the previous day, albeit it is still wet and windy. The 10.20 No.18 First Group bus arrives for Truro and on we board, me going free of charge but having to pay 60 pence again for Archie's day bus pass. Spreading his white woollen blanket across the back seat, Archie soon settles down—must keep the bus seat clean and free from his hairs, even though I had to pay for his bus fare.

Leaving the bus station at Penzance, we travel east along the sea-front with St Michael's Mount still visible through the rain across Mounts Bay. We soon leave the coast and head up the A30 towards the small town of Hayle. As we pass along the road, there are fields of blue alliums that I have never previously seen being grown commercially in Britain. Approaching **Hayle** (population 8,400), the bus makes a detour off the A30 into the centre of the historic little town, passing along the east bank of the river estuary with its wide grassy flood plains. It is thought that the Romans first occupied the harbour area for the export of tin. However, it was much later during the period of the Industrial Revolution, which saw Hayle develop as a coal importing and ore exporting port. Soon to follow, was the establishment of a number of engineering works and foundries, the best known being Harvey and Co who manufactured beam engines. During the latter part of the 19th century, the National Explosive works were established on nearby Upton Towans, which continued in the manufacture of explosives until the 1920's. A few "big bangs" have been recorded. Today, most of Hayle's industry has gone and the Town is now mainly a holiday resort. Recently, the Town and its historic harbour were included in the Cornwall and West Devon World Heritage Site (2006). At last, the rain has stopped and there are signs of the sun appearing through the clouds above—halleluiah

After a brief stop in Hayle, the bus continues eastwards along the A30. We are now approaching one of the former richest and most productive tin and copper mining areas of Cornwall and indeed the World. During the 18th and 19th centuries, the local landscape would have been covered with scores of mine workings, each with its own chimneystack and engine house that housed the steam pumping plant and winding gear. The reputation and skills of the old Cornish miners are legendary, with the establishment of specialised mining schools in the area during the 1900's. However by the end of the 19th century, the Cornish mining industry was in decline with many of the tin miners emigrating to find work overseas. Dolcoath Mine, the "Queen of the Cornish mines" near to Camborne, was at the time of its closure in 1921, the deepest mine in the world at 3,500 feet below ground level. A long way back up if you had forgotten your lunch box. The last tin mine to close in Cornwall was the South Crofty mine near Pool in 1998, albeit the headworks and winding gear at the mine are still intact. A number of ruinous chimney stacks and buildings still stand throughout this area giving testament to past tin and copper workings, but today the mining of minerals in Cornwall is a thing of the past—for the present time at least.

With another detour off the main A30 onto the A3047, our next stop is **Camborne** (population 23,000). The Town itself has a strong mining tradition. It was at Camborne in 1801 that the well known mining engineer, Richard Trevthick tested the world's first self propelled passenger carrying vehicle. This was his steam powered locomotive "Puffing Billy" that he successfully managed to ascend Camborne Hill under its own steam. This resulted in the well known folk song:

> *Going up Camborne Hill, coming down,*
> *Going up Camborne Hill, coming down*
> *The horses stand still, the wheels go around,*
> *Going up Camborne Hill, coming down*

Richard Trevthick (1771-1883) was born in Camborne and developed the Cornish Beam Engine in the early 1900's for pumping water from the depths of the local tin mines. His statue stands outside the public library in Camborne. The area of West Cornwall has traditionally, had a strong following in the game of rugby football. The Cornish Pirates RFC, having recently relocated to Camborne from Penzance, are one of England's leading clubs and attract support from all over the local area.

While travelling through the centre of Camborne, the driver has to stamp hard on his brakes to undertake an emergency stop. Every loose item in the bus shoots forward and Archie finds himself thrown off his seat onto the floor. All the passengers are quite shaken at being thrown forward, so too is the bus driver himself. It transpires that a Ford Escort had at the last minute decided to do a right-hand turn immediately across the path of our bus. Had the bus been going any faster, there would surely have been a collision. A rather sheepish car driver waves an apology (I will not mention the driver's sex) and continues on unscathed, thanks to the quick reactions of our bus driver. Looking back out of the window, there is quite a lot of rubber left on the road surface from the bus' tyres. Having enquired if everyone aboard was alright, the bus driver continues on his way through the Town. One of the other passengers does kindly enquire as to whether Archie is alright. "Only his dignity is hurt" I reply.

Leaving Camborne and on past Pool, we pass by some of the old mine workings with their engine houses and brick chimneys still standing. There must have been a number of mining communities living in this area at one time, now all long gone. It is very noticeable that a number of the local place names start with the word "Wheal".

Soon we are approaching the market of **Redruth** (population 12,400) that like Camborne, also has a strong mining tradition. There were a number of shallow mines in the immediate area of Redruth, where tin was extracted during the 18th century. A Mining Exchange for trading in mineral stock, was established in the Town in 1880, together with a School for Mines. Also, Murdock House, built by William Murdock in the 1880's was the first house in the world to be fitted out with coal gas lights. With the mining of tin long gone, Redruth has reverted back to being a market town, albeit proud of its mining heritage. In 2008 a six foot bronze sculpture of a Cornish Tin Miner was erected in the Town centre in memory of those who in past years, worked the veins of tin and copper many feet below the ground.

The bus makes its way through Redruth, passing by the sturdy red sandstone buildings that are perhaps synonymous with its past. We rejoin the A30 at Chacewater where there is an array of flags flying—there must be some celebrations taking place in the village. On we travel up the A30 to Three Milestone, where the bus diverts onto the A390 towards the cathedral City of Truro. We are passing some lush green fields with herds of grazing dairy cows. With the disappearance of many dairy herds elsewhere in the Country, it is reassuring to see that milk is still being produced in the South-West of England. At 12.00 midday, the bus drops us off at Truro bus station, the skies are grey, but at least it is not raining.

Truro—Cornwall—population 21,000

The Cathedral City of Truro (first royal charter 1589), is the administrative centre for the County of Cornwall. The port facilities on the River Truro date back to the 14th century although today there is little commercial river traffic. During the mining boom of the 18th and 19th centuries, Truro was a "stannary town" for the Cornish tin and copper mining industry and today the Royal Cornwall Museum in the City preserves the County's past mining heritage. The building of the Cathedral on the site of the 14thC St Mary's Church, was started in 1880 and completed in 1910, being in the Gothic Revival style. With the building of the Cathedral, Truro was granted city status in 1877, it then becoming the most southerly city in the UK. Within the old part of the City, there are some fine examples of Georgian architecture, which together with the high society life of the 18th century, lead to the City becoming known as the "London of Cornwall".

With Archie in tow, we make our way from the bus station up Boscawen Street past the City Hall into the City centre. After only a short walk, we reach Coinage Hall, named as a result of Truro being a "stannary town", albeit not the original building where tin and copper were assayed. The present fine sandstone building, which was built during the Victorian period, was formerly a bank, but now houses a pizza take-a-way on the ground floor and Victorian tearooms upstairs—no comment! Standing immediately outside Coinage Hall and facing up Boscawen Street, is the City's War Memorial dedicated to the City's sons that did not return after the two World Wars.

Towering above us, is the central tower and three spires of the Cathedral Church of the Blessed Virgin Mary. Walking up King

Street to the Cathedral's main entrance, we find a seat to admire the stonework, windows and carvings around the doorway of the west front. The Cathedral building was constructed during the period 1880/1910 in Gothic Revival style and modelled it is said, on the architecture of Lincoln Cathedral—there certainly is a resemblance. The building was constructed on site of the old 14thC St Mary's Church in the creamy coloured oolitic limestone brought in from Bath. Although relatively recent compared to many of the Country's other cathedrals, its external appearance is certainly in the traditional Gothic style.

There are some fine stone Georgian houses around the area of the Cathedral. One has two heads carved in stone that are incorporated high up into the external face of the building with the name "Blewetts" above the arch of the doorway. It turns out that the ground floor is a bakery selling traditional "Cornish pasties". Being lunchtime, there is a queue leading outside the shop which I join, first having tied Archie to a nearby lamppost. There is a choice of fillings but I go for the traditional meat and veg filling. Finding a seat in the Cathedral Close among the many others munching away at their pasties, I settle down to enjoy my lunch. Archie is looking at me forlornly as if saying "where's mine?". I eventually cave in and pass him a bit of my pasty.

We make our way from the Cathedral Close into the pedestrianised shopping area of Pydor Street. For those interested in retail therapy, this is the place to be when in Truro. But not for us, especially as it will soon be time to catch our next bus. Back down King Street and Boscawen Street to Lemon Street. At the top of Lemon Street is the monument to Richard Lemon Lander (1804/1834), explorer in West Africa and first to canoe down the River Niger and who was born in Truro.

* * * * * * *

Back at the bus station, we look for the stand where the No.89 bus to Newquay departs from. Our bus arrives and on showing the driver my national bus-pass and Archie's day pass, we board this time without having to pay for Archie. At 13.00 we leave Truro for Newquay and it has started to rain again.

Heading north out of Truro on the A39, we rejoin the A30 before reaching the village of Mitchell. Diverting onto the A3076 and A3058, we head past the green fields and meadows, towards the north Cornish coast and Newquay. There's some blue sky ahead and the rain has stopped—looks promising. I am trying to do some reading for my Open University course, but without much success.

Alongside the A3058 is Dairyland Farm World, a popular visitors attraction, with farm animals and machinery, various activities and displays taking place to provide entertainment especially for youngsters. I am told that the ice cream is good too. On the bus travels, through the lush Cornish countryside to Mountjoy until we reach St. Columb Minor on the outskirts of Newquay. The sun at last, is out and there is blue sky above.

As we approach the coast overlooking Newquay Bay, the traffic is starting to build up and the bus is virtually crawling along, past all the hotels, restaurants, retirement and holiday homes and other touristy developments associated with a popular seaside resort. It is a bit different to the open roads of the Cornish countryside. Nevertheless, the view across the green links and out to sea, looks interesting, with large breakers crashing down on the beach. The bus is travelling very slowly due to the amount of traffic, but eventually we reach the bus station in the centre of Newquay at 13.50 with plenty of time left in the day to enjoy the pleasures of this seaside resort.

Having made enquiries at the Tourist Information Office and picked up some pamphlets, we make our way to the B&B I had booked for the night. The Pengilley Guest house in Trebarwith Crescent, is only a short walk from the bus station and in the direction of the coast itself. The proprietor Jan, was there to greet us and leaving our kit at the Guest House, we make our way to the beach where we have the rest of the day to enjoy ourselves.

Newquay—Cornwall—population 19,600 (100,000 in summer)

Known as the "Blackpool of the West Country" and also as the "Surfing Capital of Britain", Newquay ranks as one of Britain's most poplar seaside resorts with some of the best surfing beaches in the Country. The Town is the venue for international surfing competitions with world-class surfing possible at the Fistral and Towan Beaches. The Town started to develop as a seaside resort in late 19th century with advent the of railway coming to the area, transporting visitors from far and wide to enjoy the warm Cornish climate and sea-air.

Prior to developing into a holiday resort, Newquay was primarily a fishing port. During the 15th century, funds were sought to build a "new quay", hence its name. Famous for its pilchards up to the early 20th century, fishing out of Newquay has since declined. However, the harbour still houses a small fishing fleet but the pilchards are long gone.

We reach the point overlooking Towan Beach where the grass links fall away down to the sea below. At the top, there is a stone plaque commemorating the filming of the "Magic Mystery Tour" by the Beatles that took place in Newquay during September 1967. I remember seeing the film and recall some of the shots of Newquay. The sun is now out, so it is time for an ice cream. £2.00 is a bit pricey but it was enjoyable—Archie got the tail end of the cornet. Down we walk past the pitch-and-put golf links although the course is not set out and no-one is playing today. On down we go to the promenade that overlooks the Towan Beach, to find that the tide is out. As a result, there are large tracts of the sandy beach exposed.

There is a stairway of concrete steps that lead down onto the beach from the promenade above. Archie is tugging on the lead pulling me towards the sea and I need to keep my balance. There are a lot of people on the beach enjoying themselves with fathers building sandcastles, supposedly for the benefit of their children. The sea is quite calm and with the tide out, looks inviting.

I keep Archie on his lead for a little way at first until we get to a stretch of exposed rocks where I allow him to go free. It is as if I had "opened up his cage". Off he goes chasing his ball, heading straight for the sea for a splash and then playing in the rock-pools, dropping his ball into the water and then trying to "paw" it out. He is also busy excavating long trenches in the sand attempting to bury his ball. I can appreciate that after such a long bus journey, he is enjoying his run-a-bout. We spend a bit of time here allowing Archie his fun playing in the rock-pools.

Walking along at the sea's edge, off come my shoes and socks and rolling up my trousers, in typical tourist tradition, I go for the obligatory "plodge" It is a great feeling to have the wet sand and seawater trickling between my toes. Further out to sea, there are surfers riding the breakers coming in from the Atlantic Ocean. We walk along to the towering rock stack at the east end of Towan Beach that is connected to the mainland by means of a suspension footbridge. There is a lone dwelling sitting on the top of the rock stack and it looks occupied—at least they will "not fall out with the neighbours". At low tide, you can walk underneath the bridge between the rock stack and mainland.

We face the long climb back up to the top of the headland. I am struggling a little, but Archie is helping by pulling on the lead. At the top, we are unable to continue around the top of the coast and have to come back into the Town. There is a footpath cum cycle track that has recently been developed along the line of a former railway that cuts through the rocky headland. We drop down onto this path and follow it to where it comes out onto Cliff Road further up the coast. Continuing on to Narrowcliff, here there is a fine view down to Tolcarne Beach from the promenade above. The tide is now on the turn and the breakers are starting to roll in towards the breach. There is a flurry of surfers gathering on the beach with their surfing boards preparing to ride the incoming breakers.

On we walk across the links and grassy headland that overlooks both Tolcarne and Lusty Glaze Beaches. Archie is off his lead again and is soon meeting up with other dogs. I am not sure what it is with dogs insomuch that they need to sniff the hindquarters of other dogs when first meeting up. He meets up with an Alsatian and they are soon at play—he seems to prefer playing with bigger dogs rather than those his own size. Back we walk to the promenade overlooking Tolcarne Beach. The breakers are now rolling in and there is a lot of activity on the beach, including that by the coastguards trying to rein-in a few wayward surfers.

Back we walk into the Town centre via East Street with all its hotels, restaurants, bars, gift shops and amusements and along the Crescent that overlooks Towan Beach. The tide has now covered most of the beach with waves crashing through the gap under the suspended footbridge that leads to the isolated rock stack. The sea is swarming with surfers. From the links we head up to Fore Street passing a direction arrowed sign that says "Chiropodist—30 feet"—no comment! On along Fore Street we go making a detour down to the harbour below with its lifeboat station. Then up Headland Road that leads to Fistral Beach, internationally well-known for its surfing qualities being directly exposed to the Atlantic Ocean. Again, there are a lot of surfers down on the beach riding the Atlantic breakers.

* * * * * * *

The day is passing and I am getting hungry. So it is back to the Pengilley Guest House to give Archie his dinner and to bed him down for the night. He is tired out after all the exercise and running about he has had whilst in Newquay. I make my way back to a fish restaurant that I had seen earlier overlooking Towan Beach. After a meal of fish and chips with mushy peas, I find a good pub to enjoy a couple of pints of locally brewed real ale. It has been an interesting and enjoyable day, especially with the improvement in the weather. I didn't manage to get much reading done for my OU course today. I think I will give it up as a bad job and just concentrate on enjoying our bus trip.

Chapter 3
Newquay To Taunton—Day 3

Tuesday 19th August 2008

I am up early this morning to give Archie his walk before breakfast—07.00 is early for me but perhaps not for many. The weather is at least dry but the sky is overcast and not looking good. We have a long bus trip ahead today so I will try to give Archie some reasonable exercise before we set out. Down onto the beach we head where he is soon splashing about in the sea and romping over the sands. Back up at our B&B, I enjoy a good breakfast where I share my table with an interesting chap who has just returned from Antarctica, a place that I would love to visit.

Immediately after breakfast, we make our way back to the bus station for the next stage of our trip to Exeter. Trudging uphill with the rucksack on my back, I am thankful that it is only a short distance to the bus station.

The duration of the bus journey from Newquay to Exeter is three and a half hours, the longest between connections on the whole of our bus trip to John O'Groats. As mentioned earlier in Part 1, this route is the only way out of Cornwall without using the National Express bus services, on which my bus pass is not valid. Ideally, I would have liked to break the long journey at say Launceston. However with only three buses a day on this route and a wait of some four hours between buses, my timetable would have been badly disrupted making it difficult to reach our planned overnight stop at a reasonable hour. There is therefore no other option but to go for the full three and a half hour trip, although as events turned out, we will have the opportunity to leave the bus for a five minute break at Okehampton.

Finding the correct stand for the bus to Exeter, the green double-decker Western Greyhound bus arrives prompt on time at 09.15. As previously mentioned, the "oldies" bus passes are only valid as from 09.30 each day, so there may be a problem. The next bus to Exeter is four hours later, so we are committed to boarding this particular bus if we are to maintain our timetable. On we get and there is a female bus driver at the controls. On showing my bus pass, she politely explains that it is only valid after 09.30, a fact that I already was aware of, but if I cared to pay the fare to St Columb Major, which we would reach at 09.30, it would be alright to travel free for the rest of the long journey to Exeter. I consider this very reasonable, albeit going slightly against my objectives in travelling for free across and up England. Nevertheless, I willingly paid the £2.30 fare, having the feeling that I was not the first person to attempt to travel with their "oldies" bus pass on this particular bus. However at least I don't have to pay for Archie, this being a different bus company. Thank you Western Greyhound! The only downside is that I don't get a ticket for my bus journey from St Columb Major to Exeter to add to my collection.

Climbing up to the top deck for what I hope to be good views of the Cornish and Devon countryside, off we set out of Newquay back along the sea front to St Columb Minor and then left onto the A3059 that leads onto St Columb Major. After some five miles, we pass the signs for Newquay Cornwall Airport, which now handles international flights. On we travel to St Columb Major where the road joins the main A39 that leads eventually to Barnstaple in Devon.

Here two "locals" get on the bus, one with a bull-terrier who sits immediately in front of us on the top deck, the other one at the front of the bus some three seats ahead. A bit concerned as to Archie's reactions, I move back a few seats so to create some space between us. I am pleased that I did, for they proceed to talk to each other in very loud voices across other passengers who are also travelling on the top deck. Without wanting to sound disparaging, both are what might be termed "not the sharpest knives in the box". Whilst mildly amusing, their conversation spoken in a broad south-west dialect that you cannot help listening in on, is banal. It gets around to the guy in the front seat asking the dog owner if his dog is a male or female, to which the owner replies that it is a female dog. "I have a friend with a male bull-terrier and if we could get the two of them together, then they might produce pups" he suggests, followed by "I would love to have one of the pups if she pupped—I'm sure she will pup". And on and on he goes on the same theme.

Some of the other passengers are beginning to move towards the back of the bus out of the line of the verbal banality. Whilst initially mildly entertaining, their conversation is getting tedious and detracts from our appreciation of the countryside we were passing through. The dog owner, now only some three seats in front, is turning around trying I believe, to make contact with myself so to start a conversation, knowing that I have Archie with me. I keep my gaze away avoiding any eye contact with him. I hope he isn't going to suggest that Archie and his bull-terrier bitch should mate. Why should I feel so guilty in not wanting to enter into conversation with him? Perhaps it is embarrassment on my part or may be I just can't be bothered. Please just leave me alone! (RANT 1).

One of the more interesting features I notice as our bus travels along the A39, is the Neolithic Nine Maidens Stone Row. Standing upright alongside the main road, the line of the nine standing stones that comprise the ancient monument is 262 feet in length, with the irregularly spaced stones standing between two and six feet tall. They are all aligned in a north-east direction and thought to have some astronomical or calendar function that may relate to the agricultural year. As might be expected, there are a number of myths associated with the stones, most relating to evil and demon spirits, which make interesting folklore.

As we approach the market town of Wadebridge, we pass the permanent site for the Royal Cornwall Agricultural Show that is held each year at the beginning of June. Like similar county agricultural shows across the Country, it is one of Cornwall's top social events of the year, especially for the local farming communities. Founded back in 1793, the Show caters for all interests that include the judging of cattle, sheep, horses, pigs, etc, together with sheep dog trials, show jumping events, driving competitions, flower shows, games, sports, craft shows, live music, etc, etc. All in all, a good day out especially if the weather is fine.

Next stop is **Wadebridge** (population 6,400) where the bus makes a detour from the A39 into the Town centre. Sited at the top of the Camel estuary upstream from Padstow, this pretty little town originally had the main A39 passing through. However, to alleviate the heavy congestion that occurred in the Town, a bypass was built in 1993. The stone arched bridge over the Camel dates back to 1468, although it has been subsequently widened, strengthened and improved. It still this day carries heavy traffic that passes through the Town.

Leaving Wadebridge, we rejoin the A39 travelling north towards Camelford. The route of the A39 up this section of the north Cornish coast, is known as the "Atlantic Highway" and runs from Newquay in the south up to Barnstaple in the north. There are a number of sights and places of interest scattered along its eighty mile length for the visitor to enjoy, especially along the coastal edge where small detours are necessary. We pass signs on the left pointing to Port Issac, the setting for the TV series "Doc Martin", then a little further on, to Tintagel, with its castle and associations with King Arthur and the Knights of the Round Table.

When we reach the town of Camelford, the two locals get off the bus and peace reigns! The bus then moves onto the bus station, a little further on through the Town, where there is a five minute wait. We cannot believe our eyes when we look down and see the guy with the bull-terrier stroll into the bus station and gets back on the bus, taking up his same seat on the top deck. It seems that he got off the bus for a brief walk and a cigarette. At least his companion is no longer with him and with no-one else on the bus volunteering to enter into a conversation with him, we have peace. I am still a bit uneasy though about his bull-terrier mixing it with Archie.

The market town of **Camelford** (population 2,400) sits on the River Camel and is located close to Bodmin Moor. The Town has the distinction of housing the National Cycle Museum that is located nearby in the old railway station buildings. However, the name Camelford hit the headlines back in 1988, when a major water pollution incident occurred in the town's water supply system. The incident was subsequently categorised as one of the worst pollution incidents of drinking water in the UK. It was only after a flood of complaints was received from local consumers regarding the strange taste of the tap-water, that the then water authority began investigations as to the cause. It subsequently transpired that a large delivery of aluminium sulphate, a chemical that is frequently used in the water treatment process, had been accidentally emptied into the wrong underground tank at the water treatment works. Instead of being fed into the mixing tank that formed part of the treatment process, the chemical had instead been placed into the final treated water tank that fed direct into the water supply system. The water treatment works at the time were unmanned and so it was some time before the mistake was discovered. As can be imagined, the consequences were enormous, both locally and nationally, with headlines at the time of "water supply poisoned". Even to this day, claims are being made and evidence submitted of the after-effects and on the long-term health implications on the local population. Needless to say, strict measures were immediately put in place at Camelford and procedures improved throughout the Country, so to avoid a repetition of such a serious incident.

Leaving Camelford, we continue to travel north on the A39 for a further four miles before we branch off onto the A395 leading to

Launceston. Here the bus turns right, leaving the Atlantic Highway, to travel inland with Bodmin Moor on our right. The rain is starting to fall again, and the clouds are descending over the high-ground of Bodmin Moor. Nearer to the road, we pass alongside the lush green pastures with herds of dairy cows grazing which alternate with the golden fields of wheat that are ready for harvesting.

Looking out across Bodmin Moor, the tall masts and rotating blades of a group (the collective noun I am told is a "farm") of wind turbines stand out on the horizon. I personally have mixed feelings about the effectiveness of such land-based wind turbines as an efficient means of renewable energy generation. For a start, the turbines only turn when the wind is blowing but more relevant is the cost and carbon footprint in the manufacture of these tall megaliths. For sure, global warming is a serious issue and for the sake of our grandchildren, it needs to be addressed without any further delays. But the solving of the problem of the world's excessive CO_2 gases and emissions will barely be touched by the erection of more land-based wind turbines across our countryside. I realise that by law, we need to have a minimum of 15% of our electricity supplied by various forms of renewable generation by the year 2020, but surely there must be more effective and efficient means of generating carbon-free electricity. Part of the answer could be more off-shore wind turbines with many now being proposed for areas in the North Sea. However a return on the present high capital costs of installation makes even these off-shore turbines non-cost effective, though maybe in time the technology will improve with more efficient turbines being available. Wave and tidal generation are also being seriously considered which are at least reliable over a twenty-four hour period. Nevertheless, it still leaves the question as to where the remaining 85% is to come from? I will not mention the "N" word that the politicians have until very recently, been reluctant to discuss. They are the same politicians who have failed to put in place a decisive and coherent policy on the UK's future energy supplies, despite repeated reports and warnings from professional advisers of the impending shortfall in the Country's power supply (RANT 2).

At the time of writing this passage in November 2009, proposals have just been published for the construction of ten new nuclear power stations, albeit it will be 2018 at the earliest before the first comes on line. Also at this time, the Copenhagen Conference on Climate Change is taking place, so the subject is very much in the news at this time.

Although a so-called "meaningful agreement" is reported as having being reached, this has been disputed by many nations present at the Conference, as it lacks firm legally and binding targets and dates for the reduction of CO_2 gases and emissions worldwide. The use of the word "meaningful" has been described as "political spin" and that the Conference had not done enough to prevent dangerous climate change in the future. Following the big build up to the Copenhagen Conference and high expectations, it is of serious concern that the leaders of the World's nations cannot agree on issues that could concern the continuation of the human race as we know it.

We continue along the single carriageway of the A395 eastwards with the hedgerow lined green fields on either side, before joining the A30 that comes direct from Penzance. Near this road junction is the Trethorne Leisure Farm where in addition to the usually farm related and leisure activities, they have ten-pin bowling alleys. Good entertainment if the weather is bad, such as it is today.

Taking a detour first through the hamlet of Tregadillett, we enter the market town of **Launceston** (population 7,200), located near to the border with Devon and known as the "gateway to Cornwall". The Norman castle dominates the Town that also played a major role in the Civil War of the 1640's, being loyal to the Royalist cause of King Charles. Up to 1835, Launceston was designated as the capital of Cornwall until this title was transferred to Bodmin. Located on the River Kensey, the Town figured in Daphne du Maurier's novel "Jamaica Inn". I am relieved to see the guy with the bull-terrier leave the bus here.

Some two miles after leaving Launceston, we cross over the River Tarmar and enter the county of Devon. Soon we rejoin the A30 at Liftondown and continue eastwards along the dual carriageway towards Okehampton, along which we are motoring at a good pace, bypassing a number of small villages and hamlets en-route. On the left near Broadwoodwidger, there are signs to **Roadford Reservoir**, the largest body of inland-water in south-west England. Constructed in the late 1980's, the rock-fill dam across the valley of the River Wolf holds back up to eight billion gallons when the reservoir is full. After treatment, this is used to meet most of the water supply demands of the City of Plymouth to the south. The surface area of the reservoir covers nearly 730 acres and is available for recreational use by the public, with amenities for sailing, wind surfing, fishing, camping, walking, picnicking, etc, provided. Having previously worked in the water industry, I consider that these open bodies of water actually enhance the beauty of the countryside together with providing recreation for the public in their enjoyment of the outdoors. I therefore find it difficult to accept the objections raised to the construction of new reservoirs, such as Roadford, by some of the environmental groups who do not seem to consider the benefits that are being provided to the public at large, not least the need for need water supplies. It is often the case of being dictated to by a small minority (RANT 3). It is of course, tough if you are being uprooted from your home or loose farmland as a result of a new reservoir being built, even though compensation is paid.

On we motor along the fast dual carriageway of the A30 with the dark moors of Dartmoor soon coming into sight. With the low clouds lying over them, the moors today look a bit foreboding. Soon we are at Meldon, where the bus turns off to the market town of **Okehampton** (population 5,800). With the River Okement running through the centre, the Town is on the northern edge of Dartmoor National Park with a large army training camp located nearby. Nearby too, is the site of a Roman fort, which together with the 15th castle, gives the Town some historic importance.

The bus arrives near the Town centre at 11.45 and makes a five minute stop, so the opportunity is taken for me to "stretch my legs" and for Archie to "cock his leg". After two and a half hours sitting on the bus, we need this break. Nearby is a bakers shop with an array of pastries and pies in the window, so with lunchtime approaching, I go in and ask for a "Cornish pasty". I am politely told that I am now in Devon and that because of EU protection laws, they must call their produce "traditional pasties" rather than use the word Cornish. I can understand the need to protect certain goods and foodstuffs from being exploited outside their traditional areas, but if rigorously applied to all such items, we would not for instance be able to refer to Yorkshire puddings outside of Yorkshire nor Welsh Rarebit outside of Wales. I could go on to give many more examples—perhaps it could be developed into a type of word game. Whilst not wanting to offend the Cornish people, I do think that some relaxation should be made as it is impractical to deliver freshly baked pasties only produced in Cornwall to other parts of the Country. Soon, the name of Cornish pasties will disappear from normal use, which will be regrettable. In any case, my "traditional pasty" bought in Okehampton, Devon, tastes much the same as the pasty I bought the previous day in Truro, Cornwall (RANT 4).

Climbing back up to the top deck on the bus, we head on through the Town centre, past some interesting buildings and back onto the dual carriageway of the A30. The wild and rugged high ground of Dartmoor is on our right and in today's weather, looks bleak. I can well understand why they chose this location for Britain's top security prison. I suppose that if the sun was shinning with blue skies above, it would look totally different. On we travel with stops for Sticklepath, Widdon Down and Crockernwell. At Cheriton Cross, there are a group of thatched houses together with a thatched pub. At last, the skies are brightening and there are signs of blue.

Apart from the isolated farmhouse and cottage, there are not many signs of habitation along this stretch of road. The countryside is still interesting and I have now given up on trying do any more studying for my Open University exams—it will have to wait until I get back home. The signs for Exeter are becoming more frequent and soon we are diverting off the A30 onto the A377 that takes us over the River Exe, past an interesting new footbridge that spans the River, then to the mainline St David's railway station which I had passed through two days previously, before entering into the centre of the City itself. We arrive at the bus station at 12.45 after a long three and a half hour bus ride, albeit passing through some fine and attractive countryside. We bid goodbye and thank our lady bus driver, heading for the City centre. The sun is shining.

Exeter—Devon—population 122,400

The historic Cathedral City of Exeter is the county town and administration centre for the County of Devon. The most south-westerly fortified settlement in Britain during Roman times, Exeter is at the southern end of the Fosse Way, a Roman road that traverses England ending in Lincoln. Parts of the Roman city wall still remain together with a substantial Roman bath complex, sadly not on view to the public. In 876, the City was attacked and captured by the Danish Vikings only to be retaken a year later by King Alfred the Great. Shortly after the Norman Conquest, the red sandstone Rougemont Castle was built. The Castle still exists albeit partly in ruins and up to very recently, the County Assize Courts were located within its grounds.

The Cathedral Church of St Peters was founded in 1050 with the building being completed around 1400. The Cathedral has the longest uninterrupted vault in England with the two Norman towers on either side of the nave. The Gothic west front is decorated with three rows of sculptured figures that run the whole width of the Cathedral. When in 1942 the City was bombed by enemy aircraft, the Cathedral was hit and suffered severe damage, losing most of its stained-glass windows.

During the Tudor and Stuart period, there was strong active trading in wool in the City that created great wealth. It was during this period in 1558 that the Exeter Canal was built, one of the oldest canals in Britain. With most of the City being sited on the east bank of the River Exe, access to the west bank can be gained by the ancient Butts cable ferry that is still in operation. The City still has its own port facilities although these days it is used solely for pleasure craft. More recently, the National Metrological Office of the UK was relocated to Exeter in 2004, and is now a major employer within the City.

The City has many old historic buildings. The Guildhall in the High Street is said to be the oldest municipal building in England that is still in use today. Mols Coffee House with its Tudor frontage, is in the Cathedral Close and is very popular. The Country's third oldest synagogue is in Mary Arches Street. Northernhay Gardens located near to the Castle, were first laid out in 1612 and is the oldest open public space in England. The Gardens are now set out in the Victorian design with attractive displays of flower beds, shrubs, different varieties of shrubs and trees and include many statues and memorials.

On leaving the bus station, we cross over and walk up Paris Street towards the main High Street. It would seem that there has been much redevelopment in the City centre in recent years with many new buildings, departmental stores, pedestrianised areas and pavement cafes. We reach the new shopping complex of Princesshay that was opened in 2007 and includes up to 60 retail shops. It all looks very modern and clean. We give the shopping complex a miss and follow the signs for the Cathedral. Coming out onto the greens of the Cathedral precincts, there is the statue of Richard Hooker (1554-1600), the theologian and writer who was born in Exeter and who played an influential role during the early years of the Anglican Church. Looking back to the corner of Cathedral Close from where we had come, is the black and white timber frontage of Mols Coffee House with its royal coat of arms and the date 1596 painted on its upper front. There are a lot of customers sitting outside.

Walking round to face the west front of St Peter's Cathedral, we take a rest to sit and admire the stonework and tiers of sculptured figures that decorated the main entrance to the Cathedral. The figures include most of the old kings and queens, some sitting crossed legged with others in conversation with those alongside. The Cathedral is not particularly great in height although its long nave extends a good distance. It is unusual inasmuch as the two Norman towers are sited on either side of the nave that passes uninterrupted between the towers. It is a beautiful building.

To the north-west of the Cathedral Yard is the City's Guildhall building with its ornate stone colonnade frontage. Parliament Street a little further to the south, is said to be one of the narrowest streets in the UK being only wide enough to allow only one person at a time to pass through. I am not sure how they manage to deliver large items of furniture into these houses that front onto the so-called Street.

From the west front of the Cathedral, we walk back to Mols Coffee shop on the corner of the precincts and down the cobbled Cathedral Close past the crenulated North Tower to Southernhay, with its row of Georgian houses overlooking the Green. With the number of firms of solicitors and agents occupying these houses, it would seem that this is the business quarter of Exeter.

I had allowed only an hour to look around Exeter, which was clearly insufficient time even to get a taste of what the City had to offer. It would have been nice to have had more time to visit the old Rougemont Castle, the Victorian Northernhay Gardens and the riverside area, together with some of the other historic buildings of Exeter. May be another time, so on we proceed back to the main thoroughfare of Paris Street and to the bus station for our next connection.

* * * * * * *

Back at the bus station, I look for the stand from which the No.92 First Group bus to Taunton departs. We are just in time to catch the 13.35 bus that is waiting with its engine running. On we get, with no charge for Archie. By now, Archie has now got used to the drill and heads for the back seat.

Leaving Exeter, we soon join the M5 motorway and for some ten miles, travel along at some speed until we reach Junction 28 and divert off to the village of Cullompton. I am pleased that we do not have to travel much further on the motorway, which though fast is boring and uninteresting, totally different from our bus journey across the open countryside and moorland from Newquay earlier in the day. Passing through Cullompton, the bus motors onto Willand Old Village followed by Willand New Village.

We are now back onto the narrow B class winding and twisting roads with their high hedges and walls on either side. The leafy country lanes are a pleasant change to the wide long tarmac stretches of the motorways. However, we soon join the A38 that leads first to Wellington and then Taunton. The Brendon and Quantock Hills are in the distance to the north and our left as we travel along the A38.

Leaving Devon we enter the County of Somerset, famed for its strong cider and Cheddar cheese. Travelling along the Vale of Taunton, we reach the small industrial town of **Wellington** (population 13,700) that once had a flourishing wool trade. The Town has given its name to the capital city of New Zealand and also to the "wellie boot". Arthur Wellesley (1769-18520, prime minister and victor at Waterloo in 1815, owned land in the area and took the title the First Duke of Wellington. A 175 feet high monument in memory of the Duke stands on the Blackdown Hills immediately to the south of the Town.

After a brief stop in Wellington, we travel along the A38 for the short distance into Taunton, where we will meet up with my daughter Jill, who is to provide us with our overnight accommodation. Arriving at Taunton bus station at 15.00, we have time for a brief walk around Taunton and a beer before Jill arrives to pick us up and transport us to her cottage in the small hamlet of Stolford, located to the north of Taunton.

Taunton—Somerset—population 61,400

Sited on the River Tone, the market town of Taunton is the largest town in the County of Somerset. It is also the County Town with Somerset County Council's offices being based at County Hall. Taunton has a long history dating back to Saxon times when it was a Town of some significance with its own mint, its first charter being granted back in 903. During the Civil War of the 1640's, Taunton and its Castle changed hands several times when many of the Town's historic buildings were destroyed. Later in 1685, the Duke of Monmouth crowned himself King of England in Taunton in opposition to James II, this before his army's defeat at the Battle of Sedgemoor nearby, the last pitched battle to take place on English soil. In the same year, Judge Jeffreys held his Bloody Assizes in the Great Hall of the Castle with some gruesome punishment passed down on those who supported Monmouth's cause.

Although the Keep of the Castle was demolished in 1662, the original red sandstone walls, gateways and the Great Hall itself remain, albeit more recent restoration works have been undertaken. The Castle now houses the County Museum with the Castle Hotel being built into the old walls of the Castle.

The bus station is located on Tower Street, from where it is only a short walk to the entrance of the Castle and the Somerset County Museum. We do not have time to have a look around the Castle apart from a peep through the arched gateway built into the sandstone walls that leads to the County Museum—maybe another time. Instead we walk on through the pedestrian archway of the Castle Bow under the Castle Hotel and into the busy shopping precincts of North Street.

Not wanting to stop, we cross over the road and head down Hammet Street towards the tall sandstone tower of St Mary Magdalene Church. The 15thC tower is 163 feet tall and with the bright red stonework ornately decorated with figures and carvings. The journalist Simon Jenkins in his TV documentary describes the church as "the finest in England. It makes peace with the sky and not just with a coronet, but with the entire crown jewels cast in red-brown stone". It is certainly a fine and attractive building from the outside.

Back we walk to Tower Street where opposite the Old Municipal Buildings, there is a beer garden outside the Winchester Arms public house. At the far end of the beer garden, is a replica of King Arthur's sword Excalibur, lodged as legend has it, in a block of stone. Settling down on one of the benches with a pint of beer and a bag of crisps for Archie, we wait for Jill to arrive.

Taunton is home to the UK's Hydrographic Office that is responsible for all navigational and hydrographical information around Britain's coastlines. To my mind, it does seem strange that an inland town such as Taunton should have been chosen for the work. I am sure that here is a very good explanation. The Town is also home to Somerset County Cricket Club whose ground is alongside the River Tone and with the imposing sandstone tower of St James Church providing an attractive backdrop. Remaining on a sporting theme, Taunton Racecourse is located some two miles from the Town centre.

* * * * * * *

Daughter Jill arrives just as I finish my beer—good timing. Travelling in the car with Jill, is her dog Bob, a brown and white collie and good friend of Archie. Both dogs are very excited on meeting up again and need a bit of restraining. Off we head out of Taunton, along the leafy lanes of North Somerset on the 45 minute journey towards the small hamlet of Stolford on the coast on Bridgwater Bay.

Stolford (population 97) has no real centre apart from its church that is constructed entirely out of timber, including the bell-tower. The road through the hamlet ends at the sea bank on Bridgwater Bay with the Isle of Steep Holm and the Welsh coast clearly visible across the Bristol Channel. Stolford came to the viewers' attention when it featured on the TV series "Coast" with one of the local fishermen demonstrated his technique of fishing on the mud flats of the estuary using his nets and "mud horse".

A little further down the coast, is the large monolith of Hinkley Point B nuclear power station. Commissioned in 1967, the two advance gas-cooled reactors (AGR) have a designed output of 1,250 MW. The twin magnox nuclear reactors at Hinkley Point A were shut down in 2000 and part of the grounds have since become sites of special scientific interest (SSSI). The whole issue of nuclear power generation is a contentious subject but to my mind, the station is enviro-friendly with no signs of any CO_2 emissions nor are there any large volumes of traffic transporting materials to the station. The safety record of the AGR reactors is excellent and they seem to be good enough for the French who generate some 80% of their energy needs from nuclear power. There is of course the problem of decommissioning and the disposal of the spent fuel rods but I feel sure that the necessary technology will soon be available for these issues to be resolved. What are the other practical low CO_2 alternatives to generating the bulk of the Country's electricity needs by the year 2020? (RANT 5) *

(* This ranting was written before the massive earthquake and subsequent tsunami that devastated parts of the eastern coast of Japan in March 2011 and caused severe damage to the Fukushima nuclear plant resulting in radiation leaks. Even so, my own views on nuclear power generation have not changed.)

We take both Archie and Bob down to the coast and let them off the lead so that they can have a good romp chasing each other and having a tug-of-war contest with a large stick. However, Archie being a bit older and smaller in size, soon tires and concedes. Jill has recently acquired a horse that we must go to see at the nearby stables. Called Spinney, she is a fine-looking flighty bay thoroughbred and a former racehorse. She shares her paddock with two inquisitive donkeys named Boris and Phylis who are cute-looking. Also at the stables, there are nine young fox-hound puppies that are being weaned before joining the local pack of hounds. They are a delight to watch bouncing about. Together with the pot-belly pigs and peacocks, the place is a veritable animal sanctuary.

Back to Jill's white-washed stone cottage. Built in the 1700's, the garden is packed with different varieties of fruit trees with the ripened fruit now ready for picking. After a good home-cooked meal, a glass of wine and catching up on the gossip, it's off to bed in preparation for the next stage of our journey tomorrow morning.

Chapter 4

Taunton To Swindon—Day 4

Wednesday 20th August 2008

Up early to walk the dogs—the weather is looking a bit dull. After a leisurely breakfast, we get ready for the next stage of our journey, initially to Wells. Bridgwater is nearer to Stolford than Taunton and Jill suggests that we catch our bus to Wells from here. This however, would interrupt the continuity of our bus journey from Lands End, so as far as I am concerned, it is a non-starter. Perhaps with hindsight, we should have travelled onto Bidgwater yesterday after Taunton. I think she understood the need to keep within the spirit of my planned trip, albeit reluctantly.

Off we set with Jill at the wheel, back along the narrow leafy lanes that run along the edge of the Quantock Hills into Taunton and the bus station. Saying our goodbyes, including Archie's to Bob, we find the right stand and wait for the First Group No.29 bus to Wells. Whilst we are waiting, the National Express bus to Grimsby comes into the bus station. This will be going direct virtually past my home in Lincoln. I don't give the chance to shorten our journey too much thought even though we would be arriving home that day, in comfort. In any case, I will have had to pay for the fare as my bus pass is not accepted by National Express.

Our bus to Wells arrives at 11.20, some 15 minutes later than scheduled. We soon leave Taunton behind, travelling along the twisty and narrow A361 towards Glastonbury, through West Monkton and Lyng. I seems that the driver is trying to make up for our late departure by his style of driving. Before reaching Othery, we pass Burrow Mump, a natural conical shaped hill standing at the confluence of the River Tone with the River Parrett, that flows through Bridgwater into the Bristol Channel. On the summit of the "Mump" can be seen the ruins of the 15thC St Michael's Church that was used as a sanctuary by Royalist troops during the English Civil War of the 1640's. It now serves as a memorial to the local soldiers who did not return from the two World Wars.

On we travel over the River Cary to join the main A39 that runs along the top of the Polden Hills before dropping down onto the flat Somerset

Levels, passing through Walton and then into **Street** (population 11,100). Classified as a village (albeit a large one), Street derived its name from the 12thC causeway that ran to nearby Glastonbury, along which stone was hauled for the building of the Abbey. The Village is perhaps best known as being the headquarters for the Clarks Shoe Company. Cyrus and James Clark were Quakers that set up the boot and shoe manufacturing business in Street back in 1825. As devout Quakers, all profits were ploughed back to provide welfare, housing and education for the employees. Although shoes are no longer made at Street, the Company's main offices are still located in the centre of the Village. To commemorate shoe manufacture in Street, there is a shoe museum in the Village together with a retail shopping centre called Clarks Village. The Friends Meeting House, built in 1850 and where the Clarks and local Quaker community worshiped, still stands.

About one mile further along the road from Street, we come to the Town of **Glastonbury** (population 8,800—smaller than the "village" of Street). The Town is perhaps now best known for its annual "open-air music festival", that is actually held some six miles to the east of the Town at Pilton—I must confess to never having attended, the Festival being first started a bit after my time. Glastonbury however, has a long ancient history and is the seat of many legends. Joseph of Arimathea, uncle to Jesus, is said to have visited Glastonbury shortly after Jesus' crucifixion and brought with him the "Holy Grail", the cup used at the Last Supper and supposedly containing Christ's blood. The story subsequently led to the Arthurian legends and tales of the Knights of the Round Table. Also the quest for the Holy Grail (remember the 1975 Monty Python film). It is claimed that area around Glastonbury was the Isle of Avalon, at that time standing above the marshes of the Somerset Levels, where King Arthur was brought when mortally wounded in about 540AD. It is further claimed that King Arthur and his Queen Guinevere, were both buried at the Abbey and although their graves were supposedly found in 1191, they have since been lost, leaving no firm evidence to support the claim.

Based on the visit to Glastonbury by Joseph of Arimathea, it has been suggested that the "oldest above ground Christian church in the World" was at Glastonbury, being built in and about 100AD in mud and wattle. The Abbey itself dates from the early 700's with major building works undertaken during the 10th century. At the time of the Domesday Book in 1086, the monastery at Glastonbury was recorded as the richest in the

Country. However, following the Dissolution of the Monasteries in 1536, the Abbey was stripped and left in ruins, although the Abbot's Kitchen, Gatehouse and Abbey Barn that date from the 14thC, are still standing.

As the bus drives into the Town, there is Glastonbury Tor standing above us, a natural conical shaped hill with the ruins of the 14thC St Michael's church on its summit—similar to that at Burrow Mump. Circling around the Tor, are seven roughly symmetrical ringed terraces, the origins of which are a mystery although there are a few theories. The bus continues through the centre of Glastonbury, past the grounds of the Abbey, and out onto the A39 leading to Wells.

For six miles, the A39 single carriageway highway heads across the flat Somerset Levels, past the hedge lined green pasture and fertile arable fields, to the Cathedral City of Wells. The bus driver is making up some of the time lost in the late departure from Taunton. At 12.35, we arrive at the bus station in Wells and the weather is fine and dry.

Wells—Somerset—population 10,400

The Cathedral City of Wells (first charter 1160) is England's second smallest city. Surprisingly, the accolade for the smallest city goes to the City of London, which includes the financial and business sectors with few permanent residents. Located on the southern edge of the Mendip Hills, the City can trace its past back to the Romans who established a settlement in the vicinity. In the Saxon period, it became an important centre during the rule of the Kings of Wessex. The City was later involved with events during the English Civil War of the 1640's and also during the Monmouth Rebellion of the 1680's.

Leaving the bus station, we walk up through the main shopping area of the High Street with its multitude of retail shops, to the Market Place. Being a Wednesday, it is Market Day with the entire area of the Market Place taken up with a variety of covered stalls selling fruit and vegetables, bakery and meat produce, clothing, shoes, leather items, ironmongery and tools, jewellery, craft items and many more. Medieval charters dating back over 800 years have given Wells the right to hold fairs in the Market Place. There is the traditional busyness and buzz that you usually find on market days, especially it being around lunchtime. The smell of sizzling sausages coming from one of the stalls is too tempting to just walk past, so a double sausage sandwich topped with fried onions will do for my lunch and if he behaves, Archie can have some too.

In the far corner of the Market Place, is the covered stone porch-way that leads to the Cathedral precincts. Dating from 1450 and built in the local limestone, the arch-way is called as the Penniless Porch, so named as a place for "penniless beggars" to ply their ware. Entering into the Cathedral precincts, the full vista of the magnificent

12th / 13thC Cathedral Church of St Andrew is viewed from across the Green. The elaborate stone façade of the west front that incorporates 356 figures carved in the locally quarried oolitic limestone, is one of largest of its type in world. We are not able to go inside, but from information obtained, there is stunning design of a scissors arch in the Nave that was installed in the 1340's to stabilise the main central tower. It seems that this was a unique piece of medieval engineering to resolve differential settlement of the tower foundations, all done without the aid of modern day design techniques. Inside too, is a 24 hour astronomical clock with jousting knights performing on the quarter hour. The Cathedral bells have the heaviest ring of ten bells in the World, the tenor bell weighing in at a staggering 56 hundredweight—just under three tons. With the limited lifting equipment that the cathedral builders had at the time, it must have required some effort to hoist and position these cast-iron bells.

Walking around the north side of the Cathedral, we find Vicar's Close, said to be the oldest continuously inhabited medieval street in Europe. The attractive row of stone cottages with their tall chimneys and small neat front gardens on both sides of the Close, were built to provide bachelor accommodation for the men of the Cathedral choir—could have been the original "bachelor pads" although I doubt if there would have been much "partying".

Walking back to the Market Place through the Penniless Porch, we find the Porch's twin built at the same time in the 15th century and known as the Bishop's Eye. This archway takes us into the area of the Bishop's Palace. The Palace has been the Bishop's residence for over 800 years with its high defensive walls, moat and gatehouse complete with drawbridge and portcullis. In the Palace Gardens are the springs dedicated to St Andrew from which the Cathedral takes its name. There is a charge for going into the Palace and gardens but as time is limited, we give it a miss.

I must make a point of revisiting Wells when time is not so limited and take in the architectural and historical attractions of the City. Also to take in a visit to the nearby limestone caves at Wookey Hole and Cheddar Gorge that are both to north-west of City. Back we walk down High

Street and Market Street to the bus station to catch our next connection, this time to the twin bishopric town of Bath.

* * * * * * *

The single-decker First Group No.173 bus to Bath is waiting at the stand. On we board showing my "oldies pass" and with Archie leading me towards the back seat. After walking around Wells with my rucksack on my back, I am ready to sit down for a rest. Off we set at 13.45 out off Wells and along the B3739 and twisting minor roads of rural Somerset, through the rolling green countryside, passing through the villages of Gurney Slade, Chilcompton to join the main road near Radstock. The small town of **Radstock** (population 5,300) sits on the line of the old Roman Fosseway and was at one time, the centre of the Somerset coal mining industry. Coal was first mined at Radstock in 1763 with the Town prospering during the days of the Industrial Revolution and into the 1800's. However, some 200 years later in 1973, the mine was closed although the Town's mining heritage is still preserved at the local museum in the old town hall. After a brief stop, the bus travels on through the centre, past the Town's war memorial, leaving on the A367 that heads towards Bath.

Although there are now a number of twists and turns in the A367, it roughly follows the route of the old Fosseway, the Roman military road that ran from Exeter in the south to Lincoln in the north. On we motor through the Somerset countryside until we see buildings of Bath in the distance. We reach Bath bus station at 15.00 and immediately make our way into the City centre.

Bath—Somerset—population 84,000

Although Bath has no cathedral and its population is well below 250,000, it has nevertheless, city status, this being granted by Royal charter back in 1590. Sited on the banks of the River Avon near the southern edge of the Cotswold Hills, legend has it that in about 860BC, Bladud, King of the Britons, first discovered the famous hot water springs and dedicated their curative powers to the Goddess Sul—more about this later. When the Romans arrived 900 years later in 43AD, they named the settlement that existed at that time "Aquae Sulis" (waters of Sul) and built a temple to include the bathing complex fed by the hot water springs. The Roman temple and baths still exist and form part of the City of Bath World Heritage Site (1987).

The geo-thermal springs in Bath emanate from an extinct underground volcanic system and are the only naturally occurring hot water springs in the UK, with the temperature of the spa water at 115 degrees Fahrenheit (46 degrees C). The spa resort was restored during the Elizabethan period when the health giving properties of the mineral waters were identified and publicised. From this time, Bath became a popular resort visited by the rich and famous.

In the 18th century, Bath experienced a major revival resulting in an expansion boom with many fine and elegant buildings being constructed using the locally quarried creamy-gold Bath limestone. Many were designed in the Palladian style and include the much photographed Royal Crescent, Landsdown Crescent and The Circus, the latter being laid out in three long curved terraces. During this same period, Pultney Bridge was constructed over the River Avon, which incorporates a covered shopping arcade, similar to that on the Rialto Bridge in Venice. A few years later during the early 19th century, the Bath Theatre Royal was built, one of the oldest and beautiful theatres in the Country and at which Beau Nash presided as Master of Ceremonies.

The Abbey Church of St Peter and St Paul in the City centre dates back to the early 16th century, although the foundations upon which the present Abbey is built are from the 12thC Norman church. Although being allowed to fall into some disrepair, major restoration work was undertaken on the Abbey during the late 18th century.

Closer to modern times, Bath suffered much damage from enemy bombing during the Second World War when some 19,000 buildings were destroyed or badly damaged. The bombing raids by the German Luftwaffe during 1942 on Bath and on other non-strategic but picturesque towns and cities in England were known as the "Baedeker Blitz". It is said that the raids were in retaliation to the RAF bombing of the Hanseatic League city of Lubeck in Germany and that the towns and cities targeted were chosen from the German Baedeker Tourist Guide to Britain.

Like in many other similar towns throughout the Country, Bath once had a flourishing engineering industry. This has virtually disappeared with the City now relying on mainly tourism as its main source of employment. With all its magnificent stone Georgian buildings and terraces together with Roman Baths and Abbey, there is much for the visitor to see and do in Bath.

From the bus station near the River Avon, we make our way towards the City centre, walking first up Southgate past the many attractive office buildings, shops and department stores built in the locally quarried creamy Bath limestone. Crossing over the road, we continue up Stall Street, past York Street with a slender elegant stone arch spanning over the roadway. A bit further on, we pass by the stone portico of the Pump Room and Roman Baths where inside you can "take the waters". Then around the corner, we come into the pedestrianised area of Church Street, where in front of us stands the magnificent 16^{th}C Abbey building. We spend a little time taking in the splendour of the decorative west front of the Abbey. The summer lunchtime organ recitals are advertised but we are too late and have to make do with a classical guitarist playing outside—he is very good.

Walking around the side of the Abbey, we reach the High Street, where the attractive stone fronted City Hall is located. On up to Argyle Street and along to the 18^{th}C Pulteney Bridge that spans the River Avon with its covered shopping arcade built over the old stone bridge. Heading down Grand Parade that runs alongside the River, there is an excellent viewpoint of the Pulteney Bridge with the more recently constructed weir below holding back the waters of the Avon. The waters cascading over the three semi-circular weirs with the backdrop of the bridge, make an excellent photo shot from this viewpoint. To add a bit of interest, there is a motor launch coming through the arch of the bridge carrying sightseers. Because of the weirs, this will be as far as it will be able to sail.

From the same viewpoint, we look down onto the well maintained Parade Gardens with the deck-chairs set out for those wishing to take a rest. Unfortunately for us, there is a sign at the top of the steps leading down to the Gardens indicating "No Dogs Allowed"—fair enough. Across the River, can be seen The Recreation Ground, known as "The Rec" and home to Bath Rugby Club, who currently play in the Guinness Premiership Division and who over recent years, have been one of the most successful clubs in English rugby. Behind us stands the eastern end of the Abbey. My camera is fairly clicking away. Crossing over Grand Parade and walking up to the Abbey, there is a water fountain with a young girl pouring water out of her urn. Around the stone base is the inscription "Water is Best". I am bound to agree.

Being now a bit weary and thirsty, I look around for somewhere to sit and enjoy a beer. I find a suitable hostelry that has seats outside and order suitable refreshment—its near Archie's mealtime so he can have his dinner. I have not yet arranged any accommodation for this evening, which I plan to spend in Swindon. Phoning the local Information Office on my mobile phone and requesting somewhere that is "dog friendly" they helpfully supplied me with the number of the Campanile Hotel, that although being a little way out of the Town centre, sounded ideal. Having confirmed our booking, we get back to enjoying of visit around Bath.

Making our way down Pierrepont Street, we enter the narrow North Parade Passage where a bit further along is Sally Lunn's House. Built circa 1480, it is said to be the oldest house in Bath with Sally Lunn, who was the originator of the well known Sally Lunn Bun (a light semi-sweet bread), living at the house around the year 1640. The four storied stone building with it curved bay window at ground level is now used as tearooms, there also being a small museum inside. Outside, there are many tourists milling around, making the taking of a photograph difficult. It is of course, the height of the tourist season with the City as a whole being crowded with visitors, like ourselves, so I shouldn't complain.

Walking back along the alleyways to Stall Street, we come across an open space with a large sycamore tree in the centre. Suspended from the branches of the tree, is a full sized painted pig! We had seen other full sized ornamental painted pigs elsewhere when walking around Bath and it transpired that some 108 of these pigs had been decorated and named by local artists and placed around the City during the summer of 2008 to be later auctioned. The event is called "King Bladud's Pigs", named after the legendary King of the Britons and the founder of the City of Bath way back around 860BC. The story is that Bladud had been studying in Athens when he contracted leprosy. On returning home, he disguised himself as a swineherd but found that he had passed the leprosy infection onto his pigs. Crossing the Avon, the pigs found the warm mud around the hot water springs, which they rolled themselves in as pigs do. Miraculously, the pigs were cured of their affliction and when Bladud saw this, he too took to the hot spring waters to bathe. Soon Bladud was cured of his leprosy and when he later went on to become king, he founded the City of Bath and dedicated the curative powers of the spring water to the Celtic Goddess Sul. Whilst there is no historical record of these events, it certainly makes a good story. It seems that the decorative pig suspended in the sycamore tree was named "Pig of Paradise".

Turning back towards the River along Orchard Street and down Newark Street, we head back towards the bus station, passing by a major construction site for a new Shopping Centre that will surely be of great benefit to the shopperholics of Bath. Boarding surrounds the construction site but peeping through the gaps, I can see a vast hole having been excavated, at the bottom of which machinery and workmen are scuttling around preparing for the pouring of the concrete foundations. It looks to be a major project and it's a pity the contractor McAlpines, did not put in a viewing platform for the inquisitive like myself, so to be able to observe what was taking place. Maybe they did but I did not come across it.

We arrive back at the bus station for our next connection, this time to Chippenham. We have had just over a hour to look around Bath that elsewhere was clearly insufficient to take in everything that there is to see in the City, with it elegant and historic buildings. It would have been good to have been able to visit the likes of the Royal Crescent with its fine curve of Georgian Palladium designed buildings together with the many fine gardens and parks. Had we had time, we could have hopped onto the open-top sightseeing bus that tours the City's main attractions.

* * * * * * *

Catching the 16.07 No.X31 Pickford Faresaver bus, we head out of Bath along the main A4 eastwards towards Chippenham. We are apparently not going to get much peace on this journey as there are some exceptionally noisy youngsters aboard. Although they are not being destructive, they seem to be incapable of just talking to each other, resorting to shrieking and yelling at the top of their voices. The bus driver is obviously in a difficult position though I am sure that had there been an old fashioned conductor aboard (a person of days past), he or she would have instilled some calm. I realise that economics came into the decision to dispense with conductors on buses, but on some services, there surely is a case for them to be reintroduced, if not to rescue the passengers from rowdy behaviour but to avoid damage being caused to the bus fabric. (RANT 6). However, we are in no danger of being assaulted, so I guess that we will just have to put up with the noise.

Soon after leaving Bath on the A4, we leave the County of Somerset and enter that of Wiltshire. Five miles further along the road, we come to the village of **Box** (population 3,500). Perhaps best known for Brunel's Tunnel, Box's history goes back to Roman times with the discovery of a Roman villa nearby that still has intact the mosaic floors of all its twenty rooms, said to be one of the richest collections of mosaic floors in Roman Britain. Bath stone, the shelly oolitic limestone much sought after for use as building stone, was quarried here at Box and with the opening of the Kennet / Avon Canal, the stone was transported by barge to London and beyond. The boom days however came to an end when the last of the quarries was closed in 1969. During the construction of Brunel's tunnel for the London to Bristol railway, up to 4,000 workmen were living and working around Box, most in temporary shanty towns and camps. The one and three-quarters mile long tunnel through the limestone of the Cotswold Hills from Corsham in the east to Box in the west, where the grand western portal stands at the tunnel's entrance, took five years to complete. The Rev. W.V. Awdry, author of Thomas the Tank Engine books lived at Box in his earlier years and maybe the sight of the sight of the steam trains travelling between London and Bristol gave him some inspiration for his popular children's books.

On we travel through Box along the A4 and into the market town of **Corsham** (12,000), which is sited at the eastern end of the Box Railway Tunnel. As at Box, Bath limestone has over the years been extensively quarried and although output is much reduced, the mining of limestone is still undertaken at Corsham. In the Town centre is the Elizabethan manor house of Corsham Court. Once used as a major administration centre by the Ministry of Defence during World War 2 and later during the period of the Cold War, the Court is now open to visitors.

Back onto the A4 we have five more miles to go before reaching Chippenham. The bus is running behind schedule and we have only a few minutes wait before our next connection. On reaching the outskirts of Chippenham, the bus route frustratingly, deviates off through the Town's housing estates and even diverts to the railway station before reaching the bus station itself. We arrive well behind schedule at 17.10 but fortunately the bus to our next destination, Swindon, is also running late.

Chippenham—Wiltshire—population 35,000

The market town of Chippenham sits on the River Avon with the Marlborough Downs to the east, the Cotswold Hills to the north and west, and Salisbury Plain to the south. Although there is evidence of a Romano-British settlement, the Town proper was founded by the Saxons around 600. A little later in 878 and following their defeat at the nearby Battle of Ethandun, the Danish Vikings surrendered to Alfred the Great at Chippenham.

In medieval times, the Town had an active wool industry until it was hit by the plague in 1611 and 1636. The consequences resulted in great hardship to the local inhabitants. The arrival of Brunel's Great Western Railway in 1841 attracted growth in the manufacture of both machinery for agriculture and engineering equipment for the railways. The Westinghouse Brake and Signal Company are still located in Town. Being situated on both the main railway line between London and Bristol and the A4 trunkroad, Chippenham has in recent years become more of a dormitory town for both Swindon and Bristol.

In the Town centre is the Yelde Hall. Built in 1458, the medieval timber framed building was used as a market hall, followed by the Town gaol, a savings bank, fire station, museum and now as the Tourist Information Centre. Another interesting structure in the Town centre is the Buttercross, with its pitched roof supported on six circular stone columns. Built c.1570, it was originally used for the sale of meat and diary products before being moved and re-erected as an open gazebo at Castle Combe Manor House. However in 1995 local funding enabled it to be moved again and re-erected in the pedestrianised area of the Town centre.

On Rowden Hill, there is a plaque to commemorate the spot where Eddie Cochran, the popular American rock and roll star was killed in a car crash in 1960 whilst on tour in the UK. Every year, the Eddie Cochran Festival is held in the Chippenham in memory of the singer.

* * * * * * *

Having only a few minutes between our bus connections, we have no time to explore the sights of Chippenham. The No.55 Stagecoach double-decker bus to Swindon is running some eight minutes late, sufficient for us to make our next connection. Just as well as it would otherwise be very late by the time we arrived in Swindon. Leaving the bus station in Chippenham at 17.15, the bus passes through the Town centre and back onto the A4. At least from the bus window, we are able to get a view of the old Buttercross now back standing in the Market Place, together with some of the other old buildings in the Town centre.

Out back onto the A4 and around a series of round-a-bouts before our bus gathers up speed along the A4, first to Studley and then onto the market town of **Calne** (population 14,000), that is sited on the north-western edge of the North Downs. Although dating back to Anglo-Saxon times, it was during the 18th and 19th centuries that the Town prospered by its woollen broadcloth industry with more than twenty mills operating. This is now long gone although some of the mill buildings are still standing together with many of the fine stone Georgian houses of the mill owners and clothiers. Up to the 1980's, Harris's pork sausages and other food products were prepared in Calne providing substantial employment to Town. This too has now gone but Calne has recovered with the influx of light industrial development and is now considered to be a growth area.

Nearby are a number of Neolithic structures with Avebury Stone Circle, West Kennet Long Barrow and Silbury Hill all some seven miles to the east of the Town. Maybe it is a coincidence but Calne is also at one of the corners of the "Wiltshire Crop Circle Triangle" together with Malborough and Warminster, where unexplained formations appear usually overnight in the corn fields. Some claim that these circles or formations, are made by aliens from outer space, but I would suggest that it is now generally accepted that they are in fact made by persons enjoying themselves by practicing their artistic skills in the dark of the night. It would have to be fanciful to believe otherwise.

From Calne, the bus route follows the A3102 that leads to Swindon, first to the village of Lyneham and then onto **RAF Lyneham** with its imposing entrance gates and leafy backdrop. The air force base is well known as the home of the RAF's fleet of the massive Hercules transport aircraft. The base however, is scheduled for closure in 2012 with the aircraft being transferred elsewhere. Sadly RAF Lyneham is often seen on our television these days in 2009 with the Hercules planes bringing back the bodies of the servicemen killed in Iraq and Afghanistan, all young men in the prime of their life. What is this so-called "War on Terror" all about?—why are the British troops seemingly fighting alone in the hot-spot of Helman Province?—where is the support from some of the other NATO countries, notably the French, German and Italian forces?—when will it all end? (RANT 7). It may be too controversial to make my own views known on the subject except to say that we all owe these brave servicemen, including those injured and maimed, a great depth of gratitude. *

(* When writing this passage, it is at the time of Remembrance Day 2009 when our thoughts go out to those who have paid the ultimate sacrifice, especially this year in Afghanistan when virtually every day, another death(s) is reported due to terrorist activities—"We will remember them")

The closure of the RAF base at Lyneham is understandably of some concern to the local people, many of who are employed as civilians at the base. It will be a difficult time for all should the RAF pull out altogether though hopefully the base will be re-developed to create new jobs.

On we travel along the A3102, past the lush green pastures and arable fields of ripe grain. The countryside is well wooded. After another few miles we come to the market town of **Wootton Bassett** (population 11,000). Mentioned in the Domesday Book, it was the home of Katherine Parr, the sixth and surviving wife of King Henry VIII. At least she didn't lose her head. From the bus we see the curious 17^{th}C Town Hall with its steeply pitched roof and timbered white upper storey supported on 15 stone pillars, the lower floor being open to the elements. However, Wootton Bassett is better known nationally as "the most patriotic town in Britain". Being on the road from nearby RAF Lyneham, the funeral hearses, carrying the Union Jack draped coffins of servicemen killed in action in Afghanistan, pass through the Town. Each time a funeral cortege is due, the good folk of Wootton Bassett (and others) turn out in silent tribute to that young life lost. To the tolling of a single church bell with standards / flags dipped, the cortege stops at the Town's war memorial in respect. Well done Wootton Bassett, you set an example for us all. *

(* In recognition of the tributes paid to the servicemen killed in action, the Town of Wootton Bassett in 2011 became "Royal Wootton Bassett", one of only three towns in the whole of England to have the title "Royal" preceding its name.)

On we head until we eventually reach the outskirts of Swindon, our journey's end for this day. We enter the Town along the Great Western Way, an appropriate name for such an important railway town. The bus route into Swindon travels along Station Road, past the railway station and the long line of red brick station buildings, before reaching the bus station itself at New Bridge Square in the centre of the Town. The time is about 18.00 and it is getting late, too late to think about catching a bus to our hotel for the evening that I knew as a little way out of the Town centre. In any case, I hadn't asked for directions to the hotel when I had booked our accommodation earlier in the day. A big mistake!

Resorting to have to pay for a taxi, I hail one of the cabs standing outside the bus station and ask the driver to take us to the Campanile Hotel. "Never heard of it guv" back comes his reply. After some consultations with his fellow cabbies, it transpires that the hotel has recently been taken over by another chain of hotels and has changed its name. Even then he isn't too sure of its whereabouts but heads off in the direction he has been advised by his colleagues. Thankfully, they have got it right and we arrive at our hotel some five minutes later and £6.20 lighter.

The Campanile is a fairly modern hotel located in one of Swindon's business parks, approximately two miles out of the City centre. It looks both well appointed and comfortable. It has been some time since Archie has had some exercise, so having dumped my rucksack, we head out for a walk, not knowing where we are going. Behind the hotel there is a tarmaced footpath cum cycle-way, one of the many around the Town. Having a choice, we head off in a direction that I think will be for the best.

The track takes us through the lightly wooded areas on the outskirts of Swindon, past some play areas and although it was pleasant enough to be out in the fresh air, I couldn't say where we had been, being totally enclosed by trees. Making our way back to our hotel, Archie is bedded down for the night and I make for the restaurant downstairs for a meal, to be followed by some liquid refreshment.

Back in our room, the headline news on television is about the tragic air crash in Madrid in which 153 passengers and crew have been killed. The Spanair flight had overshot the runway as a result of mechanical failure, crashing at the end in flames. The pictures shown on television are quite graphic and harrowing. On a more happier note, the other main news item is on the British successes at the Bejing Olympics where another gold medal has been won, making it 17 golds in total and putting Team GB in third position after China and the USA.

It has been a long day since leaving Jill's cottage in Stolford, although it has been most enjoyable with sight-seeing stops at Wells and Bath. Archie is now fast asleep on his blanket and I am more than ready to "hit the hay".

Chapter 5

Swindon To Northampton—Day 5

Thursday 21st August 2008

Being up reasonably early to take Archie for his early morning exercise, we head through the trees for the footpath cum cycle track behind our hotel that we had explored the previous evening. It is dry and the weather seems to be set fine for the rest of the day. We need to keep to the footpath as there are a number of cyclists using the track on their way to work. All very environmentally friendly and good exercise and at least they are not contributing to any traffic congestion. Back at the hotel, I enjoy a good breakfast from the "help yourself" breakfast bar. I much preferred to be able to select what and how much I want to eat.

When booking out, Archie gets some attention from some other guests. He takes it all in, putting on a look of "do you have anything to give me?" Off we head for the local bus to take us into the Town centre and bus station for the start of the next stage of our journey. The time is 09.20 and unless I am to fork-out for my bus fare, I have another ten minutes to wait before my "oldies pass" is valid. The buses are coming by fairly regular so it is not long to wait before the next bus came along.

Swindon—Wiltshire—population 180,000

Sited on the edge of the Wiltshire Downs, Swindon can trace its origins back to Saxon times, being mentioned in the Domesday Book. During the early part of the 19th century, the Town experienced substantial expansion brought about with the construction of the canals. This was followed with the building of the railway between London and Bristol, when in 1840 Brunel chose Swindon as the location to site his engineering workshops to service the Great Western Railway (GWR). During the 19th and the first half of the 20th centuries, Swindon continued to flourish as one of the Country's major railway towns.

A "Railway Village" was constructed by the Company to house their workers that included health-care facilities for employees and their families "from cradle to grave". This model for employees' health care was later used as a blue-print for setting up the Country's National Health Service. Steam locomotives and rolling stock were manufactured at the railway workshops for many years and by the early part of the 20th century, the Works were one of the largest in the Country. However with the end of the steam age looming, the last steam loco ever built for British Railways, the "Evening Star", was rolled out of the Works at Swindon in 1960. The engineering works finally closed in 1986. Today, part of the former engineering workshops are used to house the Steam Railway Museum that preserves Swindon's railway history.

Being designated as one of Britain's New Towns, Swindon has seen further development and expansion. With the end of the manufacture of railway rolling stock in the 1980's, other industries have since come to Swindon to plug the employment gap. These include the car manufacturers Honda and BMW, together with a number of "high tech" industries. Swindon enjoys a relatively low level of unemployment and a continuing growth in the population.

Our bus makes its way into the centre of the Town, passing the buildings of the former locomotive engineering workshops and the nearby neat rows of stone terraced houses. With little spare time, we do not have the opportunity to explore Swindon Town Centre, although it seems that it is mainly composed of retail shops—not my scene. However, it would have been interesting to visit the Steam Railway Museum and also the Railway Village Museum although I doubt if Archie would have been allowed inside. Our next destination is Oxford where I plan some time to look around, not having visited the University City previously.

Our bus arrives at the bus station in the centre of Swindon at 09.45 just as the No.66 bus to Oxford is about to leave. The next bus is in thirty minutes that will mean less time to spend in Oxford, so I desperately try to attract the attention of the driver to plead with him to allow us aboard. But the door of the bus is closed and it is reversing out of the stand. However, the driver seems to have taken pity on us as he shouts to me through the door to go around the corner where there is a stop on the main road immediately outside the station. It is only a few yards to walk and by the time we get there, the No.66 Stagecoach bus is coming out of the bus station and along the main road towards us. Onto the bus we climb with smiles all round and on showing my pass and thanking the driver, we make for the back seat to settle down for our hour and a quarter trip to Oxford.

* * * * * * *

Out of Swindon we motor negotiating what seemed to be an endless number of roundabouts. I later discovered that Swindon is famed for its number of roundabouts, the best known being nicknamed the "Magic Roundabout" and which consists of five small being incorporated into one large roundabout. On reaching the Town's outskirts, we head off along the A420 that leads to Oxford.

Soon after leaving Swindon, we cross the county divide from Wiltshire into Oxfordshire following which the bus route takes a detour off the main road into the pretty village of **Shrivenham** (population 5,500) with its many thatched stone cottages. The Village church dates back to the Norman period and nearby, the remains of a Roman villa have been unearthed. Located in the Village is the Beckett Estate and Beckett Hall dating back to the 11th century and formerly home to the Barrington family. Used by the US army during World War 2, it is now the headquarters for the Defence Academy of the United Kingdom that includes the Defence College of Management and Technology (formerly the Royal Military College of Science). Apparently, Benjamin Disraeli PM was a frequent visitor to Beckett Hall.

Back onto the A420, we travel on down the Vale of White Horse with Whitehorse Hill (856 ft) to the south that is crossed by the Ridgeway long distance footpath. After a few more miles, we again leave the A420 for the small market town of **Faringdon** (population 5,600). The centrepiece of the Market Place is the 17thC sandy coloured Old Town Hall with the Town's war memorial plaque fixed on one of the sides of the Old Hall. Facing onto the Market Place, is the 16thC Old Crown Coaching Inn with its pale pink frontage, opposite which is a water conduit fixed to an ornate rectangular stone column. On a small hill overlooking the Town, is the all—brick Faringdon Folly. The 100 feet high four sided tower with its octagonal turret at the top, was constructed in 1935 by Lord Berners. It is claimed that to date, the Folly at Faringdon is the last of its kind to be constructed in the Country.

Back onto the A420, we pass through the green Oxfordshire countryside. Soon we come to a section of dual carriageway where the bus picks up some speed, bypassing the village of Kingston Bagpuize, and then on towards Oxford itself. Stopping first at Bessels Leigh, we approach the outskirts of the University City of Oxford. Still on the A420, we enter the City along Botley Road, crossing over the River Thames and the main line railway by the station before driving into the Gloucester Green Bus Station in the City centre. The time is 11.00 and the weather is fine and sunny.

Oxford—Oxfordshire—population 165,000

Sited at the confluence of the River Cherwell with the River Thames (known as the Isis where it passes through the City), the University and Cathedral City of Oxford is nicknamed "The City of Dreaming Spires". The term was coined by the poet Matthew Arnold, with the elegant spire of the University Church of St Mary the Virgin being prominent on the skyline.

Oxford was first occupied by the Saxons and soon became a frontier town between the old kingdoms of Mercia and Wessex, later to be raided by the Danish Vikings on a number of occasions. Conflict didn't stop with the Vikings when in 1355 fighting broke out between the local townsfolk and college students over a dispute initially concerning ale, although trouble had been brewing for a number of years previous (sorry about the pun). Known as the St Scholastica Riot and lasting over two days, 93 people were killed. The uneasy relationship between the townsfolk and students, often referred to as "Town and Gown", lasted for many years up to as recently as the mid 20th century, when the Mayor was given an honorary degree by the University and the Vice-Chancellor made an Honorary Freeman of the City.

The University in Oxford was founded during the 11th century and is the oldest English speaking university in the world. It grew rapidly following the expulsion of foreigners from Paris University in 1167, with the founding of University College in 1249, Balliol in 1263 and Merton in 1264. During the period of the Commonwealth in the 1650's, Oliver Cromwell was appointed Chancellor and prevented the University from being closed down by the Puritan forces. Oxford University comprises 38 self governing colleges and 6 permanent halls and ranks amongst the top ten universities of the World. The academic year is divided into three terms, Michaelmas, Hilary and Trinity. However, it was following the uneasy relationship with local townsfolk and accusations of murder, that in 1209 some of the college academics fled eastwards, leading to the establishment of a breakaway university in Cambridge.

There is much rivalry between the two universities of Oxford and Cambridge, not least on sporting occasions. In addition to the many hotly contested annual fixtures and events, not least the annual Varsity Rugby match at Twickenham, the University Boat Race held on the Thames each year in April perhaps attracts most publicity. The four mile plus course is rowed by super-fit crews of eight oarsmen from both Oxford and Cambridge. It is an event on the national sporting calendar that attracts a very large following. The first race was rowed in 1829 and to date (2009), Oxford has won 75, Cambridge 79, with one dead heat. Oxford, you need to catch up!

The College of Christ Church, which includes the Cathedral, was established in 1546 by Henry VIII, no doubt with dubious funds obtained following the dissolution of monasteries. It is unique in that it is both one of the largest constituent colleges and is also a cathedral church that acts as the college chapel. The Dean of the Cathedral is also the Dean of the College. The Main Hall of Christ Church is a spectacular piece of architecture with its lofty hammerhead timbered roof. The Cathedral & College Choir is nationally and internationally famous, having made numerous recordings and radio broadcasts.

University Church of St Mary the Virgin was the first building of University and has one of the most beautiful spires in England, that sits above the 13^{th}C tower. The south porch is what has been described as in the eccentric baroque style with ornate spiral columns each side of the main doorway. The present church was rebuilt during the $15^{th}/16^{th}$ centuries in Perpendicular style. John Wesley, the founder of the Methodist Church in England, preached there when studying at Lincoln College. It seems that his sermons were quite controversial with the established Church of the day and "rocked a few boats". As a result, he was never invited back.

The City centre is pinpointed on Carfax at the junction of Cornmarket Street, Queen Street, High Street and St Aldate's, the word Carfax being from the French "carrefour" and meaning "crossroads". On one corner stands the Carfax Tower, a 74 feet high clock tower that is the remains of the 13^{th}C St Martin's Church. From the top of the tower, there is an excellent view over "the City of Dreaming Spires"

With the assent to the throne of the Catholic Queen Mary and the disestablishment of the new Church of England in 1555, the Anglican Archbishop Thomas Cranmer together with Bishops Hugh Latimer and Nicholas Ridley were tried for heresy against the teachings of the Church of Rome. Their trial was held in Oxford and being found guilty, the three were burnt at the stake in Broad Street. A stone cross in the road marks the spot. The Martyrs Memorial stands at the south end of St Giles, near to the spot where the three eminent Anglican clergymen died for their religious beliefs. A century later, Oxford became embroiled in the Civil War where the University's loyalty was with the King though the Town's sympathy, not unsurprisingly, was with the Parliamentary cause. During the War, the University housed the Court of King Charles, but in 1646, had to yield to the Parliamentarian Forces under General Fairfax in what is known as the Siege of Oxford.

In addition to the 38 self governing colleges and 6 permanent halls that together form the University of Oxford, there are a number of well known museums, libraries, theatres and gardens that are all part of the City.

The Ashmolean Museum was founded in 1683 and is the oldest museum in the UK. Inside, is the original collection of Elias Ashmole, the Museum's founder together with significant collections of fine art and specimens of antiquity and archaeology. These include Oliver Cromwell's death mask and Lawrence of Arabia's ceremonial dress. Other museums in Oxford include the Natural History Museum, the Museum of the History of Science and the Pitt River Museum.

The Bodleian Library (or "The Bod" as it is affectionately known), was founded by Sir Thomas Bodley in 1598 and is one of the oldest libraries in Europe. It contains over eight million volumes, stacked on 117 miles of shelving and includes every book of note published in the UK and Ireland with a legal right to request a free copy of every new book published. As a result, the number of books and length of shelving is still growing. "The Bod" is a reference library only, whereby books cannot be removed from the reading rooms. With so many volumes to store, the Library is housed at four main locations, one being the Clarendon Buildings that were formerly occupied by the Oxford Printing Press. Another is at the Radcliffe Camera, a circular building in plan with two stories and a domed roof complete with a cupola at the top and which was built during 1737/48 in the English Palladian style. An impressive building located behind the University Church of St Mary the Virgin, it has since 1860, housed part of the Bodleian Library. Why Camera?

The Sheldonian Theatre on Broad Street was designed by Sir Christopher Wren and built in 1668. "D" shaped in plan, the Theatre can seat up to 1,000 people. The roof is totally unsupported internally and with a span of more than 70 feet, it is carried by a series of bolted metal trusses. It was for many years, the largest unsupported floor / roof in existence and some 350 years later, it is still standing. On top, is the tall white eight-sided cupola that was added at a later date. The Theatre is used for music concerts, lectures, university ceremonies and conferences but not for drama productions. Not sure why.

The Town Hall in the centre of the City was built in the Gothic Revival style in 1893 on the site of the old Guildhall. Despite Oxford being a City, it is nevertheless called the "Town" Hall and in addition to being the seat of local government, it also houses the Museum of Oxford.

The University of Oxford Botanical Garden is located to the east of the City centre on the banks of the River Cherwell. Founded in 1621, it is the UK's oldest botanical garden and one of the earliest scientific gardens in the world. The Gardens contain over 8,000 different plants species representing around 90% of world's higher plant families. The Gardens, covering some 4.5 acres complete with glasshouses, are open to visitors.

One of the more famous sporting moments in Oxford took place at the Iffley Road Running Track in May 1954 when Roger Bannister, with the assistance of two pacemakers, broke the four minute barrier for the running of the mile. Since that time, running the mile in less than four minutes by professional athletes is the norm with the world record currently standing at 3 minutes 43.13 seconds. However, in the amateur days of Bannister, running a sub four minute mile was a major achievement.

Over the years, many famous people from politicians to authors to scientists, have lived in Oxford or passed through its University. Perhaps one of the best known never to have attended the University as a student, was William Morris (1877-1963), later to become Viscount Nuffield. Having lived in Oxford from an early age, Morris started off by repairing bicycles from his parents' home. In 1912, he then went on to design the "Bullnose Morris", although he had to wait until the end of the First World War before the car went into mass production, the factory being located at Cowley on the outskirts of Oxford. In 1928, the car company, Morris Motors, then started the production of the early Morris Minors, followed in 1936 by the popular Morris Eight Series I with its 943cc engine. After the Second World War, production started on the Morris Minor MM (nicknamed Moggy Minors) that was followed by the iconic Mini. Merging with Austins in 1952, the new company, the British Motor

Corporation and then by British Leyland, soon became the largest car producer in the UK, that went on to include Land Rover and Jaguar.

For various reasons, the successor Company could not compete with the world market and in 2005, the only surviving totally owned British car manufacturer went out of business. A sad day indeed for the British engineering industry which has seen manufacturing plummeting over the past 30 years. Why is it that other European countries are still competitive in this field whilst we in the UK have seen our traditional engineering industries virtually disappear? I have my own views on this matter that I will not expound upon at this time (RANT 8). At least they are still producing the New Mini at Cowley, albeit under the badge of the German company BMW.

Nevertheless, the legacy left by William Morris, the entrepreneur and philanthropist, still continues. His establishment of the Nuffield Foundation with generous financial endowments given towards education and social welfare, together with the founding of the Nuffield College at Oxford, benefits many and will keep his name alive.

There is much more to say and write about the City of Oxford and I know that I have only just touched to surface of its history, heritage and what there is to see in this City of Dreaming Spires. Having arrived at the bus station at 11.00, my intention is to spend some time looking around the City, that to my shame, I had never previously visited—especially as the sun is shinning.

From the bus station, we make our way to Broad Street and to the Tourist Information Office so to best plan our time in Oxford. Opposite is the stand for the open-top double-decker sight-seeing buses that tours around the City every 15 minutes, stopping at a number of setting down /pick up points. The City tour takes approximately 60 minutes so what better way to get a view of the sights to see in Oxford. On we hop only this time I have to pay for my fare, my "oldies pass" not being valid. After parting with £9.50, we make our way to the open-top deck to enjoy the fine weather. On the opposite side of the road is the Sheldonian Theatre with the large carved stone bearded faces mounted on stone pillars interspaced with the metal railings around its perimeter.

Off we set to a recorded commentary as we travel along. Turning left at the New Bodleian Library, we travel up Parks Road, past Wadham College and a bit further on, to Keble College and the Nuclear Physics and Metallurgy Laboratories. On the other side of the road are the University Parks and sports grounds. Turning into St. Margaret's Road, we pass St Hugh's College and Lady Margaret Hall before heading back into the City centre down Woodstock Road, passing by St. Anthony's, St. Anne's, Somerville and Regent's Park Colleges. Entering St Giles, St. John's College is on our right with the Martyrs Memorial in the centre of the roadway in front of us. Doing a "U" turn past Balliol College, we carry on into Beaumont Street, past the Ashmolean Museum that is having a facelift with part of its frontage hidden behind hoardings with a tower crane hovering above. On the other side of the road is the Oxford Playhouse that has seen such actors as Richard Burton and Elizabeth Taylor perform there. On we continue past Worcester College and down Hythe Bridge Road to the railway station, where there is a wait to pick up more passengers.

Off we set again down Park End Street, making a detour into the bus station at Gloucester Green. The recorded commentary is full of facts and information that my brain cannot take in. I just settle down to enjoy the views. Archie too seems to be enjoying the sights from the open-top deck. Along New Road, we go past Oxford Castle perched on its high green mound. Opposite is Nuffield College and a little further on St. Peter's College. Turning the corner into Castle Street and then Greyfriars and Speedwell Street, the bus heads up Aldates with Christ Church College and Cathedral on our right. Passing the Town Hall and Museum of Oxford, we come to Carfax, the City Centre with the 13^{th}C tower at one corner. There are a lot of people outside waiting to gain entry to climb the stairs to the top for a view of the City and its spires.

Turning right down the High Street, we pass the covered market on our left, followed by Brasenose College and then the University Church of St Mary the Virgin with its ornate south porch. Further on the left is All Souls College and on the opposite side of the road is University College with the Examination Rooms in which students from all the colleges sit their exams. Continuing along the High Street, we pass Queen's College, St Edmund Hall and Magdalen College. Over on the right are the University Botanical Gardens with their lines of glass-houses. Crossing the Magdalen Bridge over the River Cherwell, there are a number of punts on the water. Punting looks so relaxing, though I often wonder if ever the pole gets stuck in the clay of the river bed and the punter left clinging to the top of the pole whilst the punt itself sails on—my imagination is running away with itself.

Doing a "U" turn at the roundabout, we return back over the Magdalen Bridge and turn up Longwall Street. On the left is the site where William Morris first set up his workshops. On up past more green spaces to the University Science Area on South Parks Road, followed by the Pitt Rivers Museum and the University Museum. At the end, the bus turns back down Parks Road and heads for our drop-off point where we got on at Broad Street. An enjoyable 60 minutes viewing the sights of the City centre from the top deck of the bus—better than walking with my rucksack on my back and dragging Archie along. Having now made mention of it, the time has arrived to do just that.

Now off the bus, I try to plan my route around the City for the rest of our stay. With rucksack on back and Archie in tow, we head off past the towering bearded stone faces outside the Sheldonian Theatre. Turning into Catte Street, we come to the main entrance of the Bodleian Library. On the opposite side of the road, is the stone arch carrying the covered walkway that spans across New College Lane, affectionately known as "The Bridge of Sighs". Passing by Hertford College, we come to the open area in which is sited the circular building of the Radcliffe Camera. As with most of the other buildings in Oxford, it is constructed from oolitic limestone, similar to that used at Bath and gives off a yellowish golden appearance. Standing on its own with domed roof and cupola atop in the centre of Radcliffe Square, it is a masterpiece in architectural design. I spend a bit of time just taking in its beauty.

It was whilst I was standing admiring the Radcliffe Camera, that a gentleman came up to us and made some complimentary remarks about Archie and started to pet him. He asked what breed he was and when I replied that he was a cross, he referred to a recent news article both in the newspapers and on TV about all the problems associated with pedigree dogs. The news item highlighted all the in-breeding of dogs by established breeders so as to win show competitions, including the likes of Crufts, with terrible resulting genetic problems on the dogs themselves. The in-breeding of the traditional British bulldog is a good example but it is happening with many more breeds of dogs. There is even a talk of banning the showing of the annual Crufts Dog Show on TV because of this issue so to put pressure on the Kennel Club to sort out the problem. It is a serious issue and I personally fail to understand why certain breeds of pedigree dogs have to be produced with all the inherent genetic problems, so to satisfy the show judges. (RANT 9). I cannot imagine my scruffy half-breed winning any shows, not that I would even think of entering him in one.

We come to the High Street and walk past the frontages of All Souls, University and Queens Colleges. If we had had sufficient time, I would have like to have continued down High Street and visited the Botanical Gardens located alongside the River Cherwell—for another time. About-turn and back along High Street, past the Examination Halls, where the students must enter with some trepidation at the end of each academic year. On the other side of the High Street is the entrance to the University Church of St Mary the Virgin with the ornate spiral stone columns standing each side of the doorway. Next door, is Brasenose College with the Royal Coat of Arms, complete with lion and unicorn, carved in stone above its firmly shut doorway. Around the corner are Lincoln, Exeter and Jesus Colleges, that we walk past before returning to the High Street and the Carfax Tower sited opposite the Town Hall. There is still a big queue waiting at the Tower to gain access to the top.

Turning up Cornmarket Street past the retail and department stores, we approach St Michael's at Northgate, opposite which is Balliol College. A little further up towards St Giles and standing between the two carriageways, is the Martyrs' Memorial. Erected in 1843, the stone figures of the three martyrs, Cranmer, Latimer and Ridley, are incorporated into the Gothic style memorial. Walking further up St Giles, is the entrance to St John's College. Access into the College grounds is open to visitors so in we go for a look around—no mention of "dogs not allowed". Walking through the archway, the impressive Front Quadrangle opens up before us with its neat circular lawn surrounded by the $15^{th}C$ buildings of the former St Bernard's Monastery. The College was founded in 1555, the same year as the heresy trials of the three Anglican martyrs. Walking on through the next archway, we come to the Canterbury Quad surrounded with its elegant Italian Renaissance buildings. Continuing on through the ornate archway, we come to the Great Lawn and College gardens. There is no-one else about and it is so peaceful and quiet. Walking around the gardens with their well maintained borders and rockeries, you can understand how the tutors and students of the past and present, have been and are able to find solitude to gain inspiration in their teachings and studies. We take our time and also enjoy the surroundings.

Back out onto St Giles, across the road, is the Eagle and Child Inn that is owned by St John's College. Also known as the Bird and Baby amongst other alternatives (some unprintable), the hostelry was used as a meeting place for the Inklings, a group of writers that included J.R.R.

Tolkien and C.S. Lewis amongst others. With nowhere to sit outside, we press on around and into Beaumont Street, passing the massive stone edifice of the Ashmolean Museum with the Oxford Playhouse opposite.

Around the corner, there is the Red Lion Pub that has an outside seating area. Although very busy, we find a table and order a pint and beef sandwich. After all our walking, I am certainly ready for a rest and something to eat and drink. I have Archie's dinner in my rucksack that keeps him satisfied.

Suitably refreshed, we head to New Road and Oxford Castle that we had seen earlier from the bus. The original castle was built in 1071 and was subsequently enlarged with the construction of a ring of towers and high walls around the base of the Mound. Part of the lower walls and buildings still exist and up to 1998, were used as a prison. These have featured in a number of films and TV dramas. The buildings have since been converted into a hotel with the cells being made into guest-rooms—I hope that they have been suitably refurbished. There is a charge for going into the Castle complex called "Oxford Castle Unlocked" but you can walk up to the top of the Mound free of charge. With my rucksack and dodgy knees, I give it a miss.

It will soon be time for the next stage of our bus journey. Walking back up Hythe Bridge Street, we pass the terminus of the Oxford Canal that was constructed in 1790 to connect Oxford to Coventry. Continuing up the towpath for a short way, there are a number of canal long boats tied up, all painted in their traditional bright colours.

We have had more than four hours exploring the City of Oxford that is a fascinating place, full of interest and attractive historic buildings. We have not had the opportunity to visit any of the museums or go inside the churches or around the grounds of the many colleges, St John's excepted. I guess that you could spend nigh on a week in Oxford and still not see everything. No wonder the City attracts so many visitors, especially on a sunny day such as this in August.

* * * * * * *

Back at the bus station, we wait for our next connection to Northampton, where we shall be spending the night. The No.88 United Counties bus for Northampton drives into the station and once again, on we get. Despite being a journey of nearly two hours, the bus is a small 24 seater runabout, the type that I would normally expect to be used on short journeys across town. Nevertheless, the seats are comfortable, so at 15.20, off we head out of Oxford, north-eastwards to Northampton.

We soon pick up the dual carriageway of the A34, and are motoring along at a fair rate of knots. My reservations about the bus are unfounded as both the engine noise and suspension are quite acceptable. Crossing over the M40, we continue along the A41 into the market town of **Bicester** (population 28,700). Pronounced "Bistar" by the locals, the Town has a fast growing population with good road and rail links. The Saxons first settled here in the 6th century and the Town was used as the headquarters for the Parliamentary Army during the Civil War of the 1640's. During the 18th and early 19th centuries, the Town even had its own militia. There are some attractive old buildings in the Town centre, most constructed in the local limestone such as the medieval church of St Edburg. With most of the Town centre now pedestrianised, we do not get an opportunity to travel through it on the bus. Before leaving the Town, we pass by the Army's Central Ordnance Depot, said to be the largest in the country.

We leave Bicester on the B4100 heading north out of Oxfordshire and into Northamptonshire, to join the dual carriageway of the A43. Soon after joining the A43, we pass the **RAF Croughton** on the left with its forest of radio masts. Since 1950, this base has been used by the US Air Force as a communications base and operates one of the largest military switchboards in Europe. During World War 2, it was the base for the glider training school, many of those passing through taking part in the disastrous raid in 1942 at Arnhem, known as "Operation Market Garden".

We leave the A43 temporality, making a diversion into the historic market town of **Brackley** (population 13,400). The Normans built a castle at Brackley in the 11th century that was the setting for a meeting between the powerful barons and King prior to meeting at Runneymede in 1215. It is claimed that Brackley could well have been chosen as the location where the Magna Carta was eventually signed. Only the earthworks of the castle now remain. The Magdalen College School in the Town was founded during the 15th century so to allow the pupils of Magdalen College in nearby Oxford to escape "The Great Plague". The School, complete with its 13thC chapel and original stone buildings, is now a mixed comprehensive. At one end of the wide market place in the centre of the Town, stands the tall stone building of the Town Hall, complete with clock tower and cupola above its pitched roof. The Town's old traditional wool and lace trades have in part been replaced by more hi-tech industries. With the motor racing circuit of Silverstone nearby, Brackley has become the home of some of Formula 1's racing teams, notably Mercedes Grand Prix, which up to very recently, went under the name of Brawn GP. During the international racing season of 2009, Brawn GP won the constructors' championship with their driver, Jenson Button from England, becoming World Champion GP Driver. A tremendous achievement for the team as a whole, as at the beginning of the year, they were newly formed, did not at that time have a big-name sponsor and given little hope of winning anything.

Back onto the A34, it has started to rain—at least we are sitting comfortably in the bus. On we head towards Northampton diverting off into the villages of Syesham and then Silverstone. The name of the village of **Silverstone** (population 2,000) is known internationally as the home of the British Motor Racing Grand Prix. The Silverstone Circuit was originally a World War 2 air base for bomber aircraft, until it was taken over and developed into the world class motor racing venue. It first hosted the British Grand Prix in 1948 and every year since 1987. Although there had been some doubt about the circuit's future, it has just been confirmed that Silverstone will host the British Grand Prix until 2028 at least. In recent years there have been some notable victories by British drivers, including such well known names as Stirling Moss (2), Jim Clark (5), Jackie Stewart (2), James Hunt (1), Nigel Mansell (4), Damon Hill (1), David Coulthard (2) and more recently Lewis Hamilton (1) in 2008. On entering the village, the signs says "Silverstone—Please Drive Carefully"—rather appropriate given Silverstone's racing reputation. The houses and buildings are typical of many Northants villages, all built in the attractive golden Northamptonshire sandstone, some with moss covered stone roofs.

Back onto the A34 for a short distance before we divert off once again, this time to the ancient market town of town of **Towcester** (population 8,900). Pronounced "Toaster" by the locals, its history goes back to Roman times when it was a garrison town on the principal Roman road of Watling Street. The A5 trunkroad that runs from London to Holyhead follows the line of the old Roman road, which still runs through the centre of the Town. During Saxon times, it became a frontier town between the Kingdom of Wessex and the Viking Danelaw. Following 1066, the Normans built a castle on Bury Mount, the remains still being visible. In the times of the stagecoaches, Towcester flourished as a stopping off point for refreshments and accommodation for those travelling from

London enroute the Irish ferry at Holyhead. This all ended with the advent of the railways. Nowadays, Towcester is a bustling market town serving the local community, well known for its race course, located to the east of the Town and which hosts national horse racing events. It is said that Towcester is the "oldest continuously inhabited settlement in the Country", a claim I feel may well be challenged by some other towns or villages in England. The focal point in the wide Market Square is the Victorian Town Hall with its Italianate frontage and domed tower and spike-like spire atop—it reminds me of the World War 1 helmets worn by the German officers. The Town centre is congested with long queues of traffic, probably due to the A5 passing through the centre and it now being near rush hour.

Eventually, we are out of Towcester and back once again onto the A34, albeit not for long. Soon we are diverting off again, this time to the railway village of **Bilsworth** (population 1,800). First, we cross over the Grand Union Canal that connects London with Birmingham. The Canal was completed as late as the early 20th century with the nearby Bilsworth Tunnel being one of the longest on the British canal system. There are a number of brightly painted long boats tied up along the banks of the Canal. Then into the attractive village itself with its thatched cottages built in the rusty golden brown local sandstone. Leaving the Village, we cross under the main West Coast Railway line leading to Birmingham and Manchester. The Line was constructed in the 1830/40's under the supervision of that great railway engineer, Robert Stephenson and included the elegant high masonry arch bridge through which we pass. With the mainline bypassing Northampton, Bilsworth did have its own station, where at one time, all trains were required to stop. However the station was closed in 1960 with the express trains now speeding through at near 100 m.p.h. A little further on is Milton Malsor, with its large village green and prominent war memorial. Leaving the Village, we cross over the M1 Motorway with the long snaking lines of traffic flowing in both directions below us.

We are now entering the outskirts of the town of Northampton. First the bus calls in at the 24 hour Tesco Supermarket Store on Butts Road, Wootton. Back home, we have a similar 24 hour Tesco Superstore nearby that only closes for eighteen hours on a Sunday. I have very mixed feelings on the need for these large superstores to be kept open during the periods of the night and indeed on Sundays. Accepting the fact that some people do shop during the middle of the night and that Sundays are now the most popular shopping day of the week, folk nevertheless have only a limited amount of money to spend. If, what I would call "normal hours" were restored, I suspect that more or less the same amount of money would still be handed over at the tills, albeit the convenience of 24 hour shopping is attractive to most people. The down-side to these present opening hours is subjecting staff to work unsociable hours with little extra remuneration, together with the loss of the traditional family day on Sundays, unless a visit to the supermarket is considered to be a family occasion. I of course realise that the clock cannot be turned back, but I do have strong views about the pressures being exerted by these large superstores, especially over some of their staff, together with their suppliers and the smaller corner shops, so to achieve their extortionate profits (RANT 10). They do seem to wield a lot, maybe too much, power.

On we travel into the centre of the town of Northampton and into the Greyfriars' Bus Station that is adjacent to the large Grosvenor Shopping Centre. The time is 17.10 and after nearly two hours on the bus, we are ready to get off and stretch our legs.

The massive brick fronted covered bus station has been dubbed as "one of Britain's most hated buildings" and "a 1974 behemoth that dominates an otherwise historic town". It also featured on Channel 4's *Demolition* series of programmes and was cited as "one of the ugliest transport stations in the UK". Whilst not the most attractive of buildings, the criticism I feel is a bit harsh, it being functional, safe for pedestrians and passengers and has available all the required facilities. I can think of much worse bus stations elsewhere in the Country, not least that in my hometown of Lincoln. It is difficult to make something as functional as a bus station to look like anything but a bus station especially if it is to be under cover, unless vast sums are spent to disguise it as say a gothic castle. Crossing under the subways, we make for the Town centre. Looking back, I must admit that the western edifice of the building is over-powering and it could do without the upper storey of what I presume are offices.

Northampton—Northamptonshire—population 205,000

Northampton is said to be the third largest "town" in the Country, not as yet having achieved "city" status, despite many attempts. However, being designated "New Town" status in the 1960's, it does have a rapidly growing population that by 2020, is expected to reach 300,000. As such, it will certainly qualify. Sitting astride the River Nene, it is the historic county town of Northamptonshire, abbreviated to Northants.

First settled during Saxon times, Northampton gained its first charter in 1189. During the 11th century, the Normans built a substantial castle and town walls that were to be put to the test in a major battle in 1264. During the 12th century, the King often held his court at the castle that was at the time, of some importance. In 1328, the Treaty of Northampton was signed at the castle between English King, Edward III and Robert the Bruce of Scotland when Bruce was recognised as King of Scotland. However, during the English Civil War, the Town backed the Parliamentarians, a decision that was to rebound following the restoration of the monarchy in 1660. As a punishment for siding with the Parliamentary forces, Charles II decreed that the castle and the town walls be totally demolished. The present day railway station now stands on the site of the former castle with the only relics remaining being the rebuilt postern gate, that has been incorporated into the wall outside the station.

During the 13th century, the Town had a large Jewish community that was centred around what is now Gold Street. However, in 1277, it was alleged that some were "clipping the King's coin" and thus devaluing the currency. As a result, nearly 300 Jews were executed and the rest driven out of the Town. Harsh punishment indeed, even in those days.

The Church of the Holy Sepulchre, built in 1100, is the Town's oldest surviving building and is one of the best preserved round churches in England. The design is based on the Holy Sepulchre Church in Jerusalem and is located on Bants Lane. All Saints Church, standing dominant in the centre of the Town between George and Mercer's Rows was rebuilt in 1680 following the Great Fire of Northampton that virtually destroyed the former Norman church of All Hallows. Only the tower of the old church survived the fire. The new church was rebuilt in the style of Wren's London churches, with the eight columned portico being added later in 1801. Beneath the area around the church, there is a large network of medieval tunnels. Northampton does have its cathedral church, this being the Roman Catholic Cathedral of Our Lady and St Thomas on Barrack Road. The original church was built during the mid 19th century and extended in 1864 so to allow it to gain Cathedral status.

Behind All Saints Church and facing onto St Giles Square, is the magnificent Guildhall. Built during the 1860's in the Victorian neo-Gothic style with its tall clock tower, the ornate frontage of the Guildhall is decorated by many statues and friezes, which depict the famous people and events associated with the Town from Saxon times onwards. The building is still used as the Town Hall and for other civic purposes and ceremonies.

Northampton was for many years the Country's main centre for shoemaking and other leather industries. It was during the Napoleonic Wars of late 18th century when large quantities of footwear were required for the British Army, that the shoemaking industry in Northampton started to grow, employing many hundreds of workers. Nowadays, only a few specialist footwear companies survive with most of our boots and shoes being imported from the Far East. The heritage of Northampton's shoemaking industry is preserved at the Town's Museum and Art Gallery that also includes items of Italian art, glass, ceramics, etc.

One of Northampton's more well known landmarks that can be seen from most parts of the Town, is the tall slender Express Lift Tower. Constructed during the early 1980's for the testing of lifts, the concrete tower is 418 feet tall tapering from 48 feet diameter at its base to 28 feet diameter at the top. It is the only one of its kind in the UK. Nicknamed the "Northampton Lighthouse" and "Cobblers' Needle" the concrete tower is now redundant following the closure of the lift company's works in Weedon Road. Problems with the quality of the concrete (known as "concrete cancer") have been detected and the tower's future is uncertain but as a "historic listed building" demolition is unlikely.

There has been a diversity of businesses and industries that have since come to the Town following the rundown of the footwear industry, not least Carlsberg Brewery UK who have their headquarters based in Northampton. With good road and rail links and being in virtually the centre of the Country, the Town is well situated for further growth. This perhaps started during the 19th century with the construction of a branch from the Grand Union Canal into Northampton, connecting it with the Midlands and also the North Sea via the River Nene.

On the sporting front, Northampton is home to one of the top rugby union clubs in the Country. The Northampton "Saints" who play at Franklin Gardens to the west of the Town centre, are currently in the Guinness Premiership and have had many international players at the Club over the years. Northampton Town FC, known as "the Cobblers" currently play in Division Two and are located nearby. Also the Northamptonshire County Cricket ground is located in Abington to the east of the Town centre. All in all, Northampton is well provided for sporting venues.

The weather is not good as we make our way into the Town centre and head for our accommodation for the night. We make for the Market Square where the stallholders are packing up for the night. One of the largest open market places in the Country, Northampton's traditional market dates back to the 13th century. Enquiring where the Ibis Hotel is located, we receive directions and make our way down past the rows of retail shops that line the Drapery, past All Saints Church with its imposing portico and along Gold Street, the former Jewish Quarter, to the Ibis Hotel where we book in for the evening. The Ibis is part of the newly constructed Sol hotel / shopping / leisure complex located on the corner of Marefair and Horse Market. It is a long walk from reception to our room but on getting there, we find is well equipped and comfortable. Thankful to be able to unload my rucksack, I give Archie his dinner and I make myself a brew before heading back out again to explore a bit more of Northampton and to give Archie his evening walk.

Finding our way back through the maze of corridors of the Ibis and back to reception, we head on out to search for some green area where Archie can have a runabout. After a short walk, we find a pleasant park by the Green. There seems to be the remnants of a disused canal running through the park, maybe originally linking to the Grand Union Canal system. At the end of the park and on the other side of the busy dual carriageway, are the circular steel frameworks of two large gasometers. With the introduction of North Sea gas, these large steel structures have become redundant, with the vast majority around the Country having been demolished. Although no longer used, the steelwork of both gasometers look well maintained and it is good to see our industrial heritage being preserved. Hopefully, they will continue to survive and be able to avoid the demolition ball.

We continue to walk around the Town in an anticlockwise direction and find ourselves walking up Bridge Street back to the imposing edifice of All Saints Church. This is certainly a magnificent building reminding me a little of St Martin-in-the-Fields in London with its fine portico and tower behind. Walking down the side along George Row we come to the Town's Cenotaph and Memorial Garden dedicated to the Town's servicemen killed in action. The flags are hanging limp but there is plenty of colour in the Gardens. Further on is the 19th century Guildhall, a truly splendid building from the outside with its line of stone figures across the frontage and carved friezes above the windows. The building, constructed in the locally quarried sandstone, is complete with the traditional clock tower and balcony from which many speeches and civic announcements have no doubt been made over the years.

* * * * * * *

Time is passing and I am getting hungry. Back along Gold Street we walk, past all the take-a-ways, late-shops and off-licences towards our hotel. Finding our room and bedding Archie down for the night, I make for the restaurant. After a good meal and suitably refreshed, I return to our room to find Archie fast asleep on his blanket.

Switching on the television, ITV's series of programmes *Megastructures* is showing. The subject on this particular evening is the design and construction of the Bird Nest Olympic Stadium in Bejing. With the 2008 Bejing Olympics in full swing, the programme is both topical and of interest, certainly for myself as a civil engineer. Designed by Swiss architects and British engineers and constructed by Chinese contractors, the whole project is mind-boggling. The inner stadium that accommodates the seating area, is constructed totally in concrete. The intricate framework to the "bird nest" outer stadium has been assembled in prefabricated box-sections of steelwork to incredible precision and accuracy. The stadium, built on schedule at a total cost of $290M, is been sited on the same north to south axis of central Bejing that runs through Tiananmen Square and the Emperor's Palace in the Forbidden City.

Time for bed after a long day, albeit travelling on only two buses. Nevertheless, we have had another full day, spending an enjoyable few hours looking around the University City of Oxford. Tomorrow we head for home in Lincoln.

Chapter 6
Northampton To Lincoln— Day 6

Friday 22nd August 2008

I enjoy a bit of a lie-in this morning as my alarm clock failed to go off. After switching on the kettle for a brew, the news on the TV is that Team GB had won another gold medal at the Bejing Olympics—now 18 in total and still in third place overall. Finding our way through the maze of corridors, we eventually make the exit to take Archie for his early morning walk. We mainly retrace our steps of last evening, through the park, past the gasometers and up to and along Gold Street, back to the Ibis Hotel. I must say that the Town looks better in the early morning sunshine than it did in the damp drizzle of last night.

After breakfast in the hotel and booking out, we retrace our way back into the Town centre, past the imposing All Saints Church and up to the "behemoth" of the bus station—not my words! From my own perspective, I find the bus station itself well laid out with safe pedestrian access to the bus stands, each having a sliding glass door to prevent passengers being asphyxiated with exhaust fumes from the buses.

Our next destination is to be Leicester, calling in enroute at Market Harborough. The 10.20 Stagecoach X7 bus to Leicester arrives at our stand and on we board. On waiting to get on the bus, there is a small delay as the first passenger aboard has only a £20 note and the driver is short of change. After a bit of negotiation, the problem is eventually sorted but I could see that the driver is not a "happy bunny". At least we don't cause him a problem as we have nothing to pay. All aboard, the bus departs Northampton bus station more or less on time, heading out of Town northwards on the A508 to Market Harborough.

After some six miles, we pass by Anglian Water's **Pitsford Reservoir**. Constructed in 1956, the Reservoir is the principal source of water supply for Northampton and the surrounding area. The total surface area of the reservoir covers some 750 acres with a country park and a 7 mile cycle track being developed around its perimeter. The site has also been given SSSI status (site of special scientific interest) with a diversity of flora and fauna. I have already made comment on the recreational and environmental benefits provided by such large open reservoirs when we were passing through Devon. Whilst providing an essential resource for local water supplies, it is right that they also be developed for recreational use for the public at large.

On we trundle along the A508, passing on either side fields that only a few days ago would have been ripe with golden ears of grain. The crops have now been harvested with only the stubble remaining that will soon be ploughed back into the land. Although today the sun is shining, during the past few weeks there had been a lot of rain that would have partially flattened the crops. The wet weather would also have increased the moisture content of the grain when harvested, resulting in additional costs in the drying process. However, I understand that grain prices for the year are reasonably high and I don't hear any farmers complaining.

We pass the entrance to Lamport Hall on our right. Built during the late 17th and 18th centuries, the building has a classical stone frontage and stands in its own grounds and gardens. The gardens contain an elaborate rockery that was supposedly, the earliest alpine garden in England, together with Italian gardens and an avenue of Irish yew trees. For some 400 years, the Hall was home to the Isham family but is now under the governorship of the Lamport Hall Preservation Trust and together with the gardens, is open to the public.

A little further on at Kelmarsh, we cross the dual A14 trunk road that was recently constructed to connect the Midlands with East Anglia, a link long awaited. The road sign points to the village of Naseby three miles to the west. It was during the English Civil War in 1645 that the decisive Battle of Naseby was fought. The Battle ended in a victory for the Parliamentarian New Model Army led by Oliver Cromwell and Sir Thomas Fairfax and proved to be a turning point in the War that was to lead to the temporary suspension of the monarchy.

Travelling through the village, we pass the entrance to another of Northamptonshire's stately mansions. Kelmarsh Hall is a historic 18th century home, constructed in red-brick in the Palladian style of architecture. The Hall and its extensive parklands are open to the public and is used to host a variety of events and shows during the year. There is a big event taking place on this particular day as we pass by.

We are just sitting at the back of the bus taking in the beauty of the Northants countryside, when we are suddenly exposed to a strong blast of wind. A young woman passenger in front has just opened the top opening to the window of the bus alongside her seat without any consideration for those sitting behind. Another older woman immediately in front of me gets up and slams the window shut, giving the culprit a glowering look. Could be the start to the second battle of Naseby, but sizing up the two females, I know which one my money is on and the window stays shut. Further conflict aboard the bus is averted and peace reigns. I must admit to admiring the action taken by the second female and find it irritating that some people seem oblivious to the discomfort they may be causing to others by their inconsiderate actions (RANT 11)

Soon after crossing the county boundary from Northamptonshire into Leicestershire, we enter the market town of **Market Harborough** (population 20,800). The time is 11.00 and the bus virtually empties—must be market day. Mentioned in the Domesday Book, Market Harborough was the headquarters for the King's forces during the Civil War prior to the Battle of Naseby. Sometime later in 1841, Thomas Cook a strict Baptist and who was employed as a cabinet maker in the Town, arranged his first group travel excursion for some 570 temperance campaigners to attend a rally in Loughborough. This was by train from Leicester for which Cook negotiated with the railway company, a return fare of one shilling that also included food. Although the train journey was only 11 miles, I would guess at that time, a day trip by train to Loughborough would have been a novelty. The Town centre is dominated by the 14thC grey ashlar tower of St Dionysius' Church with its fine crocketed broach spire atop. Around the sundial on the side of the tower are the words "Improve the Time". Adjacent to the church is the timbered building of the Old Grammar School. Built in 1614, the upper storey is supported on wooden columns with the open space below accommodating the former butter market. The grammar school has since moved to other premises but the building itself is still in use. A little way further down the High Street, is the 18thC three storey red-brick Town Hall.

Leaving Market Harborough, we continue towards Leicester along the A6. After a few miles, the roadside signposts point to the village of **Foxton** and Foxton Locks. Located on the Grand Union Canal, a series of locks was required to lift canal boats and barges some 75 feet on their voyage to the West Midlands. The original series of ten ageing locks took more than an hour to negotiate, causing a great deal of frustration with the canal navigators at that time during the 19th century. At the turn of the century, a pioneering project was proposed and implemented to construct an inclined boat lift whereby two large water filled tanks were installed that counter-balanced each other as they travelled up and down the inclined slope. Canal boats were lifted and lowered in the water filled tanks reducing the time taken to twelve minutes. Opened in the year 1900, the boatlift remained in operation for only a few years before being closed in 1911 due to maintenance problems. A series of new locks have since been installed that form the largest staircase of locks on the English canal system. The old boatlift has been preserved as part of the country's industrial heritage and is open to visitors along with an adjacent museum.

Progressing on, we reach the two villages of Kibworth Beauchamp and Kibworth Harcourt, both separate parishes split by the A6 trunk road. Just after leaving Kibworth, there are two successive jolts that lift us out of our seats as the bus passes over what I would guess are poorly reinstated trenches across the roadway. I am surprised that the highway authority have not taken action against the guilty party and had the roadway properly levelled and reinstated. I could see claims coming in from motorists for damage to their vehicle's suspension and tracking systems as a result of the subsidence.

Diverting off the A6 into the village of Great Glen, we continue towards the outskirts of Leicester, first reaching Oadby and then the Leicester Racecourse at the junction with the A563 City Ring Road. The Racecourse dates back to 1773, is oval in shape and two miles in length. Both National Hunt and flat racing events are held during the year together with wedding receptions and other functions. The next race meeting is advertised for the 6th September, so need to get out the "form books"?

Newark is signed as only 39 miles, making Lincoln only 55 miles away. Unfortunately the bus routes do not go direct between Leicester to Lincoln and we need to travel via Melton Mowbray and Grantham before we reach home this evening.

The bus route continues along London Road into the centre of the City, through the suburb of Stoneygate and past Victoria Park. Along this approach into the centre of Leicester, there are some fine Victorian / Edwardian houses in what it would seem to be an up-market area of the City. Across Victoria Park, I believe that I can see the floodlight towers of Welford Road, the home ground of one of the most successful rugby clubs in England, Leicester Tigers FC. After a few more minutes, we at last arrive at the St Margaret's bus station in the centre of Leicester. The time is now 11.50. However on enquiring as to which stand our next bus leaves from, I am told that our next connection to Melton Mowbray departs from another bus station, about a five minute walk around the corner—or so I am told when asking!

Leicester—Leicestershire—population 295,000

Leicester is classified as a large city, being also the county town of Leicestershire. It is the tenth most populous city in the UK and the second largest in East Midlands after Nottingham. Situated on the River Soar, a tributary of the nearby River Trent,

Leicester's history goes back to pre-Roman times. Located on the Fosse Way that runs from Lincoln to Exeter, there was a Roman military settlement at Leicester around 50AD that later grew into a major town and trading centre of Roman Britain. To this day, evidence of the Roman period can be seen at the Jewry Wall near the City centre, where the remains of a section of the old Roman wall (70ft long x 18ft high) still exists together with parts of the Roman baths and pavements. It is understood however, that the name "Jewry" has no associations with the City's Jewish community. During the period of the Anglo Saxons, it was one of five fortified towns important in Viking Dane Law.

With the arrival of the Normans, the motte and bailey castle was constructed in around 1070 and was subsequently enlarged during the 12th century. The Great Hall, Turret Gateway and John of Gaunt's cellar still remain to this day, the site being to the west of the City centre. During the 12th century, an Abbey was built by the Augustine canons on the banks of the River Soar just north of the City centre. Cardinal Wolsey died at the Abbey in 1530, on his way from York to London to face trial for high treason. On the orders of the Henry VIII. the Abbey was closed during the 16th century with the buildings being set on fire by the Royalist troops in 1645. Now only the footprints of the walls to the former Abbey are visible in what is now Abbey Park.

Following on from the successful baronial rebellion of 1264 against Henry III, Simon de Montfort, the 6th Earl of Leicester became the de faco ruler of England and was responsible for the first directly elected Parliament. This was held in Leicester in 1265. As a result, De Montfort is credited as being the founder of modern day Parliamentary democracy.

One of the two universities in Leicester bears his name. Parliament again met in Leicester during the time of the infant King Henry VI in 1425 when conditions in London were considered "unsuitable". This meeting has been referred to as the "Parliament of Bats" as swords were banned and members instead armed themselves with wooden clubs or bats.

More than 200 years later during the English Civil War, Leicester was a Parliamentarian stronghold. In 1645, the City was however attacked by the Royalist forces under Prince Rupert who subsequently went on to sack the City and slaughter a large number of its inhabitants. Later during the Industrial Revolution, Leicester experienced unparalleled expansion resulting in a great amount of unplanned urbanisation, with the growth of the hosiery, textiles and footwear industries.

The Old Guildhall in Leicester dates from c.1390 and was part of the old walled city. Formerly functioning as the town hall, it is now used to house the City Museum. It is reported that up to five ghosts haunt the building—all have supposedly been seen. The present Town Hall was built during 1874/76 in Queen Anne style and includes a traditional tall brick clock tower. Referred to as a "Victorian Jewel" the building overlooks Town Hall Square that has an ornate cast iron water fountain as its centrepiece. In addition, the stand-alone Clock Tower in Haymarket was erected 1868 as a traffic island, with the statues of four of the City's benefactors incorporated in the stone tower, including that of Simon De Montfort.

The Anglican Cathedral of St Martins stands near the City centre near to the Old Guildhall. Consecrated as a Cathedral in 1927, the original church is Norman with a number of additions and restorations made during the Victorian period. Inside is a memorial tablet to Richard III whose original tomb was at the City's Greyfriars Church. There is much speculation as to what later became of the King's bones.

Leicester has one of the Country's largest ethnic minorities with post war immigration originating mainly from the Indian sub-continent and being drawn to the City mainly by its textile industries. The present Asian community is approximately 40 percent of the total population and is estimated it will exceed 50 percent by the year 2012. It is said that around 70 different languages and dialects are spoken in the City and outside London, Leicester must be one of the most cosmopolitan cities in the UK. This is reflected in the different faiths and places of worship, which in addition to the churches and chapels of the various Christian denominations, include Hindu, Sikh & Jain temples, mosques and synagogues.

Located on the northern outskirts of the City, is the National Space Centre. Opened in 2001 at a cost of £52M, the Centre is well worth a visit. Dedicated to the exploration of outer space, science and astronomy, the Centre has the only Russian Soyuz spacecraft on view to the public in the Western World.

Like its neighbouring city Northampton, Leicester is well provided for sporting venues. Leicester "Tigers" (Rugby) Football Club play at Welford Road to the south of the City centre. The "Tigers" are one of the top rugby clubs in the Country winning many trophies and championships over recent years with a squad of players holding many international honours. They are probably one of the best-supported rugby clubs in the Country. Leicester City Football Club's ground is nearby at the Walkers Stadium. Nicknamed the "Foxes", they currently play in the English Championship League. Cricket at County level is played by Leicestershire CCC at Grace Road to the south of the City. The Racecourse at Leicester has already been mentioned.

* * * * * * *

Being only an hour's drive away from where I live, Leicester and its sights are reasonably familiar to me, especially the "Tigers" ground at Welford Road. Not wanting to walk into the City centre with a rucksack on my back and Archie in tow, we head straight for our next connection, this time for Melton Mowbray. The five minute walk to the Haymarket Bus Station would probably be correct if you were wearing trainers and had nothing to carry. For us, it takes a little longer and results in us seeing the Melton bus pull out of the bus station just as we arrive. Nothing for it but to wait for the next bus that pulls in some twenty minutes later. We climb aboard the Arriva Fox No.5A for Melton, which pulls out of the bus station at 12.20.

Off through the City centre, under the Belgrave Flyover and up Belgrave Road / A607 northwards. For those unfamiliar with Leicester, we are now passing through the "Asian Quarter" of the City. Colourful saris are displayed in the clothing shops, spices are on sale in the food shops, there seem to be a larger number of jewellers, and most of the banks are under Indian ownership. With many of the signs above the shops written in Indian script, it is perhaps not surprising that the area is nicknamed "Little Delhi". Apart from the traditional red-brick houses, it is as if we had been transported to the Indian sub-continent.

The bus continues up the A607, along Belgrave Road and then Melton Road. A little further on, our bus route leaves the main road that continues north to join the main A46 leading to Newark and instead turns eastward into the small town of **Syston** (population 11,500). Now acting as a commuter town for Leicester, it is the location for the headquarters of the Pukka Pie Company. We rejoin the A607 at East Goscote following the course of the River Wreake towards Melton, before we again leave the main road and divert into the village of **Ashfordby** (population c.3,000). The old Horseshoes Public House in the village centre is selling Bateman's real ale. Ashfordby was best known in recent years as the location of Britain's newest deep coalmine. Opened in 1984, it was classified as one of the new generation of superpits using the long-wall technique of mining. However due to geological problems together with the fall in the price of coal at that time, the mine was closed in 1997, which must have been a major blow to the local community.

On leaving the village of Ashfordby, we join the A6006 that takes us into the market town of Melton Mowbray, arriving at the Town's bus station at 13.10.

Melton Mowbray—Leicestershire—population 25,600

Melton Mowbray is historic market Town that sits on the banks of the Rivers Eye and Wreake. During the Anglo Saxon period, there was a settlement at Melton Mowbray, which has been verified by the discovery of a Saxon cemetery. In the Domesday Book of 1086, Melton Mowbray was described as a thriving market town and having two watermills. The town's market is said to be the third oldest market in England having gained royal approval back in 1324, from which time, a market has always been on a Tuesday.

During the Civil War of the 1640's, Melton Mowbray was a stronghold of the Parliamentarian army, although it was twice attached by Royalist forces who inflicted much damage and killed many of the Town's inhabitants.

St Mary's Church near to the centre of the Town, was built during the 13th /15th centuries and is said to be the largest and most stately church in Leicestershire, with its 100 feet high tower dominant. Sir Malcolm Sargent, the highly respected orchestral conductor, was the organist at St Mary's from 1914 to 1924. Melton School dates from 1347 and claims to be one of the oldest educational establishments in the Country. "Anne of

Cleaves House" located near St Mary's Church, was built in 1384 and was used to provide accommodation for the chantry priests until such time as the Dissolution of the Monasteries during the 16th century. Although it is doubtful if Anne of Cleaves ever visited Melton Mowbray, the house was included in her estate by Henry VIII as a divorce settlement. Nowadays, it is a public house.

Melton Mowbray claims to be known as the "Rural Capital of Food"—I suspect that there may be a few other contenders for this title. However, it is the home of the famous pork pies that bears the Town's name and that now have EU Protected Status, whereby any pies bearing the name "Melton Mowbray Pork Pie" must have been made within a designated zone around the Town. In the Town's pedestrianised area, is Dickenson and Morris' "Ye Olde Pork Pie Shoppe" where the genuine product can be purchased. Stilton cheese also originates from one of the nearby villages and is still made in Melton Mowbray to this day. The village called Stilton in Northamptonshire is often thought to be where the cheese originates from but in fact was the place on the A1 highway between London and Edinburgh where the cheese was sold.

Melton Cloth, first mentioned in 1823, is a heavily milled tightly woven material that was traditionally used for the making of sailors' coats and later for the more familiar donkey jackets that were worn mainly by construction workers. The cloth has also been exported to North America for the making of "loggers cruising jackets" and "Mackinaws".

On a lighter note, the phrase "Painting the Town Red" is claimed to have originated at Melton Mowbray. In was in 1837 following a successful fox hunt, that many of the Town's buildings were liberally daubed with red paint by those celebrating the day's hunt, no doubt after a few pints of ale. Several tins of red paint had been found by the revellers and to this day, there are traces of the paint on the doors of some of the older buildings. A painting by Henry Alken named "A Spree at Melton Mowbray" records and illustrates the event.

From the bus station, we follow the signs pointing to the Town Centre. Coming out onto the pedestrianised area on Nottingham Street by "Ye Olde Pork Pie Shoppe". I tether Archie to a nearby post and go inside to purchase my lunch. What better than a traditional Melton Mowbray pork pie topped with Stilton cheese. Opposite Dickenson and Morris' shop is the Town's Market Cross and with the sun shining, I make myself comfortable on the steps of the Cross and enjoy my lunch—the pie is highly recommended and Archie too is enjoying the bits that I am giving him.

Walking on round to the busy Market Place, we cross the road to St Mary's Church on Burton Road. The 13th century church with its 100 feet high tower is certainly impressive. On the opposite side of the road are the Town's old "Alms Houses" built in the local sandstone. Adjacent to the Church, is the 14thC "Anne of Cleaves House", now a pub owned by Everards Brewery of Leicester. There is a beer garden around at the back where I can take Archie and order myself a pint of "Tiger". Another customer is sitting there enjoying a pint with his dog at his feet. It looks a bit similar to Archie and when I enquire as to what breed it is, it turns out to be another Jack Russell cross, but with a schnauzer, one of my favourite dogs. Archie and the schnauzer cross seem to be getting on alright, each doing a lot of sniffing.

* * * * * * *

It is soon time to catch our next bus, this time for Grantham. Finishing my pint and saying goodbye to the schnauzer cross and its owner, we head back to the bus station. The bus in which we are to travel belongs to a local company, Paul James Coaches of Huggles. It is reassuring to know that some of the local bus companies are still in existence, despite the "bus wars" between operators that followed bus deregulation in 1989 that ended in many of the smaller operators going out of business or being bought out by the "big boys". It now seems that a monopoly has been created between Stagecoach, Arriva and the First Group in operating most of the Country's bus services. Whatever has happened to such bus companies as Midland Fox, United Counties, Lincolnshire Roadcar, Southdown, etc. No wonder that bus fares are as expensive as they are, that is for those under 60 years of age. I would have thought the Competitions (formerly the Monopolies and Mergers) Commission would have stepped in to control the wholesale purchase of local bus companies and allow at least some competition. Bring back our local bus companies!! (RANT 12).

Onto the bus we board, showing my "oldies pass" but it seems that no tickets are issued on the Company's buses, so there will be a gap in my collection of bus tickets for our journey north. Settling down on the back seat, a thirty stone hulk of a man gets onto the bus. To my dismay, he makes his way up the aisle to the back of the bus and plonks himself on the back seat next to where we are sitting. I am sure the coach tilted slightly when he sat down, but at least the back seat is wide enough not to bother us albeit his breathing is heavy and noisy.

At 14.20, we set out from Melton Bus Station on our way to Grantham. Our driver gave an announcement over the bus's "intercom" that fares were going up next week on account of the rising price of diesel. It is a fact that fuel prices had risen in recent months because of the market forces, but I was under the impression that they had started to fall back. Still, with my bus pass, I was not going to be affected by any such rises. Perhaps the rise was in part due to the bus company being unable to be sufficiently compensated for transporting us oldies free of charge. We are soon experiencing traffic congestion with the bus inching forward at an extremely slow rate. For a relatively small town such as Melton Mowbray, the heavy congestion is surprising and it would seem that if commonplace, the Town badly needs a bypass.

At last, we were free of the congestion and moving freely along the A607, through the rolling green Leicestershire countryside. Diverting into **Waltham on the Wolds** (population c.1,000), the bus stops opposite the old parish church of St Mary Magdalene whose spire was badly damaged in the Lincolnshire earthquake of February 2008, when an earth tremor of 5.2 on the Richter scale was recorded. The top 30 feet of the spire apparently requires replacing. There are also a number of stone houses and cottages adding to the attraction and charm of the Village.

We continue along the ridge of the escarpment that overlooks the Vale of Belvoir (pronounced "Beaver"). After a short distance, we pass the brown tourist signs pointing to Belvoir Castle that can be seen sitting on high ground in the far distance. The Castle is the ancestral home of the Dukes of Rutland and is the fourth castle to have stood on the site since Norman times. The present castle, which is open to the public, was rebuilt following a fire in the early 19th century and in part resembles Windsor Castle. Advertisements are on display for a "pop concert" that is to take place in the Castle grounds at the weekend. The main group is McFly, a Brit Award winning pop group that found fame in 2004 and who have recorded many hit albums and appeared on TV on numerous occasions. For sure, there will be a big audience in the Castle grounds at the weekend.

Further on along the A607, we pass through the village of Croxton Kerrial before crossing the county boundary and entering Lincolnshire. On the outskirts of the village of Denton, stands the attractive stone gatehouse to Denton Hall and its grounds. Bypassing the Village, our bus continues its journey on towards Grantham stopping at the village of **Harlaxton**. Set back from the road is Harlaxton Manor, a large 19th century fairy-tale manor house that combines Elizabethan and Jacobean architecture. The Manor House is currently owned by the University of Evansville in the US and is available for students from the States to spend their summer semester.

We carry on along past the rolling green countryside, under the A1 trunk road and into the market town of Grantham, arriving at the Town's bus station at 15.00.

Grantham—Lincolnshire—population 34,600

The town of Grantham is located on the upper reaches of the River Witham, with both good road and rail links with the south and north. Evidence has been found of a Neolithic settlement at Grantham, with relics from the Roman period also having been discovered. During the Saxon period, records show that there was a village that later developed into a market town during the 11th century, with wool and leather being the principal trades during medieval times. Being sited on the main highway between London and Edinburgh (now the A1), Grantham became a major stopping-off point for the stage-coaches with some of the old coaching inns still standing. The Angel Inn is perhaps the best known, it being apparently used by Richard III when King of England.

Grantham played its part in the English Civil War of the 1640's. It was at Gonerby Moor, just to the north of the Town centre that Oliver Cromwell's Parliamentarians fought and won their first victory over the Royalist army.

During the latter part of the 18th century, the Grantham Canal was opened. Some 33 miles in length, the canal was built to connect the Town with the River Trent at Nottingham. However, with the advent of the railways, the use of the inland waterways declined with the Grantham Canal falling into a state of disrepair. It was eventually closed in 1936, although work has recently started on the restoration of sections of the Canal for leisure use.

With the growth in farming during the 18th century, Grantham gained importance and became a centre for the manufacture of agricultural machinery. Richard Hornsby and Sons was founded 1815 and it was this engineering company that later invented caterpillar track in 1910. Like many other British inventions, there was little interest shown in revolutionary metal tracks at the time and the patent was subsequently sold to a US company that later became the world-dominating Caterpillar

Tractor Company. A few years later and after selling the patent, the potential of the caterpillar tracks was recognised for use on the first tanks in World War One. Later the Company joined with Ruston of Lincoln and became internationally known throughout the engineering world as Ruston and Hornsby. Sadly, like many other successful and respected British engineering companies, the firm no longer exists.

The Town centre is dominated by the elegant spire of St Wulfram's Church. Built in the early 14th century and at 282 feet high, it is the tallest spire of any parish church in the Country and has been described by Simon Jenkins in his book on "England's Best 1,000 Churches" as the "finest steeple in England".

Immediately in front of the stately 19thC Town Hall in the Town centre, stands the statue of Grantham's most famous son, Sir Issac Newton. Born in 1642 on Christmas Day in the village of Colsterworth some eight miles to the south, Newton received his school education and spent much of his early life at Grantham, prior to going onto Cambridge University. He went on to become the Lucasian Professor of Mathematic at Cambridge where he developed and perfected the mathematical technique known as differential and integral calculus, albeit this is disputed by supporters of the German mathematician Leibniz. He also took a great interest in optics, philosophy and alchemy and came close to coming into conflict with the religious authorities of the day. He later went on to become Master of the Royal Mint where he resolutely pursued counterfeiters and was responsible for linking the pound sterling to the gold standard. Perhaps the most eminent scientist and mathematician the World has known, Newton died in 1727 at the grand age of 84. The Town Museum at Grantham contains a many items of memorabilia connected with Newton.

As a side note, my son Ian undertook some research during his spare time, into the family genealogy and managed by some tenuous routes, to trace our own family tree on the Newton side, back to Sir Issac. Bearing in mind our illustrious ancestor did not marry and had no children, the route went back to the 1500's and came back up along another line. I believe that most families are able, if they try hard enough, to trace their family trees back to the royal family, so perhaps I should not get too excited. In my own travels around Eastern Europe, I found that Sir Issac's name had gone before me and that foreigners had no problems with its pronunciation, especially when going through customs. At least when asked, I can claim to be related to him—it's a pity that I did not inherit his intellect. Still, enough of my illustrious ancestor and back to Grantham.

Another of Grantham's famous sons, or rather daughters, is the former prime minister, Margaret Thatcher, nee Roberts. Born in 1925 in the family home above her father's grocer shop, she spent her formative years in Grantham, attending Kesteven and Grantham Girls School before going to university. Her father's grocer's shop in the Town still stands today. Known as the Iron Lady because of her strong rhetoric of the day against the Soviet Union, Margaret Thatcher was the first female Prime Minister of the United Kingdom and resided at No.10 Downing Street from 1979 to 1990. Many of her policies were and still are controversial depending upon one's political views, but there can be little doubt that during her eleven years as the Country's Prime Minister, many major policies were introduced and changes implemented. She later became Baroness Thatcher of Kesteven in the County of Lincolnshire and now sits in the House of Lords.

Farming and food processing still plays an important part of the Town's economy, but being on the main East Coast Railway line and within an hour's travel to London, Grantham has in recent years, become an outlying commuter town for the Capital. In Lincolnshire generally, house prices are relatively cheap and the pace and quality of life is much more leisurely and relaxed than that further south.

Leaving the bus station, Archie and I set out to walk around the Town, passing by Newton's statue surrounded by the flower gardens in front of the towering Town Hall, with its tall clock tower. Following a passageway by the side of the Town Hall, we find ourselves by the River Witham. Being near its source, the River is relatively small at this point, but on its journey to the sea, it soon develops into a major waterway, passing through the Lincoln Gap and entering the Wash and North Sea near Boston. Walking along the riverside footpath, there are a number of ducks and a family of coots and their chicks swimming in the clear waters of the River. Further downstream and away from the ducks, I let Archie off his lead and quick as a flash, he is in the water. With all the travelling we had done, he deserves his swim. The footpath is also part of the National Cycle Network with Nottingham signed as 33 miles away. A little way on down the footpath, we meet another Jack Russell cross, this one crossed with a Border Terrier. Archie and the Border cross seem to be hitting it off and as it turns out, the Border cross is a female—no comment.

Walking back towards the Town, we pass through the churchyard of St Wulfram's with its elegant 14th century spire towering above us.

Then into the Town centre and Market Place where there stands an old stone cross, albeit the cross is now in metal mounted on a stone column. A water conduit in the Market Place has the date 1557 carved into the stonework and presumably provided the local population at the time with clean drinking water.

* * * * * * *

Back to the bus station for our final journey of the day, to Lincoln and home. Attempting to get back to the bus station, we are thwarted by access through the shopping arcade leading to the station being out of bounds to dogs, even those on leads. We are getting short of time, so I scooped Archie up under my arms and make a hurried exit through the covered arcade. By the time we reach the exit, I am exhausted with having to carry both my rucksack and Archie. The Stagecoach No.1 double-decker bus to Lincoln is waiting in the stand, engine running. On we hop, me showing my "oldies" bus pass only to be told by the driver, that I would have to pay 50p for Archie—we are obviously back in Lincolnshire!! The only other time that I had to pay for him was in Cornwall when at least I obtained a day pass for the one single payment.

Off we set out of Grantham bus station at 16.05 heading north up the A607. First, the bus route diverts into and through a housing estate although no passengers are picked up—a bit of an abortive diversion. Soon we are back onto the A607 passing by the attractive little village of Manthorpe and then Belton Woods Country Club, with its two championship golf courses. A little further on, there are the signs for Belton House, the home of the Brownlow family. The 17thC house has been described as one of the finest country houses in the Country and has often been visited by royalty. The architecture of the House itself is in the Carolean style with the locally quarried Ancaster limestone used on the front façade. The formal gardens include a series of follies including a gothic ruin and tower. Like many other stately homes, the cost of its upkeep became too much during the late 1990's and the house, its contents, gardens and parkland were given over to the National Trust, that is now responsible for its maintenance. All are now open to the public.

On we continue on the A607 to Barkston—the rain has just come on. After taking the left hand fork to Lincoln, a bus travelling in the opposite direction comes hurtling around a bend as we approach it, taking it very wide. It seems that there are only inches between us as we pass—another near miss or so it seems. It is probably only me panicking and that both drivers have everything under their control.

The next village has the unusual name of Carlton Scroop. The village of "Carletune" is mentioned in the Domesday Book to which in the 14th century was added the family name of "Scrope". Standing on the high escarpment above the village, is a tall steel pylon that has a multitude of radio transmitters / receivers attached. Looking like a space rocket awaiting to be launched, it is quite a landmark and can be seen from miles around. The next village is Normanton on Cliffe, albeit the village itself is at the bottom of the limestone escarpment.

The village of **Caythorpe** (population 1,200) follows next that was once the centre of extensive ironstone mine workings. In 1900, there were three ironstone mines at Caythorpe that were connected by a railway system to allow the iron ore to be transported to Sheffield. Nowadays, there are little signs of any former mining activity. Only the tall elegant spire of St Vincent's Church dominates the peaceful village with its limestone buildings and cottages. Although I am familiar with driving my car along this road, I am finding that travelling by bus is much more enjoyable and relaxing, being able to appreciate the rolling countryside and attractive villages that straddle the bus route.

We next pass through the tree-lined village of **Fulbeck** (population 450), composed mainly of stone built houses and cottages together with the fine stately Fulbeck Hall. Built during the 18th century, the Hall is home to the Fane family. The tall wrought iron gates are still standing at the entrance to the Hall's long driveway. The Hall also houses the Arnhem Museum, the building being requisitioned by the army during the Second World War and used as the headquarters for the 1st Airborne Division. It was in 1944 that the Division took part in the unsuccessful raid on the Dutch town of Arnhem, known as "Operation Market Garden".

A little further along the road, we cross over a cutting that carries the A17 that heads eastwards to Sleaford, Kings Lynn and Norwich. Until the recent bypass was built, this busy trunk road passed through the small village of **Leadenham** (population 400) resulting in severe traffic congestion. With its handsome church complete with its tall elegant spire, coaching inn, manor house and array of stone dwelling houses, peace and tranquillity has returned to the Village.

The "National Shoe Box Grand Prix" is held on the slopes of the escarpment above Leadenham in April of each year. This has become a popular event where each competitor enters their individually designed wheel-mounted cardboard shoe-box that is not to be more than one pound in weight. Automotive power is not allowed. The object is for the shoe-box to travel of its own accord, down an inclined ramp on a straight line as far as possible. The winner is the person whose shoe-box travels the furthest distance unassisted. Another crazy competition that the British have created—maybe one day, we might have an international shoe-box grand prix with all the razzmatazz that goes with that of Formula One Grand Prix.

We next pass through the twin villages of Wellingore and Navenby and then along the top of the limestone escarpment, heading north towards Lincoln. The view to the west is across the Trent Valley with the cooling towers of Cottam Power Station in the far distance, discharging tall plumes of water vapour high into the atmosphere. Much closer and sited on the edge of the escarpment, is the cliff-side village of Boothby Graffoe, the name being taken by the radio presenter / comedian who at one time, hosted his own radio show. Across the sloping heathlands to the east, the combine harvesters are gathering in the last of the grain as we pass by.

These arable fields of the Lincolnshire heaths are vast with many of the hedges having been ripped out some years ago. This has in turn led to serious soil erosion creating mini dust storms in dry weather when the fields are not in crop. In a drive to maximise yields and productivity, the local farmers have perhaps sacrificed the long-term productivity of their lands. With the destruction of the hedgerows, they have also destroyed the local flora and fauna, especially the bird-life. A number of footpaths have also been ploughed up despite protests from ramblers and the like. Although there are moves afoot to replant some of the hedgerows and set-aside land for conservation, much irreversible damage has already been done. As supposedly "guardians of the countryside" I feel that the local farming fraternity have much to answer for in not properly maintaining the countryside, especially in these areas of rural Lincolnshire (RANT 13). I do have some friends who are local farmers. If they ever read this narrative, I fear that relationships may be a little strained.

A little further on, we pass through the village of Waddington, adjoining which is the large base of **RAF Waddington**. First opened in 1916, the RAF station was the base for the heavy Manchester bombers during World War 2, one of the many bomber bases located in Lincolnshire known then as "Bomber County". During the Cold War, it was one of the main bases for the Avro Vulcan delta aircraft that carried the UK's deterrent at that time. The last Vulcan squadron was disbanded in 1993, which apart from briefly participating in the Falkland's War, were thankfully never required for action in warfare. Since the early 1990's, RAF Waddington has been the home to the Nimrod and AWAC surveillance and intelligence aircraft. With the intended closure of nearby RAF Scampton, it is proposed that the RAF's aerobatic's team, The Red Arrows, will be transferred to Waddington. In the first weekend in July of every year, the RAF's International Air Show is held at Waddington. Aircraft from air forces from all over the World are displayed and perform in front of more than 150,000 visitors. The skies to the south of Lincoln are certainly busy and noisy over that particular weekend. So too are the roads to Waddington, with traffic congestion being a serious problems over that particular weekend.

Still on the A607 we continue along the edge of the limestone escarpment to Bracebridge Heath. Here our bus makes a detour around the housing estates, before passing by the tall stone water tower over the Water Company's service reservoirs that provide storage for most of Lincoln's water supply. The descent into Lincoln Gap is down Cross O'Cliff Hill, so named because of the Eleanor Cross erected at it base at the former St. Catherine's Priory. This was the first of the twelve stone crosses subsequently erected by King Edward I to mark the overnight stopping points of the cortege carrying Queen Eleanor's body in 1290. The Queen died just outside Lincoln and her body taken to Charring Cross in London for burial. Three of the elaborate stone crosses that were erected enroute to London are still standing, with the bottom section of the Cross from St Catherine's being on display in the grounds of Lincoln Castle.

Ahead of us is the magnificent Lincoln Cathedral standing on the limestone escarpment on the northern side of the Lincoln Gap, through which the River Witham passes on its way across the Lincolnshire Fenlands to Boston and the Wash. Entering into the City of Lincoln, our No.1 bus motors down the long High Street that follows the old route of the Roman Fosseway that connected Lincoln with Exeter. A section of the old Roman road has recently been uncovered and is on display under a glass walkway. As at most times of the day, the traffic is moving slowly down the High Street but eventually we reach the City centre, crossing over the railway level crossing that, with its frequent closing, is partly responsible for the slow moving traffic. Passing by the front of the

Central Railway Station, we at last reach the main bus station in Lincoln, the time is 17.30.

In my haste to get off the bus, I forgetfully leave my camera sitting on the back seat of the bus. Thankfully one of my fellow passengers draws my attention by pointing to it. With all my photographs on the camera's memory card since starting on my journey from Lands End, its loss would have been a disaster. Outside the bus station, my wife Florence is waiting in the car to take us home. Can't wait to get there—I guess Archie too.

Lincoln—Lincolnshire—population 34,600

The cathedral city of Lincoln and county town of Lincolnshire, is sited within and on either side of the Lincoln Gap, through which flows the River Witham. The limestone escarpment on either side, rises to some 200 feet above the lower areas of the City with the Cathedral sitting on the high ground to the north and dominating the City skyline, especially at night when floodlight. It was John Ruskin who wrote:

> *"I have always held and proposed against all comers to maintain that the Cathedral of Lincoln is out and out the most precious piece of architecture in the British Isles"*

Those who have the impression that Lincoln is flat have another surprise when first visiting the City, especially if walking up Steep Hill to the Cathedral.

It has been established that there was an Iron Age settlement by the Brayford Pool in the lower area of the City during the 1st century BC. When the Romans arrived in AD48, they initially built their fortress on the high ground to the north and as their army moved northwards, the Lindum Colonia was subsequently established for army veterans and their families. Sited at the northern end of the Fosseway where it joined Ermine Street that in turn ran from London to York, Lincoln became a major Roman settlement. To this day, there is visible evidence of the Roman occupation with sections of the walls and gateways to the Colonia still to be seen. In particular, the 3rdC Roman archway, now known as Newport Arch, is the oldest intact archway in the UK under which traffic still passes, albeit it was temporarily dislodged in 1964 when a high-sided lorry tried to pass underneath.

During the Viking period of the 9th and 10th centuries, Lincoln became one of the principal towns under Dane Law and had its own mint. With the arrival of the Normans following the Norman Conquest in 1066, a castle was built in 1068 on the high ground previously occupied by the Roman Colonia. Initially constructed in timber, the fortifications to the castle were later improved to include stone ramparts, two mottes and a fortified barbican as the main entrance, the stone being plundered from the town walls left by the Romans.

At the same time, work started upon the construction of the Cathedral. Dedicated to St Mary the Blessed Virgin, the original building was completed in 1092. Following an earthquake in 1185, the Norman cathedral was severely damaged leaving only the west front standing. Rebuilding work commenced almost immediately. Rebuilt and extended in early English Gothic style, the spire on the central tower was some 525 feet high. At that time, it was the tallest man made structure in the World, overtaking even the Great Pyramids of Egypt. However, because of structural problems the spire was taken down in 1549 and not replaced. Lincoln Cathedral remains the third largest cathedral in the UK, after St Paul's in London and York Minster. Inside, the lofty stone vaulting and magnificent carved stone screen, are breathtaking. The octagonal Chapter House was used during the time of Edward I to hold meetings of his parliament.

Within the Angel Choir at the east end of the Cathedral, there is mounted atop a stone column, the famous (or infamous) Lincoln Imp. There are various legends associated with the stone Imp, but maybe it was the work of a mason just bored with carving angelic figures. However, the Imp has become a symbolic figure in Lincoln with a local jeweller, James Usher, earning a lot of money with the production of silver figures depicting the Lincoln Imp. Today, Lincoln City Football Club are known as "The Imps". Also inside the Cathedral, is the Country's only memorial to the RAF's Bomber Command of World War Two. Lincolnshire was the home of many bomber squadrons that set out across the North Sea to attack enemy targets, including the famous Dam Busters. Like many others, I feel that it is shameful and a disgrace that the bravery of these bomber crews of World War Two has not been recognised by the erection of a national memorial. More recently, the Cathedral was used for the filming of "The Da Vinci Code" doubling as Westminster Abbey and also for "Young Victoria".

To the south of the Cathedral and overlooking the lower parts of the City, is the Bishop's Palace. Built during the late 12th century, it was at that time, one of the most important buildings in England and often received visits by royalty, including those made by Henry VIII and James I. However, during the period of the Civil War, it was sacked by the royalist troops and never restored. Today, the grounds and ruins are maintained by English Heritage and open to the public.

Returning back to medieval times, during the 13th century Lincoln was the third largest and one of the wealthiest city in England. This was the period of the "wool trade" during which time Lincoln prospered being one of the Country's largest staple ports for the export of wool. Two Battles of Lincoln were fought, each centred around the Castle, the first in 1141 that concerned the conflict between King Stephen and Queen Matilda for the throne of England. The second was between the rebel barons and King John that lead to the signing of the Magna Carta in 1215. One of the four remaining copies of the Magna Carta is on display within a dedicated exhibition centre that is housed within the Castle grounds.

During the 12th century, Lincoln had a sizable Jewish community. However, following an incident in 1255 known as "The Libel of Lincoln" where the Jews were accused (probably unjustly) of murdering a young boy, they were all expelled from the City. At this time, there was much resentment nationally against the Jewish communities. The 12th century stone and timber building known as Jew's House and Jew's Court, still stands at the bottom of Steep Hill.

During the 14th and 15th centuries, Lincoln fell into decline. The "Dissolution of the Monasteries" in the 16th century saw the seven monasteries located within the City close, together with a number a smaller abbeys. During the English Civil War of the 1640's, Lincoln changed hands a number of times between Royalist and Parliamentary forces, with many of the City's buildings being badly damaged, including the Bishop's Palace and some of the stone effigies on the Cathedral.

Lincoln again started to prosper with the advent of the Agricultural and Industrial Revolutions of the late 18th and early 19th centuries. A number of engineering companies that were subsequently to become nationally and internationally well known, were established in the City. These included Ruston and Hornsby who manufactured diesel gas engines and later gas turbines, Ruston Bucyrus, the excavator and crane manufacturer, along with Gwynes Pumps, Clayton's, Proctor's and Wm. Foster's. It was at the works of Wm. Foster's that the first ever tank was designed and built for use in World War One. Codenamed "Water Tanks for Mesopotamia" to confuse enemy spies (hence the word "tank"), the tanks used the caterpillar metal tracks invented by Richard Hornsby of

Grantham. One of the original WW1 tanks built at Wm. Foster's factory, named "Flirt", is on display at the City's Museum of Lincolnshire Life. Most of Lincoln's engineering manufacturing base has disappeared over recent years except for the manufacture of large gas turbines, albeit the future of these is uncertain.

Another incident of note occurred in 1904/05. This was an outbreak of typhoid that affected more than 1,000 of the City's population and resulted in 113 deaths. The epidemic was linked to the City's water supply, which was found to be severely polluted from untreated sewage effluent. Clean drinking water supplies had to be brought in by rail tanker from Newark and chlorine used for the first time in the UK to disinfect the water supply, prior to developing a new supply of drinking water for the City's population.

Descending from Castle Square down Steep Hill (the gradient is 1 : 4 in places), passed the historic half-timbered buildings and the Jew's House at the bottom, the visitor enters the narrow Strait before coming to the top of Lincoln's long High Street that extends nearly two miles to the South Common by St Catherine's. A little way down from the Strait, is the 16thC Stonebow / Guildhall. The southern gateway to the lower area of the City and at one time fronting onto the River Witham, the Guildhall Chambers above the archway are still used by the City Council for its meetings. Housed within the Guildhall, is Lincoln's civic insignia, said to be the finest outside London and which includes a priceless sword presented to the City of Lincoln by King Richard II. Further down still, is the 12thC High Bridge over the River Witham where it passes through the City centre. With the black and white 14thC half-timbered houses sitting atop, the Bridge is said to be the oldest bridge in the UK with buildings over it. The archway below where the River passes under the bridge, is known as the "Glory Hole".

Where the River Witham turns to flow eastwards through the Lincoln Gap, is the Brayford Pool from which Lincoln derived its name during the pre Roman period. Now developed into a marina with outdoor cafes and bars along its edge, the new University of Lincoln buildings can be seen across the waters of the Pool from its northern banks. The University was opened in 1996 and to date, accommodates more than 8,000 students on a variety of degree courses.

There are a number of museums etc, in Lincoln. "The Collection" housed in a recently constructed purpose-made building, contains an array of items of archaeological interest and was one of four finalists for the 2006 Gulbenkian Award. The adjoining Usher Gallery is dedicated to items of art and literature and contains memorabilia associated with Alfred Lord Tennyson, the Poet Laureate, who was born and lived nearby in the rolling Wolds of rural Lincolnshire. The Museum of Lincolnshire Life concentrates more on the County's industrial archaeology and contains one of the original WW1 tanks manufactured at Wm Foster's Works in Lincoln. Within the grounds of the Castle, is the exhibition centre depicting the story behind the Magna Carta, with Lincoln's original copy on display beneath a glass case. There is also the Sir Joseph Banks' Conservatory at the Lawns Complex next to the Castle. Banks, the renowned naturalist and botanist, was another of Lincolnshire's famous sons who sailed with Captain Cook on his voyages during the 18th century. On these voyages, he identified and brought back species of plants from all over the World, especially from Australia. At the Lawns is a hot-house glass conservatory dedicated to Banks that contains many tropical and subtropical plants.

Lincoln has over the years, been the home to a number of well known people. The actors John Hurt and Jim Broadbent both belong to the Lincoln area, together with the orchestral conductor, Sir Neville Marriner and radio broadcaster, Steve Race. Going back a bit further in time, George Boole, the pioneer of Boolian algebra and the binary notation that would later be used for computer programming, was born in the City in 1815.

There is much to see and do in the historic City of Lincoln, but without doubt, the busiest period of the year is at the time of the Christmas Market, held during the first weekend of December of each year. Started in 1982 and based on the Christmas market of Lincoln's twin town, Neustadt an der Weinstrasse situated in the Palatinate wine growing area of West Germany, it has grown to become the largest Christmas market of its type in Europe, with over 200,000 visitors coming to Lincoln over the four day period. Held in the grounds of the Castle and around the Cathedral in the uphill area, the smell of the gluhwein and bratwurst sausages is all pervading.

For the past forty years, Lincoln has been my home and I am naturally proud of its history, heritage and what it has to offer. As such, I make no apologies for extolling its virtues and recommend a visit to those who have never been before. For Archie and myself, we are to take a break from our bus travels northward across and up England, as the August Bank Holiday Weekend is approaching.

* * * * * * *

Friday 23rd to Wednesday 27th August 2008

Whilst I had enjoyed my journey so far (I can't speak for Archie), I was nevertheless pleased to be spending a few days at home, especially with the busy Bank Holiday weekend approaching. With all the bumping about whilst travelling and sitting about on the buses, my bones were weary, my knees aching and backside sore. The break would also mean no rucksack to hump about, no anxieties regarding accommodation or bus connections. Also, the bus services over the Bank Holiday weekend and the Sunday would be restricted and accommodation difficult to find. A few days at home would allow me to catch up with my Open University work and complete my next course assignment.

My knee replacement operation had been rescheduled by the local hospital in Lincoln for the 3rd September, so I didn't have too much time before I set out again to complete the next section up to Berwick. I planned to continue our bus trip on the coming Thursday, hoping to reach Berwick by midday on the Saturday, thus allowing me sufficient time to prepare myself for my knee op. As fate would have it, we had been notified that our boiler had been scheduled to be replaced early in the week, so at least I would be at home to see that done, although there was little involvement by myself apart from making cups of tea. Time to relax and cut the grass and best to be away from the Bank Holiday traffic and congestion.

At the weekend, the Olympic Games in Beijing were coming to an end, with a spectacular fireworks display at the end of the closing ceremony. The UK athletes and competitors had performed exceptionally well at these Games, coming fourth in the overall rankings behind China, the USA and Russia with 19 golds and a total of 47 bronze, silver and gold medals. We had come out ahead of the Australians, the Germans and particularly the French. The Lord Mayor of London, Boris Johnson, was there at the closing ceremony to accept the handover for the next Olympics to be held in London in 2012. An event we all await with pride and anticipation.

On television over the weekend, was Martin Clunes' programme "One Man and His Dogs". On the programme, it was given that a dog's DNA matched that of a wolf by some 99%. Always thought that Archie's pedigree was in doubt, now I know. Also that dogs became "man's best friend" some 15,000 years ago, although I doubt if they would have been pampered as much in those days. For certain, there would not have been any "Pedigree Chum" about. Perhaps not too surprising was the fact that there are estimated to be 7 million dogs currently kept as pets in the UK, all descending from over 400 different breeds, the majority being half breeds and Heinz 57s.

Over the weekend, there were a series of music concerts being held at the Castle, which is not too far away from where we live. Aled Jones, Haley Westenra and the Bootleg Beetles were all performing, with the amplified sound of the music being carried well beyond the confines of the Castle's walls. At least we didn't have to pay to listen. The final day ended in a fine display of fireworks that set Archie off on a barking frenzy. The period of Guy Fawkes is always a nightmare at home.

At church on Sunday morning, one of the hymns was "One more step along the world I go". I was tempted to change the words to "One more bus along the road I go". For myself and Archie, it may have been more appropriate. Lincoln City (The Imps) lost again on Saturday. So far this season, they have yet to pick up any points and sit at the bottom of their league table. Early days though!

Me and Archie by the Signpost at Lands End

Entrance to Visitors' Centre at Lands End

Towan Beach, Newquay

West Front of Exeter Cathedral

Cascade on River Avon, Bath

Radcliffe Camera, Oxford

Issac Newton's Statue, Grantham

Bus to Lincoln

Lincoln Cathedral from Castle

Humber Bridge from Barton

South Bay and Harbour, Scarborough

Durham Cathedral from River Wear

"Angel of the North", Gateshead

The Tyne Bridges, Newcastle

The "Coast and Castles" Bus, Alnwick

Alnwick Castle

The Royal Tweed Bridge, Berwick

Chapter 7
Lincoln To Scarborough—Day 7

Thursday 28th August 2008

Time to set off again on our travels north up to Berwick-on-Tweed. I am up early to give Archie his early morning walk before catching our bus to Scunthorpe.

Nearby where we live is a large well-maintained cemetery that provides a pleasant early morning walk for Archie. Within the grounds is a military cemetery with its rows of Portland-stone headstones and memorial cross. There are approaching some 200 war graves, all immaculately maintained. Most are of servicemen who died from their wounds received during World War 1 when repatriated to the military hospital in Lincoln. The inscriptions on the headstones depict various regiments of the British army, together with those of Australia and Canada, their servicemen being buried here too, together with a Polish soldier. Some were as young as 19 years of age, still just boys. Other headstones are dated 1919, a year after the armistice, for soldiers were never able to return home due to their injuries. "Their Name Will Live Forever".

Having had his early morning exercise and me my fried breakfast, we are ready to set out again on our journey north. My wife drops us off at the Lincoln City Bus Station to catch our first bus to Scunthorpe. In my narrative, I have made a number of references to the various bus stations we have visited. Some are simple but functional bus stands; others that include shops and the necessary services, are well designed and provide for the comfort and safety of passengers. However, in my own opinion, the bus station at Lincoln comes at the bottom of the pile. It is dark, dank and dangerous. Constructed in concrete during the 1970's without much regard for the comfort of passengers, it is soon scheduled for demolition when funds allow, with a new improved station being built as a replacement. It cannot come too soon.

The 09.35 No.100 Stagecoach bus to Scunthorpe roars into the bus station, the noise of its exhaust echoing around under the concrete roof.

On we both board, me going for free, Archie costing me 50 pence. I don't understand why a national firm like Stagecoach need to differentiate between the bus services in Lincolnshire and the rest of the Country as regards fares for dogs. Apart from The First Group in Cornwall, I have not been charged for Archie to travel anywhere else so far (RANT 14). Maybe I should not make too much of an issue over this point in case the Company change their policy and make a charge throughout the Country for dogs to travel.

Off we set, along Carholme Road and past the old grandstand and racecourse alongside the West Common that up to the mid 1960's, was where the Lincoln Handicap was run. Traditionally the first flat race of the horse racing season, the event was transferred to Doncaster following the closure of the racecourse at Lincoln. As we head out along the A57 towards Saxilby, up in the blue skies above, the RAF's air acrobatic team, the "Red Arrows" are practising, leaving behind them their trailing coloured vapour trails. The "Red Arrows" are currently based at RAF Scampton located just to the north of Lincoln, although there are plans for them to move to RAF Waddington, some eight miles to the south. During the last World War, RAF Scampton was the base for 617 Squadron, better known as the "Dam Busters" and later during the Cold War, for the Avro Vulcan delta wing bombers.

The bus route along the A57 follows the old Roman Foss Dyke that is today still used as a navigation canal linking the River Trent with Lincoln and the North Sea via the River Witham. Constructed by the Romans in 120AD, the Canal is the oldest navigable canal in Britain. Most of the craft using the Canal these days are pleasure boats, some sizable and expensive. Reaching the village of **Saxilby** (population 3,800) the bus turns off the A57 and into the Village itself. A Roman camp was located near to the Village with the parish church of St Botolph's dating from the 12th century. Today Saxilby is a large commuter village for Lincoln. There are two brightly painted long-boats tied up alongside the canal bank opposite the old Sun Inn as we travel along Bridge Street.

The Sun Inn at Saxilby figured in a grim murder that took place in late 1805 on a nearby country lane between the Village and Drinsey Nook to the west. The incident, that has since become local folklore, concerned a local navvy called Tom Otter, who murdered his newly wedded wife Mary on the night of their marriage. Mary was carrying Tom's child although it subsequently turned out that he was already married. The murder weapon he used was a wooden hedge-stake with which he inflicted terrible wounds on the body of his unfortunate wife. Mary's body was brought to the Sun Inn where it lay until Otter was arrested. It is said that the bloodstains on the step of the Sun Inn could not be removed no matter how hard the steps were scrubbed. Otter was tried, found guilty and his body hung in chains from a gibbet at the site where the terrible act took place, now called Tom Otter's Lane. For many years afterwards, the locals claimed that they could still hear the rattle of his chains from the gibbet and few dared to venture down the Lane during the hours of darkness. All sorts of ghostly tales arose from the incident including the cries of a newborn baby in the room at the Sun Inn where Mary's body lay. The murder weapon itself, which was in the possession of a local innkeeper, was supposedly cursed with evil spirits. Eventually the Bishop of Lincoln ordered that the hedge-stake used in the murder, be destroyed and burnt in front of witnesses.

Our bus does a circuit of the Village, passing by the 12th C St Botolph's church before setting out along the B1241 through the Lincolnshire countryside towards the village of Sturton by Stow. On the way, we pass the signs for the Bransby Rest Home for Horses, a rescue centre for horses, ponies and donkeys. Nearly 300 animals are housed at the stables at any one time, many being brought in following incidents of neglect and cruelty. Reliant on charitable contributions, the Centre does some excellent work in the rescue, rehabilitation, re-homing and retirement of these horses, ponies and donkeys. Operating for over 40 years, it is open to visitors most days of the week.

Reaching Sturton by Stow, we cross over the former Roman road, Tillbridge Lane that runs down to and at one time crossed over the River Trent into Nottinghamshire. Along the Lane is the site of the 14th C Palace of the Bishops of Lincoln, with now only grassy mounds indicating where the building once stood. On we head out to the attractive and historic little village of **Stow** (population 400). Dominating the village, is the large Saxon / Norman Minster Church of St Mary's. There has been a church on the site since the 7th century, the original being burnt down by the Danish Vikings. The present church with its square tower was built during the 10th century and was the Cathedral Church of Lindsey until the cathedral at Lincoln was built in the late 11th century. Still referred to as the Mother Church of Lincolnshire, it has the tallest Saxon arches in the whole of Europe. Outside the Church, is the Village's old "whipping post" complete with hand irons and which dates back to 1784.

On we head out of Stow towards the next village of Willingham by Stow and Gainsborough. Across to the west, can be seen the cooling towers of the large Trentside coal-fired power stations of Cottam and West Burton, the white plumes of water vapour ascending high into the skies above. As we pass through the Lincolnshire countryside, the last of the cereal crops are being combined, this being a little later than usual, due no doubt to the recent wet weather. The fields of maize and beans look good but have yet to be harvested.

Joining the A156 at Lea, it is only a short distance before we enter the town and inland-port of **Gainsborough** (population 20,100), the time is 10.25. Sharing the same name with the famous painter, the very name Gainsborough conjures up an image of beauty and attractiveness. However, even the local townsfolk would agree that visitors and any art aficionados would be disappointed. Gainsborough is an inland port sited on the east bank of the River Trent and prospered during the industrial periods of the 19th and 20th centuries with the manufacture and production of steam engines, boilers, agricultural machinery and food processing equipment. Flour-mills also sprung up along the banks of the River. In its heyday, Gainsborough was one of the largest inland ports in England. Sadly, both Marshall's Britannia engineering works and Whitton's flour mills are now closed, with retail parks and offices established in their place. The former riverside wharf areas have recently been redeveloped into pedestrian areas with pavement cafes along its length.

One of the major towns in the old kingdom of Mercia, it is purported that it was at Gainsborough that King Canute tried to turn back the tide. This may have some merit as the "Aegir", a five foot high tidal bore that starts at the Humber, travels up the Trent as far as Gainsborough, where the tidal surge dies out and "turns back". An 11th century earthworks motte and bailey fortress did at one time exist on the high ground overlooking the Town, though this fell into disrepair many years ago and is now overgrown with little to be seen. Without doubt, the main attraction and place of interest in the Town, is the Old Hall. Built in the 15th century, the large timber-framed strong house is considered to be one of the best preserved medieval manor houses in Britain. Visited by both Richard III and Henry VIII, the property is now under the jurisdiction of English Heritage and open to the public.

Stopping to pick up passengers at the main bus halt on North Street, we head out of the Town past the ground of Gainsborough Trinity FC, along Morton Terrace and onto the A159 towards the steel town of

Scunthorpe. On we travel first passing through the village of Blyton that has still managed to retain its old style of red telephone box with its heavy metal door and small glass windows. No doubt BT's reason for the removal of most of the old telephone boxes was because of high maintenance costs and vandalism. Nevertheless, I feel that these old red boxes were part of our British heritage and like the old "Doctor Who" type blue police boxes, I regret seeing their removal (RANT 15) No doubt it is because of so called "progress" but at least it is good to see some of the old red telephone boxes preserved in the small rural villages like Blyton, where perhaps the scourge of vandalism is not a serious problem as it is in our larger towns and cities.

Being harvest time, albeit the tail-end, there is still a lot of activity taking place on the land in gathering up the rest of the arable crops. Combine harvesters are working in the fields with accompanying tractors and trailers that are collecting the grain alongside the combines. Other machinery is collecting up the loose straw and bundling it into large circular bales for picking up later. Unfortunately, we get behind one of these slow moving tractors and trailers that seems to be travelling for some distance on the same road that our bus is travelling on. On the single carriageway, twisty rural roads of Lincolnshire, there is no chance of overtaking. Eventually, the tractor turns off towards its farm, and our bus picks up speed.

On we travel through the village of Laughton and then between woodlands of pines and silver birch trees to Scotton and Scotter, making a detour along narrow country roads into the villages. Being still the school holidays, a number of youngsters board the bus and our peace is shattered with their yelling and shouting. Young people these days don't seem to be able to converse in normal tones of volumes—maybe we were the same when their age although I suspect not. I really am becoming a "grumpy old man"—must try to be more tolerant and not rant on about such matters.

On we go to Messingham with its well maintained war memorial and interestingly named pub called "The Bird in the Barley". I notice one of the street names is "Temperance Street", presumably all the residents were at one time teetotallers—perhaps not anymore! Approaching Bottesford, we cross from Lincolnshire into the newly formed administrative county of North Lincolnshire, previously part of the county of Humberside, which was by popular request, abolished in 1996. With the traditional rivalry between the north and south banks of the Humber, Hull and

Grimsby in particular, the former County was never popular with most of the inhabitants. The same has happened elsewhere in the Country and I cannot understand why the politicians don't listen to the views of the local people before implementing such unpopular changes (RANT 16). On a much larger scale, the EU is another good example of the electorates' views not being listened to, but I will not start on the subject on the lack of democracy of the European Union, as it would fill this book.

We arrive in the major steelworks town of Scunthorpe, called "The Industrial Garden Town" because of its well maintained parks and gardens. It is also often referred to a Sunny Scunny—not sure why as the sun shines no more on Scunthorpe as it does on towns elsewhere. As we travel down Ashby Road on our way into the Town centre, we pass by the Civic Hall and Festival Gardens with their flower borders a blaze of colour. We reach the bus station in Scunthorpe at 11.20, leaving us some fifty minutes for a brief walkabout.

Scunthorpe—North Lincolnshire—population 72,500

The name "Scunthorpe" comes from the old Norse word *Escumetorp* that appeared in Domesday Book and meaning "Skuma's homestead". Often unfairly the butt of music-hall jokes because of its name, the present day Town was originally composed of five villages, those of Scunthorpe, Frodingham, Crosby, Brumby and Ashby. The Borough received its municipal charter in 1936 when it was included in the "Parts of Lindsey in the County of Lincolnshire", similar to the Ridings of Yorkshire. In 1974, the County of Humberside was formed, to be eventually abolished and be succeeded in 1996 by the County of North Lincolnshire, in which Scunthorpe is the principal town. Scunthorpe has also suffered because of the four-letter word that follows the "S" insomuch as that AOL's obscenity filter will not accept the Town's name. Known in the computing world as the "Scunthorpe problem", it is still ongoing at the time of writing this book.

Scunthorpe is sited on the limestone escarpment that extends southwards to Lincoln. Underneath lies on a rich bed of ironstone that together with the limestone above, is the main reason for the emergence of the iron and steel industry in the Town.

Apart from being worked by the Romans, ironstone mining was not commenced on any large scale until the mid 19th century that ultimately led to the development of the present iron & steel industry in the Town.

Cast iron was first produced in 1862 at the old Trent Ironworks to be followed by the establishment of a number of other ironworks, notably Frodingham, Appleby, Redbourne Hill and Lysaght's at Normanby Park. Steel was first produced in 1890 using the old Bessemer open-hearth type furnaces, which were subsequently replaced by the more modern and efficient basic oxygen blast furnaces. There are four of these blast furnaces, affectionately named "Mary, Bess, Anne and Victoria" after the four British Queens and which tower over the rest of the steelworks. They can be seen from miles around, especially at night-times when giving off a red glow and are part of the Scunthorpe scene. The Town's motto that is included on its coat of arms, is "The Heavens reflect our Labours" perhaps making reference to the glow in the night-time skies. Also included on the coat of arms, is the fossil "*gryphoea incurva*" known as the "devil's toenails", which is found in abundance in the local rock formations.

Although the number of employees have shrunk from the 27,000 employed in the 1950/60's to the 4,000 / 5,000 today, the steelworks are still the major employer in the Town. Now part of the Indian Tata Group, the works specialises in the manufacture of high-grade quality steels including rail sections and cable wire. However, the iron mines are now all closed down as the local ore had only a 20% iron content, with much higher grades of iron ore now being imported from abroad that even allowing for the costs of transportation, is deemed to be more economically viable. I do wonder if this would be the case if other factors, including environmental issues, were taken into account. During the heydays of the steel-making industry at Scunthorpe, there were a large number of associated engineering industries in the Town. With the subsequent decline in steel-making, many of these industries have either closed down or cut-back their output. However, the Scunthorpe Steelworks are still considered to be the major integrated steelworks in the whole of the UK and with the efficiency measures introduced over recent years, should remain competitive against foreign markets.

Scunthorpe being a relatively new town, does not have many old buildings. The oldest is St Lawrence's Church, built during the Middle Ages with its squat tower, it is located near to the Town's hospital. The imposing former church of St John the Evangelist, built in the local Frodingham ironstone at the end of the 19th century, is located in Church Square near to the Town centre and shopping precinct. Due to falling numbers in the congregation, the church was closed in 1984 and remained so until the year 2000 when the building was reopened as the Town's Visual Arts Centre. The North Lincolnshire Museum, located near to the railway station, is well worth a visit, especially if one's interest is in geology, where there is an excellent collection of rocks, minerals and fossils, many obtained locally.

A number of well-known names have come from or have been associated with the Town. Such people include Joan Plowright, the actress, Donald Pleasance, the actor and perhaps Scunthorpe's favourite son, Tony Jacklin, winner of the British Open Golf Championship in 1969 and the US Open the following year. Ian Botham, the international cricketer and more recent long-distance walker, lived in nearby Epworth on the Isle of Axholme and when at home and not on the cricket field, played football for the "Iron", Scunthorpe United FC. Epworth was also the birthplace of the founder of Methodism, John Wesley, who born in 1703, was brought up in his clergyman father's rectory along with his brother Charles, the hymn writer, and seventeen other brothers and sisters. Meal times must have been interesting.

Leaving the bus station, we walk around the back and into Church Square where work has recently been undertaken in repaving the open area with patterns of coloured paviors. Opposite is the former Anglican church of St John the Evangelist that is now used to house the Town's Visual Art Centre. It would have been interesting to be able to have a look around the Centre, but not today with Archie. The tower of St John's church stands high over the Square with the soft brown ironstone and creamy limestone edgings to the building, adding to its elegance.

It has started to rain so we make our way to the adjacent pedestrianised shopping precinct where outside a café and under cover of an overhanging canopy, I find a table to sit at. Being late morning, I order coffee and scones—Archie can have a bit of my scone. On this Thursday morning in August, there are few people about in what is Scunthorpe's new and modern main shopping area. Soon it is back to the bus station for the next stage of our journey, this time across the Humber to Hull.

* * * * * * *

Finding the right stand, we wait for our bus to Hull to arrive. In rolls the mauve coloured double-decker No.350 Stagecoach East Yorkshire bus and on we board, at least this time I don't have to pay for Archie. Off we set leaving the bus station at 12.10, heading out of Scunthorpe northwards via Winterton Road and along the A1077. On the bus travels, passing by the works and offices of the industrial estates with the four blast furnaces of the steelworks clearly visible to our right, then up the slope of the escarpment past Dragonby and on towards Winterton.

At Dragonby, the former offices, head-works, workshops and welfare facilities that served the former ironstone mines are still standing, albeit now empty and abandoned. Back in the 1970's, I had cause to visit the underground workings as a result of my work. The mine workings below ground are relatively shallow with access by a long sloping tunnel driven from ground level. Once underground, the workings are vast, with at that time, large mechanical face-shovels and dump-trucks operating on the extraction of the iron ore. The headroom is some twenty feet with pillars being left at suitable intervals to support the stone roof, leaving adequate access for the machinery to operate. The scene is totally different to that of a traditional coalmine. Together with the nearby mine at Santon, the underground workings have spread out over the years to cover an area of some six square miles and from where many thousands of tons of the local Frodingham ironstone have been extracted since the mines were opened in the late 1940's. In 1980, the mines were closed on economical grounds as already mentioned, although they were kept open for a short period to allow inspections to take place so to monitor the conditions below ground. There are still vast reserves of iron ore left underground although it is suspected that most of the workings are now flooded. Perhaps one day when market conditions permit, the mines may be reopened.

Reaching the top of the escarpment, our bus leaves the A1077 to make a detour into the large village of **Winterton** (population 4,800). Perhaps drawn by the availability of the local ironstone and sited on Ermine Street, Winterton's past can be traced back to Roman times. A number of relics have been discovered, including the presence of a Roman villa complete with mosaic floors and pavement. A lead-lined stone coffin was also unearthed, complete with skeleton that also dates back to the Roman period. Nowadays, with its four pubs and limestone houses, the Village is mainly home for commuters working in Scunthorpe. Stopping outside the Cross Keys to pick up passengers, we head out of the Village northwards towards the Humber, along the narrow country lanes. As experienced earlier on in the day, the combines and baling machines are busy working in the fields harvesting the remainder of the cereal crops.

We cross over the main A1077 road to call in at the small but attractive village of **Winteringham** (population 1,000). Sited at the northern end of the Lincoln Ridge and overlooking the Humber, it was here that the Romans crossed the River Humber by means of a ferry (or so it is supposed) when travelling along Ermine Street on their way north from Lincoln to York. Many of the buildings are constructed in the local limestone, complete with red pantile roofs.

Leaving the Village, we soon rejoin the A1007, this time heading eastwards, above and then alongside the south bank of the Humber. From the high ground, there is a good view across the Humber to Yorkshire, the River being approximately one mile wide at this point. With the River Trent and the Yorkshire Ouse discharging their waters into the Humber, the River carries the drainage water from most of Central England and Yorkshire. We also get our first view of the magnificent Humber Bridge that spans the Estuary between its two tall concrete towers—more later. Immediately alongside us is Read's Island, so named after the brothers who first farmed there. Up to fairly recently, cattle were grazed on the Island, but with changes in the tidal flows of the River and recent heavy flooding, the Island's size has been substantially reduced. It is now an important RSPB site for avocets. Previously treeless, it would seem that there has been some recent activity in planting a few new trees.

On we travel along the south shore of the Humber until we reach **South Ferriby** (population 600) that is located on the River Ancholme where it enters the Humber. At one time, as the name would suggest, a ferry operated across the Humber to North Ferriby on the north bank. It is also alleged that illegal contraband was brought ashore here in days gone-by. Passing by the cement works that takes its raw materials from the nearby chalk escarpment of the Lincolnshire Wolds, we cross the bridge over the River Ancholme that is lifted when boats need to pass under. Thankfully, the bridge is down and there is no hold-up as we pass by the Hope and Anchor public house—it is sometimes interesting to speculate how pubs obtained their names.

Immediately leaving South Ferriby, the bus climbs the steep incline to the top of the chalk Wolds, again giving us good views across the Humber and of the Humber Bridge especially. Crossing over the cutting that carries the access road to the Humber Bridge, we enter the market town of **Barton-upon-Humber** (population 9,400). Dating back to Saxon times, there is a fine example of a Saxon tower at St

Peter's Church, now closed. Only literally a few feet away is St Mary's Church that is still open for regular worship, posing the question as to why two separate churches should be built so close together—must have been on either side of the old parish boundary. For many years, bicycles were manufactured at Barton but no more. Chad Varah, founder of the Samaritans, was born in the Town, where also Issac Pitman of short-hand fame lived for many years.

It is worth mentioning that in Barton's twin town of Barrow upon Humber, just four miles to the east, lived John Harrison, the man who perfected the marine chronometer and who was able to solve the problem of establishing longitude whilst at sea. Although not born at Barrow, Harrison's family moved there in the late 1690's, whilst he was still a young boy. It was at Barrow that Harrison set up his workshop that was to lead to him resolving the problem for which the "Board of Longitude" had made substantial prize money available, this in order to improve marine navigation and prevent the then appalling loss of shipping. The availability of an accurate timepiece that could be used at sea would resolve the problem of the determination of longitude, that Harrison, a self-taught man, eventually managed to do after much hard work and fighting against bigoted opposition. He died in 1776, having spent his lifetime in perfecting his original designs to the satisfaction of the Board, who begrudgingly eventually awarded him the full amount of the prize money. This had been made in instalments but in the end totalled £23,065, making him a rich man albeit he was too old to enjoy much of it. His four time-pieces, H1, H2, H3 and H4 are on display at National Maritime Museum at Greenwich in London.

Stopping in the Barton's wide market place, the bus travels down to the railway station and to the top of Barton Haven before returning back to the market place and proceeding out of the Town towards the Humber Bridge. Joining the A15 Humber Bridge access road, our bus speeds down the dual carriageway towards the giant concrete towers at the south end with the suspension cables of the Bridge itself, stretching out in a catenary across the wide waters of the River Humber. It is truly a magnificent sight and an engineering masterpiece. Down below us on the left, are the old early 18th century brickworks and clay pits that have now been developed into a country park and nature reserve. The starting point of Lincolnshire's long distance footpath, the "Viking Way" can be seen below, heading west along the River bank. The footpath is some 130 miles in length and finishes at Oakham by Rutland Water.

As a civil engineer by profession, now retired, I am obviously biased in my praises of the **Humber Bridge**, that gracefully spans the wide waters of the River. Opened by the Queen in July 1981, it was at that time the longest single spanning bridge in the World and retained that title for some 16 years. Although the accolade has since been claimed by bridges elsewhere, it is still ranks fifth in the World (as in 2009) and is the longest single span in the U.K. The Bridge's main span is 4,626 feet (1,410 metres) with side spans of 1,739 feet on the south side and 919 feet on the north, making its total length 7,284 feet, nearly one and a half miles. The height of the slender hollow concrete towers on both sides is 510 feet with the bridge deck having a clearance of 98 feet above the waters below. Work started on site in 1971 with the construction of the piers to the towers and cable anchorages, the foundations to the tower on the south side proving very problematic due to the poor ground conditions. Each of the two suspension cables is composed of nearly 15,000 wires that could if joined together, twice encircle the World. Unlike the corrosion being experienced with the cables on the Forth Road Bridge, recent checks at the Humber Bridge have established no similar problems. Designed by Freeman Fox and Partners and constructed by Sir Wm. Arrol & Co, the final cost was near £150 million. Tolls are still charged for vehicles crossing the Bridge (£2.70 each way for cars in 2009) to pay off the loan debt and which are still controversial, especially now as the tolls for the Forth Bridge have been abolished by the Scottish Parliament. Nevertheless, drivers of the 2,000 plus vehicles that cross the Bridge each day between Barton and Hessle, obviously prefer to pay the tolls rather than take the 50 mile detour via Goole upstream. It is certainly much faster than crossing by the old steam-paddle ferryboats, the Lincoln Castle and the Tattershall Castle, which the Bridge replaced. Those who do not want to pay the toll can always walk across via the footways provided on each side and enjoy the views.

As we set out to cross the Humber into Yorkshire, Archie has come to life as he smells the water and has his snout pressed hard to the window. There are fine views of the River Humber below, on which there is some shipping sailing to and from the inland ports of Yorkshire and the Midlands. At the centre point of the Bridge, the cables come sweeping down to near deck level before ascending again in an arc, high up to the top of the concrete towers. At the Hessle end of the Bridge, are the tollbooths through which our bus has to pass. I presume that there must be a charge for service buses that use the Bridge and that this is reflected in the bus fares, which neither Archie nor myself have to pay. Below on the left at the Hessle end, is the visitors centre and viewing area that provides an excellent photo shot of the Bridge from the north bank.

We have now entered Yorkshire, or rather the East Riding of Yorkshire. Turning eastwards at the roundabout immediately after the Bridge crossing, we head down the A1106 into the dormitory town of **Hessle** (population 14,800). Each Whitsuntide, the Hessle Feast is held. Dating back to the early 1800's, it is said that it is "an event of enjoyment that is embraced by the whole community of Hessle and when people all gather to celebrate the coming summer". A good time no doubt, is had by all.

Continuing down the tree-lined Boothferry Road and past the sign informing us that we are now entering the City of Kingston upon Hull, we come to the magnificent new KC Stadium where both Hull City Football and Hull Rugby League Clubs play their home games. The initials "KC" stands for "Kingston Communications", as the Stadium was funded from the proceeds of the sale of the City's municipally owned public telephone system. On we travel down Anlaby Road, passing the Royal Hospital and into the centre of the City, where our bus finally comes to a halt at the new Paragon Interchange. Opened in 2007, the new development has preserved the façade of the old Victorian railway station whilst providing an integrated transport hub for rail and bus travel. It is certainly impressive. The time is 13.20.

Kingston upon Hull—East Riding of Yorkshire—population 258,700

The City and port of Kingston upon Hull is the largest town / city in East Yorkshire and since 1996, has been a Unitary Authority with its own self governing City Council. Located aside the River Hull where it joins the Humber Estuary, it is thought that the site has been occupied since Neolithic times. However, it was in 1299 that the City received its first Royal Charter from Edward I, when it adopted the name "King's Town upon Hull".

During medieval times, the City flourished, trading with the Hanseatic League towns of the Baltic area. In 1642, the Royalists placed a siege on the City that sided with the Parliamentarians. This precipitated the beginnings of open conflict between the two sides in the English Civil War. More recently during the last World War, Hull was the most heavily bombed city outside London, with up to 95% of houses being destroyed or badly damaged.

During the 18th and 19th centuries, Hull was a major whaling port and continued as one of the Country's premier deep-sea fishing ports until the Cod Wars of 1975/76 that involved disputes at sea with Icelandic trawlers. The outcome of the fishing dispute with Iceland has lead to a decline in the deep-sea fishing industry in Britain and in Hull in particular. The former flourishing fishing industry at Hull has now virtually disappeared, although the port still remains very busy, handling container cargos with roll-on roll-off ferry services sailing across the North Sea to Rotterdam and Zeebrugge.

With the general industrial decline of the engineering and chemical industries in the local area, unemployment levels in Hull are well above the national average, resulting in the usual social problems. The phrase "Hull, Hell and Halifax in that order" is often quoted, more by people outside the City. Much redevelopment work has taken place in recent years, especially in the area of the former docklands along the banks of the Humber where the large Prince's Quay shopping complex has been built. The recently opened submarium "The Deep" on the banks of the Humber, is claimed to be the only one of its type in the World, although I am not sure if this is strictly true as I visited a similar submarium a few years ago near Perth in Australia. Nevertheless, it is certainly different and well worth a visit.

Alongside "The Deep" is the tall tidal surge barrier that controls water levels in the River Hull at times of flooding. Most of the City is built on low-lying alluvial deposits that are only six to twelve feet above sea level. More than fifty percent of the City is below the high water mark. During the severe flooding of 2007 that affected the Country as a whole, up to twenty percent of homes in Hull were flooded resulting in them being uninhabitable for months and in some cases, more than a year. With rising sea levels forecasted over the coming years, there has been much debate and head-scratching as to what the solution might be to the problem. For sure there will be some tough decisions to be made by the authorities to protect their City.

One of the oldest buildings in Hull and dating from the early 14th century is Holy Trinity Church, its walls being composed of medieval brickwork. Although a City, Hull has no cathedral but Holy Trinity is the largest parish church in England, based on floor area. There has been a Guildhall building in Hull for many years with the present building complete with its tall tower, dating from 1907. It is still used by the City Council for the meetings. The imposing City Hall with its domed tower, dates from the early 1900's and is used to host concerts and other gatherings. The Maritime Museum in the City centre is another imposing building from the Victorian / Edwardian period and houses exhibits and artefacts from Hull's past as a whaling and fishing port. Again, well worth a visit and it's free.

Until very recently, Hull had its own municipally owned telephone system that was totally independent of British Telecom and its predecessors. Set up in 1902, it was operated and managed by the City Council up to as recently as 2007 before it was sold to a private company. The cream coloured telephone boxes contrast with the familiar red boxes found throughout the rest of the Country. As mentioned previously, the network is now owned and operated by the private company Kingston Communications who purchased the stock and assets from the City Council, part of the proceeds going towards the construction of the new KC Stadium on Anlaby Road.

Being a City of more than a quarter of a million inhabitants, Hull is well provided for by theatres and other venues of entertainment. The City Hall has already been mentioned but there are many more. With well known Hullensians that include poet Philip Larkin, play-writers John Godber and Alan Plater, and the actress Maureen Lipman, the City has a strong literary and theatrical reputation. The University of Hull with some 16,000 students, also adds to the culture of the City.

Perhaps Hull's most famous son was William Wilberforce, a native of the City and Member of Parliament for Hull from 1780 to 1784. He continued as a M.P. representing Yorkshire and Bramber for a further 41 years to 1825. It was Wilberforce that worked tirelessly for 26 years in promoting his Bill for the abolition of slavery throughout the then British Empire, which eventually resulted in the passing of the "Slavery Abolition Act of 1833". Suffering ill health, Wilberforce died three days after the Act was passed, his life-long work completed.

On the sporting scene, Hull has three top-flight football clubs, one association football and two rugby league football. Hull City FC, the "Tigers" recently gained promotion to football's Premiership League starting with some shock results, albeit later struggling near to the bottom. The two rugby league clubs Hull FC, the "Airlie Birds" and Hull Kingston Rovers RLFC, the "Robbins" are located on different sides of the River Hull, with both having their loyal and partisan following. Hull has a long tradition in the game of rugby league that commands strong support throughout the City and derby matches between the two clubs creates much passion amongst supporters. Clive Sullivan was one of the game's greatest players, playing for both clubs and captaining the Great Britain international team. He was the first black player to captain an England / British international team and is remembered by one of the main thoroughfares of Hull being named after him.

* * * * * * *

At the Paragon Interchange, our next bus to Scarborough is due in five minutes time. Being the time of day and having visited Hull on a number of occasions in the past, I decide that we should catch the bus that is due in rather than spend time walking around the City. With due respect to Hull, time by the seaside will be more enjoyable, although perhaps Archie might enjoy a brief walk.

Even at this time of the day in the early part of the afternoon, there is a large number of people waiting to catch the Scarborough bus, nearly all being "senior citizens". How I dislike that description. It turns out that they are all heading for Bridlington for an afternoon out by the seaside, using of course, their bus passes for a free trip. There had recently been some publicity in the national press about Scarborough Town Council complaining that the bus pass scheme was under-funded by the government and that the Council was having to pay out nearly £1 million a year to subsidise the free bus travel from the likes of Hull. It was reported that this was having a marked effect upon the Council's spending budget and cuts in other services would have to be made, such as getting rid of the dog wardens, which is a bit of a strange comparison. Needless to say that the Government denied that there was a problem. It was further reported by the bus company Stagecoach, that "*free bus passes for the over 60's were causing a problem. The "free-loading wrinklies" were taking up places on buses, leaving no room for paying customers, making the bus services uneconomical*". Oh dear!! However, I think that I prefer the term "free-loading wrinklies" to that of "senior citizens" which in my opinion, seems very patronising. (RANT 17).

The double-decker East Yorkshire No.121 bus soon pulled up alongside the stop and on we get, fighting our way aboard with the other "free-loading wrinklies"—also no charge for Archie. There being no seats left downstairs, we go up onto the top deck where at least we will have a good view of the countryside that we will be passing through. With everyone settled down, the bus pulls out of the Paragon at 13.25.

Amongst the general chatter and hubbub, I hear, to my dismay, the chap on the seat behind start speaking into his mobile phone. It seems that when people speak into their mobiles, they seem unable to do so in a quiet or even normal tone of voice. His voice is particularly loud and virtually the whole of the top deck can overhear his conversation, which is far from being brief. It seemed that he is having trouble with his car, that has amongst other faults, developed a hole in the petrol tank. He was apparently having problems in fixing it and paying for the cost of repair. Sympathetic as I might be towards his plight, the expense and inconvenience that he is being caused, I do not want to hear about all the ins and outs that have caused the problems, the arrangements he was making to have it fixed and how he is going to raise the money. I am sure that the time he is spending on his mobile phone would have seen the repair completed. Why is it that when some people use their mobile phones, they do not seem able to speak in normal tones and seem unable to keep their conversations brief and to the point (RANT 18). Maybe he was hoping the rest of us on the bus would take pity on him and have a whip-round.

We drive out of Kingston upon Hull heading north along Beverley Road that is lined with some fine buildings and then on the A1174. After only some eight miles, we enter the medieval market town of **Beverley** (population 29,200), passing by the old Racecourse and 17thC Grandstand, where there are a large number of horseboxes gathered for the coming Friday's race meeting. Then on into the Town centre, where stands the imposing 13thC Minster Church that was built in the medieval Gothic style, the original church having been destroyed by the Vikings (a destructive bunch of hoodlums). Settled by the Saxons and occupied by the Vikings, Beverley was at one time the tenth largest town in England and also one of the richest. With its Minster, it became one of the most important centres of Christianity in Northern England, attracting pilgrims from far and wide. Initially supporting the Royalist cause, the Town changed hands a few times during the English Civil War. In the 18th century, Beverley became the county town for the East Riding of Yorkshire and the main market town for the surrounding area. The Minster, although not a cathedral, has its own suffragan bishopric and is regarded as the most impressive "church" in England. Beverley Grammar School that was founded in 700AD, is the oldest state school in the whole of England. One of the School's notable alumni, was Thomas Percy who was involved in the "gunpowder plot" of 1605. Today, Beverley is a bustling market town, especially on Saturdays and also on race-days, attracting large numbers of visitors. Its medieval buildings and elegant stone Georgian houses, make the Town very appealing to the eye.

Our bus passes by the old 15thC medieval stone-arched gateway, signed North Bar Without—not sure what is missing! The Bar is the only surviving one of five Bars that protected the Town from undesirables. It would seem that we are still in the telephone area of Hull as all the telephone boxes are the same cream colour. After stopping in the Town centre to pick up more passengers, our bus continues northward on the A164 towards Driffield.

On we travel, through the village of **Leconfield** and past the RAF station that is the base for the MoD's Defence School of Transport, together with a squadron of Sea King helicopters. These are in frequent use in "search and rescue" operations, especially along the Yorkshire coast. On the bus goes, through the pleasant and attractive villages of Beswick, Watton and Hutton Cranswick. They are "muck-spreading" in the fields alongside the road, providing a whiff of good-old country air. We could even smell it inside the bus.

We reach the busy little market town of **Driffield** (population 11,500) with the "Welcome" sign proclaiming the Town to be the "Capital of the Wolds". We have indeed left behind the flat low lying lands of the area around the Humber and have arrived in the rolling landscape of the chalk Wolds of East Yorkshire. The Town lies nestled on the edge of the Yorkshire Wolds, near to the source of the River Hull and at the head of the Driffield Navigation Canal. There was once a Norman castle at Driffield though there is little to see of it today. The one big event of the year is the Diffield Agricultural Show held on the showground of each July. It is reputed to be one of the Country's largest one-day agricultural shows. Being a Thursday, today is Market Day with the Town centre and Market Place closed to traffic. As such, there is a need for our bus to make a detour literally "around the houses".

The time is 14.30 and we stop for some six minutes immediately alongside a Total filling station so to allow for a change of drivers—the view could have been better than that of gazing out onto the forecourt of a filling station. However we are soon on our way again, joining the A614 that leads to Bridlington. I am conscious that Archie has had little exercise since leaving Scunthorpe and rather than continue on the bus for another hour and forty minutes to Scarborough, I decide that we will leave the bus at Bridlington to explore the seafront and beach there.

After passing by the village of Nafferton, we are stuck in a line of traffic of some thirty plus vehicles, behind a slow moving tractor and trailer. The combines are out working in the fields with the tractors transporting the loose grain to the grain-store back at the farm. I have already today ranted on about these slow moving farm vehicles not pulling over to allow traffic to pass and here we have another example. It seems that we are stuck in this slow moving queue for ages trundling along at twenty miles per hour, with the line of vehicles behind growing all the time. Eventually, the tractor turns off and we gather up speed. We can't see the bus driver from the top deck, but I don't think that he is too happy to be crawling along for so long a time with a tight time schedule to meet.

Next is the village of **Burton Agnes** (population 500)—must introduce her to Boothby Graffoe in Lincolnshire. Every year, the village holds a scarecrow festival that sees the village and surrounding area adorned with fancy designs of scarecrows, many of them put together by children. In the village is Burton Agnes Hall, an Elizabethan manor house constructed in brick during the early 1600's and rated amongst the top twenty country halls in England. It was until recently the ancestral home of the Boynton family. The imposing three-storey gatehouse also built in brick, stands in front of the Hall with the original driveway passing underneath. The Hall and its grounds are now administered by a Preservation Trust, with the house and gardens being used for events and special occasions, including open-air concerts. Immediately adjacent to the Hall is a Norman manor house built in 1170 that like the Hall, is a Grade 1 listed building. A family of ducks are enjoying a swim on the Village's duck pond as we pass through, which gets Archie excited.

Further along the road after passing through Carnaby, we are again held up in a line of slow moving traffic, this time behind a caravan and a slow moving lorry—must not rant on again about this matter. We are approaching the seaside town of Bridlington shortened to just "Brid". We need a break and I had already made the decision to get off the bus here to give Archie some exercise. Our bus arrives at the Town's bus station at 15.10 and off we get along with all the other "free-loading wrinklies".

Bridlington—East Riding of Yorkshire—population 33,800

The seaside resort of Bridlington sits on the coast of the North Sea in the East Riding of Yorkshire. The eastern coastline along this part of

Northern England is known as the Holderness coast, stretching down to the Humber estuary and having the highest rate of erosion in all Europe, a real problem of disappearing coastlines. The Town also has a small harbour that is currently one of the Country's main shellfish ports.

It is claimed that Bridlington was a Roman station with coins found in the area and a Roman road passing nearby. In the early 12th century, an Augustinian priory was founded and subsequently visited by Henry V. However the priory fell into decline with the Dissolution of the Monasteries during the reign of Henry VIII. During the English Civil War, Bridlington supported the Royalist cause with Henrietta Maria, Queen to Charles I, landing her army on the coast by the Town in 1643.

Bridlington is divided into two parts, the "Old Town" approximately one mile inland and "Bridlington Quay" on the coast itself. The Old Town contains the Town's historic market and Priory Church of St Mary, site of the former Augustinian priory. Bridlington Quay is home to the Town's tourist area and harbour. The first hotel in Bridlington opened in 1805 and with the arrival of the railways in 1846, Bridlington quickly developed into a popular seaside resort, with the towns of West Yorkshire within easy reach. The long curving promenade and ornamental gardens are supported by a high masonry seawall and sit well above the sandy beach that in turn is protected from erosion by a series of timber groynes that run out into the sea.

The harbour is the home port to the Town's fishing fleet and includes the RNLI's lifeboat station. The nearby Spa was reopened in 2008 after a multi million pound redevelopment and is used as a concert venue together with other functions. The many tourist attractions that are traditionally associated with the seaside are concentrated to the north of the harbour and include all the funfairs and other pleasure activities. For 2008, a London Eye type big wheel called the "Eye on the Bay" has been erected on the seafront. This is 130 feet in diameter and is fitted out with 24 pods. It dominates the seafront.

Immediately to the north of the Town, is Flamborough Head, a promontory of hard chalk that projects eastwards into the North Sea. Together with the nearby Bempton Cliffs, they form an important RSPB reserve for the breeding of gannets and puffins. The promontory is cut across by a Bronze Age ditch known as Danes Dyke, a hand excavated cutting some two and a half miles in length. Flamborough Head was the scene of a small naval battle in 1779 that involved two British Navy vessels against four vessels of the American Continental Naval Squadron, lead by John Paul Jones. The British naval vessels were escorting a convoy of 50 plus ships from the Baltic. The time was that of the American Wars of Independence and France had provided support to the American Squadron with the supply of ships—typical! With the Americans hoping to capture some of the convoy ships as a "prize", the ensuing engagement between the two navies resulted in the flagships on both sides being lost, including the *Bonhomme Richard* that was captained by John Paul Jones. However during the battle at sea, virtually all the ships of the convoy managed to sail away to a safe port. The result was that there was no real winner but importantly, the convoy of ships had been saved. Various attempts have been made over the years to locate the remains of the *Bonhomme Richard* off the coast at Bridlington. To date all have been without success but with modern computer-aided technology, this may happen soon.

Archie has got a sniff of the sea air and is anxious to get onto the beach. Leaving the bus station, we make our way to the seafront where the "Eye on the Bay" is standing overlooking the beach. The sun is shining and the skies are blue. Being still in the August holiday period, there are a lot of people about and the pods on the big wheel are all full. The tide is in and as such, the beach area is much reduced by the high tide. We also find that access onto this section of the beach near to the tourist area is banned for dogs. I have no problems with this except that if Archie is to get onto the beach and go for a swim in the sea, we will have to walk nearly a mile along the promenade to an area where dogs are allowed.

The walk along the curving promenade that sits well above the beach, is enjoyable with the ornamental gardens above and plenty of activity taking place down below on the beach and in the sea. Unfortunately, I have to carry my rucksack all the way. We are heading towards the promontory of Flamborough Head that with its white chalk cliffs, can be easily recognised. The white-painted tourist "road train" pulled by a tractor-type engine rolls past and I am tempted to get on board, but it doesn't stop. Eventually, we get to a point along the coast where the promenade ends and we can go down onto the beach, although I need to keep Archie on his lead, for at least a little while longer.

The beach itself at this point, is a mixture of sand, shelly fragments and small rounded stones, easy enough to walk along though maybe a bit hard on the bare feet. The sea looks inviting so I slip Archie off his lead and in he rushes for a swim, enjoying being smothered by the waves that are not too high. A mock-up wooden pirates galleon comes sailing by carrying holiday-makers up the coast from the harbour. Overhead, a yellow Sea King helicopter (probably from RAF Leconfield) is hovering above us, presumably out on routine exercise, as there does not appear to be anyone in trouble. Everyone on the beach gives the crew a wave.

It is soon time to make our way back to the Town centre to catch the bus to our destination for the evening, Scarborough, which is only a few miles further along the coast. Back we climb up to the promenade, Archie leaping onto the stone wall overlooking the beach. I have learnt from previous experiences to keep him on the lead. The "road-train" comes past us again but again does not stop, we obviously aren't at the right pick-up locations. We stop for an ice cream and I at least enjoy a sit down with the rucksack off my back. Archie is pulling away on his lead wanting to be back onto the beach, but he will now have to wait until we get to Scarborough. Pity that we don't have sufficient time (or energy) to visit the harbour area and the recently developed Spa building. Bridlington seems a nice resort and I must make a point of visiting it again in the near future

* * * * * * *

Back up at the bus station, there were a number of "free-loading wrinklies" waiting to catch the bus back home, to Hull in particular. Our No.121 East Yorkshire bus to Scarborough arrives, another double-decker no doubt brought into service to carry all the FLW's. On we board and up onto the top deck to the back, only to be joined on the back seat by, what I might describe as two "dodgy characters". We leave the bus station at 16.35 and soon banknotes are being exchanged along with hushed whispers between these two dubious characters alongside me. I pretend to ignore it all but cannot help my eyes drifting back across to the other side of the seat. I can't hear what is being said—I must learn to mind my own business.

Heading out of Bridlington and picking up again the A165, we cross the boundary between the East Riding and North Yorkshire. Reaching the small village of Reighton, at first sight, sheep appear to be grazing on the roundabout, only they are not real live sheep but only look-alike models. Here we divert down a narrow scenic road that leads down to the coast overlooking Filey Bay, where there is a large static caravan park at Reighton Sands. From the top deck of the bus, there are good views of the countryside with combine harvesters still working in the fields in the late afternoon. Across the fields and in front of us, the coastline stretches south to Flamborough Head, with the surface of the sea to our left sparkling in the bright afternoon sunshine.

Returning back up to the main road, we continue a little further along the A165 before diverting yet again down towards the coast, this time to the large Primrose Valley Caravan Park. Primrose Valley is a popular holiday venue especially for young families with all the necessary facilities available. The Filey Golf Club lies alongside the site. A number of families with young children leave the bus here before we again head back up to the main road, this time heading away from the coast along the narrow country lane leading to the village of Hunmanby. Crossing over the railway line, we pass through the Village and onto Muston, before dropping back down to the coast and into Filey.

We arrive at the seaside town of **Filey** (population 6,800) at 17.20, time is getting on although the sun is still high in the sky. In past years, the Town had an active in-shore fishing fleet, especially during the period of the herring boom. The uniquely patterned Filey "gansey", a hand knitted navy-coloured pullover, was traditionally worn by the local fishermen. However, it was in the mid 1800's that Filey was first developed into a fashionable holiday resort when some fine houses were built. During the 20th century, the Town became the home of one of Butlin's Holiday Camps, which later closed in 1984 due to the availability of cheap holidays abroad. However, recent redevelopment work has revamped the former site to accommodate 600 holiday homes for private ownership. With an excellent sandy beach, Filey continues to be a popular destination for seaside holidays and long may it continue to be so.

Leaving Filey, we continue along the A165 on towards Scarborough. I had not realised when catching this particular bus from Bridlington, that it was scheduled to do a tour of all the caravan parks along the coast leading to Scarborough. First we make a detour to the Blue Dolphin Park and Crows Nest. The American Circus is in "town" that must provide a popular attraction to the many young families staying at the nearby caravan parks. Diverting inland to the village of Cayton, we head back to the coast and the Cayton Bay Caravan Park. Back onto the main road again and there is a herd of highland cattle grazing in the adjacent fields. Against the backdrop of row upon row of static caravans, they look a bit out-of-place.

At long last and after doing a tour of virtually all the sites of static caravans and holiday homes along this particular coastline, we reach the outskirts of Scarborough. Motoring past one of the Town's main golf clubs and university campus, we head along Ramshill Road under Oliver's Mount and across the bridge over Valley Road into the Town centre. Our bus stops outside the Brunswick Centre, a large recently constructed indoor shopping complex. The time is 18.00 and we must first find our accommodation for the evening and book in before it gets any later. After making a few enquiries, we eventually find the Skikero B&B / restaurant in Falconer's Square which is hidden away off Falconer's Street and not far from the bus station itself. I don't know why I experienced such difficulty in finding it, being off the main thoroughfare of Falconer's Street. On arriving at the B&B, there seems to be a problem. Evidently a small area of the ceiling in the room allocated had fallen in with the proprietor being concerned that I would find it unacceptable. On looking at the damage, which was a relatively small hole in the ceiling, I quickly reassured her that it was quite acceptable, especially as I did not want to search for alternative accommodation at this late stage in the evening. It was otherwise a nice room with a good view.

Dumping my rucksack, giving Archie his dinner and having a quick wash to freshen up, we head out for a walk along the beach. The Grand Hotel, that large building overlooking the South Bay, is only a short walk from our B&B. So with the sun still shining we make our way past the Hotel, down to Valley Road and onto the beach. The tide is out and at this time of the day, there are not too many people about. So I let Archie off his lead and he is away like a rocket straight into the sea and splashing about in the waves. After spending so much time on the bus today, he is enjoying his freedom off the lead.

Scarborough—North Yorkshire—population (50,200 resident—110,000 in summer)

The seaside resort of Scarborough is centred around a rocky headland that juts out into the North Sea. Either side of the headland are the sandy beaches of South Bay and North Bay. Below the headland on which stand the ruins of the medieval castle, is the harbour from where a small fleet of inshore fishing boats are based together with the RNLI lifeboat station. Scarborough is the largest and probably the most popular holiday resort on the north east coast of England with safe sandy beaches and a variety of activities suitable for all ages.

Evidence of Stone and Bronze Ages settlements have been found in and around Scarborough with a signal station being located on the high headland during the Roman period. It was the Vikings who first established a firm settlement in Scarborough in the 10th century. However, a rival band of Vikings under the leadership of Hardrada, King of Norway, invaded Scarborough in 1066 (a date familiar to most for happenings further south) and had all the buildings burnt to the ground. Not to be deterred, the inhabitants soon rebuilt the Town, with an imposing strongly fortified stone castle constructed during the 12th century on the rocky headland, some 250 feet above sea-level. The final fortifications to the castle were completed during the mid 14th century and must at that time have provided some measure of security to the local inhabitants.

In 1318, Scarborough was again attacked, this time by the Scots under the leadership of Robert the Bruce. During the English Civil War of the 1640's, the Town was twice under siege by the Parliamentarian forces with the castle changing hands seven times. Advancing forward to 1914, Scarborough was bombarded from the sea by the German navy during World War 1, one of the very few incidents of hostile activity on British soil during the First World War. A number of buildings were damaged and shells were reported to have landed up to three miles inland. For a town of its size, Scarborough has had its fair share of hostilities over the centuries.

The Town's first Royal charter was granted by Henry I in 1100, to be followed by another charter in 1253 which "gave permission to hold a fair every year from the 15th August (Day of the Assumption) to 29th September (Michaelmas Day)". This was held continuously for some 500 years until the 18th century. The "fair" is remembered in folklore by the song that became very popular in recent years by the pop duo, Simon and Garfunkel :

> *Are you going to Scarborough Fair?*
> *parsley, sage, rosemary and thyme*
> *Remember me to one who lived there*
> *She once was a true love of mine*

It was in 1626 that the acidic waters of the Spa were discovered running out of the cliffs to the south of the Town. The reported health giving qualities of these waters soon attracted many visitors to Scarborough that resulted in the Town becoming Britain's first seaside resort. Bathing machines were first recorded on the beaches in 1735 and with the coming of the railway in 1845, the Town increased in popularity, especially with families from the towns of the West Riding of Yorkshire. The Town continued to develop with the construction of some fine hotels and the elegant terraces of Regency and Victorian houses, that to this day still grace the seafront above the South Bay, the Spa and South Cliff Gardens.

In 1827, an iron footbridge was built to span the deep Valley to give easy access between the Town centre and the South Cliff Promenade. The bridge was known as the "Penny Bridge" because of the 1d toll charged for pedestrians. The bridge is still very much in use today although the one penny toll is no longer charged. At the north end of the footbridge is the Grand Hotel that stands dominant over the South Bay. Built in 1867, it was at that time one of the largest hotels in the World, with 4 towers to represent the seasons, 12 floors to represent the months of the year, 52 chimneys for the weeks of the year and 365 bedrooms for the days of the year. In plan, it is "V" shape, being built during the Victorian period. The Grand still remains popular and well used. To the south of the footbridge and at the foot of the cliffs, is the Spa Complex that includes the Palm Court made famous during the 1950 / 60's by music concerts broadcasted on BBC radio each week by Max Jaffa and his Palm Court Orchestra. I am old enough to still remember them, albeit only just.

In 1993, the Town became national news. Following very heavy rains, a section of the unstable cliffs to the south of South Bay started to slip down into the sea. Unfortunately above these cliffs was the Holbeck Hall Hotel and when the landslips started, the Hotel and gardens, bit by bit, slid down the slopes onto the beach below. There were some dramatic photo shots taken at the time of the large Hotel building gradually disintegrating and tumbling down the slopes over a period of days. It must have been heart breaking for the owners to watch.

Most of the entertainment and nightlife in Scarborough is centred around the harbour area of the South Bay with a variety of restaurants providing cuisine for all tastes. There is also a fish quay and fish market at the harbour that takes in the catches brought ashore by the inshore fishing fleet. Below the headland on which still stands the ruins of the historic castle, is Marine Drive, a Victorian roadway and promenade leading around to the North Bay that traditionally is more quiet and peaceful than that at the South Bay. The large gardens of Peasholm Park are just behind. In the evenings of the summer months, a mock marine battle takes place on the boating lake, replicating the Battle of the River Plate of World War Two. As a youngster when on holiday in Scarborough,

I was enthralled watching the mock sea battle taking place, although if we are honest, we are all children at heart.

As one of Britain's premier seaside resorts, there is a variety of activities and things to do and see for holidaymakers. There are a number of theatres and cinemas in the Town that provide plenty of evening entertainment during the summer months. There are also a number of art galleries and museums in the Town together with pleasure parks and funfairs to keep everyone happy. For the shopaholics, there is the pedestrianised area of the High Street together with the new Brunswick Shopping Centre in the Town centre that has five floors of some thirty six stores. Scarborough has won a number of awards and accolades over recent years including the best resort for "Beach Donkeys" in 2009. For those interested, the inhabitants of Scarborough are known as "Scarborians".

Down in the Valley almost underneath the Penny Bridge, is the circular stone building of the Rotunda, which was constructed in 1824/26 under the supervision of William Smith, known as the "Father of English Geology". The Rotunda was reopened in 2008 as "The William Smith Museum of Geology" and houses many interesting rock, mineral and fossil specimens together with other geological items. It was Smith who prepared the first geological map for England, Scotland and Wales that was subsequently referred to as "the Map that changed the World". He lived in Scarborough for a period of his later life when the Rotunda was constructed.

For the sporting minded, Oliver's Mount to the south of the Town centre is the venue for motorcycle racing events during four weekends of each year. The twisty two and a half mile circuit is composed of public roads that wind their way up and down the hill and requires much skill to negotiate. For cricket followers, the Yorkshire County Cricket Club play some of their home fixtures at the ground on North Marine Road, with the annual Scarborough Cricket Festival being held at the end of each season. There are also two principal golf clubs in the Town and Ganton Club to the west has hosted major tournaments in the past such as the Ryder Cup and Walker Cup. The Town's football club did enjoy a spell in the Football League during the 1990's but following relegation and financial difficulties, was wound up in 2007.

Down on the beach with the tide in retreat, Archie and I are enjoying the late evening sunshine, walking along the firm sands under the Spa Complex. Used for racing horses during the 1800's, these sands are normally covered when the tide is in. Archie really does enjoy the sand and sea and is making up for the time spent today on the bus. I am getting hungry not having eaten much all day. I am also ready for a beer. So off we set, back along the beach of the South Bay with the Grand Hotel towering above us and the castle sitting on the promontory ahead. As we approach the more popular area of the beach, we climb up to and walk along the low-level promenade. Much to his dismay, Archie is now on his lead.

Around the Bay we walk, past the cliff funicular railway, past the many amusement arcades, bars and restaurants to the harbour area. In the sand on the beach below, some artistic person has created two large "sand sculptures" of a fish and boot-home. They are very good and being left unattended, it is good to see that they have not been destroyed by some mindless hoodlum—or at least not yet.

Taking a walk around the harbour, a pleasure boat is discharging its passengers from a sailing trip out to sea. At least the sea is calm so they should have had a smooth trip. Opposite the harbour on the other side of the road, is the King Richard III pub / restaurant that has an outside seating area. It is reputed that King Richard stopped here when visiting Scarborough. Finding a table and tethering up Archie, I go inside to order a beer and a meal, a Fish Supper including mushy peas. At last it arrives at my table together with the rhubarb crumble, all of which cost £6.95—really good value. Archie is waiting for some of my fish giving that "remember me" look. I give in and pass him down a small piece.

Suitably refreshed after my meal and beer, we make our way back up to our B&B, the sun has now disappeared and it is getting dark. Up the steps we walk to the viewing point at the top of the funicular that overlooks the harbour and the South Bay. It now being dark, the coloured lights of the harbour area below provide a sparkling illumination effect, reflecting in the waters of the sea. Then back to the Skikero to watch some television before we go to bed. Switching on the tele, there seems to be a problem with the picture, so tonight I will have to go without knowing what national crisis has taken place today. I recall what my Grandfather would often say "switch the radio on Mother, we might be at war!" It seems an age since we left Lincoln on our journey today via Scunthorpe, Hull and Bridlington to reach Scarborough. It's been a long but interesting and enjoyable day.

* * * * * * *

Chapter 8
Scarborough To Alnwick—Day 8

Friday 29th August 2008

Another new day and the sun is shining. Despite the squawking from the seagulls outside, I had a relatively good night's sleep, so we are up early for a walk along the beach before breakfast. It is a beautiful morning with clear blue skies above. Down we go onto the beach where at this time of the morning, few people are about. The tide is out too, as it was yesterday evening when we arrived. So there are the hard flat sands below high water mark for Archie to romp about over and chase his ball. The air is so fresh and clear that you can appreciate why people come to Scarborough for their holidays. It may be different when it is raining. Having spent some time on the beach, we make our way back past the Rotunda that houses William Smith's Geological Museum, up to the Skikero in Falconer's Square for breakfast. This is in their Italian Restaurant and is well prepared, presented and satisfying. Archie being suitably exercised and fed too, we are now ready for the next stage of our "bus trip".

There is no dedicated bus station in Scarborough, which for a seaside Town of its size, is surprising. On arrival the previous day, we were deposited at a stand alongside the roadway at the back of the Brunswick Shopping Centre with no signs or information boards for the benefit of visitors. On making enquiries as to where the bus for Middlesborough, our next destination, leaves, I am given a number of options but recommended to head for the railway station, where there are a number of bus stands. On reaching the railway station, I am informed that the Middlesborough stand is back across the road in Westborough. Having finally arrived at the right place, I do wonder how many other visitors to the Town have the same problems.

The single-decker Arriva No.X56 bus for Middlesbrough pulls in alongside the bus stand and on we board yet again. There is a seat by the emergency exit on the bus that has plenty of legroom that we "bag". The journey to Middlesborough is some two and a half hours, so we need to make ourselves comfortable. The bus fills up, mainly with "free-loading wrinklies" and there is an "oversized person" who seems to want to move across to the seat we are occupying. We sit firm and hum "*We shall not be moved*". With everyone aboard, the bus finally pulls away at 09.50.

Out of the Town we travel, through the suburb of Scalby and past the impressive new ground and clubhouse of the Scarborough Ruby Football Club. After passing thorough the small village of Burniston we head north along the A171 that runs a little way inland from the coast itself. Nevertheless, it is nice rolling countryside that we are travelling through with the heather clad Yorkshire Moors to our left. The heather is in bloom with the Moors appearing as a blanket of purple. The road soon starts to climb upwards and we are travelling across the heather covered moorlands when a passenger gets up to leave the bus with his shopping. He is elderly and does not seem too sure of what he is doing. It is in the middle of nowhere with no buildings nearby and I wonder if he has got off at the right place. However, in the far distance, I do notice at the end of a farm track leading from the bus stop, there is a small white painted cottage. Surely he is not going to walk all the way across the moors carrying his shopping? Maybe he is. On a bad day these moors must be formidable—they breed them "tough up North"!

Our bus continues across the Moors that in today's fine weather, have an attractive wildness about them. After a little while, we come to the minor road that leads down to Robin Hood's Bay. Here we leave the main A171 and turn down the narrow twisting country road, hoping that there is nothing coming in the opposite direction.

We arrive back at the coast and continue along the road a little way until we reach the picture-postcard fishing village of **Robin Hood's Bay**. The first record of the village was in 1536 during Henry VIII's reign, although earlier settlements were probable. Any association with Robin Hood of Sherwood Forest fame, is dubious and it is suggested that the name may be derived from legends relating to ancient forest spirits. During the 18th century, the secluded village became a notorious haven for smugglers and fights were frequent between the villagers and local revenue men with contraband being cunningly transferred between hidden boltholes via secret passageways. Fishing from the Village reached a peak during the middle of the 19th century but has since dwindled. Robin Hood's Bay is today is a very popular tourist destination and is well known to long-distance walkers with the Coast to Coast Footpath from St Bees on the Cumberland coast ending here, a distance of some 190 miles. Also the Cleveland Way passes through the Village. Situated on the edge of the cliffs overlooking the North Sea, the narrow twisty roads lined with the fishermen's cottages and totally unsuitable for traffic, lead down to the small harbour. Our bus stops well above the old village, so to allow passengers on and off.

There are a number of people waiting to board at Robin Hood's Bay and the bus fills up to maximum capacity with some standing. Archie is on my knee so to vacate the seat beside me that is soon occupied. Off we set up the hill, back towards the main road. With a full load of passengers, the bus is struggling even in first gear. We wonder whether it is going to make it and if we might have to disembark to lighten the load. However, after much high-pitched whining from the bus's engine, we finally make it and continue along the B1447 towards Whitby. Again, we were passing through some lovely countryside with occasional views of the coastline and the sea.

At 10.50, we arrive in the historic fishing port of **Whitby** (population 13,600) situated at the mouth of the River Esk. The Town was founded as long ago as 656 when Oswy, the Christian King of Northumbria, started the building of the Abbey. The first abbess was Hilda, a remarkable lady who was later to be venerated as a saint. In 867, the Abbey was destroyed, again by those terrible Vikings, but later rebuilt high up on the headland on the south side of the river estuary, where it still stands to this day. For the fit, there are 199 steps leading up to the Abbey from the harbour, known as the "Church Stairs". In the 18th century, Whitby became a centre for shipbuilding and whaling with the first whaling ships setting sail for Greenland in the mid 1700's. At this time, there was much trade in the shipping of alum from Whitby that was mined nearby and was used in the curing of leather and fixing of dyes as well as for medicinal purposes.

Whitby jet, the black mineraloid found in the cliffs around the Town, has been mined since Roman times and was especially favoured as mourning jewellery by Queen Victoria. The manufacture of jewellery from jet became one of the Town's main industries in the mid 19th century and became popular all over the World. The reserves of jet have long since been depleted although the past is preserved in the Town's Museum that has a large collection on the archaeology and social history of jet. On the literary front, Bram Stoker used Whitby as a setting for Dracula's arrival in Britain in his popular novel that also included various pieces of Whitby folklore. Perhaps Whitby's most famous resident was Captain

James Cook, who although born a little further north of the Town, did live and served his apprenticeship as a seaman sailing on colliers out of Whitby, before embarking upon his three epic round-the-world voyages in the 1760/70's.

Our bus travels down to the Town's bus station located near to the harbour. Above us stand the ruins of the Abbey that are outlined against the blue skies. In front of us is the busy harbour with a fair amount of activity taking place on the quayside. At the bus station, most of the passengers leave, giving relief to the bus's suspension and engine. I would have liked to join them and been able to explore the Town that is such a popular tourist stop and holiday destination. However, we need to reach Alnwick tonight and have another long day's travel ahead of us.

Leaving Whitby behind, our bus joins the A174 that follows the coastline to Sandsend before cutting back inland for a short distance. There are excellent views to the west across the North Yorkshire Moors with the Cleveland Hills behind. We pass a sign post pointing to Ugthorpe, that sounds of Viking origin. A little further on, the bus makes a detour into the small and beautiful fishing village of Runswick, that like a number of other villages along this stretch of coastline, clings to the cliff sides. The steep hills on either side of the Village and wide sandy beach of Runswick Bay below, make it another picture postcard scene and popular with visitors.

Leaving Runswick behind and rejoining the A174, we next visit another small picturesque fishing village clinging to the coastline. **Staithes** sits within the steep sided valley of the Roxby Beck where it flows into the North Sea. Besides its popularity as a tourist destination and also with artists, the ancient Jurassic cliffs surrounding the Village are a great attraction for geologists where many fossils can be found and the Earth's history can be diagnosed. The Village also has associations with Captain Cook for it was at Staithes that he first worked as a grocer's assistant before deciding upon a career at sea. Because of the steep narrow road that leads down to the harbour, the bus only go as far as the high area above the Village, where some passengers get on board.

Immediately on leaving Staithes, we rejoin the A174 that follows close to the coastline for a short distance. Near the village of Boulby, we pass the large surface workings to the deepest mine in the UK and the second deepest in Europe. At 4,600 feet deep, Boulby Mine was developed in 1972, to produce potash and presently supplies over half of the Country's needs, mainly for use in agriculture. It is still working at full capacity where there are vast resources of potash still underground. As a by-product, rock salt is also produced for use as a road de-icing agent during the winter months.

Continuing along the A174, we pass through the villages of Loftus and Brotton with the Cleveland Hills now prominent to our left. Immediately to our right is what seems to be a perfect conical green grassy hill rising some hundred feet above the surrounding ground level. It looks as it could have been man-made but it would have required a lot of effort to build it up to this height. Maybe it has some ancient pre-historic significance but there are no "brown signs" to say so. The road starts to descend down into the Tees valley with the industries of Teesside being visible in the distance ahead.

We are now coming into the market town of **Guisborough** (population 18,100), pronounced "Gizbra" by the locals. Guisborough Priory was built during the 12th century for the Augustinian community but was destroyed at the time of the Dissolution of the Monasteries during the reign of Henry VIII—the vandal! The ruins are still standing and are maintained by English Heritage. The Town enjoyed prosperity with the discovery of iron ore in the nearby Cleveland Hills during the industrial revolution of the early 1800's, with many fine buildings and houses erected. Today, Guisborough is mainly a commuter town for Middlesbrough and Teesside, although regular markets are still held in the wide cobbled area of Westgate in the Town centre.

Leaving the Town, Guisborough Forest is on our left above which stands the stately peak of Roseberry Topping. Rising to 1,049 feet, it dominates the surrounding area and with its distinctive half-cone shape peak and jagged cliff-face that has lead to comparisons with the much higher Matterhorn in Switzerland, which does seem to be stretching things a bit too far. Roseberry Topping was held in reverence by the Vikings who gave the Hill its name. It was also a favourite stomping ground of James Cook, who in his earlier years, lived nearby. A memorial to Cook stands near to the summit. However, it was in 1914 that the profile of the summit was substantially altered by a landslip, probably as a result of the extensive ironstone workings immediately beneath. From the summit, which is crossed by the Cleveland Way long-distance footpath, there are magnificent views on a clear day across the Tees Valley and to the Pennines.

Continuing on under the northern escarpment of the Cleveland Hills, we approach the outskirts of Middlesbrough. Many years ago, the area could be recognised from afar by the "red cloud" permanently hanging over it. This cloud has long gone together with, sadly, a lot of the Town's industries. Travelling into the Town's centre via Ormesby Bank and past the housing estates leading to the dockside area of Cargo Fleet, our bus passes by the Riverside Stadium, home of Middlesbrough Football Club. The lattice steel towers of the old Transporter Bridge can be seen above the tops of the buildings as we come into the Town centre and bus station. The time is 12.00, midday. It would seem that there has been a lot of redevelopment of the Town centre undertaken in recent years that appears to be a great improvement of what existed previously. The bus station in particular is worthy of praise.

Middlesbrough—North Yorkshire—population est. 190,000

Middlesbrough is a large industrial town on the south bank of the River Tees near to the river's estuary into the North Sea. Over the past century or more, the Town's great steelworks, chemical plants, shipbuilding and fabrication yards have all contributed to Britain's prosperity. However with the number of recent closures, Middlesbrough today is no longer a heavy industrialised town with the Corus steelworks now virtually closed down and shipbuilding an activity of the past. At least the large chemical complexes on Teesside still exists.

Originally included in the North Riding of Yorkshire, Middlesbrough was part of non-metropolitan County of Cleveland up to 1996, but by popular demand, the County was abolished and now Middlesbrough exists as a separated Unitary Authority. Note also that the name is spelt "brough" without the "o" after the "b" and not "borough" as is the usual spelling for other English towns.

The Town's original name was Middlesburgh after the church of St Hilda's that was founded in 1119. This was later known as Middlesbrough Priory that was home to the monks from the Benedictine Order. During the Middle Ages, there was little activity in the area with Middlesbrough being described in 1801 as a hamlet with only 25 people. However, the potential for development as a port for the shipment of coal from the Durham coalfield was seen and by 1830, the Town had grown substantially, especially with the extension of the railway line from nearby Stockton.

Then in 1850, ironstone was discovered in the Cleveland Hills, which initially resulted in the production of pig-iron in 1853 at Bell Brothers Ironworks. This was to be followed with the production of steel in 1889, with a new company being founded that was to become famous worldwide, Dorman Long. It was at Dorman Long's factory in Middlesbrough where the design and fabrication of the steel sections required for the Sydney Harbour Bridge was undertaken, with the new bridge on the other side of the World erected in 1932. A few years earlier, they had designed and constructed the New Tyne Bridge at Newcastle that is a smaller version of the landmark steel arched bridge in Australia.

Middlesbrough is well known for its bridges. In 1911, the Transporter Bridge was built by the Cleveland Bridge and Engineering Co between Town and Port Clarence on the north bank of the River. The bridge is unusual insomuch as a cable-hauled cradle transports vehicles across the River between two massive lattice steel towers that stand 225 feet high on each side of the Tees. Its total length is 850 feet. The Bridge still exists and is in everyday use despite rumours brought about by the TV comedy drama series *Auf Wiedersehen Pet* of it being shipped to Arizona in the USA. Another well known landmark on the banks of the Tees, is the Newport Bridge that is sited a little further upstream and which was opened in 1934. Again it is an imposing sight of a steel structure where the central roadway section is lifted so to allow shipping to pass underneath. Although still carrying traffic on the main road across the River and into the Town, the central section can no longer be lifted and which creates an obstacle to large ships sailing upstream to Stockton.

Another development in the area during the 19th century was the discovery of rock-salt and other similar minerals in the underground Permian deposits. The development for the extraction and processing of these minerals led ultimately to the foundation of the large chemical industries that exists to this day on Teesside. Mention has already been made of the large potash mine at Boulby.

At one time, there were a number of large shipyards that lined the banks of the Tees. Again these are no more although some of the yards have been used for fabrication work on North Sea oil rigs. Now not too far away in the Tees' estuary, a colony of seals breed close-by to the sandy beaches that provides a contrast to the heavy industry and chemical works further up stream.

Being a town that grew during the period of the Industrial Revolution, there are not many ancient buildings in Middlesbrough. The oldest domestic building is Acklam Hall that is located some two miles south of the Town centre. Built in 1680, it was the home of the Hustler family for 300 years before becoming an educational establishment after being acquired by Middlesbrough College. The Hall is the Town's only Grade 1

Listed building and is set in 40 acres of grounds. The Town Hall located in the Town centre, is an imposing structure with its tall clock tower. On the cultural front, the Middlesbrough Institute of Modern Art opened in 2007 and contains a large art collection of works by Picasso, Andy Warhol, Henri Matisse and Damien Hirst. The Dorman Long Memorial Museum is over 100 years old and together with the Transporter Bridge Visitor Centre, preserves some of the Town's industrial past. There is also Captain Cook's Birthplace Museum dedicated to the famous explorer and navigator and who in 1728, was born in the village of Marton, now a suburb of Middlesbrough.

In recent years, the Town centre has undergone much redevelopment with the construction of new shopping malls and arcades. Even the Town's football club has relocated from its former old home at Ayresome Park to a brand new Riverside Stadium sited on the banks of the Tees. The University of Teesside that was built around the former Constantine Technical College, was founded in 1992 and is located near to the centre of the Town.

* * * * * * *

I have arranged to meet up with my brother Ken in Durham City, which is our next stop. Rather than spend time walking around the streets of Middlesbrough and with the bus to Durham due in five minutes time, we head for the stand with the No.X1 above it. Had time allowed, I would have liked to have taken a walk to the Transporter Bridge that could be seen towering over the nearby houses together with its Visitor Centre. The single-decker Arriva No.X1 bus for Durham arrives and once again, on we board. Apart from his romp on the beach at Scarborough this morning, Archie has not had much exercise over which I feel a bit guilty. However, once in Durham, we will have the chance for a good long walk by the river.

Leaving the bus station at 12.05, off we head along the A66 that follows the south bank of the Tees out of Middlesbrough. We soon reach the Queen's Campus of Durham University that is located in Thornaby on the south side of the River. In 2009, the Campus was linked to the Town with the erection of a dual bow-string pedestrian bridge over the Tees. The double arch of the Infinity Bridge reflects in the waters below as we pass by. After stopping at the Campus, we then cross over the road-bridge to the north bank and into the ceremonial county of Durham and the market town of **Stockton-on-Tees** (population 80,100). A market has been held in Stockton since 1310, which at the time possessed a castle, until it was totally destroyed and dismantled by Cromwell's forces following the English Civil War. The former site of the castle is now one of the Town's shopping centres. It was the advent of the railways that brought fame to Stockton with the first steam drawn train in the World travelling between Darlington and Stockton. This was in 1825 when George Stephenson set his newly developed steam engine, Locomotion No.1, to haul the open carriages carrying up to 600 passengers the 26 miles between the two towns. The gauge between the two rails adopted by the Stockton and Darlington Railway Company was that used for the horse drawn wagon-ways of the North East for the hauling of coal. This was 4 feet 8½ inches wide and has been used as the international standard rail gauge ever since. As a result of all this, the Town has the oldest railway station in the World. Stockton also has the widest High Street in the whole of England with the imposing 18th century three storied Town Hall dominating the centre. It was also at Stockton's market that Michael Marks of M&S fame first set up his stall and when asked the cost of items on sale, is reputed to have replied *"Don't ask the price, it's a penny"*.

Our bus stops opposite the 18th century parish church of St Thomas alongside of which is the Town's impressive white limestone war memorial. Leaving Stockton on the A177, we head northwards towards Durham. To the east can be seen the tall chimneys of the large chemical complexes centred on Billingham, which forms part of the Borough of Stockton. One of the major chemical companies on Teesside was ICI, a major UK company that has recently been sold to a Dutch conglomerate. I fail to understand what is happening to British owned manufacturing and production? It seems that we are letting all our well established and successful companies be taken over by foreigners who do not have the same motives to create jobs in this Country as say British owners might have. Look too what has happened to the Corus Steelworks on Teesside, now under Indian ownership and also to Cadbury's, recently taken over by the US company Kraft. Something should be done to at least restrict this wholesale takeover of UK industry (RANT 19). Maybe we have something to learn from the French on such issues.

On we travel along the A177 through the village of Thorpe Thewles, towards **Sedgefield** (population 4,600), a pleasant little town with wide streets and cobbled areas and which was once a centre for the former mining industry in County Durham. For a number of years, the Town and local area had the former Prime Minister Tony Blair, as its Member of Parliament. It was in May 2003 while he was Prime Minister, that Mr Blair invited to Sedgefield the US President at that time, George W Bush, to enjoy a pint at the local pub, the Black Lion. The event was well covered by the international media and for a day, Sedgefield hit the world's headlines. Sedgefield has its own racecourse at which a number of national hunt horse racing events take place during the year. Our bus stops outside the Black Lion but unfortunately not long enough to get off for a pint and a bag of crisps.

Our bus continues on through the former colliery villages of Coxhoe and Park Hill, bypassing as we travel along the A177, a number of other former pit villages such as Fishburn, East Hetton, Trimdon and Cornforth. Some 30 years ago, these villages had their own mine, pithead, chapel, local pub and more importantly, own close knit community that supported each other through the hard times. Now that the mines have been closed, I often wonder what became of these hard working coal miners and their families. Even the tall slag heaps at the pit-heads have disappeared. Work down the pit was a hard and dangerous occupation and it is perhaps a good thing that we no longer have to send men down into the depths of the Earth to hack-away at the coal face. For sure, I would not want a son of mine to go down there. Nevertheless, for many of these traditional mining communities, it was a way of life and the pit closures of the 1980's especially must have been hard for them and for some, meant leaving the area to seek work elsewhere. No doubt some stayed and are probably still living in the villages that they were brought up in. These people were a special breed and it is sad that their communities have been broken up. The wholescale closure of the coal mines in the 1980's was perhaps implemented at the time for political reasons, although with the reduced demand for coal as a result of the need to cut back on CO_2 emissions, undoubtedly the outcome would sooner or later have been the same. Whilst my sympathies and support would have been with the miners, it is a question of balance between the loss of jobs and break-up of the mining communities as against sending men into the bowels of the Earth working in dangerous and unhealthy conditions. I am not sure where I really stand on this one.

Passing through Park Hill, I note that the local pub is called "The Kicking Cuddy" which for uninitiated is translated to "Kicking Donkey". Passing over the A1 motorway, we continue through Coxhoe, another former mining village before reaching Shincliffe, an up-market village on the outskirts of the City of Durham that has been designated a conservation area so to preserve its historic character. We cross the old masonry arched bridge that spans the River Wear and head on down towards the City itself, passing the University Sports Grounds on the way. We arrive at the bus station in Durham at 13.10 where I had pre-arranged to meet up with my brother Ken who lives in the City and who is waiting for us as the bus pulled in.

Durham City—County Durham—population 43,000

The cathedral city of Durham and county town for the ceremonial county of Durham, is sited on the River Wear where it makes a tight meander below the high promontory upon which sits the historic Cathedral and Castle.

Although evidence suggests that there has been a settlement here since the 2nd century BC, it was in AD995 that the present City was founded, when the monks from Lindisfarne brought the body of St Cuthbert to Durham as its finally resting place. St Cuthbert, who died in 687 was famed for his miraculous healing powers.

Although an earlier building had been erected by the monks, the present Cathedral was founded in 1093. Named "The Cathedral Church of Christ, Blessed Mary the Virgin and St Cuthbert of Durham" which is now shortened to just "Durham Cathedral", the building sits on the high peninsula that overlooks the River Wear and dominates the skyline of the City. It is regarded as one of the finest Romanesque cathedrals in Europe and marked the beginning of Gothic ecclesiastical architecture. Besides being the resting place for St Cuthbert, it is also that for the Venerable St Bede of Jarrow. On the main door of the Cathedral, is the medieval bronze "Sanctuary Knocker". Tradition has it that any fugitive managing to reach and hold onto the "Knocker" was given refuge in the Cathedral for up to 37 days, thus gaining respite from their pursuers, no matter what the reason for their misdemeanours. The original "Knocker" that is in the form of a medieval bronze mask, is now in the Cathedral Treasury with only a replica now on display on the main door.

Because of Durham's geographical and its strategic location, it became an important defence post for England against the Scots. As a result, the City had a large degree of independence from the King, who was based away down in London. This all gave rise to the emergence of the Prince Bishops, who enjoyed extraordinary powers of a Bishop Palatine (or Prince of the Church) on account of secular principalities for which they were responsible. They held their own parliament, raised their own armies, had their own court system, issued charters, levied taxes and collected revenues and even had their own mint. A comment was made at that time of there being "Two Kings of England, one of the Lord King of England wearing a crown and the Lord Bishop of Durham wearing a mitre". However, many of these powers were curtailed by Henry VIII to be followed later by their total removal under the Reform Act of 1832. Nevertheless, the County of Durham is still known as "The Land of the Prince Bishops" as displayed on the "Welcome" signs when driving into the County.

The 11th C Norman Castle at Durham is a good example of an early motte and bailey castle. Like the Cathedral on the opposite side of the Palace Green, it stands high on the rocky promontory overlooking the River Wear down below. It has the distinction of being the only Norman castle never to have been breached and has withstood many an attack by invading forces in its long history. Over the centuries, the Castle was used as the Bishop's Palace (or residence and office), this being until the earlier part of the 19th century when the last of the Prince Bishops, William Van Mildert made Bishop Auckland his primary residence. During the period of the Commonwealth, the Castle was confiscated by Cromwell and sold to the Mayor of London who let it fall into disrepair, albeit it was later restored back to its original state. With the establishment of the University in 1832, the Castle has since been used by University College. As a result, the Castle has been in continuous use for the past 900 plus years.

With mention of Cromwell, during the period of the English Civil War, the City remained loyal to King Charles, but as a consequence, suffered much damage both during the War and later during the period of the Commonwealth. This was due mainly to the abolition of the Church of England, upon whose institutions the City depended upon for its economic survival. In the aftermath of the Civil War, the Cathedral was closed by Cromwell and used to incarcerate some 3,000 Scots prisoners who were captured after the Battle of Dunbar in 1650. Some 1,700 perished whilst imprisoned in the Cathedral, a bad chapter indeed in the history of this magnificent building. Graffiti inscribed by these prisoners-of-war is still visible on the interior faces of the Cathedral walls. Following the restoration of the Monarchy in 1660, major works commenced upon the restoration of the Cathedral and the Castle, as elsewhere in City.

Just to the west of the centre of Durham, is Neville's Cross. Now a suburb of the City, in the October of 1346, it was the site of a major battle between the English and the Scots. England under Edward III was preparing to attack France, which subsequently led to the start of the Hundred Years War. Under the *Auld Alliance*, the King of France, Philip VI, asked King David II of Scotland to create a diversionary force by attacking England from the north. This David agreed to do, marching first with some 12,000 men on Carlisle then Hexham, before reaching the outskirts of Durham. To his surprise, there was an English army waiting for him at Durham albeit consisting of only 5,000 men. Nevertheless, the English had the better ground and employed superior tactics over the Scots that resulted in a decisive victory for the English, even though greatly outnumbered. Many of the Scottish nobility were slain and King David captured, only to be released some 13 years later after a substantial ransom had been paid. It was Lord Neville who erected a stone cross at the site to commemorate the battle, hence the name Neville's Cross.

The medieval city of Durham was made up of Cathedral, Castle and administration buildings on the high ground of the peninsula, with the outlying areas below, known as the "township", that included Gilesgate, Claypath, Elvet and Framwelgate. The area between the Cathedral and Castle is known as the Palace Green, with The Bailey below and to the east. To this day there are still many fine Georgian buildings on The Bailey that are used by some of the colleges. Except for the Gatehouse, the former castle walls were removed around The Bailey by the Victorians after "much remodelling and beautification" of the City. The whole of the City centre has now been made a conservation area with many Grade 1 & Grade 2 Listed buildings. In 1986, the area around the Cathedral and Castle was designated as a World Heritage Site.

The bridges that span the River Wear in Durham are worthy of mention. They include three old stone arched bridges, that when travelling downstream, are Elvet Bridge originally built 1153/95, the newer Prebends Bridge built 1772/78 and Framwelgate Bridge built in the 15th century. When Sir Walter Scott visited the City, he was inspired to write his poem "Harold the Dauntless" of which the first five lines are carved into a stone tablet on Prebends Bridge. The poem begins:

> *Grey towers of Durham,*
> *Yet well I love thy mixed and massive piles*
> *Half church of God, half castle against the Scots*
> *And long to roam those venerable aisles*

The graceful reinforced concrete Kingsgate Footbridge that spans across the River between the high ground of the Cathedral and New Elvet, was erected in 1966. Designed by Ove Arup, it is said to be one of his favourite bridge designs, On the west side of the City spanning high across the wide valley and seen from just about everywhere in the City, is the multi-arched Victorian brick viaduct that carries the main London to Edinburgh railway line. A triumph of Victorian civil engineering.

Mention has already been made of the University of Durham. Founded by Bishop Van Mildert in 1832, the University now consists of sixteen separate colleges, not all of which are located in the City itself. It was the first university to be established in England following that of Cambridge, albeit some 600 years later. As a result, Durham ranks third after Oxford and Cambridge as an institution of higher education.

The City is in the heart of the Durham coalfields that at one time, provided the County's main employment, with just about every village having its own mine, pit-head and brass band. Each year on a Saturday in July, the Durham Miners' Gala would be held when the miners of each village would parade behind their own colliery banner, lead by their own brass band. They would parade past the old Royal County Hotel in Old Elvet where a senior member of the Labour Party would take the salute. This would be the Prime Minister of the day if Labour were in government. After the march-past, the miners and their families would adjourn to the old racecourse by the riverside for something to eat and drink, with rides on the funfairs and games played, usually football of course. The local public houses did a roaring trade. Although all the mines have now closed, the annual Gala is still held albeit at a much reduced level, with Tony Blair, who was born and educated in the City, taking the salute when Prime Minister. Even today, it still remains one of the largest socialist trade union events in the World.

Rowing is a main sporting activity that takes place on the waters of the River Wear, there being a number of clubs along the banks of the River, many associated with schools and colleges. A number of important regattas and head-to-head races take place each year that attract crews from far and wide.

Archie is pleased to stretch his legs after being so long travelling on the buses. Me too. With Ken leading, we make our way down to the riverside footpath that follows the Wear with the Castle and Cathedral towering above us. It is a lovely tree-lined walk that takes us past the popular viewpoint of the Cathedral standing high above the weir that crosses the River. Further on is the masonry arched Prebends Bridge. From here, we walk up the banks to the old churchyard of St. Oswald's before crossing over the Kingsgate Footbridge that spans the River, high above the water level. Passing the Heritage Centre, we are now entering the Cathedral area and Palace Green. One of the popular photo-shots is to have your photo taken holding onto the Sanctuary Knocker on the main door of the Cathedral. Ken duly obliges to take my photo holding onto the Knocker with one hand and Archie on his lead in the other. Across on the other side of the Green, is the Castle, still in use today in providing accommodation for college students. On a clear day such as today, there are some excellent photo opportunities to be had in this historic conservation area of the Palace Green.

Leaving the Palace Green via Saddler Street, we make our way down to Old Elvet, crossing over the historic Elvet Bridge with rowing boats for hire on the River below. It is well past one o'clock and we need refreshment. There is a pub, the Swan and Three Cygnets that has an open area with tables where we can sit with Archie. After more than three hours on the buses followed by a long walk to explore the sights of Durham, a pint of beer is most welcome. Unfortunately, the pub does not have any light refreshments so we shall have to make do with a bag of crisps. Suitably refreshed, we make our way back across the River through the Market Place and down Silver Street, over the Framwelgate Bridge, to the bus station. On our way back, we pass a pork-butcher's shop and being hungry, buy ourselves a savaloy and stuffing buttie (a local delicacy) and another bacon buttie filled with fried mushrooms at £1.00 each—not bad value for these days. Munching on our butties and pleased I am not where I might meet someone I know, we make our way to the bus station for the next stage of our journey, this time to Newcastle.

* * * * * * *

We catch the same number bus as we travelled up on from Middlesbrough, the 1X to Newcastle that departs at 14.50. I have had nearly two enjoyable hours exploring Durham and chatting to my brother Ken, though I haven't got rid of him yet, as he joins us on the bus for a short distance to where he lives, using of course his oldies bus pass. I do wonder if anyone actually pays a bus fare during the daytime off-peak periods, with cash actually being handed over to the driver. The interior of the bus is littered with loose pages of the local free newspaper. I am not sure where they have all come from, there must be pages from twenty plus copies of the newspaper that have been scattered all over the floor of the bus. Why do people do this? (RANT 20). Maybe the delivery boy or girl had discarded their undelivered copies not wanting to return them to the newsagent. Whoever was responsible, it would probably be for the driver to clear up the mess when he reached his terminus.

Off we head leaving the City centre, travelling up the old North Road, first under the tall railway viaduct, towards Shire Hall, the County Council's offices. Back in the 1950's I was employed by a firm of civil engineering consultants based in Newcastle where one of the projects I was employed upon was assisting in the structural design and preparation of drawings for this large office complex. It is nice to see it still standing albeit the architecture is typical 1950's and uninspiring. On up the hill we travel past the University Hospital to the former pit village of Pity Me, where we say goodbye to Ken. There are a number of theories as to how the Village came to be named "Pity Me", a rather sad and forlorn name suggesting sympathy. However one of the more popular suggestions is that the name is derived from the Norman-French word for a small lake "petit mer". Another is the place where the black slurry waters from the local pit were discharged, namely Pithead Mere. Take your pick.

We are now travelling along the A167 that used to be known as The Great North Road, heading towards the market town of **Chester-le-Street** (population 24,000). Arriving at the town's outskirts, the bus travels down Front Street into the Town centre. Chester-le-Street sits along the line of an old Roman road that continued north to Newcastle, hence the name "le-Street" that has a Norman derivate. For 113 years, the body of St Cuthbert lay in the monastery at Chester-le-Street where the monk Aldred made the first translation of the Bible into old English, over 400 years before John Wycliffe's translation into the vernacular English. From medieval times, a primitive game of football was played every Shrove Tuesday between the "upstreeters" and "downstreeters" along the length of Front Street, which at that time was the main road north. More than four hundred players took part in the game that lasted over a five-hour period. Not without reason perhaps, the game was finally outlawed by the police in 1932. In the Town centre, stands the former church of St Mary's and St Cuthbert, now used as a museum. The church hall was used in 1936 to provide accommodation for the "Jarrow marchers" on the first night of their "Crusade" to the Palace of Westminster in London to draw attention to the high levels of unemployment and extreme poverty being suffered in the North East and on Tyneside in particular. It took 22 days for the marchers to reach London only to be refused an audience by the Prime Minister of the day—a shameful disgrace!

Immediately to the east of the Town centre alongside the River Wear, is the new Riverside Ground for the Durham County Cricket Club. Durham CCC was admitted to First Class County Cricket status in 1991, the most recent of the 18 major clubs that make up the English cricket structure. Since being admitted at senior level, they have twice won the County Championship title and have supplied some well known names to the England team. Across the River Wear from the Ground, sits the 14thC Lumley Castle, now used as a hotel with adjoining golf course.

After a brief stop, we leave the Town centre and pass the "brown signs" indicating the way to Beamish Outdoor Museum, that is located only four miles to the west of Chester-le-Street. The "Living Life Museum of the North" as it is called, is a 300 acre site on which has been created a small town and colliery village complete with pithead, both dating back to 1913. Everything is so realistic and authentic that is like taking a step back in time of one hundred years. Also on the site is a manor house that dates back to 1825. There is plenty to see and do at the Museum that will take in most of the day. It is well worth a visit.

We continue northwards along the A167 into the town of **Birtley** (population 11,400). Prior to its closure, the former brickworks at Birtley employed a high proportion of the town's workforce. Birtley bricks were used throughout the North East for the construction of houses and for use on other buildings. The Birtley Ironworks also provided much employment for the local population and was supplied with coal from the neighbouring coalmines. Although alternative employers have moved in to fill the employment gap, there are few in the manufacturing sector. Continuing along Durham Road, the main thoroughfare through Birtley, we reach the large intersection with the A1 motorway, underneath which the bus passes to continue along the A167 towards Gateshead and Newcastle.

Almost immediately, we see on the high ground ahead, the iconic figure for the North East—the **"Angel of the North"**. Sited on a small hill that overlooks the A1 motorway, the steel statue stands 66 feet high with a wingspan of 178 feet. Completed in 1998, it is the largest man-made sculpture in Britain. The total amount of steel used in the construction of this impressive figure was 220 tons, which has been left unprotected, giving it a weathered rusty-brown appearance. The Angel is intended to represent the heavy engineering and steel industries of the North East and though now viewed with some affection, when first erected, it was met with a lot of criticism. An acquaintance told me of his grandson visiting the site of the "Angel" in early December and was obviously very impressed. When Christmas came, he had penned new words to the well-known carol.

> *When shepherds watched their flocks by night*
> *All seated on the ground*
> *The "Angel of the North" came down*
> *And glory shone around*

Onwards our bus continues along the route of the old Great North Road into the metropolitan borough of **Gateshead** (population 78,400) entering first the suburb of Low Fell. It was at Gateshead Fell (now Low Fell) that the forces of William the Conqueror defeated the combined forces of Malcolm, King of Scotland, and Edgar the Atheling in 1068. Gateshead was first mentioned in 623 by The Venerable Bede, who resided in nearby Jarrow, with the earliest record of any coal mining activity in 1344. The Town's first ironworks was established in 1747 with the manufacture of ships' anchors and chains. Sir Joseph Swan, inventor of the light bulb, lived on Kells Lane in the Town where he had his house wired for electric light, the first domestic installation in the World. The Town grew rapidly during the 19th century following the Industrial Revolution, with the further establishment of more heavy industry, including locomotive works and a wire rope factory that supplied submarine telegraph cables. However, with a number of factory closures, unemployment became a serious issue in the 1920/30's. As a result, the Team Valley Trading Estate was developed for light manufacturing industries and distributors, one of the largest still in the UK.

Over the years, Gateshead's image has not been good, it being described by J.B. Priestley as "having been designed by an enemy of the human race". An article some years ago in Daily Telegraph, reported of a woman applying for a visa to the UK, being denied entry into the Country because she gave as her reasons for entering the Country, as wanting to visit Gateshead. Her reasons were considered by the visa officials as "not credible". Whilst the Town's past reputation may have in part been justified, much has changed in recent years, with the development of the Gateshead Quays on the south bank of the Tyne. This includes The

Sage, an impressive modernistic venue for music and performing arts, designed by Sir Norman Foster. Also the Baltic Centre, where former flour mills have been converted into a centre for contemporary art, and the prize winning Millennium Footbridge, nicknamed the "Blinking Eye" that was opened in 2001. The Gateshead International Stadium is used for international athletics events and football of all codes including rugby league and American football. Both Brendan Foster and Steve Cram, Olympic gold medallists, are from the Town and have helped in the promotion of these international athletic events. The Trinity Centre muti-storey car park that was used for the filming of Michael Cain's film "Get Carter", dominates the Town centre, which on the admission of the Town authorities, is an eye-sore and is soon to be demolished.

We continue into through Low Fell, past Saltwell Park on our left. The extensive well laid out and maintained Park is a popular venue for local people, with the imposing Victorian mansion of Saltwell Towers standing central in the Park. There are some fine Victorian / Edwardian houses in this area of the Town as we pass by. On down the hill we travel towards the Town centre and the River Tyne itself.

We cross the River by the iconic bow arched Tyne Bridge, a smaller and earlier version of the Sydney Harbour Bridge in Australia. It is one of the symbols of Tyneside together with the High Level Bridge and low-level Swing Bridge. From the Tyne Bridge, we get good views downstream on our right, of the new Millennium Footbridge and reflective curved shape of the Sage building that is sited on the south bank of the River. Immediately upstream to our left, is Stephenson's High Level Bridge that carries road traffic on its lower deck and the mainline railway across its upper deck. Below us is the Swing Bridge, now painted in red and white and on the site of one of the earliest crossings of the Tyne between Gateshead and Newcastle. All are set against a background of the glittering waters of the Tyne itself that travel a further eight miles to its estuary at Tynemouth and the North Sea.

> *"The Tyne, the Tyne, the coaly Tyne—the Queen of all the Rivers".*

It has been many years since the last collier left the Tyne bound with a cargo of coal for the south-east. In fact these days, coal is imported from overseas, which now gives the saying "taking coals to Newcastle" a different meaning.

Whenever I travel up to the North East and cross over the Tyne Bridge, or the High Level Bridge if on the train, a lump comes to my throat. I am coming home to the place of my birth, upbringing, schooling and training. Although I lived away from Tyneside for a number of years, I still have my roots here and I am still proud to call myself a "Geordie".

Once across the Tyne Bridge, we enter into the City of Newcastle itself, where our bus leaves the main A167 and diverts into the City centre via Pilgrim and Blackett Streets, then on past Eldon Square (more on that later). The bus route takes us along Percy Street before turning into the Eldon Square Bus Station. Much has changed since I lived in the area with many new buildings replacing those that I was familiar with. Still, I am looking forward to exploring some of the City within the limited time that I have available. The clock is showing 15.45 and once off the bus, we make our way into the City centre.

Newcastle upon Tyne—Tyne and Wear—population 274,000

The historic City and Metropolitan Borough of Newcastle upon Tyne, sits on the north bank of the Tyne at the lowest point where the River can be bridged. Since 1400, the City has had separate County status although geographically, it is part of Northumberland. From 1974 however, it has been included in the geographical area of Tyne and Wear, which with the traditional rivalry between Newcastle and Sunderland, has never been a popular name with the local people of Tyneside and Wearside. It is much the same as that which existed on Humberside. As a mark of its popularity, in 2007 Newcastle was voted the best City in the North by the Daily Telegraph newspaper.

The City has been known by a number of names throughout the ages, including Pons Aelius by the Romans, then Monkchester prior to the Normans, who gave the City its present name of Newcastle, sometimes referred to by its Latin name Novocastria. Nowadays, the locals simply refer to the "Toon" although this is in contradiction to its city status. Note that there are no hyphens between the words Newcastle, upon and Tyne. The local pronunciation of the word "Newcastle" needs to be explained. Unlike other places in the UK with the same name, the emphasis is very much on the last syllable "castle", blinking your eyes and head-butting at the same time. No true Geordie would pronounce it differently.

Newcastle is sited on the line of Hadrian's Wall where it ran for some 73 miles across the breadth of Northern England from near Carlisle to the appropriately named Wallsend some four miles to the east and down-river of the City. During the times of the Romans, a timber bridge built on stone piers was erected across the Tyne at this point, with a settlement being developed on the north bank, hence the name Pons Aelius. This bridge must have been well constructed for it lasted until 1248 when it was destroyed by fire. It is said that the construction of Hadrian's Wall was not necessarily a defensive barrier against invasion but more to control unwanted immigration by the Scottish Picts from the North into Roman England—I could make some comment here, but on reflection, better not go there!

After the Romans left, the area became part of the powerful Anglo-Saxon kingdom of Northumbria. Due to its strategic position, it was the Normans who built the first castle that gave the City its name "Newcastle". A wooden castle was initially built in 1080 by William the Conqueror's son Robert, as the Country's northern defence against the invading Danes and rebellious locals. This was soon followed in the 1170's by the construction of the present stone Keep that stands 80 feet tall. During the mid 13th century, the Black Gate was built, complete with drawbridge and portcullis, followed by the Town Walls that ran for two miles around the Town and stood 25 feet high. The Black Gate (now a museum) and some small sections on the old Walls, still stand to this day.

With its solid stone Keep and fortified Town Walls, Newcastle was England's northern fortress during the Middle Ages and was defended against attacks from the Scots on a number of occasions. The City became an important centre for wool trading and in 1400, was created a self-governing county with its own sheriff. Some 240 years later, Newcastle supported the Royalist cause in the Civil War, that resulted in the City being besieged and eventually sacked by Parliamentarian forces based in nearby Sunderland, probably the start of the long-term rivalry between the two towns.

During the 16th century, Newcastle was the centre for the local coal mining area and developed into a major port, gaining a monopoly for the export of coal to the rest of England. Hence the expression *"taking coals to Newcastle"*, that was first recorded as being quoted in 1538. Loading the coal from the banks of the River onto the southern bound colliers, was undertaken by a group of elite boatmen known as the "Keelmen". Based in Sandgate on Newcastle Quayside, this closely-knit community had their own traditions and customs. They worked hard transferring twenty tons at a time to the London bound colliers waiting mid-river via their uniquely designed timber keel-boats. The well known folk song is dedicated to them.

> *As I came thro' Sandgate, thro' Sandgate, thro' Sandgate*
> *As I came thro' Sandgate, I heard a lassie sing*
> *O weel may the Keel Row, the Keel Row, the Keel Row*
> *O weel may the Keel Row, that my laddie's in*

The days of the Keelmen started to decline in the early 1800's with the construction of the timber coal staithes that allowed coal to be loaded direct from the banks of the River into the waiting colliers. The coal was brought in from the local pits via horse drawn coal wagons along the rail-tracks of the wagon-ways.

During the 19th century, Newcastle together with the whole of Tyneside was a power-house of the Industrial Revolution that included shipbuilding and repair together with many other heavy engineering industries, such as the manufacture of armaments and steam turbines. Even into the 20th century, Tyneside itself was one of the largest shipbuilding and ship repair centre in the World. My own father, grandfather and uncles all worked in the shipyards on the Tyne in the mid 1900's and I too started my career as a civil engineer working in the yards. As such, there is a strong family tradition associated with shipbuilding and repair on Tyneside.

Sadly, during the 1970 / 80's, virtually all the yards and factories on the Tyne were closed down with the loss of many jobs and associated skills that were difficult to replace. Because of lack of investment in the future and need for a short term profit (mainly from accountants and investors), we, as a Country, have lost our traditional engineering base together with the skills required for the manufacture of equipment and heavy goods. Why is it that countries such as Germany, can prosper with such a strong engineering industrial base where much investment is allocated to skills training for employees? There is much talk about the reintroduction of apprenticeship schemes and training in engineering skills in this Country and maybe it might get off the ground, but we have a lot of catching up to do. The recipe for a strong economy cannot be solely based upon banking and service industries, as perhaps we have discovered during the recent economic collapse in 2008/09 (RANT 21).

Having lost most of its heavy engineering industries, Newcastle today is predominately a business, education and cultural centre. There are two large universities in the City. The University of Newcastle (formerly Kings College and part of Durham University) was founded in 1963 and is one of England's leading establishments for higher education. Northumbria University, which was founded in 1992 from the former Polytechnic College (where I studied back in the 1950's), also excels in excellence. As might be expected for a city of its size, there are a number of museums and galleries including the Great North (Hancock) and Discovery Museums and Laing and Turner Art Galleries. There are also some well-established theatres that are supplemented by music and cultural festivals.

Over recent years, the City has gained a reputation for its nightlife, especially in the Bigg Market and Quayside areas where there is a wide selection of restaurants, pubs and clubs. Although now not my scene, they are popular venues for stag and hen parties where dress is optional and different!! The City even has its own "Chinatown" centred on Stowell Street and complete with a Chinese archway. For shop-a-holics, the new indoor Eldon Square Shopping Centre, one of the largest indoor shopping centres in Britain, will not disappoint. Nearby, is the old indoor Grainger Market, with its collection of traditional shops and stalls.

Newcastle is well known for the fine architecture of some of its buildings. The neo-classical developments in the 1830's by Grainger and Dobson in the City centre has won many accolades with Grey Street being voted in 2005 as England's finest street. "Grainger Town" encompassing Grainger Market, the Theatre Royal, Grey, Dean, Clayton and Grainger Streets together with Eldon Square (now partly demolished—more on that later) includes 244 listed buildings. Standing some 135 feet above on his stone column at the top of Grey Street, is Earl Grey himself, or at least a statue of him. Born locally, the Earl was Prime Minister at the Time of the Reform Bill in the 1830's. Another piece of fine architecture from the 19th century is Newcastle Central Station with its neo-classical façade and entrance portico. Opened by Queen Victoria in 1850, it was the first covered railway station in the World from which the design of many other railway stations around the World was based. The Queen unfortunately did not care for Newcastle and was "not amused" by it all. It is said that she even kept the curtains of her rail carriage drawn closed when approaching Newcastle by train.

Newcastle has two cathedrals, albeit neither can be classed as one of England's old traditional cathedrals. Located near the Keep and Black Gate, the St. Nicholas' Anglican Cathedral, complete with its 15th century lantern tower, was originally a parish church until 1882 when it received cathedral status. St Mary's Roman Catholic Cathedral, opposite the Central railway station, was similar upgraded to cathedral status in 1850.

Going back a bit further in time, there are some interesting 15th century Tudor timber buildings down by the Quayside, with their upper stories leaning out over the pavements. Bessie Surtees' House is one where it is said that Bessie, the daughter of a wealthly merchant of the City, eloped and married against the wishes of her father, a local lad John Scott, who was later to become the 1st Earl of Eldon. Her father's subsequent thoughts may have been interesting. More or less adjacent, is a similar building where I once worked as a designer draughtsman, with the uninteresting name of Derwent Buildings. Opposite is the old Guildhall that used to house the Coal Exchange, where shares were bought and sold in the local mining companies of the day, before they were all nationalised and brought under the umbrella of the NCB.

In the Quayside area of Sandgate, where the Keelmen used to live, there are many fine merchants' houses. But perhaps most impressive of all are the three Tyne Bridges. The oldest is the High Level Bridge that was designed in 1849 by Robert Stephenson, son of George. It spans the steeply sided Tyne valley between Newcastle and Gateshead carrying both a roadway on its lower level and the mainline railway across its top deck, another first of its type in the World. Immediately downstream and at River level, is the brightly painted Swing Bridge that was constructed in 1876 on the site of the former timber Roman bridge. The Bridge is so named because it "swings" or pivots on its mid-river central axis, so to allow shipping to pass through. You better not be in a hurry if the Bridge is about to open. Towering above the Swing Bridge and immediately downstream, is the impressive steel arch of the New Tyne Bridge. Designed and build by Dorman Long of Teeside in 1928, it was the forerunner to Australia's Sydney Harbour Bridge, the design of which in most respects is the same, only that the bridge in Sydney is a bit bigger. Together, the three bridges have become a symbol of Newcastle and indeed of Tyneside.

Within a distance of five miles and within the City limits, there are a total of ten bridges that cross the waters of the Tyne. At the furthest point downstream, is the Gateshead Millennium Footbridge and nicknamed the "Blinking Eye" because of its method of opening so to allow shipping to pass under. Upstream of the High Level Bridge, is the Queen Elizabeth

II Bridge that carries the new Tyne and Wear Metro, Britain's first light rail transit system and which was opened by Queen Elizabeth in 1981. This is followed by the King Edward VII Rail Bridge, which was opened in 1906 as an alternative crossing to the High Level for mainline rail traffic. Next is the newly constructed concrete Redheugh Road Bridge that carries the A109 and which replaced the two previous bridges, one being a steel trestle bridge designed by Thomas Bouch of Tay Bridge fame. The steel arch of the New Scotswood Road Bridge follows, built in 1967 and replacing the stately old Chain Bridge that is referred to in the popular Tyneside anthem "Blaydon Races". Scotswood Railway Bridge is next though this was taken out of use in 1982 and no longer functions as a bridge crossing. Finally, there is the newly constructed Blaydon Bridge, a concrete structure spanning the River that carries most of the road traffic on the A1 that now bypasses the City to the west.

To the north of the City centre and travelling out along the old Great North Road, is the Town Moor. Larger than Hyde Park and Hampstead Heath combined, the freemen of the City have the historic right to graze their cattle on the Moor. In June of every year, the "Hoppings" come to the Town Moor, this being the largest travelling funfair in Europe and traditionally coinciding with the old work's holidays of "Race Week". As a youngster, I remember them well and looked forward with much excitement to spending the pennies my Mother gave me on the various rides.

St James' Park is nearby, home to Newcastle United Football Club. Football is more of a religion on Tyneside than just a sport. There are hundreds of football clubs at all levels throughout the area, each playing in their own league. However, top of the tree is Newcastle United Football Club, who still play in Gallowgate district of the City. Established in 1892, the "Magpies", so named because of their black and white strip, have a long and proud tradition. It is however some time now since they won the FA Cup three time in five years. This was in the early 1950's when I was still living on Tyneside and regularly watched them on Saturday afternoons when we used to stand on the open terraces. I can still recite most of the team, that included Jackie Milburn, Joe Harvey, big Frank Brennan, the Robledo brothers, et al. How times have changed and with their present performances on the pitch, it is perhaps just as well that they have some of the most loyal supporters in the Country. More recently, the Newcastle Falcons Rugby Union team, whose ground is at Kingston Park, Kenton, have had some success, with the game of rugby seemingly attracting more support on Tyneside. Whilst on the subject of sport, mention should be made of the Great North Run that takes place in October of each year. Claimed as the World's most popular half-marathon, the runners start in Newcastle itself before crossing over the Tyne Bridge to finish on the sea-front at South Shields. Over 50,000 competitors now take part in an event that was originally devised by Brendan Foster in 1981, with the winners of the men's race completing the thirteen mile course in less than one hour.

Some mention here should perhaps be made of the Geordies and their unique dialect. The name "Geordie" denotes only those who were born and brought up within no more than five miles of the banks of the Tyne. It does not include folk further north in the Northumbrian coalfields and certainly not the Makems from Wearside. There are a number of suggestions regarding the derivation of the word "Geordie". My own favourite is at the time when King George II's army was marching north to put-down the Jacobite Rebellion of 1745 and was looking for volunteers. Always being up for a fight against the Scots, the men of Tyneside signed up for the "King's shilling" in their hundreds to support the King's cause. From that day, they were known as "King George's Men", later shortened to "Geordies". The local dialect is what might be termed as being distinctive. It originates from the old Anglo-Saxon language with a strong Scandinavian influence and unless you are from the area, is difficult to understand when spoken with a strong accent. Such expressions as "canny bairn" (nice youngster), "I'm gannen hyem, hiney" (I am going home, my dearest one), "hoy it doon th' netty" (flush it down the toilet) or "hadaway yer bugger" (I don't believe what you are saying) are all part of the local language. I am not aware of any college courses as yet on how to speak Geordie, but who knows what the future holds.

Tynesiders and folk from the North East of England in general, are proud of their locally brewed beer. Like football, it is one of the favourite topics of conversation amongst the menfolk, especially in the pubs themselves. Newcastle Breweries used to be the main brewer in the City, with its well-known "blue star" logo that used to hang outside pubs that sold its beer throughout the North East. Newcastle Brown Ale, known affectionately as "Newky Broon" was first brewed in Newcastle in 1927 and is sold worldwide. However, since the acquisition by a well known Danish Company, brewing has been moved away from Newcastle to Tadcaster in Yorkshire, another loss of one of the area's traditions brought about by foreign companies.

Leaving the Eldon Bus Station, Archie and I head for the Haymarket and the Church of St Thomas the Martyr, one of the City's principal churches. It is claimed that St Thomas' is the only Anglican church in the Country without a parish. Immediately outside the Church, is a very moving war memorial depicting soldiers saying farewell to their families before leaving for war. Behind, is the City's Civic Centre. Built in 1967, the tall tower of the building has a decorative and pleasing curved top. A carillon of 25 bells is housed within the tower and used to play local folk songs on the hour.

We head down Northumberland Street, now pedestrianised and much improved from when I remember it being choked by traffic congestion. The pavement cafés placed in the middle of the once busy roadway, are a big improvement. I take the opportunity to take a seat at one of the tables for a cup of coffee and a scone. Afterwards we continue a little further down Northumberland Street, turning the corner at the Northern Goldsmiths with the large gilded golden clock still suspended out from the corner of the building, high over the street below. Around the corner and into Blackett Street, we walk past Grey's Monument with the Earl and pigeons atop. I want to see what has happened to Eldon Square following the development of the new Shopping Centre, that we saw briefly when arriving by bus.

On reaching the Square, my heart sinks with despair. Where on three sides once stood the elegant neo-classical terraced buildings as designed by Dobson, two sides of the Square have since been demolished. This was done to accommodate the new Eldon Shopping complex that incorporates the dreadful architecture of the 1960/70's. The one remaining terrace of Dobson's original buildings looks out of place. The new development has resulted in an act of urban development vandalism. I understand that at the time, there was much opposition to the proposed changes, but it seems that the developers got their way and brought in the demolition ball and bulldozers. I somehow doubt if they would have succeeded in today's climate for the preservation of our heritage. The damage done is now irreversible but with some innovative thinking and planning for the then new shopping development, most of these fine buildings could have been saved, albeit the cost may have been a little more. No doubt, the lure of money and profit was strong than the preservation of our urban heritage. How did they manage to get away with it? (Rant 22). I guess that the local people of Newcastle are now used to what now stands and some will not even remember the former Eldon Square. Sadly, I do. At least the green open space has been preserved, with the war memorial still located in the centre of the Square.

After a short stop, we make our way back past Grey's Monument and up Northumberland Street, where the fire brigade are collecting for a local charity. Parting with my spare pennies, we are back at the Haymarket to catch our final bus of the day to Alnwick, the Duke's town.

* * * * * * *

Our bus leaves from the Haymarket Bus Station, which adjoins the Eldon Square Bus Station where we arrived. On making enquiries on the times of the buses to Alnwick and where they leave from, I am left total confused. It seem that there are a number of alternatives but we need a bus that goes direct. Seeing a bus with "Berwick" on its destination sign, I ask the driver if it is going via Alnwick. "Why aye man" is the reply, so on we board. The Arriva single-decker No.505 bus soon pulls out of the Haymarket Bus station, the time now being 16.35.

Off we head northwards along the old Great North Road, past Lord Armstrong's monument, the university buildings, Exhibition Park and the green open spaces of the Town Moor. The Chinese Circus is in town and is encamped on the Town Moor where in June every year, the "Hoppings" are held. After a mile, we approach the upmarket suburb of Gosforth, (pronounced "Gosforeth" or "Gosfuth" depending upon your upbringing). There are certainly some fine and expensive houses. On we travel along Gosforth High Street and past the Regency Centre, a large business park that was developed in the late 1970's. At the time, it was the largest office complex in Europe covering an eleven acre site. Northern Rock, presently owned by the government (i.e. us) have their headquarters here.

We stop to pick up some passengers, four of which are teenagers that seem unable to talk at normal sound volumes. The dialect that they are speaking is also very strange and certainly not from the Tyneside / Northumberland areas. As I have experienced elsewhere on my travels with such loud mouthed individuals, their conversation is usually banal and I don't want to listen to what is being said. I really am not interested in their plans for the weekend and the quantities of beer they hope to consume. To make matters worse, the guy sitting immediately in front of me has been on his mobile phone since leaving Newcastle although the four loudmouths are drowning out his phone conversation. The joys of bus travel! I have had too many rants already over these issues so I will not repeat myself. I feel that I really am becoming an intolerant "Grumpy Old Man".

A little further on, we pass by McCracken Park, still the home to Northern Rugby Football Club, where I visited on many occasions as a player of the opposition. Further on still, we pass the entrance to Gosforth Park, home of the Newcastle Race Course. The main race of the season at the Newcastle course is the Northumberland Plate, nicknamed the Pitman's Derby. First run in 1833 on the Town Moor, the Race is held in June of every year and is just over two miles in length around the oval shaped course at Gosforth. The traditional works' holidays in the North East was Race Week that coincided with the big race of the Northumberland Plate, held on "Plate Day". The week also coincided with the "Hoppings" on the Town Moor. There used to be a permanent camp for the local Boy Scout troops at Gosforth Park, where I spent many a happy weekend, especially on race days. Maybe it is still there.

We soon join the dual carriageway of the main A1 trunkroad that now bypasses Newcastle to the west of the City. Here we are gathering up speed, bypassing the former mining village of Wideopen, then out into the open countryside crossing over the county border and into Northumberland, England's most northerly county and home of the 14/16th century Border Reivers. After a few miles, the highway drops down into the small valley of the River Blyth, passing on our left Blagdon Hall, home to Lord Ridley. A little further on, the A1 arcs around and passes the attractive country village of Stannington with its study sandstone houses and ancient church. Soon after, the new trunkroad veers off to the west and across the valley of the River Wansbeck. In the far distance to the northwest can be seen the outlines of the heather-clad moors of the Simonside Hills that stand over the Coquet Valley, nestled in which is the delightful small country town of Rothbury.

Instead of continuing along the main trunkroad, our bus diverts onto the route of the old Great North Road, down past the ruins of the 14[th]C castle and over the old sandstone road bridge that crosses the River Wansbeck, into the market town of **Morpeth** (population 14,000). The time is 17.10. Since 1981, the Town has been the administrative centre and county town for Northumberland. It first received its charter to hold a market in 1199, which is still held every Wednesday. Prior to the construction of the new A1 bypass, the Great North Road passed through the Town centre, which was the cause of severe traffic congestion. Prior to the advent of motor vehicles, Morpeth was a popular stopping point for horse-drawn stage coaches and there are still a number of old coaching inns in the Town. There are also some fine buildings in Bridge Street and Newgate Street that include the Town Hall designed by Sir John Vanburgh. Admiral Lord Collingwood, Nelson's Second in Command at the Battle of Trafalgar, lived in Morpeth and his house still stands near the Town centre. The Town's oldest building is the 13thC Chantry that is now used as a tourist office. Opposite is the 17thC free-standing stone clock tower, past which, is the large open space of the market. Sitting on the banks of the River Wansbeck, there are some excellent riverside walks, especially in springtime.

At one time, the Town's bus station was alongside the open market area by the River, which entailed travelling through the Town centre. The new bus station has now been re-located to the east side of the Town, which meant that we would not see much of the centre of Morpeth, a pity. Nevertheless, I still have my memories when I used to cycle here and beyond, on day trips into the countryside back in the 1950's.

Today is the 29th August 2008. Little did I know when passing through Morpeth with the River Wansbeck looking so quiet and tranquil, that in just eight days time on the 6th September, the Town would experience some of the worst flooding in recent years, with river-side defences breached. Over the previous day, the 5th September, more rain fell within a 24 hour period than the average rainfall for the whole month. In parts of the River's catchment area, the amount was even more than double the monthly average. Peak river flows were the highest on record. The resulting torrent that came down the narrow valley of the Wansbeck devastated the low-lying areas of the Town and put severe loading on the old stone bridge that carries the main road across the River. Fortunately, there were no casualties but up to 1,000 buildings and residential dwellings were badly affected by the floodwaters with most of the streets awash. Although flooding of my own home is something I have never experienced, my sympathies do go out to the folk who have to clear up after the muddy floodwaters have receded. The mess and water damage must be hard to cope with.

After a short stop at the Town's bus station, we once again head northwards, past Dogger Bank and up the hill out of Morpeth, back along the old Great North Road. The four teenagers are still ranting on about matters that I am not in the slightest bit interested in. If it were some juicy gossip, then maybe! At least the chap with the mobile left the bus at Morpeth.

We soon rejoin the dual carriageway of the A1 trunkroad before reaching the junction with the A697 that heads northwest towards Wooler and the Scottish border at Coldstream. We continue due north up the A1 that now has reverted back to a single carriageway. To our right is the former mental hospital, now closed, which at one time accommodated a large number of patients. On we travel up the A1 through the open countryside with names on the signposts bringing back memories. Signs to places such as Widdrington, Ulgham (pronounced Uffham) where my Grandmother once lived, Causey Park and Longhorsley are all familiar. As we approach the Coquet Valley, I can see on the skyline, the purple clad Cheviot Hills that form part of the Northumberland National Park.

Once again, we leave the main highway of the A1, diverting down into the Coquet Valley and the village of **Felton** (population 1,000). A new road bridge has been constructed over the River Coquet to replace the 16th century stone arched bridge that is now closed to road traffic. The Village itself is typical of many Northumbrian country villages with its church, pub and virtually all the buildings, including the new houses, constructed in the local dark sandstone. Only the village hall, built out of brick, does not conform. The B6345 passes through the Village with the road signs pointing to Acclington, Amble and Warkworth to the east and Longframlington (note the 15 letters) and Rothbury to the west. Stopping briefly in the Village centre outside the Stags Head, our bus continues on its way north again.

We are soon back onto the dual carriageway of the A1 heading for Alnwick, our final destination of the day. Bypassing the village of Newton-on-the-Moor, we continue along the dual carriageway at a reasonable speed. However, we make yet another diversion, this time to the former mining village of **Shillbottle** (population 1,350). Coal mining first started at Shillbottle in the early 1700's, the local mines being some of the most northerly of the main Northumberland coalfield. However, after more than 250 years of mining, the pits were closed in 1981 with similar consequences as experienced elsewhere among the mining communities. nevertheless, the Village still flourishes although I am not sure if there is much local employment. At least the four teenagers get off the bus here and peace reigns, albeit we do not have very far to go now before we reach Alnwick, only another three miles.

Leaving the village of Shillbottle, we head along the minor road that leads to Alnwick, crossing over the A1 trunkroad and into the town of Alnwick itself, following the route of the old Great North Road. Sitting admiring the views as we drive through the outskirts of the Town, I realise too late that we have just passed the hotel where we will be staying for the evening. Had I realised in time, I would have got my things together, including Archie, and got off the bus here, saving ourselves the walk back. Never mind, at least it is a fine evening with bright blue skies. Down into the Town centre we travel and eventually reach the Town's bus station. The time is 18.00 and I think we have both had enough bus travel for the day. Pleased to be able to stretch our legs (in Archie's case to cock his leg), we head back along the way we came, back up the road towards the Oaks Hotel where I have booked our accommodation for the evening.

It is a pleasant walk back from the bus station through the town centre, down Market Street, past the Town Hall and along Bondgate Within, through the old stone gateway and up Bondgate Without. Virtually all the buildings are constructed from the locally quarried sandstone with no garish shop frontages, all very pleasing on the eye. A little further on, we pass the Town's war memorial where above us on top of a small hill, stands the Tenantry Column with the Percy Lion on top. At last we reach the Oaks Hotel, some three-quarters of a mile from the Town centre and situated near to the roundabout where the road to Alnmouth branches off. The hotel looks very pleasant from outside and when shown to our room, is very comfortable and well appointed within. I seem to have made a good choice. I am certainly pleased to be able to put down my rucksack and freshen-up under the shower. Archie seems to have had enough too and curls up on his blanket in the corner of our bedroom. Not having eaten for some hours, I am feeling hungry and make my way to the outside restaurant, it still being light and a pleasant summer's evening. There seem to be a wedding party staying at the Hotel with much noise and merriment. After an excellent meal and a couple of beers, I take Archie out for his late evening walk before going to bed. I think we both will sleep well tonight.

It has been a long, though pleasant and interesting day since leaving Scarborough this morning, calling in at Durham to see my Brother and exploring parts of my home town of Newcastle. Travelling through Durham, Tyneside and Northumberland today, has certainly brought back memories of my earlier years when living in the North East of England, albeit much has changed during the intervening years. Nevertheless, it's good to be back where my roots are.

Chapter 9
Alnwick To Berwick—Day 9

Saturday 30th August 2008

Today is the final day of our bus journey across England. After a good night's sleep, I have a long soak in the bath, before giving Archie his early morning walk. The skies outside are a bit grey but at least it is not raining. The news on morning television is a bit depressing with the Chancellor of the Exchequer, Alistair Darling, saying that the UK's economy is heading for its worst recession in sixty years, most of which has been caused by the greed of international bankers and fund managers. It is also reported that a family of three have fallen 200 feet from Sharp Edge ridge in the Lake District, with one fatality. Having been over Sharp Edge myself on a few occasions, it is a challenging rocky traverse, which if weather conditions are bad, can be dangerous. The other news item is that the female governor of Alaska, Sara Palin is to partner John McCain as vice president in the forthcoming US presidential elections against Barack Obamha and Hilary Clinton. Well at least it balances things out gender-wise.

Breakfast at the Oaks is a good selection of fruit followed by local Craster kippers topped with lemon, red berries and a sprinkling of parsley, all very well presented and served with the usual "there ye gan" from the waitress. Although kippers are still smoked at Craster, the herrings are brought in from afar, not sure where, but they are certainly not landed locally. Although very tasty, somehow they do not seem to look or taste the same as I remember when I lived in the area. I recall reading something about the EU having interfered with the smoking process, but maybe I am mistaken.

After an excellent breakfast, I pack our kit for the last time on this section of our bus trip, and book out. The Oaks has turned out to have been a good choice and I am well satisfied with the accommodation and meals served at the Hotel. The time is 09.30 and we set out for a walk into and around the historic town of Alnwick, before catching our bus to Berwick.

Alnwick—Northumberland—population 7,800

Described in the magazine Country Life as being *"the most picturesque market town in Northumberland and best place to live"*, the historic and market Town of Alnwick sits on the south side of the River Aln that meanders through pastures below the walls of Alnwick Castle. The name of the Town is pronounced as "Anick" with the letters "l" and "w" silent.

Dating back to early settlements in the 600's, the Town became of significant importance with the building of the Castle in 1096, immediately following the Norman Conquest. A number of battles and border conflicts were fought in and around Alnwick, mainly against the Scots and their allies. In the First Battle of Alnwick in 1093, Malcolm III of Scotland was killed nearby which was followed by the capture of William the Lion of Scotland in the Second Battle of Alnwick in 1174. Alnwick was later prominent in the Wars of the Roses in the 1460's when it changed hands a number of times. Alnwick Castle has been over the centuries and still is, the home to the Earls and Dukes of Northumberland, the Percy family, who during the medieval times were one of the most powerful families in England, especially up in the far North. Henry Hotspur, immortalised in Shakespeare's *Henry IV*, was the eldest son of the 1st Earl of Northumberland and who performed heroic deeds in battles, mainly against the Scots.

During the 15th and 16th centuries, Alnwick Castle was extended and further fortified to withstand attacks and sieges. The extensive ramparts of the Castle, which still stand to this day, incorporate the main entrance and barbican, lion arch and middle gateway and six fortified towers, all encircling the outer bailey and the original inner walls and Castle courtyard itself. Along the tops of the battlements on the walls, are stone figures of soldiers that are sized smaller than life-size, so to fool the enemy into thinking that the castle walls were higher than they actually were—I'm sure the Scots were not that dumb! In more peaceful times of late, the Castle has, in addition to being the home of the Dukes of Northumberland, been used as a teachers' training college for females and more recently, to house US college students. It is after Windsor Castle, the largest inhabited castle in England and has in recent years been used as the setting for a number of films, including the *Harry Potter* films and the *Blackadder* TV comedy dramas. The Museum of the Northumberland Fusiliers is housed within the main central block of the Castle.

The Town itself was partially fortified with town walls that encircled most of its perimeter. Parts can still be seen today including the Bondgate or Hotspur Tower, through which motorised traffic still passes between Bondgate Within to Bondgate Without. Also the Pottergate Tower at the top of Pottergate on the western side of the old Town. There are many interesting old sandstone buildings within the central part of the Town, especially in Narrowgate, Fenkle Street and Bondgate Within. The stone Market Cross in the Market Place that is overlooked by the Market Hall, gives the Town its historic identity. Nearby is the Bailiffgate Museum that contains a collection of local artefacts and paintings associated with Alnwick and the surrounding area.

Immediately outside the town walls on a small hill to the south, stands the Tenantry Column, which was erected by the Duke's grateful tenants in 1816. Standing 83 feet tall, the stone column is topped by the Percy Lion complete with horizontal tail, the symbol of the Percy family. On the other side of the Town, is the Lion Bridge that carries the B6341 over the River Aln. Constructed in 1773 to replace an earlier bridge that was destroyed by a flood, this solid sandstone three-arched bridge has been designed in the "castle style" of architecture, matching that of Alnwick Castle itself that stands immediately above. Incorporating central and end turrets and castellated battlements along its length, this ornate structure has the life-size Percy Lion standing at the central point of the bridge looking towards the Castle above.

In recent years the Town has attracted many people visiting the Gardens at Alnwick Castle, that were first initiated in 2001 and developed by the present Duchess of Northumberland on a 42 acre site adjacent to the Castle. The elaborately laid out Gardens are said to be the most visited gardens in the Country after Kew and Wisley. Costing many millions of pounds, the Gardens have over the years been improved and extended and now include the main fountain and grand cascade, one of the World's largest tree houses, ornamental flower gardens and the infamous poison garden that contains species of poisonous and illegal plants, such as cannabis and opium poppy. I guess that security is high. The inspired gamble taken by the young Duchess back in 2001, would seem to have paid off with the Gardens now having become a major tourist attraction. They now belong to a charitable trust

It is perhaps not surprising to find that Alnwick, being a traditional county town supporting country sports, has two world-renowned makers of fly fishing tackle located in the Town. The Town also is home to one of the largest second-hand bookshops in England. This is located in the rather ostentatious-looking old railway station on the south side of town that was built in the style befitting a Duke and his visitors. Sadly, trains no longer pass through the station.

One of Alnwick's annual events is the Shrove Tuesday Football Match, also known as "Scoring the Hales", that is played by teams from two parishes within the Town. Prior to the game commencing, the football is processed down to the pastures from the Castle with the Duke's piper leading the way playing the Northumbrian pipes (to my mind more melodious that the traditional Scots bagpipes, but maybe I am biased). The winning team is the first to score two goals or "hales". Another annual event is the Alnwick Fair, held during the summer period. It is a re-enactment of the old medieval fair in which the town residents dress up in authentic costumes.

We have some spare time before our bus is due to leave, so we take the opportunity to explore a bit of the Town. Leaving our hotel, we walk back into the centre of Alnwick, passed the Tenantry column with the Percy Lion atop, and through the stone archway of the Bondgate Tower into Bondgate Within. Continuing down Narrowgate towards the Castle, we pass some interesting and well maintained old stone buildings in this area of the Town. Passing by Pottergate, we can see the stone tower and archway at the top of the street. At the bottom is a polished granite water fountain, complete with conduit and cast iron street lamp fixed to its top. We soon come to the main entrance and barbican of Alnwick Castle itself. It does look very impressive and well fortified against attack with the smaller than life-size stone figures standing on the battlements above. These days, rather than having to physically battle your way in to gain entry, it is just a question of paying the admission charge. Much less hassle.

We continue past the Castle forecourt down the B6341 towards the Lion Bridge that crosses over the River Aln. It is only a relatively narrow footpath, but it is littered with dog sc**t that to avoid treading in, we have to walk along the roadway. I am about to start on a subject that really does get me very annoyed, especially as a dog owner myself. It is not the dogs' fault that they foul the pavements, but that of their irresponsible owners who cannot be bothered to pickup. I like the majority of other dog owners, carry around with me a few small light plastic bags that are readily slipped into my coat pocket. To pick up Archie's mess after him is not a problem, especially as these days there are plenty of red bins specially provided for dog faeces. The few selfish owners who cannot and in some cases will not, clear up after their dogs, are getting us all a bad name. Do they not consider others, especially children who are likely tread in their dog's mess and young parents who will contaminate the wheels of their children's pushchairs? Do they not consider the subsequent health hazards that could arise? Have they no pride in their town or city? To those irresponsible idiots, I would say "if you can't be bothered to clear up after your dog, don't own one!" (RANT 23). The imposition of fines is not the answer as these individuals are rarely caught, especially when walking their dogs at night-time. Even when challenged, as I have done on occasions, there is often a lot of abuse given back. It also seems that for some, having a dog of a certain breed is a macho status symbol that often implies irresponsibility in looking after their pets. Somehow, more control needs to be imposed on those owning dogs. Extreme measures may be necessary if owners do not comply with the simple requirements of looking after a dog, such as confiscation of their pet. There is talk of micro-chipping all dogs and making new owners undergo a proficiency test, similar to that when collecting a dog from a rescue centre. At least this would be a start if it were possible to implement.

Back to Alnwick and the Lion Bridge. For a road bridge, this is really a most ornate yet appealing structure, with its castellated parapets, circular turrets and the Percy Lion with its horizontal tail, perched on a stone plinth at the bridge centre. The masonry features on the sides of the bridge add to its character and are in keeping with the Castle that stands immediately above. The bridge with the Percy Lion and Castle in the background, provides an excellent photo-shot. Prior to the town of Alnwick being bypassed, the Great North Road at one time passed through the Town centre and across the Lion Bridge for those travelling north towards Berwick. The single carriageway of the bridge must have caused a lot of congestion at the time.

Following our visit in August 2008, the severe flooding that occurred during the following week caused some undermining of the bridge foundations that has affected the stability of the masonry structure. As a result, the bridge and this section of the B6341, has been closed off to traffic and as at the time of writing, has not yet been reopened. When visited in August, the River Aln looked so tranquil and peaceful. It is difficult to imagine how the situation can so dramatically change due to the powers and forces of nature.

Whilst at the Lion Bridge admiring the views, a young couple are also here looking across the green pastures up to the Castle above. Then a comment from the male in his strong southern accent, "better than most of the piles of stones around here". Whilst Alnwick Castle does rank among the best, they had obviously not been to Bamburgh or to Lindisfarne. Maybe he was just trying to be provocative and controversial, but using the words of Peter Kay, the comedian, "what a knobhead!"

Negotiating our way past all the dog sh**t back up to the Castle's main entrance, we retrace our footsteps back along Narrowgate before diverting up the narrow lane of Fenkle Street and into the Market Place. There are some interesting buildings and shops surrounding the open square of the market place with the large sandstone market hall, known as Northumberland Hall, standing on the opposite side. Near to the middle of the square stands the medieval Market Cross that consists of a carved crosshead mounted on a stone column that in turn stands on an eight-stepped octagonal stone plinth. Although today is not market day, the place is still very busy. Across from the Market Place is Market Street in which stands another ornate stone water fountain with horse trough attached. The sign says "St Michael's Wishing Well" although the carved stone figure above the fountain, is that of St George slaying the dragon. Archie is gasping for a drink.

* * * * * * * *

We are now back at the bus station ready for the final stage of our bus trip across and up England. On enquiry as to which stand the bus leaves, I am directed to the wrong queue only to find our bus arriving on the other side of the bus station. A quick dash across to the correct queue means that we are last to board a near full bus. Never mind, we find a seat on the top deck of the Arriva No.501 double-decker bus that is scheduled to travel the "Coast and Castles" route from Alnwick to Berwick. At 10.45, we pull out of the bus station at Alnwick and head back towards the Oaks Hotel before deviating left on the A1068 towards Alnmouth. Opposite us on the top deck is a young Polish couple, chatting away in their native tongue. Having spent a little time in Poland, I try to pick up some words they are saying, but without any success. I must stop ear-wigging and concentrate on admiring the scenery. Archie too is interested in where we are heading and has got himself into the right position to look out of the bus window.

The bus travels down towards the coast, calling in at Alnmouth Station, which is situated on the main London to Edinburgh line. Of all the high-speed trains passing through, I would guess very few will actually stop here. Unfortunately, the bus does not go into the picturesque fishing village of Alnmouth itself, which is a pity. Once a major port for the export of grain and with a history of smuggling, Alnmouth today is a popular holiday resort, sitting at the estuary of the River Aln, with its golden sandy beaches stretching along the coast.

After a brief stop at the railway station, we proceed through the village of Lesbury and onto a narrow road leading to the coastal village of Boulmer and **RAF Boulmer**. The Station is presently the principal location for the RAF's air surveillance and control systems (ASACS) and has the responsibility for the 24 hour per day monitoring of the UK's air space. The Station also houses the RAF's School of Aerospace and is home to No.202 Squadron that operates the search and rescue missions throughout Northern England, employing Sea King helicopters. There has been talk of closing the Station down and transferring all activities elsewhere, but for the time being at least, Boulmer has been reprieved as is to remain open for a little while longer.

After leaving Boulmer, the bus route takes us back onto the B1339. We pass the signs for Howick Village and Howick Hall down a minor road leading off to our right. Howick Hall is the ancestral home to the Earls Grey since 1319, including the second Earl who became Prime Minister and after whom is named the blend of tea. The present Hall was rebuilt in 1782 and is set in extensive gardens that are claimed to be among the top five coastal gardens in England. A good time to visit the gardens is in May / June when the rhododendrons are in full bloom.

However, we continue a little further along the B1339 before turning off down another minor road that leads to the small picturesque fishing village of **Craster** (population 350), that is renown for its kippers. During the 19th century, Craster was perhaps better known for the hard basalt whinstone that was quarried to produce kerbstones and street cobbles for use on the streets of London. A new harbour was built specifically for the shipment of the locally quarried whinstone stone and sandstone. However, the quarries that provided work for many of the local folk, were closed in 1939 and are now given over as a nature reserve. More or less at the same time, the end of the North Sea herring boom of the 19th and early part of the 20th centuries, saw significant reductions in the catches of herring landed at Craster that were smoked to produce kippers. Although the herring fishing fleet has now long gone, the smokehouses at Craster still exist, using the traditional curing methods to produce the famous

"Craster kippers". The smell from the smokehouses is intoxicating. Sadly, we do not get a whiff of it in the bus.

Looking northwards along the coastline, the ruins of Dunstanburgh Castle standing out like fingers pointing up to the sky, can be seen. Built during the 14th century by the earl of Lancaster, it saw much action during the Wars of the Roses between the Houses of Lancaster and York. Set on a headland overlooking the North Sea, the original castle was the largest in Northumberland, even Alnwick. Ravaged by war and years of neglect, most of the former castle is today in ruins. The Castle can only be accessed by foot and from Craster, it being reached by following the scenic coastal footpath for a mile along the sea cliff tops. On a fine day, it is a very rewarding walk. This coastal footpath forms part of St Oswald's Way, the 97 mile long footpath recently established, starting at Holy Island, passing through Rothbury and finishing on Hadrian's Wall.

Had we more time, I would have got off the bus at Craster to explore the harbour and smokehouses and taken a walk along the coastal footpath towards Dunstanburgh Castle. Something else to do on another occasion. Leaving Craster, our bus winds its way along the narrow country roads towards the village of Embleton, with the ruins of Dunstanburgh Castle still clearly visible to our right for most of the way. Stopping briefly at Embleton, we can see the old water pump in the middle of the village green and the fortified pele tower next to the church.

Leaving on the B1340, we soon divert off again down the narrow country road that leads to the village of **Newton-by-the Sea** (population 250). Split between High Newton and Low Newton, the village is popular with visitors all the year round. A bumpy narrow road leads down to the picturesque little village of Low Newton where the cream-washed cottages overlook the village green and the 18th century Ship Inn that has its own micro-brewery. The small church of St. Mary's, constructed from corrugated steel sheets is still in use. The golden sandy beaches and bay have been popular with wind-surfers for many years. Perched on the cliff tops to the south, we can still see the finger-like ruins of Dunstanburgh Castle across the bay, standing out against the skyline.

Leaving High Newton, we return back up to the B1340 and continue along to Swinhoe before returning back to the coast, to the little fishing village of **Beadnell** (population 550). The Village has the unique distinction of having the only harbour on the whole of the eastern coast of England, facing westwards, although I suspect that this might be challenged. Directly overlooking the small harbour are two large circular limekilns, now owned by the National Trust. In the Village centre is the attractive sandstone 18th century parish church of St Ebba, together with the 16th century fortified pele tower that is now part of the local hostelry, the Craster Arms. However, Beadnell is best known locally, at least, for its fine beaches with a number of holiday homes and caravan parks, swelling the village's summer population.

From Beadnell, the bus route takes us along the North Northumberland Heritage Coast to the fishing village and resort of **Seahouses** (population 1,800). Popular with visitors during the summer months, the Village still has its own small fleet of boats and remains active as a fishing port with regular boat trips that operate from the harbour to the Farne Islands, weather permitting. Our bus takes us into the village centre where the large war memorial is the centre point of a roundabout. There seem to be plenty of fish-and-chips restaurants in the Village.

Leaving Seahouses, our bus continues northwards along the coast. Looking out to sea over the tops of the sand dunes, the dark outlines of the **Farne Islands** can be seen. The Farnes are a group of twenty plus small islands located between two and five miles offshore. The Islands are formed from the igneous Dolerite rock of the Whin Sill, with the hard basalt cliffs having withstood the pounding of the North Sea over the centuries. During the 7th century, the Islands were visited by St Aiden and St. Cuthbert, soon to be followed by St. Aethelwold. Over the years, there have been many shipwrecks on the Farnes even though there are three lighthouses, all of which are now unmanned. Perhaps the most well known incident concerning the Farnes, was in 1838 when the sailing ship Forfarshire went aground in stormy weather and fog, on the Farne's Harker Rock. Hearing the cries for help, the keeper of the Longstone Light, William Darling and his twenty-two year old daughter Grace, took to the seas in their wooden rowing boat in an act of great bravery and saved nine lives. The name of Grace Darling is now immortalised as one of the great heroines of all times and her act of bravery is part of local folklore. She is buried nearby in Bamburgh with the lifeboat at nearby Seahouses named after her. The Farne Islands are one of the Country's most important bird and seal sanctuaries. Over 250 different species of birds have been sighted and recorded on the Farnes, of which the most abundant include artic terns, guillemots, kittiwakes, shags and herring gulls. The Islands are also home to a large colony of grey seals and their seal pups that number over six thousand. There are now no permanent residents on the Farnes with the Islands being under the close jurisdiction of the National Trust.

Continuing along the Heritage Coast, we next approach the village of **Bamburgh** (population 500), with its imposing castle standing on the rocky plateau on the basalt cliffs of the Whin Sill, high above the Village and overlooking the beach and sea. The site was the seat of the Anglo-Saxon Kings of Northumbria until devastated by the Vikings. The Normans built new fortifications on the site that still forms the core of the present Castle. Badly damaged by artillery during the Wars of the Roses in 1464, the Castle fell into decline over subsequent decades, until bought and restored by the local Victorian industrialist, Lord Armstrong, whose descendants are still the owners. The massive square structure of the 12thC Keep is the central point with the surrounding walls and towers giving the Castle an impregnable appearance. The view of the Castle from the north and along the beach is one of the best photo-shots in the whole of England. At home, I have an oil painting of 1889 of the Castle from this vantage point that is a much-prized possession. The Village of Bamburgh is equally attractive and interesting. In the churchyard of the 13thC church of St Aiden's, is the grave of Grace Darling, the heroine of the SS Forfarshire rescue on the Farnes. Above her grave stands an elaborate memorial complete with stone canopy. Opposite the church is the Museum in which the main feature is the original 21 foot wooden fishing coble that was rowed by Grace and her father on that fateful night in 1838.

After a brief stop in the Village, giving us an opportunity to admire the magnificence of the Castle above us, we are on our way again, this time heading inland and leaving the coast behind. With all its historic interest, scenic beauty and beaches of golden sand, it is a little surprising that this stretch of the Northumbrian coastline is not more popular with tourists from outside the North East of England. But there again, any influx would spoil its wild attraction. Although blue skies are common, the temperatures are not always very high, especially when the winds from Scandinavia blow across the North Sea onto this exposed coastline.

Still following the B1342, we pass the mash flats of Budle Bay and then past fields where the ripened corn is being harvested. Up a side road, a tall tapering stone round tower with a conical top is visible and arouses some interest. However on later inspection of the local Ordnance Survey map, it is shown as a disused windmill. On we trundle across the main London to Edinburgh railway line before crossing over the A1 trunkroad and into the village of **Belford** (population 1,100). Prior to the railways and being on the Great North Road, the horse-drawn stagecoaches used

Belford as a watering-hole. Now the A1 bypasses this picturesque village although there is still plenty of activity. The 18th century Belford Hall is constructed in the Palladian style of architecture and sits in extensive parkland. The Hall has recently been renovated and converted into residential flats, albeit superior apartments. The local fire station has a practice tower constructed from stone, rather than the normal brick. At bit OTT, but at least it is in keeping with the village's other stone buildings. The Rev John Wesley, founder of Methodism, preached in the main street at Belford in 1826. His subsequent recorded comments were that "the hearers were seriously attentive and a few seemed to understand what was spoken". The signpost shows Berwick to be another fifteen miles.

We are soon back onto the A1 moving north, albeit slowly. We are once again stuck in a long line of traffic behind a large slow-moving vehicle and running fifteen minutes behind schedule. At least moving slowly allows us to obtain better views of **Lindisfarne** (also known as **Holy Island**) that has now come into view across the bay. The monastery on Lindisfarne was founded by Saint Aiden, who had been sent from Iona on the west coast of Scotland in AD635 at the request of King Oswald. He was to establish the Christian church in Northern England. Later, St Cuthbert, Northumberland's patron saint, would become Abbot and Bishop of Lindisfarne, when during the early 700's, the famous illuminated Lindisfarne Gospels were prepared at the monastery. However, the monks' peaceful way of life was soon to be severely disrupted by the Vikings. Their barbarous raids on Lindisfarne and their devastation of the surrounding areas caused much consternation. "Never before has such terror appeared in Britain as we have now suffered from a pagan race" wrote the scholar Alcuin. Eventually, the monks left the Island with the remains of St. Cuthbert who is now buried in Durham Cathedral. Following the Norman Conquest, the priory was re-established as a Benedictine monastery. However, as elsewhere throughout the Country, the Abbey fell victim to Henry VIII's purge of the Dissolution of the Monasteries in 1536 and today stands as a ruin. The 16thC Lindisfarne Castle sits on a high rocky basalt outcrop of Beblowe Crag that overlooks the bay and harbour. The Castle was mainly built from the stone of the Abbey after it was closed by Henry VIII. After a period of neglect, the Castle and its gardens were renovated by Sir Edward Lutyens in the early 1900's. It is the Castle that can be seen from some distance inland. Considered as the birthplace of Christianity in Northern England, Lindisfarne today has become a centre for Christian revival with pilgrimages being made across the sands from the mainland. The Island is accessible by car across the causeway at times of low tide, but at high tides is totally cut-off from the mainland. There is a small village on the Island with two pubs. There is no police presence on the Island and in previous years, the pubs never shut when the tide was in. For many years, Lindisfarne was mainly a fishing and farming community. Today, it is mainly tourism and the production of Lindisfarne Mead that provides employment for most of the Island's residents.

Passing the turn-off to Beal and the Island of Lindisfarne, we continue past the fertile pastures of the Northumbrian countryside still following behind the long slow-moving vehicle in front. The drivers behind are getting frustrated and attempts are made to pass that might well lead to an accident. Why does not the driver of the slow-moving vehicle pull-over? We next reach **Haggerston Castle**, now a large mobile home and caravan park that occupies the 250 acre site. Of the original 13thC castle, only the tower remains, the castle allegedly having been cursed and set on fire on at least three occasions. During the late 19th century, the Haggerston Estate was owned by Mr Christopher John Leyland, who rebuilt the main house and developed the gardens. His brother sent him six hybrid trees that he had had cross-pollinated back at the family home in Wales. These were the fast growing conifers, Cupressocyparis leylandii that were later to be propagated, grown commercially and sold in every garden centre and nursery in the Country. To some, they are a menace, especially when allowed to grow to excessive heights and block out light.

After passing a sign for Oxford, our bus again diverts from the main trunkroad down the route of the old A1 and into the former coalmining village of **Scemerston** (population 1,000). Geologically, the coal seams were among the earliest coal formations in Britain and do not form part of the Northumberland coalfields. At one time, there were extensive colliery workings in the area together with factories for the manufacture of bricks, tiles and lime. All have since closed and the parish has reverted largely back to agriculture for its livelihood. The bus stops at the Village's war memorial, although no one gets on or off. On we continue down the wide main street that at one time carried all traffic travelling between Newcastle and Edinburgh.

Picking up the A1167, we enter the small seaport town of **Tweedmouth** that is situated on the south bank of the River Tweed and which is now part of Berwick itself. The Tweed is one of Britain's prized rivers for salmon fishing and being at its estuary, the Town celebrates every year Salmon Week, a tradition dating back to medieval times during which the "Salmon Queen" is appointed. Once a busy port with its own foundries that were supported by the local coalfields and lime workings, Tweedmouth today is principally a dormitory town for its much bigger neighbour on the other side of the River.

Crossing over the graceful concrete arched Royal Tweed Bridge that spans the River, we enter into the historic border town of Berwick-upon-Tweed, the final destination for our bus trip across and up England. Our bus takes us through the Town centre before terminating outside the mainline railway station. Archie has been lying by my feet on the floor of the bus for the past few miles and when we get up to leave, I notice some white-matter sticking to the fur of his brown coat. Further examination shows that it is chewing-gum that some irresponsible person has discarded on the floor of the bus. I could have used a more descriptive adjective and noun for the *?*?* responsible, as it is well stuck to his fur. On leaving the bus, I attempt to remove this dreadful substance from his coat but find it well adhered. Having been able to remove some, I need to get out my scissors to cut away the rest, leaving a small partial bare patch on his coat. I am very annoyed that firstly, I had to pull away with my fingers gum that someone had spat out of their mouth and secondly, that I had to cut away part of Archie's coat to remove it all. What a disgusting habit! If people have to chew gum, that seems to be popularised by certain football managers, why can't they wrap the discharged remains in paper and dispose of it properly (RANT 24). You can't help noticing these days down the length of most high streets, that the pavements are covered in circular grey patches that pot-mark the whole surface of the footpath. Have these irresponsible idiots no consideration for others? Have they no pride in their town or city? If the chewing of gum in public places cannot be banned altogether, as it is in Singapore, then I would suggest imposing a 1,000% tax on the substance that could in turn be used for cleaning up the mess on our pavements.

Having removed the gum from Archie's coat, placed it in an appropriate receptacle and washed my hands, we set out for a walk around Berwick before catching our train back home. The time is 12.50.

Berwick-upon-Tweed—Northumberland—population 11,800

Berwick-upon-Tweed is the most northerly town in England, with the Scottish border only two and a half miles to the north. Sitting on the north bank of the River Tweed at its estuary, it is a market town with a long history, mainly comprising the conflict between the English and the Scots. Berwick was an extremely wealthy port during the 12th and 13th centuries, exporting wool, grain and salmon, trading with merchants from Germany and the Low Countries.

However because of its wealth and strategic location on the border between England and Scotland, Berwick was very much central to the wars between the two countries during these medieval times, changing hands on thirteen occasions between 1147 and 1482. Under Scots rule in 1120, the Town was made into a Royal Burgh with its own mint set up for Scottish coinage. However, following the signing of a pact with the Scots and France, Berwick was attacked and sacked by Edward I's army in 1296, with a large number of the Town's population put to the sword. From this time, the Town fell into decline from in former halcyon days. With continued fighting between the Scots and English, the ownership of the Town fluctuated between the two countries, until it was finally recaptured in 1482 by Richard, Duke of Gloucester, later to become King Richard III of England.

Under English rule, Berwick was developed into a garrison town. During the Elizabethan period of the 16th century, vast sums were spent upon the construction of new ramparts and fortifications to withstand artillery bombardment from the Scots. These defensive walls some two and a half miles in length, encircled the whole Town and were constructed using the Italian design of wide battlement ramparts, being 35 feet high and including a number of towers around their perimeter. They are undoubtedly the finest of their type in the UK and still remain largely intact to this day, being accessible on foot for their whole length.

In 1603, the kingdoms of England and Scotland were united and James VI of Scotland became also James I of England. On his way south to receive the English crown at Westminster Abbey in London, Berwick was the first of the English towns to greet the new King. Although Berwick was made into a County Corporate as part of England in 1551, the Town was never formally annexed to England. Even under the Act of the Union in 1707, Berwick remained a separate entity although it did remain within the laws and legal system of England. It was only in 1853, that Berwick eventually lost its partial independence and was included for administrative purposes in with the County of Northumberland.

There is a curious but true story of Berwick having been at war with Russia up to recently as 1966. When the declaration of the Crimean

War against Russia was proclaimed in 1853, it was signed by "Victoria, Queen of Great Britain, Ireland, Berwick-upon-Tweed and all British Dominions". However, when the Treaty of Paris was signed in 1854 to end the War, the name of Berwick-upon-Tweed was omitted, probably because of its loss of independent status. As a consequence, the small British town of Berwick remained at war, at least technically, with Russia, one of the most powerful nations of the day. This state of war continued for another hundred years until an official from the then Soviet Union visited Berwick to sign a declaration with the Town's Mayor, to declare an end to hostilities. The Mayor is reputed to have said to the Soviet official "Please tell the Russian people that they can sleep peacefully in their beds". It's a nice story although some of the facts and legalities have since been questioned.

The Borough of Berwick-upon-Tweed was created in 1974 but further local government reorganisations in 2009 saw the borough status abolished and most of the Town's functions transferred back to Northumberland County Council. In that same year, an unofficial poll was held among the voters of Berwick as to whether they wished to remain as part of England or be transferred to Scotland. Approximately 60% voted for transfer to Scotland, mainly, so it is claimed, because of the better health and social service benefits obtainable in Scotland as a result of devolution, which is undoubtedly true. It is perhaps worth noting that the Scottish county of Berwickshire has not since 1482 included the town of Berwick within its boundaries.

At one time there was a castle at Berwick, which is not surprising due to the Town's strategic importance and location so close to the Scottish border. The original 12th Castle was sited on a high knoll overlooking the River, immediately to the west of the railway line. However, with the construction of the Town ramparts in the 1500's and the uniting of the two kingdoms in 1603, the castle's importance waned with the structure being virtually demolished for building stone. During the latter part of the 19th century, it was further demolished to make way for the railway, with the present railway station standing on the site of the Great Hall of the old Castle.

One of the buildings in the Town to benefit from the stone taken from the Castle, was Holy Trinity Church that was the only church in the Country to be built during the period of Oliver Cromwell's Commonwealth in the 1650's. Built in the Puritan style without a steeple, the Church originally had no stained glass or any other decorations.

John Knox preached here during his ministry for whom a special pulpit was built. The parish church of Holy Trinity continues to be used for regular worship and is located in The Parade. On the other side of The Parade across from Holy Trinity, are the Old Barrack Buildings that were built in 1712/21 and were one of the earliest purpose-built infantry barracks in England. Previous to this, soldiers were billeted in people's homes and other places, which resulted in many problems. Today the Barracks are maintained by English Heritage and house the Regimental Museum of the Kings Own Scottish Borderers

Moving into the Town centre, the fine Guildhall complete with clock-tower looks up the wide expanse of Marygate where the weekly markets are still held. The Guildhall that is referred to as the Town Hall, was built in 1750 in the traditional Classic style of architecture, originally housing on the top floor the Town's prison.

Perhaps the most poplar photo-shot of Berwick is that of the three bridges that span the River Tweed. The Old Bridge was built on the orders of King James in 1610/24 and is 1,164 feet in length incorporating fifteen sandstone arches. It still carries light road traffic to this day. The Royal Border Bridge is the tall masonry railway viaduct that was designed and the construction supervised, by the well known civil engineer, Robert Stephenson. The Bridge, which was opened by Queen Victoria in 1850, is 2,160 feet long with 28 arches carrying the bridge deck some 126 feet above the River. For its day, it was quite a feat of engineering and still carries the busy main-line railway between London and Edinburgh. The most recent of the three bridges, is the Royal Tweed Bridge that was built in 1928. The graceful reinforced concrete arch spans 361 feet across the Tweed and at that time was the longest concrete span in the Country. The structural design was by L.G. Mouchel and Partners, a consultancy firm of civil engineers based in Newcastle, with whom I started my career in civil engineering. The Bridge carried the main A1 highway until the 1980's, when the Town's bypass was built.

J.S. Lowry, one of Britain's best loved painters and well-known for his paintings of "match-stick men" depicting mainly northern industrial scenes, was a frequent visitor to Berwick. From the mid-1930's until his death in 1976, he painted a number of scenes in Berwick and considered buying Lion House that is located alongside the Town walls. A Lowry Trail has recently been established that follows for most of its way, the Elizabethan walls around the Town. Along the Trail, there are eighteen information boards depicting the sites for some of his paintings and drawings, on which are include reproductions of his finished works.

The local football team, Berwick Rangers, is unique in that playing their football at Shieldfield Park in the North East of England, they participate in the Scottish Football League. Had they been in one of the English leagues their furthest away match could have been nearly five hundred miles away at Plymouth, whilst their fixtures against Scottish clubs are much closer to home. Being a relatively small club, the "Borderers" most impressive win was that against the mighty Glasgow Rangers in the Scottish Cup in 1967, said to be one of the biggest cup shocks in world football.

We haven't too much time to spend looking around Berwick before catching our train home. We will be back in Berwick sometime in the very near future to start the second stage of our bus journey up through Scotland to John O'Groats when hopefully we shall have a greater opportunity to explore the Town more thoroughly.

From the railway station where our bus completed its journey from Alnwick, we walk down Castlegate, past the polished-granite fountain, through and under the stone archway of Castlegate into the main shopping area of Marygate. Immediately facing us at the bottom of the wide street, is the imposing $18^{th}C$ Town Hall complete with its tall steepled clock tower. Being a Saturday, there are a number of market stalls out with their coloured canopies strung out above. We make down West Street past some interesting shops towards the River and the $17^{th}C$ Old Bridge that still carries vehicular traffic albeit in one direction only. Heading along the Quay Wall that runs above the River, we pass by a line of imposing Georgian houses that may well have been the homes of past trading merchants.

Continuing on towards Wellington Terrace, we stop and look back to the three magnificent bridges that span the Tweed. In the foreground is the Old Bridge that dates back to the early 1600's. Immediately behind is the concrete arch of the Royal Tweed Bridge, that up to the 1980's carried the main road traffic of the A1 highway. In the distance are the high masonry arches of Stephenson's Royal Border Bridge, built in 1847 and still carrying the main railway line between London and Edinburgh. It is a classic sight and would be even better from a higher vantage point.

On the point overlooking the wide River estuary is the start of the Town's ramparts or battlements, which encircle Berwick to the north and west. Here is Fisher's Tower that can be accessed to provide a better view across the bay to the pier. The scene is the subject of one of Lowry's paintings and is titled "The Pier". A little further on, we come to the Russian Gun. At one time, the riverside fortifications bristled with artillery to defend the harbour entrance. None now survive but the Russian Gun, with its long cast-iron barrel mounted on its wheeled gun-carriage, was brought back from the Crimean War in 1856 as a trophy and placed on the ramparts at Berwick. On closer inspection, the double-headed eagle of the Russian Tzar can be seen embossed on the top of the barrel. At this point there is a fine view across the estuary to Tweedmouth and Spittal on the south side of the River.

Continuing around the ramparts, we pass the access road leading up to the three storied Lion House, so named because of the stone lions at the entrance gate. It is said that J.S. Lowry contemplated buying Lion House as his Berwick residence though the purchase never transpired. Here we come across one of the information boards on the Lowry Trail, titled "The Lions". Alongside is the Gunpowder Magazine that dates back to 1749 and supplied the defensive artillery along the walls. We are walking along the top of what seems to be high grassy embankments until we see the large vertical drop of the masonry walls on the attacking side. I need to keep Archie on his lead as he seems to be very curious on what is below us and it is a long way down. We come to the Windmill Bastion, part of the original fortifications. Beneath the walls is a football pitch that is yet again the scene of another of Lowry's paintings titled "The Football Match". His painting is shown on the information board.

The ramparts continue around to the Brass and Cumberland Bastions finishing at Meg's Mount, the site of the old Castle. However, time is pressing and we need to get back to the railway station. We leave the ramparts at the Windmill Bastion and drop down onto The Parade near to the entrance of the 18th century Barracks. Across The Parade, is the parish church of Holy Trinity that was built during the period of the Commonwealth in the 1650's. Walking into the churchyard, the outside of the building is quite plain, representing the Puritan times of that period, although there is a certain beauty to it. Immediately on the opposite side of the road, is another large church, that of St Andrew's of the Church of Scotland.

Walking down Church Street, we return back to the Town Hall and Marygate. Not having had anything to eat since breakfast, I find a local butchers shop that sells the traditional Scottish lamb mince pies. When heated, they are delicious. Munching on my pie with Archie giving me the "eye", we make our way back up Castlegate to the railway station for the final stage of our journey home.

* * * * * * *

We have about fifteen minutes to spare before our train to Newcastle arrives. On going to the station ticket office, I find it closed with a notice saying that due to an unprovoked verbal assault by a travelling customer, the clerk had decided to temporarily close the ticket booth. On further questioning, it seems that a male of foreign origin requiring a ticket had become very aggressive, intimidated the female clerk, causing her to become distressed. I don't know the circumstances of his annoyance, but I am sure it wasn't necessary for him to upset the lady who would have just been doing her job. Had he difficulties in understanding the language, that was his problem and provided no excuse to become abusive. However, whilst an unpleasant experience for the female ticket clerk, there was a glass window between the two, preventing any physical contact. There are a few passengers waiting to buy tickets but to her credit, the lady clerk comes back to man the ticket booth in sufficient time for us to buy tickets before our train arrives.

For some reason I could not buy a ticket that would take me all the way home to Lincoln, but only as far as Doncaster, where in between changing trains, I would need to purchase another for the final stage home. I am not going to question the reason why, as the lady behind the glass is still recovering from her earlier verbal assault. Having purchased my single fare ticket, which at £49.00 comes as a bit of a shock, we make our way across the bridge and down to the platform for the southern bound trains. At least Archie goes for free. At the bottom of the stairs is a plaque stating that the Great Hall of Berwick Castle once stood on the site of the railway station and that in the Great Hall on the 17th November 1292, "the claim by Robert Bruce to the crown of Scotland was declined and the decision in favour of John Baliol was given by Edward I before the full Parliament of England and a large gathering of nobility and populace of both England and Scotland". Is this the same Edward referred to in the Scots newly-found anthem "Flower of Scotland"?

We don't have long to wait before our London bound train draws into the station, arriving on time at 14.12. Fortunately it is not too busy so we are able to get a seat by the window in the "quiet coach" that means no mobile phones—hallelujah! With hindsight, I should have selected a seat on the eastward facing side of the train, from which the views are more interesting. Off we set across the Royal Border Bridge that looks down to the other two bridges across the Tweed and the Town itself. Soon picking up speed, we race through the Northumbrian countryside, with the castles of Lindisfarne, then Bamburgh seen in the distance to the east. Drawing closer to the coast, the small seaside town of Alnmouth is passed. It does not seem too long before we are drawing into Newcastle Central Station, only forty-five minutes after leaving Berwick. Remaining on board, we are off again, this time over the River Tyne across the King Edward VII Rail Bridge through Gateshead with the "Angel of the North" standing out against the skyline. Soon we are slowing down for Durham, where from the railway viaduct sited high above the River Wear, there is a magnificent view across to the Cathedral and Castle. It had taken only sixty minutes to cover by train what had taken more than four hours to travel by bus over the past two days.

On we speed through Durham County, stopping at Darlington, and then the relatively flat countryside of Yorkshire before reaching York. No views of York Minster from the train. As I have already mentioned, I would have liked to have to visited York on my trip north from Lincoln, but the bus connections prevented this. Leaving York, it is not long before we are slowing down again as the train approaches Doncaster. Here we need to leave for our next connection. The time is 16.20.

On leaving the main-line train, we head for the ticket office to purchase a single ticket to Lincoln. On enquiry, I find there is no direct train to Lincoln due for some time, which will mean that we shall have to change again at Retford. After a relatively short eighteen minute wait, our train to Retford arrives, which is only a journey of some fifteen minutes. Being a weekend, we find that on arrival at Retford, there are maintenance works being undertaken and the railway line through Retford to Lincoln has been closed for the period of the works. A bus shuttle service has instead been laid on to transfer rail passengers to Lincoln via Gainsborough. So it seem that we shall be finishing our journey by bus, which seems rather appropriate. The only problem now is that we shall have to wait some forty minutes before the shuttle bus arrives. Being so close to home, the long wait is a bit frustrating. Nevertheless, the wait provides an opportunity to give Archie some exercise and also to try to remove what is remaining of the chewing gum on his coat before we get home. At least it is a fine and warm evening.

At last our bus arrives and at 17.30, off we head leaving Retford through the Nottinghamshire countryside, then across the River Trent into Gainsborough, where we had been three days earlier. Back on the A156, we take the direct route through Torksey and Saxilby towards Lincoln. At last we see Lincoln Cathedral standing high on the limestone escarpment in the far distance—nearly there. It is not long before the shuttle bus is pulling into the car parking area of Lincoln Station. Having telephoned in advance, my wife Florence is waiting to pick us up and take us home. The time is 1830 and I am looking forward to a relaxing soak in the bath.

Tomorrow is Archie's birthday when he will be eight years old. We must arrange some sort of celebration for him after what he has been through, although I suspect that he has enjoyed the experience. It would be interesting to hear what he would say if he could talk—or maybe not.

In three days time, I will be due to go into hospital to have my second knee replacement, so any plans of continuing our bus journey north through Scotland to John O'Groats will need to be put on hold for the time being at least. Nevertheless, I will be able to get on with the planning of the next stage, which allowing for the winter period to pass and the longer days to arrive, is likely to be in the Spring of 2009. Unfortunately, I shall not be able to use my bus-pass for the journeys up through Scotland, as Gordon Brown restricted its use to England only. Nevertheless, I should be grateful for that. At least Archie will travel free—or so I hope!

PART 3

SCOTLAND—to JOHN O'GROATS

Chapter 1
Prepartions And Travel Up To Berwick—Day 10

Saturday 25th April 2009

"Back on the Road Again"—would be an appropriate song to accompany this book.

A few things have happened since my trip last August between Lands End and Berwick-upon-Tweed. For the second stage of my bus trip, I was now equipped with two new knees and fully bionic, thanks to the doctors and nurses at Lincoln County Hospital. In February, earlier this year we went on a round-the-world trip, taking in Australia for a family wedding in Melbourne, both islands of New Zealand and finally Los Angeles in the USA. In total, there were 5 long-haul flights and each time I was asked to step aside when I passed through airport security with the buzzer sounding as I walked through the X'ray machine. I guess the security staff are well accustomed to travellers with artificial limbs and joints, but for me it was at first a little embarrassing and a bit disconcerting. At least, I know that there is some metal down there.

You might be wondering what we had done with Archie whilst we were on our "round-the-world" trip, which lasted some 4 weeks. Good friends of ours, who have two small white poodles called Tiffany and Tamara, had volunteered to look after him. It turned out that he was in his element with two female dogs at his side all day. It was quite noticeable when we returned, that he did not want to leave and for some days after, was downcast. Your holiday is over Archie and you're back on the "bus trip".

There was some planning to be done for this second stage of my bus trip. I had previously decided to follow the route up the east coast of Scotland, taking in Edinburgh, Dundee, Aberdeen, Inverness and Wick to John O'Groats, ending up at Thurso. Besides being well served by local bus services, there are some splendid sandy beaches up this eastern coastline that I knew would be enjoyed by Archie. Sorting out the bus routes and timetables was relatively easy, including the stop-over locations. As on the first stage of my journey, I was intent on calling in on as many places of interest that I could reasonable take in, allowing adequate periods of time for exercising Archie between individual bus journeys. Again, this fell into place relatively easy, calling in at cities and towns such as Dunbar, Dunfermline, Perth, Arbroath, Montrose, Banff, Elgin, Dornoch and Wick.

The next step was to arrange overnight accommodation. Previously, I had contacted the local Tourist Information Offices to enquire for B&Bs that would accept dogs. It was when I was "surfing the net" on my computer, that by chance, I came across a most useful web-site called "bedandbreakfastsearcher.co.uk" This site lists a good range of accommodation at various locations and towns in the UK that may be selected from basic B&Bs to upmarket hotels. More importantly for myself, it also has a special requirements box that includes "dog friendly" accommodation. By clicking the appropriate boxes, I was able to bring up an accommodation list in each of my overnight stops that would accept Archie, together with charges and availabilities. Booking was also on line, so great, problem solved. I would subsequently find out that everything had worked out fine, although out of courtesy, I did send each of my overnight stays an e.mail warning them that I would be bringing a "small well behaved dog"—well you have to give a good impression. One of the hotels did send back an e.mail saying that they looked forward to seeing me and my "canine friend"—a different turn of phrase.

Finally, there were the arrangements I needed to make to get Archie and myself to the starting point on this second stage of my trip, Berwick-upon-Tweed, where I had ended my trip last August. Also to get back from the far north of Scotland on completion of our journey. The train was the obvious option, so back onto the computer to look at timetables and costs. Getting to Berwick from Lincoln was no problem, with changes at Doncaster and Newcastle. Also getting back from Thurso, the most northerly rail station in the UK, was relatively easy, with changes at Inverness, Perth, Edinburgh, Doncaster and Retford. Equipped with a senior rail pass that I had purchased for my trip in August 2008, and by booking on-line in advance, I was pleasantly surprised at the cost of fares charged. These were £23.55 up to Berwick and £50.00 back from Thurso to Lincoln. The only drawback was that I was committed to travelling at specific times and dates and that I needed to book in advance. Because of the distances and time to be spent travelling on the return journey, I decided to break my train trip back home staying overnight at Inverness.

Also to have a short break in Newcastle to exercise Archie. With the use of my "flexible friend" and pressing the appropriate keys on my computer, within two days, my rail tickets arrived in the post—all very impressive!

So equipped with rucksack containing mine and Archie's kit and luggage, on Saturday the 25th April 2009, we are ready to set-off. Our rail journey up to Berwick is just over four hours, even allowing for a sojourn in Newcastle, so it will be near midday before we board the train in Lincoln. This gives me an opportunity to exercise Archie before we leave. One of his regular walks is a bridle cum cycle path (part of the A1 National Cycle Path), just to the north of Lincoln. When they are at their home base at RAF Scampton, the Red Arrows can often be seen practicing in the skies above this bridle path. At this time in late April, the crop in the adjoining fields is rapeseed oil, with the crops being over two feet high. Off the lead, Archie is fine, but should he see a rabbit or squirrel (worst still a cat), he will be off giving chase, although because of his barking, he never gets anywhere near his quarry. This morning, he has seen a rabbit and gives chase into the fields and soon gets lost amongst the crops. Despite my calling, he does not return, at least not immediately. It seems like five frantic minutes later when he sheepishly appears back on the bridle track, much to my relief—the little b*****r. Had he not, at the very least, we would have missed our train and at worst, I would not be writing this book. As a rule, he will not let you out of his sight and can usually be relied upon to come back without any calling. This particular morning is the exception to the rule and perhaps he has genuinely got lost among the crops that towered over him. For sure, he is now firmly back on the lead.

So at last we set out on the 11.54 train from Lincoln Central to Doncaster. Unusually for a Saturday, the two carriages of the train are full, with a large party of young men dressed in fancy outfits, intent on having a good weekend. In fairness, it is all good humour and makes the hour long journey all the more entertaining. I am not sure in what state they will be later in the evening though, but who am I to say too much, having been there myself on a few occasions in my earlier days. I guess that growing old makes you less tolerant and perhaps forgetful.

First we travel through Gainsborough and on to Doncaster, where after a short wait, we board the main east-coast line National Express train to Newcastle. When booking my rail tickets online, I had also reserved seats where possible, in case the train was full. Having boarded the correct coach (inevitably at the wrong end) and fought my way to where my reserved seat is, I find it occupied. Why bother reserving a seat in the first place. Not wanting to get into a confrontation (I must be getting old) I quietly slide into another seat that was unoccupied and had been reserved from London. Maybe the passenger had got off before Doncaster. For sure, I am here to stay until Newcastle.

Whilst relaxing in my seat, a gentleman with an Eastern European accent (it turned out he was Latvian) approaches me with his camera and asks if he can take a photograph of Archie. In his own words, he says "We do not have dogs like him in my country" I knew that here was something different about you, Arch!! Needless to say, I am happy to oblige, especially as I have previously worked in Latvia and have some happy memories of that Country and the people I met.

You see and meet all types of people whilst travelling both on the trains and buses.

A few seats in front and facing in my direction, is a woman of dubious age, questionable weight and not in contention for any glamour awards. Nothing wrong with that except that she spends most on her time in full view of those travelling, covering her face with some hideous dark coloured make-up, including jet black eye-shadow. I feel sure that many of us have been in a position where we don't want to watch what is going on but can't help doing so. Try as I might, I concentrate on looking out the window to watch the passing scenery, but my eyes keep wandering back like magnets, to the goings-on of this woman. When finished putting on her make-up, she is on her mobile phone to some poor unfortunate person, giving them a hard time and threatening to take them in hand. One look from this woman would have been enough. The whole coach is intrigued and guessing what the poor unfortunate on the other end of the phone has done to deserve such treatment. Pleased it wasn't me.

On the train rolls at 100 + mph through the flat countryside stopping at York and Darlington. Sitting up by the window watching the passengers get off at Darlington, a familiar face passes by the carriage window. Who can mistake the crazy smile on the face of Vic Reeves of "Vic and Bob" and "Shooting Stars" fame. There is a further stop at Durham, with a splendid view from the train across the River Wear of Durham Cathedral and Castle.

Then on towards Newcastle. Travelling by train, we cross the High Level Bridge over the River Tyne, with the iconic arch of the New Tyne

Bridge downstream on our right, before entering Newcastle Central Station. For me, crossing over the Tyne into Newcastle is always a bit of an emotional moment.

So as to give Archie some exercise, we break our journey at Newcastle. This gives me a chance to explore the quayside area of the City that I have not visited for a number of years. We walk down the steep stairways that supposedly Dick Turpin rode up on his horse Black Bess many years ago, where half way down there used to be a barbers where I used to get my hair cut—now long gone, that is both the barbers and my hair. Down we walk onto the Quayside with the green latticework arch of the Tyne Bridge looming high above on one side and Stephenson's double-decker High Level Bridge on the other side. The low level Swing Bridge painted red and white is immediately in front. The sight of all three bridges at this level is awesome, it being the symbol of Tyneside.

For a period during the early days of my career, I had worked in a design office that was located in one of the timber faced Tudor style buildings down on the Quayside. The frontage of this building leans outwards and overhangs the pavement. During Tudor times, the former inhabitants supposedly threw their rubbish and the contents of their bedpans from the windows into the streets below. This practice has of course long ceased, although sadly there is still too much litter and discarded rubbish lying scattered on the streets and pavements in the area. Walking Archie on his lead amongst all the discarded food lying on the ground is a nightmare and it is hardly his fault in wanting to pick up the half-eaten burgers and chips. Why cannot people use the litter-bins provided and the population as a whole take more pride in their towns and countryside? We need to bring back a "Keep Britain Tidy" campaign, like we had in the 1960's. (RANT 25)

The historic half-timber Tudor buildings are well preserved and maintained, but like most of the other buildings around the Quayside in Newcastle, are now mainly eating and drinking establishments. It appears that Newcastle has over recent years become a mecca and favourite destination for stag and hen parties. I have my own opinions over this change, and perhaps as an "oldie" they reflect those of my own generation. But I remember the Newcastle I grew up in with its individual shops and traditional pubs. It is a steep climb from the Quayside, back up Dean Street and the Side, past the house where Admiral Collingwood was born in 1761, to the Cathedral. From here, it is only a short walk back to the railway station, where we are to catch the train to Berwick.

We are back on the train, which is the "Cross-Country" train from Birmingham to Aberdeen. With one change at Birmingham, you can travel the 700 mile route from Penzance up to Aberdeen across the country and avoiding London. That must be some journey. By chance, I managed to find a seat in the "quiet coach" although typically there is a passenger that has just started up a conversion on his mobile phone. Can't you read the sign dumb-head! Fortunately, the train guard is on hand and gives the offending passenger a bit of a rollicking—quite rightly too.

We are heading north non-stop to Berwick, through Morpeth and then with the beautiful Northumberland coastline passing by on our right. After approximately 40 minutes, we are crossing the River Tweed with the two road bridges on the right and into the historic Town of Berwick-upon-Tweed. On getting off the train, my first act is to find the B&B that I had booked. This is at Miranda's Guest House in Church Street, near to the Town centre. Here I am welcomed by Robin, "mein host", and able to dump my kit.

My potted guide to Berwick has already been given in Part 2, which was the termination point of my trip from Lands End in August the previous year. So I am not going to be repeating what has already been written on Berwick.

I need to phone home to my wife Florence to let her know of my whereabouts. On getting out my mobile I find that my phone has been barred from making out-going calls, by my mobile phone company. A couple of weeks prior to leaving, I had experienced problems of overcharging, which the company had accepted was their mistake—computers get blamed for everything. The appropriate adjustments and measures were put in place, or at least that is what I had been told. Not able to use my mobile phone, I have to resort to using the coin-operated public phone and to ask Florence to sort out the problem. It subsequently transpires that the agreed arrangements had not got through to the company's computer and as a result, a bar had been put on my phone until such time as the original amount had been paid. This I am reluctant to do but without all the details of my account with me, I am "over a barrel". It is not until I reach Inverness where I am able to get the assistance at the local O2 shop, that I eventually get the bar lifted. Fortunately, for the time being at least, I am able to receive incoming calls. Modern technology is fine when everything works and computers are programmed to take the correct instructions, although the problems encountered usually come down to human error. It seems that these days we have become far too reliant on computers and have lost the mental ability to use our brains in certain everyday issues (RANT 26).

After taking Archie for a walk around the Town walls and across the Tweed bridges into Tweedmouth and back, I bed him down for the night and go out in search of both solid and liquid refreshment. Being a Saturday, most places are busy, but eventually, I find a hostelry that suits my needs. Then to bed, looking forward to tomorrow and the first stage of our bus journey up through Scotland.

Chapter 2
Berwick-Upon-Tweed To Edinburgh—Day 11.

Sunday 26th April 2009

After a reasonable night's sleep, I am woken at first light by the loud constant screech of the local seagulls. Thankfully, we are here only for one night. I suppose the locals must be used to their noise.

Being a Sunday, the bus service out of Berwick is operating to a Sunday timetable, with the first bus leaving at 07.55 hours to be followed by the next some four hours later. Too early to be served breakfast, Robin has kindly put me up a take-away brunch which is waiting to be collected—I was very grateful to him for taking the trouble.

At this time of the morning on a Sunday, there is no-one else about and I am the only person waiting at the bus stop from which the Edinburgh bus departs. Nor are there any other dogs waiting to board. I am beginning to wonder whether I have got the right time and place, so it is therefore with some relief that I see the Perryman's bus appear from around the corner with "Edinburgh" displayed as its destination.

My next destination is to be Dunbar, approximately one and a quarter hours bus ride from Berwick, where I planned to make a stop before journeying on to Edinburgh. Berwick is of course, in England with the Scottish border being a few miles to the north. I did wonder whether by showing my English bus pass to the bus driver, I might be allowed a concessionary trip, say at least up to the border, if not further. On showing my pass to the driver, his reply is "nice try" and I have to pay the full single fare to Dunbar. So much for free bus travel the length and breadth of England, although this is perhaps being a bit pedantic.

After picking up a few more passengers, the bus heads out of Berwick northwards on the A1 trunk-road. A strange looking guy gets on the bus and sits on the back seat on the opposite side to me. Looks like he has been sleeping rough, but at least he keeps to himself. After two miles, we cross the English / Scottish border with the flags of St Andrew flying on our left and those of St George on our right for traffic travelling in the opposite direction. We are now in Scotland, the land of the heather, lochs and glens, not to mention the haggis and of course whisky. Many famous people have come from Scotland, including some eminent engineers and scientists. For a country of its size, I guess that the Scots has made a large contribution to modern-day civilisation.

On up the A1 we travel through Berwickshire, following the scenic coastline to Burnmouth, with Archie taking in the views of the sea from the backseat window of the bus. The scenery is enhanced by the fresh Spring greenery of the trees and the bright yellow of the gorse bushes. We then take a deviation off onto the A1107 into the picturesque fishing port and holiday resort of **Eyemouth,** (population 3,400) with its natural harbour at the mouth of Eye Water. During the 17th and 18th centuries, smuggling contraband goods was rife along this coastline, being relatively close to mainland Europe. However, a disaster occurred in 1881 when during a severe storm, 189 fishermen were drowned trying to reach the harbour entrance. It is in July of each year, that they hold the Herring Queen Festival—a well advertised and popular event, although I would have thought it a bit of a dubious title to be known as the "Herring Queen". Unfortunately the bus did not journey down to the harbour.

Next along the coast to Coldingham and **St Abbs**, named after the Northumbian Princess St Aebbe who founded the nearby monastery. It is a popular scuba diving centre with an offshore natural underwater marine reserve. I am tempted to get off the bus here and explore the rugged coastline up to St Abb's Head, with the red sandstone cliffs rising to 300 feet above the sea that provide nesting ledges for numerous seabirds. Unfortunately, the Sunday timetable does not allow this to be fitted into my schedule, although with a heavy rucksack and dodgy knees, it is probably for the best.

Out of St Abbs and up the B6438 into the village of Reeston and back along the A1 following the main east coast railway line to Grantshouse, Cockburnspath and into East Lothian. A little further on sited on, the edge of the coast, is the Torness Nuclear Power Station (commissioned in 1988)—then on towards Dunbar.

On approaching Dunbar, there are the signposts for Spott, which was the site of the first battle of Dunbar in 1296 when Edward I of England defeated the Scots army in the early stages of the Wars of Independence. The second Battle of Dunbar in 1650 took place near Doon Hill. It was here that Cromwell's English Parliamentarian troops inflicted a surprise defeat upon the larger Scottish Covenanter army that was loyal to the Stuart King Charles II and who had been proclaimed King of Scotland the previous year.

We arrive in the fishing port of Dunbar after an hour and a quarter bus trip from Berwick. At Dunbar I plan a two hour plus break, so to allow for a quick look around the Town and give Archie some exercise.

Dunbar—East Lothian—7,700 population—former Royal Burgh (1532)

Getting off the bus in the High Street by the whitewashed 17thC Tolbooth House with its steepled octagonal tower (now the Tourist Information Office), we walk past the house where Dunbar's illustrious son, John Muir was born in 1838. John Muir emigrated to the USA at a young age and was an eminent botanist, geologist, engineer and writer. With the help of President "Teddy" Roosevelt, he was responsible for the setting up of one of the first national parks of America, Yosemite in California.

At the top of the High Street, is the impressive red sandstone Lauderdale House, which was built in the 18thC by the Earl of Lauderdale. Turning eastwards and following the signs for the harbour, the road leads to a grassy headland that overlooks the New Harbour (built in 1842). Also, the ruins of the medieval castle, strategically sited on the craggy headland at the southern end of Belhaven Bay. The first castle was constructed in the local red sandstone during the 11thC and was in use until the 16thC, before being slighted (deliberately ruined). Catches of fish are still landed at the New (Victoria) Harbour, although there has been a significant reduction in the number of fishing boats from former years. A RNLI lifeboat station based in the New Harbour is still operational; it is the second oldest in Scotland.

From the grassy headland above Belhaven Bay, the **Bass Rock** can be seen on the horizon some 7 miles to the north. This is best viewed from North Berwick further up the coast. The Bass Rock is a volcanic plug (igneous intrusion) rising near vertical some 350 feet above sea level. Its surface area covers approximately seven acres and in the past has served as a monastic retreat, fortress and prison, one of the prisoners being John Blackadder of the Covenanting martyrs. A lighthouse was constructed under the supervision of David Stevenson in 1902 and is still functional, albeit unmanned. The island which is now uninhabited, is an SSSI (Site of Special Scientific Interest), housing the world's largest single gannetry, with an estimated 150,000 gannets on the Rock. Sir David Attenborough has described the Rock as "one of the wildlife wonders of the world", and he should know. From the coastline the Rock appears as a white blob on the horizon, which is a result of years of droppings by the gannets and the other sea birds. The Rock also figures in Robert Louis Stevenson's (cousin of David, the lighthouse builder) novel *Catriona* and also in Bruce Marshall's novel *Father Malachy's Miracle*. An interesting, but for most days of the year, an inaccessible place, with the heavy sea swell restricting any landing by boat.

Having spent a little while taking in the views from the headland and eating some of my brunch under the bright blue skies of Dunbar, I stroll down to the New Harbour that is now used principally as a marina. Then on towards the Old (Cromwellian) Harbour constructed in 1650 with its cobbled quaysides. At the southern end, there is a painted stone metrological station with the inscription "Presented to the Fishermen of Dunbar to whose perilous industry the Burgh owes so much of its prosperity". It is dated 1856 and above the barometer is an alabaster carving of a fisherman saying goodbye to his wife and children as he boards his fishing boat. It is a very fitting memorial to the fishermen of Dunbar that, sadly, has been seriously neglected in recent years. I suggest that a bit of TLC is required by the Town Council.

We walk on towards the sandy beach and rocky outcrops, to the south of the Old Harbour. The tide is out, so Archie enjoys himself splashing about in the rock pools and racing into the sea. He likes burrowing into the sand and excavating long trenches so to bury his ball. He is soon at work like a young child, with sand flying out behind him.

Soon it will be time to catch the bus for Edinburgh, so up we climb from the beach to the tall red sandstone kirk overlooking the sea front. Being that time on a Sunday morning, the congregation were assembling for Sunday morning worship. Then on we walk, along Queen's Road, back onto the High Street where at the southern end is the old Parish Church, now closed (hopefully only temporarily) following a fire. Time for a coffee and a muffin before the No.6 bus to Edinburgh arrives.

One of Dunbar's other claims to fame is that up to 2005, the local brewery, Belhaven Brewery (established 1719), was the oldest and only surviving independent brewery in Scotland. It has since been taken over by the Suffolk brewers, Greene King, but I am informed that with the recent closure of a number of other Scottish breweries, it is now the only traditional brewery (i.e. other than micro-breweries) left in Scotland. It is hard to believe that the Scots have to import the bulk of their beer from outside their own country. However I do recommend the Belhaven Best, a smooth honey coloured pale ale with a 3.5% alcohol content.

* * * * * * *

On the dot of 11.30, the No.6 Edinburgh bus arrives. From the outside, it appeared to have all the windows painted over with adverts, but from the inside at least, the passengers could see out. Asking for a single fare to Edinburgh, I am told that the cost is £4.10. It was a bus fitted with a coin slot receiver with which I am not familiar. So in went five one pound coins, only then to be told by the driver that no change is given—?*?*$*!! or words to that effect. Maybe there is a sign, but watching me put in the last one pound coin, I do think that the driver could have warned me—maybe it is because I am English or am I being unreasonable? (RANT 27). It so happens that I do have a 50p coin in my pocket and could have reduced my losses to 40p instead of 90p.

Then it is out of Dunbar, onto the A1 and into East Linton with its row of old almhouses. The bus travels on over the River Tyne (not where the Geordies live) and then after a short distance we make a deviation into the market town and former Royal Burgh of **Haddington** (population 8,800). A former mill town, it is now the administrative centre for East Lothian. It was in Nungate, on the opposite side of the River Tyne to Haddington, that John Knox, the great Protestant reformer, was born in 1505. There are many fine buildings in the Town, including some 18thC town houses, constructed in yellow / grey sandstone, all a testimony to its former prosperity, with few brick buildings.

Out of Haddington along the A199 to Macmerry (sounds a jolly place), Tranent and Wallyford. It is here heading south along the main east coast railway line, that we see a steam train in its green livery pulling 8 coaches, the engine being of a similar design and class to the Flying Scotsman. Maybe it was the Flying Scotsman steam locomotive itself, which from my train spotting days I recall being of the A3 Pacific Class, built 1923 and designed by Sir Nigel Gresley for the LNER Company (No.4472 subsequently changed to No.60103 in the 1950's—some further useless data unless you are a steam train nerd). I must admit though, to being very pleased to seeing some of our industrial heritage being preserved and still operational. Hats off to all those enthusiasts who give up their time to ensure that our industrial past is preserved for future generations to see and appreciate. During the 1960's and 1970's, much was scrapped and demolished with little thought given to preservation—perhaps during these times there was not the same interest or enthusiasm. We need more characters like the late Fred Dibnah to keep interest alive in the saving of our industrial heritage, not just engineering machinery but buildings too. Let us be proud of our past achievements in which Britain was once known as the "Workshop of the World" and "Made in Britain" was a seal of good quality—Rule Britannia!! (RANT 28)

Back to my bus trip with Archie. At this point, I must make the comment that this particular bus journey is not one of the most comfortable, in fact it turns out to be perhaps the most uncomfortable of all the bus journeys that I was to experience on my Scottish trip. The bus suspension is suspect, the engine noisy, with the seats and upholstery worn and dirty. The vehicle has certainly seen better days. This is not helped by a teenager who is sitting in front of me, having his feet stretched out and his scruffy trainers parked on the seat facing him. Heaven only knows what he had been treading in. Why are people so lacking in consideration to others? I wish that I had the courage to say something to him. As many would say, "they would not do it in their own homes"—or perhaps they might!! (RANT 29)

On we travelled through **Musselburgh** (population 22,000). Situated at the mouth of the River Esk, Musselburgh is said to be the oldest town in Scotland, being settled by the Romans back in 80AD. The 16thC tollbooth dominates in the centre of the High Street. Musselburgh is the largest town in East Lothian—it also has its own racecourse.

Since leaving Dunbar, the skies have turned grey, a bit like the town of Musselburgh itself with its drab housing estates through which the bus deviates. Why did planners and local councils in the past condemn their tenants to live in such unattractive houses all to the same unimaginative design? For a little extra money, the external design of these plain, very ordinary houses could easily have been made more pleasing to the eye. Although folk might have been unable to afford to take out mortgages to buy their own homes, they still had to pay rent and deserved more. I know that there was a housing shortage in the 1950's and families were grateful for their own home, but surely? The immediate post war period is not known for its architectural excellence and unfortunately, it is a legacy that we now have to live with, not just in Musselburgh, but at many places elsewhere in the UK (RANT 30). At least the flowers planted along the banks of the River Esk give some colour to the Town, especially the yellow splash of daffodils.

The bus route then follows the coastline of the Firth of Forth with open views across to Fife. Soon Portobello (an unlikely Scottish name) we reach with its own beach and promenade and very much up-market housing where some of the more wealthy business folk of Edinburgh obviously reside. Then into the City proper, passing the large Meadowbank Sports Stadium that was used in 1970 and 1986 to host the Commonwealth Games. The Stadium's capacity is 16,500 and has proven too large for present-day requirements. After much controversy, the current proposal is to relocate and to demolish the existing stadium so to allow for the construction of high-density housing on the available land—hopefully to an acceptable architectural design and layout. On along London Road past the terraces of some fine four storey Georgian / Regency stone houses, arriving at St Andrew's Square in the City Centre at 13.20.

Edinburgh—Capital City of Scotland—472,000 population

The Scottish Gaelic name for Edinburgh is *Dun Eideann* or *Din Eidyn* that means "Edwin's Fort" after the 7thC King of Northumbria. The name gradually developed through the English language into Edwinesburch and then Edinburgh. It is also known as the *Athens of the North* due to the design of some of its buildings and the City being a major centre of learning and culture. More down-to-earth, it is also referred to as *Auld Reekie* due to the polluted smoky atmosphere in past years, now, thankfully, long gone. It has been Scotland's capital since 1437 and is the Country's second largest city after Glasgow. Edinburgh was listed as a UNESCO World Heritage Site in 1995, with its many historic buildings and monuments.

Over the years, there have been numerous books, guides and other sources of information written on the history and culture of the City, including the castle, palaces, churches, museums, monuments and the many other buildings of interest. Also of the City's parks, gardens and zoo including its unique landscape and geology. Outside of London, it is perhaps the most visited city in the UK and attracts large numbers of visitors from all over the world, not least during the period in August of the annual Edinburgh Internal Festival, which includes the Military Tattoo and the Edinburgh Fringe.

To give a potted history of Edinburgh, as I have done with other places visited on my travels, would not do justice to Edinburgh and all that there is to see and do in the City. I therefore propose only to describe my wanderings and ramblings whilst walking around the City Centre and Royal Mile during my brief stop. My wanderings are in any event, curtailed by the fact that I have Archie in tow and am unable to take him inside the many buildings of interest we walk past. So, here goes.

Thankful to be off the bus, which as previously said, was not the most comfortable of bus rides, I make my way into the centre of St Andrew's Square to sit down to eat the rest of my brunch Robin had made up for me, and to plan out my time in Edinburgh. Being a Sunday, there are a lot of people about enjoying the Gardens, but nevertheless, I find somewhere to sit. I have booked into a hotel in Leopold Place, which is on London Road, along which our bus has just travelled a few minutes earlier. However, the earliest booking-in-time is 14.00, so I have some two hours plus to fill in before I can deposit my kit at the hotel.

St Andrew's Square is at the eastern end of George Street with Charlotte Square being at the western end. The elegant Georgian houses, most of which are now banks and commercial offices, were constructed during the late 1700's to the design of the young architect, James Craig and formed the development of what is known as the New Town. The pattern created by the street layout, which includes the area between Princes Street and Queens Street, was planned to resemble the Union Flag. The New Town contains what many today consider to be the finest examples of Georgian architecture in the world, which I can well understand. The official residence of Scotland's First Minister, is in Charlotte Square.

From St Andrew's Square it is a short walk down to Princes Street, the main shopping area for tourists in the City. Unbelievably, virtually the whole length of Princes Street is closed to traffic due to roadworks, which I subsequently find out is for the laying of a new tramway system—also new water and gas mains. With the original tram-tracks having been removed in the 1950's, it is amazing how events turn full circle. Normally, Princes Street is very congested with traffic but somehow, the buses, taxis and cars seemed to be coping—may be a case for the future pedestrianisation of the area? The first phase of the new tramway system is from Leith to Edinburgh Airport, the cost being £512M. Forgive me for saying this, but you could have a fleet of taxis standing by on a permanent basis to ferry the folk of Leith to the airport, for substantially less than half a billion quid!! But maybe it needs to be seen from an environmental viewpoint.

Walking between the fenced off roadworks (it was good to note that the contractors were working on a Sunday, in what I would assume to be to minimise disruption), I enter the sunken gardens that run the length of Princes Street. The Gardens, as I understand, were begun in 1816 on bogland that had once been the Nor Loch that had earlier been drained. Some 250 feet above us, stands the Castle, which is perched on top of the extinct volcanic basaltic plug from some 450 million years ago. The Castle is the symbol of Edinburgh and has been of great importance throughout its history.

In the western section of the Gardens, there is the floral clock, composed of about 20,000 plants. The Winter Floral Clock for 2008/2009, is, according to the plaque, dedicated to the "250th Anniversary of the birth of our national poet and cultural icon Robert Burns—born 25th January 1759, died 21st July 1796". Burns was only 40 year old when he died, but he had a full and "interesting" life, leaving a lasting legacy not just for Scotland, but for the rest of the World. Remember him when you sing *Auld Lang Syne* at New Year, or rather Hogmanay. Burns of course, spent most of his life in Aryshire and Dumfrieshire in the south east of Scotland, part of it, surprisingly employed as an excise man.

We are now walking eastwards, between the Royal Scottish Academy and the National Gallery of Scotland, the latter housing a large number of paintings by famous artists worldwide and then on towards the Scott Monument. Nicknamed the "Gothic Rocket", the monument with its neo-gothic spire was erected in the 1840's following the death of Sir Walter Scott and is one of Edinburgh's most famous landmarks. It was designed by a joiner / draughtsman called George Kemp and is 200 feet tall with 287 step to reach the topmost viewing platform. There is a marble statue of Scott under the canopy of the central arch, together with 64 statuettes of characters from his various novels, housed in niches within the monument itself. Even if I had not had Archie with me, I don't think I would have made it up the narrow stairways inside the monument. Instead, as the sun is again out, I sit on one of the many benches and enjoy the view and watching people walk by. At least three different people stop to make a fuss of Archie, to which he unashamably responds by sitting up with his forelegs in the air waiting for a tit-bit—show off!! Perhaps if I had a tin, I might be able to make a bob or two.

On consulting the street plan, I set off down Leith Street to Picardy Place, then a short walk along London Road, past all the fine Georgian terrace houses I had seen earlier from the bus, to my overnight accommodation at the Richmond Hotel on Leopold Place. I had warned them previously that I would be bringing a small (well behaved) dog with me to which they had responded saying that they looked forward to seeing me and "my canine friend". I am met by friendly staff and shown to my room that thankfully, is on the ground floor, this being well furnished, clean and comfortable. Being able to deposit my rucksack and freshen-up, we set off to explore more the sights of Edinburgh City.

I have been to Edinburgh many times in the past, especially when I lived on Tyneside, being only just over two hours drive away—depending on how fast you drove. Many of my trips were to the Scotland v England rugby internationals at Murrayfield. In those days, it was mainly standing with never any problems between the rival fans. All good friendly banter. Perhaps my most memorable moment from those internationals (and there were a few) was when in March 1980, England defeated Scotland to win the Calcutta Cup, Triple Crown and Grand Slam under the captaincy of the great Billy Beaumont. The score was 30-18 with new boy John Carleton scoring three tries. What a team England had at that time. Rose Street in the City centre was swarming with English supporters that night. However, I digress.

One place that I had never visited on my previous visits, was Carlton Hill that overlooks the eastern end of Princes Street. My hotel being located immediately below the Hill, off Archie and I go up through the park opposite and over the Royal Terrace, appropriately named with its stately Regency houses built from the local stone. On up we walk, thankful that I had been able to drop off my kit at the hotel, until eventually we reach the top. The views from the top are magnificent, especially on a fine day as it was on that Sunday in April. The view was recently short-listed as one of the best views in Britain.

Looking southwards are the crags of Arthur's Seat, formed from the vents of a former volcano. At this time of year the banks are partially covered in bright yellow gorse. Immediately below Arthur's Seat is the Palace of Holyrood, the Queen's residence when she is in Edinburgh. It was also used by Bonnie Prince Charlie as his headquarters prior to his defeat at Culloden in 1746. The present Palace was built during the 17thC in the Palladian style and is a masterpiece of elegance. Adjoining the Palace, is the 12th/13thC Abbey, now in ruins. A little further to the west, can be seen the new Scottish Parliament Building, completed in 2004 (following a big over-spend) and housing the Country's 129 MSPs. The design of the building is said to be innovative and to resemble an upturned boat, using traditional materials. However, I have not been up close to the place and from the top of Carlton Hill, I would not want to comment on its design and or its appearance.

Turning around now to look northwards is the Firth of Forth, with its waters gleaming in the afternoon sunshine. The view is towards the Port of Leith and out over the Firth to Fife. The Forth Road and Railway Bridges are too far upstream to be clearly distinguished. To the west is Princes Street with the clock-tower of the old North British Hotel in the foreground and the Castle set high on the crags behind. All well worth the short climb to the top of Carlton Hill.

When we (that is Archie and myself) were walking up the Hill, we could hear the continuous thumping of drums. There was no skirling of the pipes, so it was unlikely to be a pipe band. It was only when we reached the top that I observe a large gathering of people performing what it seemed some sort of pagan ceremony. Intrigued, I see a number of the participants dancing some form of ritual and carrying on high around in a circle, one of their own stretched out prostrate. For the uninitiated such as myself, it seems to be a bit bizarre. It was some days later when I bought a newspaper, that I saw a photograph of the Beltane Fire Festival that was held on the 31st April (some five days later) on Carlton Hill and involved some 300 performers celebrating the end of winter. Maybe what I had witnessed was participants practicing for the event.

Sited at the top of Carlton Hill, is Scotland's unfinished National Monument, also known as "Edinburgh's Disgrace". It is a 12 column portico modelled on the Parthenon in Athens to commemorate the Scots who were killed during the Napoleonic Wars. Unfortunately, funds ran out during the mid 1820's before it could be finished and it has been left in its present state for the past near 200 years. Proposals to complete the Monument have met with mixed receptions over the years. Also on the summit, is the 106 feet tall tiered circular tower dedicated to Lord Horatio Nelson, victor of Trafalgar in 1805. At this time, the Tower is being renovated and is covered in scaffolding and sheeting and so, out of sight.

Down the steep steps of Carlton Hill to Waterloo Place and then up North Street over the railway bridge, to High Street which is better known as the Royal Mile. There is a substantial gradient down the High

Street from west (the Castle) to east (Holyrood Palace). This is a result of glacial action, with the glacial deposits being laid down (known as the tail) as the glacier travelled eastwards over the basaltic plug of Castle Rock.

On the corner is the Tron Kirk with its tall spire and the traditional assembly point for Hogmanay revellers. We now turn westwards and walk uphill passed the old Royal Exchange on one side and St Giles Cathedral on the other. The present Cathedral dates from the 15thC and the exterior is distinctive by its square tower with the delicate eight arched crown spire that dominates the Edinburgh skyline. The Cathedral has seen many troubled times during its history, not least during the period of the Reformation in 16th Century, when there was a change from Catholicism to Protestantism. During this period, many of the precious relics were swept away. It is known as the High Kirk of Edinburgh and the Mother Church of Presbyterianism. Strictly speaking, it cannot be called a cathedral as the Church of Scotland has no bishops. The High Kirk contains the Chapel of the Order of the Thistle, Scotland's chivalric Company of Knights headed by the Queen.

Immediately outside the Cathedral in the middle of the High Street itself, a crowd has gathered to watch a street performer doing his act. He is wearing a kilt but is bare-chested, exposing his arms and chest that are covered in tattoos. I am not sure what his act is as I do not want to stop and watch. I like to think that I am fairly broad-minded and at another time in a different place, his act may well have been worth watching. But we are supposed to be a Christian society with standards and morals to match, at least that is what I believe most of us set for ourselves. For this bare-chested tattooed guy to be performing on a Sunday afternoon immediately outside the High Kirk of Edinburgh was in my mind disgraceful. I am not an advocate of the Lord's Sunday Observance Society, but even in today's lax society, this is an offence to my own and I am sure many others' moral standards and I cannot understand why the City Authorities apparently allow it to happen (RANT 31).

Pressing on up the Royal Mile with Archie still in tow (I'm not sure if he is enjoying this) we pass many eating and drinking establishments. It is a problem keeping him from picking up discarded food on the pavements. Perhaps one of the best known hostelries is Deacon Brodie's Tavern, established in 1806 and named after one of Edinburgh's more infamous characters. Deacon William Brodie was a respected citizen of the City being a cabinet maker and locksmith during the mid 18thC.

However he lead a double life of crime in that he made duplicates of the keys he cut for clients and used them to burgle their homes. Eventually he was caught and hanged in 1788 after trying to bribe the hangman. His story inspired Robert Louis Stevenson to write his novel *The Strange Case of Dr Jekyll and Mr Hyde*. The ale sold there is quite good too.

To the left and down George IV Bridge, there is the Greyfriars Kirk and Kirkyard that date back to 16th century. Many of Edinburgh's past dignitaries are buried here and the graveyard contains some elaborate memorials and headstones. One of the memorials is to the Covenant Martyrs of Edinburgh erected in 1706 to "about an hundred of Noble Gentlemen Ministers and other noble martyrs" who died for their religious beliefs. There is also the gravestone to "Greyfriars Bobby", the faithful Skye terrier dog that maintained a continuous vigil by his master's grave for some 14 years before its own death in 1872.

On up the Royal Mile past more touristy-type shops and eating places, on to the Scotch Whisky Heritage Centre at the top. Unfortunately, Archie is not allowed inside which I guess is fair enough although I would like to have made a call, having an interest in the subject. We are now at the Castle Esplanade, laid out in 1753 and where the Military Tattoos are held in August of each year. It is many years since I was last at a Tattoo, which is quite a spectacle. I gather that these days you have to book well in advance if you require a seat. Participating bands come from all over the world and perform their music on a variety of different instruments. At the end of the evening, the massed pipes and bands are followed by a lone piper way above on the Half Moon Battery playing a lament to fallen comrades—a very moving experience.

At the far end of the spacious parade ground is the Gatehouse leading into the Castle itself. On the north side of the Esplanade is a statue to General Haig of First World War fame. Some two years previous, I visited the Fields of Flanders in Belgium, walked around the British and Commonwealth cemeteries and learnt of the ineptitude of the Generals in charge that resulted in thousands of our young soldiers being sent to their unnecessary deaths. I therefore ask the question why we still revere such individuals and I can think of many other statues that have been taken down in recent years, especially in Eastern Europe since perestroika. At least Haig's statue is hidden behind scaffolding.

There has been a Royal Castle on the site since the 12thC with many changes over the centuries. Few of the present buildings within the Castle walls pre-date the 15thC except for St Margaret's Chapel that dates from the 12thC and is the oldest building in Edinburgh. Among the other buildings are the Royal Palace and the 15thC Great Hall, together with buildings housing the Scottish National War Memorial and War Museum. The entrance to the Castle, or Gatehouse, was constructed in 1888 more as a cosmetic addition and is flanked on either side by two of Scotland's national heroes, Robert the Bruce and William Wallace. The Portcullis Gate a little further in, was constructed in the 16thC following the Lang Siege (1571-1573) and was the Castle's front line defence.

At 1300 hours precisely, the One O'Clock Gun is fired, this first being enacted in 1861 as a time signal for the ships anchored in the Firth of Forth. The Castle was used as a garrison up 1923 when the Army moved out to alternative barracks in the City. It is now under the control of Historic Scotland and in 2008, was Scotland's second-most-visited tourist attraction. This is after the Kelvingrove Art Gallery and Museum in Glasgow, the Falkirk Wheel being a close third behind Edinburgh Castle.

I have been around the Castle on numerous occasions in the past and it is well worth a visit, as the numbers of visitor each year testify. However, because of time and having Archie in tow, we make our way off the Castle Esplanade, down the narrow Ramsay Lane and passed the tall interesting old houses to the top of The Mound. The National Gallery and Royal Academy buildings are both built on top of The Mound that was created as a result of spoil from the development of the New Town. This links the Old Town of the area around the Royal Mile with the New Town of Princes Street and George Street across what was formerly the depression occupied by the Nor Loch.

We then descend down the steep stone stairs by the National Gallery to the eastern end of Princes Street Gardens. From the bridge over the railway that tunnels under The Mound, there is a good view of Waverley Station. Time for an ice cream, though at £2.00 for a simple cornet, it is a bit expensive. Still, it is nice to be able to sit down in the Gardens, relax and enjoy the sunshine. More people wanting to pat Archie and are asking what breed he is. Comments such as he looks like Basil Brush or an Alsatian with short legs, are now getting a bit wearing. There are now a lot of tourists about and the place is getting quite congested, especially with Princes Street being closed—although I should remember that we too are tourists and part of the general melee.

It is now just after 17.00 and I have just missed by a few minutes, the closing for the day of the Tourist Information Office at the new complex off Waverley Bridge. Why you might ask do I want to call in at the Tourist Office at this late stage of my visit? Because I have an addiction to picking up free leaflets and pamphlets that one day might be of use!! Not today in Edinburgh. So off back along Princes Street past the Scottish Records Office Building with its portico frontage and statue of the Duke of Wellington outside. Down Leith Street, first stopping for a pint of the amber nectar at the Aussie Walkabout, and then along London Road, back to the Richmond Hotel.

Being tired and exhausted with all the walking around the City, I take time out for a rest at the hotel. Switching on the TV, the news is soon on. The big news item of the day is the spread of swine fever / flu from Mexico and the USA that was being predicted to reach pandemic levels across the world. To date, 100 plus people have died of the disease in Mexico and there are reports of cases in the UK and Scotland in particular. Urgent measures are being made to combat the potential outbreak, which thankfully has not at that time materialised. Also in the news is that Jensen Button in his Braun GP had won the Bahrain Formula One Grand Prix, which followed wins in the previous two races. What a start for the season for him and the newly formed Braun GP team that is based in Brackley, Northants, that we passed through on the English section of our trip. Finally, the London Marathon had taken place earlier in the day with a record time of 2 hours, 5 minutes and 10 seconds achieved by the winner.

Archie seems to be exhausted too and is soon curled up on his blanket. After feeling more revived, I set out in search of some much needed refreshment, both solid and liquid, there being plenty of suitable establishments in the near neighbourhood. I do not have far to go and am not to be disappointed.

Chapter 3
Edinburgh To Dundee—Day 12.

Monday 27th April 2009

I am up reasonably early to take Archie for his walk in the park across from our hotel. The day doesn't look too bright with light rain falling—the weather forecast had not been too good so maybe they have got it right. At the hotel, continental breakfast is served which turns out to be substantially more than the average continental breakfast provided at many hotels. This will see me through the best part of the day.

With a packed kit, we make our way back to the Bus Station off St Andrew's Square, the main bus terminus in Edinburgh. The entrance into the bus station from St Andrew's Street is not readily seen with the station itself hidden behind the buildings. However as bus stations go, it is well laid out and passenger friendly. The bus that we will be leaving on is the Stagecoach No.X54 bus to Dundee, departing at 10.10. I have decided to visit Dunfermline on the other side of the Forth, so we will not be travelling the whole way.

After a short wait, the X54 bus arrives, which turns out to be a long distance coach with all the usual comforts. The single fare for the 50 minute journey is £4.90, which is more than I expect, especially as the bridge tolls had been abolished for the Forth crossing the previous year. Off we set, first along George Street, lined with its stately buildings and then onto Queensferry Road that also has some very desirable dwellings along its length. Then out of the urban area of Edinburgh, along the A90 to Queensferry itself and onto the Forth Road Bridge.

On crossing over the Firth, the **Forth Rail Bridge** can be seen on the right. Known by the rail authorities as simply "The Bridge" without an identification number, the railway bridge is an internationally recognised landmark of Scotland and was the first major structure in Britain to be constructed wholly from steel. The design is based on the principle of cantilevers, with the longest span being 1,710 feet. The three trapezoidal lattice-work towers reach a height of 340 feet, with the total length of the Bridge being 8,296 feet. Fifty five thousand tons of steel was used in its construction together with eight million rivets. Sadly 75 men lost their lives in the construction of the Bridge, Health and Safety being a low priority in those times. The Bridge was opened by the then Prince of Wales, in 1890 who drove home the last rivet, gold plated of course. The term "Painting the Forth Bridge" frequently used to denote a never-ending task, is incorrect for such a working practice never existed on the continually painting of the Bridge. It has, however, a crew of workmen permanently employed on its maintenance and a recent report gave the Bridge an estimated life of another 100 years, at least.

The bus is of course, crossing over on the much newer **Forth Road Bridge**, opened by the Queen in 1964. The design principle is that of a suspension bridge, with a span between the two towers of 3,298 feet, at the time the longest outside the USA. The two 512 ft high concrete towers support the two suspension cables carrying the road deck, some 200 feet above the waters of the Firth. Recent inspections of these cables have revealed corrosion is taking place and that the cables have lost up to 10% of their strength. By 2019, a new bridge crossing will be necessary. An extensive programme of dehumidification is being installed to slow down the rate of corrosion of the cable strands. However, with increasing traffic levels, a new road bridge across the Forth is required and design has already started upon a new three towered cable stayed bridge that is to be sited immediately upstream of the existing road bridge. At an estimated cost of £2,300M, construction of the new bridge is due to be completed during 2016. It is perhaps of interest to note that the same civil engineering contractor, Sir William Arrol & Co Ltd, was employed both upon the construction of the present Road Bridge as was some 70 years previous, upon that of the Railway Bridge immediately downstream. Up to 2008, tolls were levied for crossing the Forth Road Bridge but have since been scrapped by the Scottish Parliament.

On over the Bridge our bus travels, with fine views looking up the Firth albeit the skies are looking a bit grey, into the Kingdom of Fife and the naval dockyard town of **Rosyth** (population 13,000). In the early 1900's, Rosythe was developed as a garden city and port for Dunfermline. With the build-up of the German naval fleet prior to WW1, the naval dockyards were established in 1909 and were a key naval base during both World Wars and were used for breaking up the German Fleet following its surrender at Scarpa Flow in 1918. In more recent times, the dockyards have been used to refit the nuclear submarines—that is until 2003 when this work was transferred to Devonport near Plymouth.

Although the naval base was closed in 1994, the privately run dockyards are still in use to fit-out and service the Navy's surface vessels, with the new Queen Elizabeth Class aircraft carriers due to be assembled at Rosythe.

After the detour into Rosyth, the bus journeys along the B980 and reaches the bus station in Dunfermline at 11.00.

Dunfermline—Fife—45,000 population—former Royal Burgh (1153)

My first impression of the Town, or rather City, is that it is larger than I had first expected. Prior to 1437, it was the Capital of Scotland with its history going back before 1,000 AD. It was in Dunfermline where the much sought after damask linen and silk was woven. The mills that housed the hundreds of clattering looms are now all closed, with many of the buildings having been converted into offices or up-market apartments.

Having orientated myself as to which way to go, we set off in the drizzle, down Bruce Street past the tall City Chambers with its baronial style turrets, calling in at the Tourist Information Centre opposite. Here the staff are most helpful and provide me with a useful free guidebook to the City. Nearby, is the Abbey Church, monastic buildings and Royal Palace, the latter two now being ruins. It was back in 1996 that my nephew Andrew and his wife Nikki got married at the Abbey. It brings back memories.

The Abbey Church with its 12^{th}C Norman Nave, was rebuilt in 1820's to accommodate a growing congregation. The Abbey houses the tomb of Robert the Bruce (1274-1329), with many of the Scottish royals also buried at the Old Abbey. The circular arched Norman doorway is of particular interest. On a stone within the Abbey's crowded graveyard, there is a plaque commemorating the 158 citizens of Dunfermline that died in the cholera epidemic of 1832. Adjoining the graveyard are the red sandstone ruins of the 11^{th}C Monastic Buildings. Across the road are the ruins of the 13^{th}C Royal Palace where in 1600 King Charles I was born, the same King that was beheaded in London in 1649. Both buildings are now under the guardianship of Historic Scotland.

Across the road from the Abbey is Pittencrief Park, which was presented to the City in 1902 by Dunfermline's most famous son in modern times, Andrew Carnegie (1835-1919), the US steel baron and philanthropist. Carnegie was born in Dunfermline and left for the USA at an early age, never to forget his roots. The City has benefited handsomely from his many generous legacies. These included the library, public institutes, churches, colleges, sports facilities and not least, Pittencrief Park itself, which is now administered by the Cargenie Dunfermline Trust. Carnegie was know to say "To die rich was to die disgraced". His statue, erected by public subscription, stands in Pittencrief Park.

Within the Park are the ruins of Malcolm Canmore's Tower, built during the 11th century and depicted as the main emblem on the City's coat of arms. Malcolm III, known as Canmore (1058-1093), decided to make Dunfermline his capital. Perched on a high rock overlooking the Tower Burn, now only the base remains of the Tower. Malcolm was married to Margaret, later to become St Margaret due to her piety and devotion to the Catholic Church and for her involvement in the founding of the monastery at Dunfermline. The foundations marking her chapel are at the east end of the New Abbey.

Pittencrief Park is well worth a visit, with its ornate and formal gardens and the Tower Burn cutting a deep valley through the Park, known as the Glen. The wrought iron Louis Carnegie gates and the circular stone doocote (dovecote) are also worth seeing.

Off now back towards the City centre, the light rain having stopped. We walk past the City Chambers built in 1879 in the French Gothic baronial style with rounded turrets, and constructed in the local grey coloured sandstone. The tall fine steeple includes a clock face on each of the four sides, so to be seen from anywhere in the City. On up the pedestrianised High Street to the Old Guildhall, opposite which is the 17thC Mercat Cross with the unicorn sitting on its top. Here I am stopped by a female traffic warden and seemingly face interrogation—as to what breed my dog is, how old is he and what is his name. She is really very nice and makes quite a fuss of Archie—he seems to be getting used to it now.

* * * * * * *

On up we go, around the corner back to the bus station, to catch our next bus, the 12.05 to Glenrothes. After a short wait, the X54 Dundee bus shows up. I could have stayed on the bus all the way to Dundee, which crosses over the Tay Bridge. However, I want to visit Perth and also my lodgings for the night are at Longforgan, some five miles to the west of Dundee. This will mean travelling back on myself. So, I ask the driver for a single to Glenrothes, to be told the fare is £5.00—again more than

I had expected and no concessions for oldies, but at least Archie goes for free. Off we travel out of Dunfermline (which I have taken an liking to), past Dunfermline Athletic Football Club's ground at East End Park, to Crossgates and the dual carriageway of the A92. Then onto the New Town of Glenrothes.

Glenrothes—Fife—39,000 population—New Town

As we arrive in Glenrothes, the skies are grey and it is raining again. We have some 30 minutes to wait before our next bus to Perth, so there is little opportunity to look around, not from what I understand there is much to see. The coffee shop is out of bounds as I cannot leave Archie tethered to some post. So we are confined to wait a miserable half-an-hour in the glass bus shelter with the rain beating down, until such time as the Perth bus arrives. Perhaps unfairly, this wait in the bus shelter has coloured my impressions of Glenrothes, which are not great.

Glenrothes is one of the New Towns built immediately after the Second World War, to accommodate the local mining community following a number of pit closures in the area. When the new super-pit at Rothes Colliery opened in 1957, it was hoped that this would provide much needed employment for the Town. Unfortunately, due to geological problems, the coal mine closed some four years later.

The Town then became a centre for electronics and hi-tech industries and has since been established as the hub of Scotland's "Silicon Glen". It was also made the administrative centre for Fife, all of which helped with levels of local employment.

Glenrothes was unfortunate enough to receive the "Carbuncle Award" for 2009, as the most dismal town in Scotland, following a vote by the Scottish public. When the most notable landmarks for the Town are given as factory chimneys and railway viaducts, this hardly helps. My own observations from the bus would seem to verify this Award, although I think I have seen worse elsewhere in Scotland. You may remember that I made a "Rant" over what I felt was the unimaginative housing designs and layouts of the planning authorities in the immediate post-war years. One plus point however, was the colourful floral displays on the many roundabouts that all New Towns seem to be blessed with. I believe that the Town's parks have also won awards in the past.

* * * * * * *

Eventually, the No 36 Stagecoach double-decker bus to Perth arrives. Thankful to be aboard and on our way again, we leave Glenrothes at 13.15. Maybe it is because we were leaving, but the rain has stopped. The bus route is back onto the dual carriageway of the A92 for a little distance before diverting off onto the B936 into the attractive village of Freuchie and then Falkland.

Unfortunately, the bus doesn't go into the centre of the historic town of **Falkland** (population 1,200), maybe because of the narrow roads. I had visited the former Royal Burgh of Falkland some few years previous and climbed the Lomond Hills that overlook the Town. Falkland Palace was a popular residence with the Scottish kings, with good hunting grounds nearby, with Mary Queen of Scots making frequent visits to the Palace. Built during the 16thC, the architecture is in the French Renaissance style.

The Palace and grounds are located in the centre of Falkland, amongst the other historic buildings of the Town, including the Bruce Fountain. In 1970, the old town was made a conservation area with the interesting architecture of the old stone buildings being in the Scottish baronial style. The weaving of linen was the main industry in the 19thC, but now there is little manufacturing left.

The bus route skirts around the Town centre, then out along the B936 through the wooded countryside of the Eden valley to Dunshalt. Then it crosses the A91 into the small town of **Auchtermuchty** (population 2,000)—try saying that when you have had a few whiskies. When the comedian Rich Hall told folk he was going to Auchtermuchty, they said "wear a fox hat"—think about it, the old ones are always the best! The Town was a Royal Burgh (1517) and can trace its origins back to 350AD. Textiles once provided the main employment, but now most of the residents commute. Auchtermuchty is well known from featuring as Tannochbrae in the latest TV series *"Dr Finlay's Casebook"* as written by A.J.Cronin. As might be expected, there is the Tannochbrae Tearoom situated in the Town centre. The Scottish country-dance musician Sir Jimmy Shand, was from Auchtermuchty and in the High Street, there is a statue of him in his kilt and playing the accordion. I wondered if anyone has though of rigging up speakers in the High Street with Scottish country-dance music being played. From the bus, it seems to be an attractive place to live. There is also an impressive war memorial in the Town centre.

Our double-decker bus travels up the High Street, out of Auchtermuchty and along the B936 through some attractive rolling Fife countryside. The yellow gorse is standing out against the green of the hillsides. On we travel to Grange of Lindores before joining the A913 leading to Newburgh and eventually Perth. We are leaving Fife and entering Perth and Kinross. The bus travels onto Abernethy, with its 11thC 74 feet tall round tower, similar to those seen in Ireland and then past the "Scottish Off-Road Driving Centre" (sounds fun) at Aberargie. On joining the A912, the next bus stop is Kintillo with its line of attractive cottages, before crossing over the River Earn and into Craigend. We are soon driving past the "Welcome to Perth" sign.

Perth—Perth and Kinross—43,000 population—former Royal Burgh (1153)

We arrived at Perth Bus Station at 14.30 and make our way to the Tourist Information Centre that has recently been relocated in Mill Wynd off St Paul's Square. After picking up some pamphlets and town map, we set off to explore the "Fair City on the Tay".

Officially, Perth is no longer defined as a "city", this following a move by a set of bureaucrats in the 1990's that has relegated Perth to "town" status, an act that has infuriated its proud citizens. Moves are afoot to have this overturned and with its long history and tradition, hopefully this will succeed. For my part at least, I shall refer to the City of Perth.

Having studied the map, off we set down Methven Street to the honey-coloured sandstone Episcopalian Cathedral of St Ninian's on the corner with Atholl Street. Consecrated in 1850, it is said that St Ninian's was the first cathedral to be constructed in Britain since the Reformation in the 17th century. Following the brown signs, we make our way up Hay Street to Balhousie House, that with its fine wrought iron gates, is now the regimental headquarters and museum of the Black Watch. This famous regiment was formed in 1739 by General Wade to keep the peace within the Highlands and has been involved in action throughout the world. After a quick peep inside the entrance, we walk through the gardens and onto the North Inch behind.

The North Inch, like its counterpart the South Inch, is common land bounded on the west side by the River Tay, that is said to be the largest river in the Britain. On the east side of the Inch, is Bells Whisky's Sports Centre with its large domed building. At one time, the City of Perth had two large whisky distilleries, Bells and Dewars. Although the name of Perth still appears on their labels, there is sadly no whisky now distilled in the City. Their names still remain however, as sports centres, the Dewar Centre being the main ice rink for the sport of curling in Scotland.

The North Inch, which covers some 100 acres of grassed parkland, was the scene of the Great Clan Combat in 1396 and now accommodates a set of rugby pitches (not much has changed over the years), together with a golf course. On the look-out for errant golf balls and avoiding the hallowed turf of the rugby pitches, we make our way across the Inch to the River Tay, with its fast flowing peaty-brown waters. Archie is itching to get into the water, which is flowing a bit too fast to be safe. Nevertheless, I do let him in for a paddle whilst he is still on his lead. Following the flow of water, we make our way down the tarmaced footpath to Smeaton's elegant nine arched Old Bridge (also known as Perth Bridge). This was completed in 1771 using the local red sandstone. On the eastern abutment, is shown the various flood levels that have brought devastation to the City over the years.

Continuing down the riverside walk alongside Tay Street on the eastern side of the River, we pass a number of fine stately old sandstone houses and buildings, including the Kirk of St Matthew's with its tall slender spire towering over the glittering waters of the Tay. Behind, is the 15thC Kirk of St John's the Baptist, with its unusual steepled tower that also dominates the skyline. Perth is often referred to as "Saint John's Toun" after the name of its kirk, and a name still retained by the City's football team, St Johnstone FC. Further down from St Matthew's, is Water Vennel, a small lane connecting Watergate to Tay Street. The term "Vennel" is unusual to us English, it being a Scottish name for a passageway between the gable ends of two buildings. Maybe a "snicket".

Continuing down on the pleasant and well laid-out riverside walk alongside Tay Street and past the much more recent Queen's Bridge, is the imposing colonnaded frontage of the Sheriff's Court building on the right. I presume that the City's registry office must be inside for there was a wedding party gathered underneath the colonnade—at least there is now some blue in the skies above.

I had previously read of the 15thC Greyfriars Monastery (now totally demolished) and the 16thC burial ground off Canal Street, so I decide to investigate. It appears that there had been some riots at the time of the Reformation, with all four monasteries being totally destroyed in 1544 when "several martyrs suffered death ". These martyrs together with other dignitaries, were supposedly buried in the cemetery. Unfortunately, the wrought iron gates to the old burial ground are chained and padlocked.

So on we plod down Princess Street towards the South Inch. I was now being to feel the weight of my rucksack and I am ready for a break.

After a brief rest under the trees of the South Inch that line Marshall Place, we set off again back to the bus station for the next stage of our journey. First along King James Place, which is overlooked by the fine crown spire of St Leonard's in the Field, opposite which is a statue to Sir Walter Scott. Not quite as elaborate as the one in Edinburgh, but nevertheless standing proud against the backdrop of the South Inch. On we trod under the railway bridge back to the bus station. I am thankful for a hot drink and sandwich at the station café before we catch our next bus.

Perth is perhaps lacking in the presence of old historic buildings that I would have expected in a city with such a long illustrious past. Perhaps this was due to most of them being demolished in the many conflicts over past years. However, there are a number of some more recent fine sandstone buildings in the City that make up. It is nevertheless, an excellent centre for retail therapy, with a pedestrianised High Street and a large mix of different types of shops. At least that is what I am told as being a typical male, they are places I try to avoid and don't visit.

Although we are not travelling in that direction, some two miles to the north of Perth is one of Scotland's most hallowed and historic sites, Scone Palace. It was in the 9^{th}C when Scone was made the centre of the Scoto-Pictish Kingdom with the coronation of all the Scottish kings taking place there. Up to 1296 on their coronation, the Scottish kings were seated over the Stone of Scone (or Destiny), a block of red sandstone measuring 26 ins x 16 ins x 10 ins and weighing 336 lbs. Legend has it that the Stone was used as a travelling altar by St Columba on his missionary travels around Scotland and that it had been brought to Scone from Dunstaffnage in 838, by the first king of Scotland, Kenneth MacAlpine (was this MacAlpine's first civil engineering contact?). It was when Edward I of England invaded Scotland in the late 13^{th}C, that he had the Stone removed to Westminster Abbey, where it remained until the 1990's. That is apart from 6 months in 1950, when it was stolen as a prank by some students who accidentally broke it in two. In 1996, it was agreed that the Stone should be sent back to Scotland and kept in Edinburgh Castle, where it still remains. There is still some speculation as to whether the Stone is the original Stone of Destiny over which all the Scottish kings were crowned.

* * * * * * *

Our next bus is the No.16 Stagecoach to Dundee, which leaves at 16.30. We are not going as far as Dundee today, as I have booked overnight accommodation at Longforgan, a village some five miles to the west of Dundee. Off out of Perth on the A90 dual carriageway, before the bus diverts off at Glencarse onto a B road into the village of St Madoes and then following along the north shore of the Tay Firth to Errol and Grange. On each side of the road, there are newly born lambs in a number of the pasture fields. Elsewhere, there are large semi-circular polythene tents known as poly-tunnels, that cover the area and which I gather are used for the growing of soft fruit. Dundee is of course, a major centre for jam making.

Turning back up on the B953 towards the A90, the bus once again takes a diversion, this time into the village of Inchture with its red sandstone houses and church, only to do an about-turn and come back out via the same point. Then along the A90 for a short distance before turning off into the village of **Longforgan,** our overnight stop. Getting off at the post office (the village has been fortunate to avoid the recent closures of post offices), we walk to the 17thC Coaching Inn where I had previously booked accommodation for the night. The owners have converted what were the stables into bedroom units similar to that at motels These are well furnished, clean and comfortable, each room named after a local castle. Ours was "Broughty" being a castle to the east of Dundee.

Before settling down for something to eat and drink, I take Archie for a walk into the village. Immediately outside the Longforgan Coaching Inn is the village's old mercat cross which may well have been moved in recent years. Further back up the main street and past the post office, is the village kirk with some interesting ancient gravestones. One was dated 1777 and had a skull, bones and an hour-glass carved beneath the family coat-of-arms—not sure of the significance. We go through the lytch gate of the graveyard and can see the waters of the Firth of Tay, shimmering in the evening light. There are some attractive stone cottages in the village, including one that has a thatched roof. The spring flowers in the cottage gardens are particularly colourful.

We head back to the Coaching Inn where I give Archie his dinner and bed him down, before going myself for some much needed refreshment—I have eaten very little since breakfast. The Inn has a good menu so I choose some traditional dishes (when in Scotland, etc, etc,) and order as a starter, haggis, tatties and neaps with whisky butter, followed by local salmon, garlic butter and vegetables, with apple pie and ice cream to finish. I am not disappointed with either the quality nor quantity of the dishes served—all excellent value for £9.95. The beer on tap is Belhaven Best, from Scotland's sole surviving brewery in Dunbar, where we had been the previous day. There are four Geordies in the bar apparently on a golfing holiday, telling jokes in their broad Tyneside accents and obviously enjoying themselves. They perhaps don't realise it, but I am ear-wigging and understand everything that is being said. Better not repeat some of their jokes although some are very funny.

Back to my bedroom apartment suitably refreshed, I settle down to watch some television before turning in. Julia Bradbury is on the box revisiting some of Alfred Wainwright's Lakeland walks. This week, she is climbing Blencathra via Sharp Edge in the north east of the Lake District, near Keswick. Having climbed all the 127 peaks over 2,000 feet in the Lakes, my favourite is undoubtedly Blencathra. The routes up, especially over Sharp Edge, are challenging and the views from the top on a clear day, are exceptional. Also it is not usually swarming with other fell walkers. So it is with some enjoyment and nostalgia, that I watch her undertake the ascent of my favourite peak in the Lakes.

Arthur's Seat and Holyrood Palace, Edinburgh

St Giles' Cathedral, Edinburgh

Forth Road Bridge

Smeaton's Bridge over River Tay

RSS Discovery, Dundee

Desperate Dan Bronze Figures, Dundee

Fishermen's Cottages, Arbroath

Town House, Union Street, Aberdeen

Elgin Cathedral

The Riverside, Inverness

A Bus Stop with a View, Invergordon

Bus to John O'Groats

The Plaiden Ell (Stone), Dornoch

Signpost at John O'Groats

Harbour at John O'Groats

Archie at Bridlington

Archie on Beach at Dornoch    Free Loading Old Wrinkle and Archie

Chapter 4
Dundee To Aberdeen—Day 13.

Tuesday 28th April 2009

Up early for breakfast and to walk Archie before catching the 08.10 No.16 bus into Dundee. The skies are grey with a cold wind blowing up the Tay—at least it isn't raining. There is quite a crowd waiting at the stop for the Dundee bus, obviously off to school and work. When the bus does arrive and everyone has boarded, it travels the length of the Village, does a "U" turn and travels back out via the same route it came in to rejoin the A90. I hadn't checked, but I presume that there is only one way in and out at Longforgan. I could have boarded the bus some minutes later on its return trip out, then again, I may not have got a seat.

Back onto the dual carriageway of the A90, we pass more of the giant poly-tunnels I had seen the previous day. The bus then deviates through the dormitory town of Invergowerie to pick up more passengers before entering Dundee City proper. Then along Perth Road past the tall tenement housing blocks and the Public Library, a very prominent building in red sandstone, before reaching the City centre and bus station. The time is 08.50 and still relatively early in the morning, for me at least.

Dundee—Tayside—142,000 population—former Royal Burgh (1214)

Dundee is Scotland's fourth largest City and is known for its "three j's"—jam, jute and journalism. Journalism and the making of jam still flourish within the City, but the manufacture of jute has long ceased. As too, has its shipbuilding industry. For more than 100 years, the jute industry flourished with the majority of workers in the City employed in the mills. Until 1912, Dundee was a major whaling port with whale oil being used in the process of jute manufacture. Gradually, production of jute was transferred to the Indian sub-continent and in the 1970's, the last jute mill in Dundee was closed.

Dundee also had a thriving shipbuilding industry—my uncle used to work as an engineering draughtsman in the Caledonian Yard. Scott's ship, the *RRS Discovery*, was build at Dundee. Like elsewhere throughout the UK, shipbuilding is virtually a thing of the past with the yards on the Tay being closed in the early 1980's.

Jam making and in particular marmalade, was first started in Dundee in 1797 by Janet Keiller. The Company is now world-known. The publishers DC Thompson & Co, have their offices and printing works in Dundee, and publish a variety of newspapers, magazines and children's comics. The Dandy and The Beano are particularly well known with such characters as Desperate Dan, Denis the Menace, Keyhole Kate, Lord Snooty, Beryl the Peril, Korky the Cat and many more, who feature in both comics—they bring back memories of past years. So too do Wilson of the Wizard and Alf Tupper of the Rover. The imagination, creativity and humour are perhaps a testament to the character of the Dundonuans.

From the bus station, we made our way into the City centre, past the Episcopalian Cathedral of St Paul's. The Cathedral is located on the site of Dundee Castle (now long gone) with the statue of Adam Duncan at the front. Admiral Duncan (1731-1894), who was born in Dundee, led the British fleet in the defeat of the Dutch fleet in 1797.

On up to the pedestrianised City centre, where there are bronze figures of a different type on the pavement in front of the City Chambers—those of Desperate Dan, his Dawg and Beryl the Peril complete with her catapult. Across the City Square are the linked churches of St Mary's and the Steeple Church. The original 14th C Parish Church of St Mary's was subdivided after the Reformation. Now only the tower survives and is the oldest building in the City. I must appear to be lost as I am approached by one of the City's guides, who couldn't be more helpful—I enjoy his friendly chat. I must admit to being impressed by the redevelopment of the City centre. From my memories when I last visited the City some 40 years previously, it was not a place you would want to spend much time in.

With directions from the City guide, we head for the quayside and the *RRS Discovery*, used by Captain Robert Falcon Scott on his Antarctic expedition of 1901/04 and which is now permanently berthed in Dundee. The custom-built ship was built in the Dundee shipyards in 1901 and has now returned home. The adjoining visitors' centre is still closed, but we are able to walk around the dry dock in which *RRS Discovery* is berthed.

The vessel is quite an imposing sight, especially at close quarters though I would have loved to have gone aboard. With some imagination, you could picture the ship trapped in the Antarctic ice, with its frozen rigging glistening against the blue southern skies.

From the quayside looking upstream, there is a good view of the **Tay Railway Bridge**, which was completed in 1887 following the collapse of the original bridge in 1879. The original Railway Bridge built the previous year in 1878, was at that time, the longest railway bridge in the world, being just under two miles in length. It was when a train was crossing on a stormy night in December 1879, that the high girders gave way and collapsed, throwing the train with all 75 passengers and crew aboard, into the cold, dark, murky waters of the Tay. No-one survived and the incident is still known as Britain's worst rail disaster. Faults in the design, shoddy construction and poor workmanship in the manufacture of the ironwork used in the bridge's construction, were subsequently found to be the cause of the disaster. Some of the stumps of the stone piers of the original, ill-fated bridge can still be seen above the water line. The new Railway Bridge is some 2¼ miles in length.

William Topaz McGonagall (1830-1902), who lived most of his life in Dundee, is said to be "the world's worst poet" and Dundee's best remembered nobody. Today these remarks can be considered a bit unfair. For sure, during his lifetime, he was impoverished and the butt of cruel jokes. However, since his death, there have been at least 12 books published of his poems and life, and today he has become a bit of a celebratory. It is a pity he could not have enjoyed the fame during his lifetime. He is perhaps, best known for his two poems of the first railway bridge that crossed the Tay at Dundee. The first of these poems is titled *"The Railway Bridge of the Silvery Tay"* and followed the construction of the original railway bridge across the Firth in 1878, the first verse being:

> *Beautiful Railway Bridge of the Silvery Tay*
> *With your numerous arches and pillars in so grand array*
> *And your central girders, which seem to the eye*
> *To be almost towering to the sky*
> *The greatest wonder of the day*
> *And a great beautification to the River Tay*
> *Most beautiful to be seen*
> *Near Dundee and Magdalen Green*

His second poem is titled "*The Tay Bridge Disaster*" and followed the collapse of the original bridge a year later in 1879. The two penultimate verses are:

> *So the train mov'd slowly along the Bridge of Tay,*
> *Until it was about midway,*
> *Then the central girders with a crash gave way,*
> *And down went the train and passengers into the Tay,*
> *The Storm Fiend did loudly bray,*
> *Because ninety lives had been taken away,*
> *On the last Sabbath day of eighteen seventy nine,*
> *Which will be remember'd for a very long time.*
>
> *As soon as the catastrophe became to be known,*
> *The alarm from mouth to mouth was blown,*
> *And the cry rang out all o'er the town,*
> *Good Heavens! The Tay Bridge is blown down,*
> *And a passenger train from Edinburgh,*
> *Which fill'd all the people's hearts with sorrow,*
> *And made them turn to pale,*
> *Because none of the passengers were sav'd to tell the tale*
> *How the disaster happen'd on the last Sabbath day of eighteen seventy nine,*
> *Which will be remember'd for a very long time.*

Not bad for a self-taught man of little means. Perhaps he lived before his time for I know his works would have been more appreciated today. I have read a lot worse, especially some of the modern day rubbish. Perhaps McGonagall did achieve some sort of fame during his later life as he is buried in Greyfriars Kirkyard in Edinburgh.

Looking now downstream to the east, the much newer **Tay Road Bridge** can be seen. This carries the A92 from Fife into Dundee and is 1.4 miles in length. It consists of 42 spans between a series of piers and carries two carriageways in each direction together with a central walkway. Off we walk in the direction of the Road Bridge, along the paved walkway along the banks of the Tay and under the Bridge itself. We continue down the quayside to where the docks and shipyards once stood with all the associated noise and activity. Now everything is silent, apart from the wind whistling up the Tay. We walk across the footbridge that crosses Victoria Dock and which leads to a newly developed shopping complex. There is the old North Carr Lightship in the Dock and the 19thC sailing frigate *Unicorn*, both being rebuilt. A notice in front of the shopping complex says "No Dogs Allowed". I have no problem with that, so we skirt around and head back towards the bus station.

* * * * * * *

Today, we are heading for Aberdeen with stops at Arbroath and Montrose on the way. On making enquiries as to which stand the Arbroath bus was leaving, I am told that this is back at a bus stop in the City Square. Apart from the local town service buses, I would have thought it reasonable to think that all buses travelling outside the City would have left from the bus station itself. However, off we trudge, past St Paul's Cathedral, Desperate Dan and his companions, back into the City Square. We don't have long to wait before the 10.10 No.39 Stagecoach bus for Arbroath appears.

The bus route takes us along Arbroath Road to Broughty Ferry, a suburb of Dundee where the jute barons had their mansions, past two huge wind turbines towering against the skyline and onto the A92. The Firth of Tay is on our right as we pass many more of the giant poly-tunnels. Evidently, Dundee enjoys the warmest temperatures of all Scotland's cities, it being the only city facing south. After 11 miles, we see the signs for Carnoustie, the home of one of Scotland's world famous golf courses, with the Open Championship having being played there seven times in past years. Scotland is of course the home of golf with the Royal and Ancient Golf Club of St Andrew's being on the other side of the Tay. Shortly afterwards at 11.00, we reached Arbroath.

Arbroath—Angus—23,000 population—former Royal Burgh (1214)

From the bus station, you can see the old red sandstone abbey on the hill above—we will try to make a visit, if time permits. Off we set into the Town centre and along Keltie Street and down East Grimsby Street towards the harbour.

Historically, the Town is best known for the "Declaration of Arbroath" in 1320, when Scotland asserted its independence as a separate kingdom with its people free to choose their own king, rather than being a feudal land controlled by England. It also set out the Country's right to the use of military action if unjustly attacked by foreign forces. It has been suggested that the rhetoric used in the Declaration had an influence on the drafters of the United States Declaration of Independence. The document has certainly played an influential role in the history of the Scottish national identity throughout the ages, with a pageant held each year involving a re-enactment of the signing of the Declaration.

Down at the harbour, which also serves as a marina for yachts, a small number of fishing boats are tied up. Over the recent years, the size of the fishing fleet has suffered with the introduction of fishing quotas by the EU, with many of the boats having to be decommissioned. Formerly known as a whitefish port, shellfish are now landed at the quayside. At the far end of the harbour, is the Bell Rock Lighthouse Signal Tower, which was built in 1813 to provide a means of communicating with the keepers of the lighthouse out at sea. The Signal Tower is now a museum and visitor centre. Also there is the RNLI lifeboat house with its offshore lifeboat still operating from Arbroath.

During the late 19thC and early 20thC, Arbroath was well known for the production of jute and sailcloth, with over 30 mills operating in the Town employing over 4,000 people. It is believed that the sails for the Cutty Sark were manufactured at Arbroath. Much like elsewhere, all the mills have since been closed.

The Town is of course, also the home of the "Arbroath Smokie" (smoked haddock), a speciality that has the name protected by EU law, insomuch that the name can only be used if the "smokies" are processed within 5 miles of Arbroath itself. Down on the quayside, you can smell the smoke of the curing process from the smokehouses. Whilst "taking in the air" outside one of the smoke-houses, the proprietor comes up and asks if I would like a look inside. Needless to say, I am delighted to take up his offer and having tethered Archie to a suitable post, I go with him inside.

Not unsurprisingly, it is quite smoky inside with little natural light. The smokehouse is a family-run concern and have been producing "smokies" for many years. The hesian covers over the simple rectangular oven (approximately 6 feet x 4 feet) are rolled back and a cloud of smoke from the curing process hits the space above. Inside the oven are racks of filleted haddocks suspended vertically on skewers with their mouths wide open, hanging over the bright red glow of an open wood fire. The dangling haddocks are left in the oven for approximately 40 minutes being cured by the smoke from the oak log fire below. The heavy hesian covers over the top are kept continuously damp to create a dense steam.

At the same time, herrings are being cured in a smaller side oven from the same heat source, to produce kippers. In the past, the fish being cured were caught and landed by local fishermen. With the contraction of the local fleet, fish are now transported in from Peterhead, the Orkneys and as far afield as Norway and Iceland. Emerging into the fresh air outside the smoke-house, the smell of the curing fish is still in my nostrils and on my clothes. I only wish that I could have bought a smokie to eat there and then, but they first have to be cooked and I don't fancy carrying any in my rucksack on the bus. I may receive a few comments and odd looks if I do.

From the smokehouse, we walk along past a row of fishermen's stone cottages, each one painted in a different colour and then onto the beach. Archie is again at home digging in the soft red sand, coming up with his nose plastered in sand. The tide is out so he has to go without his usual dip in the sea.

We continue along the coast to the end of the cottages where a grassy knoll towers over the seafront. At the foot of the knoll, there stands two pairs of solid rectangular stone pillars on either side of the road, all four being painted white. There does not appear to be any information or signs as to the purpose of these pillars nor what they represent. No doubt I shall find out one day.

With my dodgy knees, we climb up the grassy knoll where from the top there are great views along the coast and out to sea. Turning around and looking inland, are the ruins of the red sandstone Abbey. Off we set across the grassy tops towards the Abbey, the sun is now high in the sky and shining. First along a street of fine solid red sandstone houses that seem typical of the area, before we reach the Abbey.

Built and consecrated during the early part of the 13thC, it was here in 1320, that the Scottish Parliament met to draft the Declaration of Arbroath. The work in putting pen to paper, was undertaken by the Abbot of Aberbrothock, as Arbroath was known at the time. The Abbey fell into disrepair during the 16thC with its red stone being reused in the construction of many of the local buildings. It was not until 1951 that the Abbey again came into the news when the Stone of Destiny, stolen earlier from Westminster Abbey, mysteriously turned up on the altar.

Having walked around the perimeter of the Abbey to the main entrance and gateway, we head off downhill back to the bus station to catch the 12.30 No. 39 bus to Montrose. There is a nice little café at the bus station for eats and refreshments.

Before leaving Arbroath, it should be mentioned that the Town is the birthplace of David Dunbar Buick (1854-1929), who was the founder of the Buick Motor Company in the USA. He did however leave Arbroath at the age of two when his parents emigrated to America. It has also been the home to the 45 Commando Unit of the Royal Marines since 1971.

* * * * * * *

From the bus station, the bus to Montrose travels uphill past the Abbey where I had been some 30 minutes previous—if I had realised, I could have caught the bus from outside the Abbey and saved some shoe leather. The distinctive smell from the smoke-house is still on my clothes—lovely. The bus route joins the A92 leading to Montrose via Inverkeilor and following for most of the way the railway line to Aberdeen. To the right, the 14^{th}C Eithie Castle can be seen standing by the edge of the coast and which is claimed to be the second oldest inhabited castle in Scotland.

Sitting at the other end of the back seat of the bus, is a young girl listening to music on her ipod with her feet stretched out and resting on the seat in front. As on the bus to Edinburgh a few days ago, it seems that these days, it is acceptable practice to put your shoed feet on seats where others will sit, despite the fact that dirt (or worse) could be left on the upholstery to spoil unsuspecting passengers' clothes. I do wonder how this youngster would have reacted if her clothes had been soiled by some other person's inconsideration. Again I should say something, but don't.

Having travelled for some 30 minutes along the "Angus Coastal Road", we arrive at the port and coastal resort of Montrose at 13.00—lunchtime.

Montrose—Angus—11,000 population—former Royal Burgh (1153)

The bus drops us off in the High Street in the centre of the Town, there being no dedicated bus station in Montrose. We cross the road and walk down the broad High Street, said to be the widest high street in Scotland. A statue to Joseph Hume stands in the centre of the High Street facing the clock on the sandstone building of the Guildhall. Then down a tree-lined footpath that passes through the old kirkyard and leads to the Tourist Information Office and Museum on Panmure Street. The Office and Museum are housed in an attractive stone building, with two Doric columns on each side of the main entrance. As elsewhere, the staff at the

Centre are most helpful, recommending that I spend my short time in Montrose with a visit to the coast and beach.

Having picked up a town map, we set off across the Mid Links towards the sea. The Mid Links in Montrose comprises a series of garden parks that form a green corridor, running parallel to the High Street. The garden parks were instigated by a local man called George Scott during the 19thC who turned what was *"a quagmire in winter and a dust bowl in summer"* into a series of nine individual elegant Victorian gardens that cover nearly 20 acres. The garden parks were recently restored in 2005 and include a fitting war memorial in the Hope Paton Park. The bandstand, so often a common feature of Victorian parks, was demolished in 1953 and has not yet been replaced.

Walking through the Panmure Gardens and past Burn's statue, with the Montrose Academy and its golden dome immediately to the south, we reach Marine Avenue and soon Archie gets the scent of the sea. Deviating off onto a cycle track that follows the old railway line, we soon arrive at the grassy Links of Montrose that are used as a golf course. Being a public space, I presume that it is alright to cross, keeping a careful eye out for any airborne golf-balls. At last, we reach the Pavilion and Splash Area on the coast. Although the skies are blue, there is a strong cold wind blowing in off the sea, resulting in the place being deserted. It is high tide, but the stretch of sandy beach looked attractive and under more pleasant conditions, we could have gone for a walk along the sands. However, we need to be back in the Town centre to catch the bus on the next stage of our journey. So off we set back across the Links, down India Street and India Lane and across Scott Park with its memorial to George Scott, back onto the High Street, in time to catch the bus to Aberdeen.

Had time permitted, I would have liked to visited Montrose Basin, located to the east of the High Street. The Basin, used during Romans times as a safe harbour, is a shallow water estuary some two miles in diameter and is the largest inland salt-water basin in the UK. It now serves as a wild-life reserve and is an important habitat for the mute swan and pink-footed geese during the winter months. During the summer months, ospreys are sometimes seen. The Basin drains into the River South Esk, where there is a small port and lifeboat station, together with a recently unveiled statue to Montrose's war hero "Bamse". He was a large St Bernard's dog from Norway (Bamse meaning Bear), who arrived aboard a Norwegian minesweeper during World War II. He saved the life of a Norwegian officer and generally looked after his fellow sailors, especially if any confrontations took place. He was everyone's favourite in Montrose at that time, especially the schoolchildren, who mourned his passing in July 1944.

It was during World War II, that Montrose served as a major air force base for pilots from all over the Commonwealth and other allied nations, flying sorties to enemy occupied Norway. As a result, the Town was bombed on more than one occasion by enemy aircraft. Finally, it should be mentioned that Montrose has the 5th oldest golf course in the World.

* * * * * * *

Now onto Aberdeen, a long three hour bus ride that follows the coastline of Angus and Aberdeenshire. At 14.20, the No 107 double-decker bus arrives. On we jump having to pay £8.00 single fare to Aberdeen—no concessions and seeming expensive even for Scotland. At least Archie again went free. By now, he knows where we normally sit and heads for the back seat. This subsequently turns out to be a mistake on this particular long journey.

We travel out of Montrose and onto the A92 following the coast, calling in at St Cyrus with its holiday camps and swarm of mobile homes. It would appear that the area of the coast is a popular holiday destination. Next, we arrived at the pretty fishing village of Johnshaven, where the bus makes a detour down to the harbour, the driver having to make some difficult manoeuvres around the tight bends of the narrow streets.

A little further on, the bus stops to pick up passengers at Benholm, where it would seem there is a home for the handicapped, as some with their carers, get on the bus. I am always full of admiration for the patience and attention shown by the care workers towards those under their charge. Then on along the A92 to Gourdon, another picturesque fishing village along this Angus coast, with its harbour well below the level of the main road. Again the bus makes a detour down to the harbour with some difficult manoeuvres for the driver. It would appear that this area too is a popular holiday destination.

Then onto and through Inverbervie, where the road bridge over the River Bervie is under re-construction. We were now in Aberdeenshire. Leaving Inverbervie, the bus passes fields full of fresh daffodils and narcissi, a glorious sight. However, these are matched by other fields of bright yellow, only the crop is rapeseed oil, an obnoxious smelling crop, especially to all asthma suffers. On along the A92 through the oddly named villages of "Roadside of Kinneff" and "Roadside of Catterline" with the road verges full of yellow daffodils. Just before we reach Stonehaven, the ruins of the 14thC Dunnottar Castle can be seen to the left. Sited on the precipitous rocky headland overlooking the sea, this was the location for the filming in 1990 of Shakespeare's Hamlet. It is also the ancestral home of the Keith family, where the Scottish crown jewels were hidden during the period of the Commonwealth in the 1650's and subsequently smuggled out to prevent them falling into the hands of Cromwell's forces.

The bus route now follows a short length of dual carriageway before diverting through a housing estate and passing the Mackie Academy. It is at this point that a man in his twenties gets on the bus and walks up to the back where an attractive sixth-form schoolgirl is sitting at the other end of the seat. He seems to be a bit "lacking" but approaches the young lady saying that his shoulder is hurting and will she give him a massage. Expecting her to say no, or words to that effect, he sits down on the back seat and much to her credit, the young lady starts to massage his shoulder. Maybe they know each other, but it is a generous act for her to do this in public, although I suspect that she feels a bit uncomfortable. However, when we reach the Town centre, a friend of hers gets on the bus that gives her the excuse to join him and move seat.

We reach the Town centre of **Stonehaven** (population 9,600) at 15.20. I have on a few occasions in the past, visited Stonehaven where my Mother-in-law did live during the 1980's. Stonehaven was once the county town of Kincardineshire, but in 1975, the County was abolished and the Town is now incorporated into Aberdeenshire. In the past, Stonehaven had a large fishing fleet and with its safe harbour, prospered during the herring boom of the 1800's. Today the Town is benefiting from the oil boom, housing overspill population from Aberdeen. Two annual events take place in Stonehaven, which attracts great crowds. One is the Fireball Fesival that is celebrated every hogmanay with a procession through the Town. Also Stonehaven has its own Highland Games that are held in annually in July. Finally, one of Stonehaven's more famous sons, Lord Reith, the first Director General of the BBC, was born in the Town.

I am due to be in Aberdeen by 18.00 so unfortunately, do not have time to revisit the Old Town, its market place, the old tollbooth and historic harbour. It is a pity, especially as it is market day. I do however note that Robertson's bakery and cake shop where my Mother-in-law once served, is still in existence.

Leaving Stonehaven after a change of drivers, I still have the guy with a sore shoulder sitting on the back seat of the bus opposite me. I am praying that he will not try to make conversation with me and ask that I give him a massage. Thankfully, he keeps himself to himself. However, sitting on the back seat of a double-decker bus with its engine at the rear, is proving to be a bit uncomfortable. The heat transmitted from the engine is warming up the seat and it is becoming a little unbearable. We now have been on the bus for more than an hour with a further two to go. Archie is lying on the floor and away from the heat of the engine. Sensibly, I should move seat but by now the bus is fairly full. So I decide to stick it out.

We are back onto the A90 dual carriageway heading for Aberdeen. First stop is Bridge of Muchalls, then a detour into the village of Newtonhill, back up onto the A90, followed by another detour into the villages of Downies and Portlethen. At last, the guy opposite gets up to leave, first hesitating and then trundling down the aisle to leave the bus. Relief!

Back on the dual carriageway of the A90, we soon pass the Welcome to Aberdeen sign, albeit it is still some 5 miles to go to the City centre. The roadside banks leading into Aberdeen are bright yellow with daffodils and narcissi—a splendid sight and I am fortunate insomuch that in a few weeks time, they will all be gone. It is said that some years ago, a city official grossly over-ordered a consignment of daffodil bulbs for the City Parks Department, which resulted in bulbs being planted in just about every public place. I am not sure if this is true, but they have multiplied over the years to give the fantastic displays enjoyed today by all. It is nevertheless, a good story. During the summer months, I understand that the colour is maintained with roses blooming all over the City. On ten occasions in recent years, the City has been the winner of "Britain's Best City Bloom Award".

On down our bus travels, across the road bridge over the River Dee and into Aberdeen City, also known as the "Granite City" and more recently as the "Oil Capital of Europe". The bus takes us past the docks where the support vessels for the North Sea oilrigs are anchored. We have at last arrived at the City Bus Station, the time is 17.30. My rear end is fairly baked from the heat of the bus' engine. It is the first time that I have experienced the problem sitting on the back seat of the bus. Maybe there is something lacking or missing in the insulation over the bus' engine, but whatever it is "Sitting in the hot seat" now has a new meaning.

I have previously arranged to meet up with my brother-in-law Mike with whom I will be staying the night (it was mentioned earlier that Mike's dog Bramble, is Archie's dad). Our agreed rendezvous is at the nearby main railway station, this being a convenient pick-up point. I don't have far to walk or long to wait before Mike arrives.

Aberdeen—Aberdeenshire—202,000 population—former Royal Burgh (1153)

Aberdeen is Scotland's third largest City and the busiest port in the U.K. Sited between the mouths of the Rivers Don and Dee, the City is comprised of two former burghs, Old Aberdeen with its historic cathedral quarter and the City Centre located around the site of the old castle and harbour on the Dee. Aberdeen is known as the "Granite City" because of the locally quarried grey granite used in the construction of many of the City's institutional / public buildings and residential houses. More about this later. The City has a strong maritime heritage, with shipbuilding and fishing providing much of the local employment during the 19^{th}C and early 20^{th}C. These industries still flourish albeit on a smaller scale.

The development of the North Sea oil-field has created an economic boom and earned the City the nickname the "Oil Capital of Europe". The relatively recent discovery of oil off the north-east coast of Scotland in the 1970s has had a substantial affect upon the local economy. It also contributes some £10 billion to national revenues. Many of the major international oil companies together with associated business, have been attracted to locate to the City, my brother-in-law Mike being employed by one such company.

Spot on time, Mike arrives at the railway station to pick me up in his car. First a quick tour of the City centre. From the railway station, we drive to Union Street, the main street and shopping area in Aberdeen, which is graced by many fine grey granite buildings. These include the 19^{th}C Town House with its baronial style turreted tower that dominates Union Street. Around the corner in Broad Street is the Marishal College Building with its grey granite façade decorated with colourful heraldic shields above the main entrance. Constructed during the 19^{th}C with its row of ornate mini spires at rooftop level, it is said that the College is the second largest granite building in the World—I don't know which is the largest. Once you get used to the grey granite, the façade is very impressive. Previously owned by the University of Aberdeen (founded in 1495), the Marishal College building is no longer used as a centre of learning, now being used as offices by the City Council.

We drive around the corner into Upper Kirkgate and past St Nicholas Kirk with its tall Gothic spire. During the Reformation, the Kirk was divided into two, with the West Church and East Church still functioning for worship. On we go past the fine granite building that houses the City's Art Gallery. Constructed during the 19thC, twin fluted Doric columns stand either side of the main entrance. On past the imposing statue to William Wallace and around into Union Terrace, with its fine terraced houses overlooking the sunken gardens below street level.

We head back onto Union Street and down to Castlegate, where stands the 17thC Mercat Cross, one of the largest of its type in Scotland. The stone column of the Cross, which is surmounted by a unicorn, stands on an elevated platform that is itself supported by a round arcaded stone structure. Around the top of the arcade, is a frieze of oval panels each containing a portrait of the ten Stuart kings. Nearby in Castlegate, is the Mannie Water Fountain. Constructed in sandstone, water used to spout from the green-man type heads at the four corners of the fountain, which provided the first piped public water supply to the City centre. At the top of the fountain is the metal figure of the "Mannie" itself, a semi-clad young man.

Continuing on our tour of the City, we head for the harbour and to Victoria Dock. With the advent of North Sea oil, the docks have become a hive of activity, providing facilities for servicing and repair together with the victualling of the oilrig support vessels. At this time, there are a number of support vessels with their specially designed superstructures complete with helicopter decks, moored in the harbour. Motoring around the harbour area, it is evident that many oil related businesses have recently set up their bases here. Across at the Albert Dock, the recently modernised fish quay and market still flourishes, with fish of all types being landed, processed and sold. In accordance with its maritime tradition, there is a RNLI lifeboat station by the harbour at Aberdeen.

We then motor out to the coast, where the sandy beaches stretch between the Dee and Don and beyond. Although there is a cold wind blowing in from the sea, we walk some way along the soft golden sands, invigorated by the sea air. Archie is again enjoying himself, digging in the sand and splashing about in the waves. With all the facilities along the sea front, it is obviously a popular place during the summer months when no doubt, the air temperatures are a bit warmer. I am not so sure about the sea temperatures that even during the summer months, are probably at "brass monkey" levels.

The sea air has given us an appetite, so it is back off into the City centre to Mike's favourite fish and chip restaurant, the Ashvale. Being hungry, we order a "whale portion" consisting of a one pound (in weight) piece of haddock, complete with chips and mushy peas. Served on a large plate, both helpings are beautifully cooked, more than plentiful and of course, fresh. Half way through our meal, the waitress comes over with another helping of fish saying that the chef had thought that we had been "short changed" with the size of the original serving of fish and will we accept this piece to make it up. We are both dumbfounded as our original serving was more than enough, but we gratefully accept and manage the extra portion of fish between us. It is one of the best fish and chipperies that I have been to and the charge is very reasonable too. The popularity of the restaurant perhaps speaks for itself.

Where Mike lives is some six miles west of the City centre, heading towards the Grampian Mountains and Royal Deeside. More than fully satisfied with our meal, off we head along Queen's Road past the elegant grey granite houses that give a silvery sparkle in the evening sun, this due to the quartz and mica minerals in the granite itself. Nearby, is the Rubislaw Quarry, an intrusion of igneous Diorite granite, which for more than 300 years, provided the grey granite used in the construction of many of the buildings in Aberdeen and further afield too, including the Houses of Parliament and Waterloo Bridge in London. It is worth mentioning that the locally quarried grey granite does not weather and retains its fresh new appearance when used as a building material.

Unfortunately, we do not have time to visit the historic parts of Old Aberdeen with its 14th C St Machar's Cathedral, King's College Chapel complete with crown spire and Old Town House. Perhaps another time. It is of interest that Aberdeen has three cathedrals, the Church of Scotland's St Machar's Cathedral, the Episcopal Church's St Andrew's Cathedral and the Roman Catholic's St Mary's Cathedral, the latter two being constructed during the 19th century.

* * * * * * *

By the time we reach Mike's house out at Elrick, the sun is beginning to set over the foothills of the Grampian Mountains to the west. Being a clear evening, it is a spectacular sight. After a glass (or two) of Mike's best malt whisky, I am ready for bed—Archie too. It has been a long but enjoyable day.

Chapter 5
Aberdeen To Inverness—Day 14.

Wednesday 29th April 2009

Mike is an early riser, so it is up at 06.15, for me an unearthly hour. After a bite to eat, Archie and I are driven into the centre of Aberdeen for the next stage of our journey. Saying goodbye to Mike, we set off for a walk around the City centre before catching our next bus to Banff. The time is 07.30 and it's raining, albeit only lightly. Although he is at home splashing about in water, Archie does not enjoy walking in the rain and has to be dragged around on his lead. He is not a happy dog and lets you know it.

Walking past Burns' statue that overlooks the Union Terrace Gardens, we head towards the Art Gallery. At this time of the morning, everywhere is closed including the Gardens. Then on to St Nicholas' kirk, past the Marischal College buildings and the Town House, to the Mercat Cross and the Mannie water fountain in Castlegate. It is a good opportunity to take some photographs and thankfully, the rain has stopped. Even at this time of the morning, Union Street is very congested. Next, we walk past St Andrew's Episcopal Cathedral, its diocese reaching up to the Orkney Islands. Heading now down Shiprow past the Maritime Museum (it would have been nice to have been able to look around inside), we make for the bus station to catch the 08.35 bus to Banff, our next destination.

The No.305 Stagecoach Bluebird coach for Inverness turns up on time. Climbing on board, Archie, rucksack and all, I was told that the single fare to Banff is £10.50, with no concessions for oldies—the highest so far. At least it is a comfortable single-decker touring coach. Settling down on a seat near to the back (someone had beaten me to it), we head north out of Aberdeen, the roadside verges and central reservations awash with yellow daffodils. No wonder that Aberdeen has won the Best City Bloom Award so many times.

Leaving the City on the A96, we soon turn north onto the A947 leading to the village of Dyce and eventually Banff. The road to the international airport at Dyce however, continues further along the A96 in the direction of Elgin and Inverness. Immediately after Dyce, the road crosses the River Don, which if you blink, will be missed. The guy who had beaten me to the back seat and sitting immediately behind me, starts coughing—rather badly. Only hope that he doesn't pass anything on especially with all the news in media about swine flu. Hopefully, he has only a bad cough.

On along through the rolling countryside through Newmachar to Old Meldrum, with its Glen Garioch whisky distillery. Continuing along the A947, we reach the village of Fyvie. Here the bus leaves the main road, crosses the River Ythan and diverts along a minor country road past Fyvie Castle to Tifty (hope that the spelling is correct), before rejoining the main road to Banff. There are "brown signs" pointing to the Castle Trail. It does seem that there are a number of castles in this area of the Grampian foothills, with Huntley Castle only a few miles to the west.

On we travel into the agricultural and market town of **Turriff** (population 4,500), with its rows of red sandstone buildings. The locally quarried sandstone has been used in the construction of most of the Town's buildings including the Clydesdale Bank with its Gothic tower and also the "Auld Post Office Museum". There is another imposing 16thC Mercat Cross in Castle Street. It is believed that Knights Templar had a base nearby during the 13thC.

Continuing northwards through farming country and crossing into Banffshire, we reach the Solway coast at **Macduff** (population 4,000), a busy little town with its 18thC deepwater harbour and fishing fleet. Within the harbour, a number of fishing boats are tied up. On one side is the local boat yard complete with fabrication shed and at the end of the pier stands the lighthouse. Our bus makes a detour through the Town centre where there is a stop for a change of driver. Then back along the sea front and up to the white painted Doune Church, which stands dominant on high ground overlooking the Town and the harbour. Standing alongside the Church, is the impressive octagonal granite tower built in 1920 as the Town's war memorial. There is also a marine aquarium in the Town that is worth a visit.

The road then crosses John Smeaton's seven arch sandstone bridge over the River Deveron, which was constructed in 1799 to replace previous bridges that had been swept away by floods. Once over the River, we are in the Royal Burgh of Banff. The No.305 bus continues onto Inverness, our eventual destination today, but we take a break to explore and stretch our legs—in Archie's case, to cock his leg. The bus drops us off in Low Street, there being no bus station as such, in Banff.

Banff—Banffshire—3,800 population—former Royal Burgh (1372)

Prior to 1975, Banff was the county town of Banffshire. The Scottish settlers also gave its name to the town in Alberta, Canada. Since 1975, it has become part of the expanded county of Aberdeenshire, although Banffshire still exists as a Lieutenancy area.

On Low Street, there is the Town House with the 16thC Mercat Cross and old iron cannon standing immediately outside. Inside the Town House is the Information Office where I pick up a map of the Town. Across the street is the elaborately carved stone water fountain complete with a crown spire, similar to that of St Giles in Edinburgh, albeit smaller. Parallel to Low Street, but at a much higher level, is High Street—makes sense. Off we climb up the steep cobbled Straits Path to High Street, or Upper Town. Here there are a number of 18thC stone houses, each with it own design of doorway and gable end. Also a bakery that is selling some mouth-watering pies—will visit later.

Walking along Castle Street, we reach the grounds of the old castle. There is very little now remaining of the castle, only the remnants of its outer walls. However, from the high ground, there are excellent views across Banff Bay to Macduff and down to the harbour. Off we set again, past the Masonic Lodge building down to the Quayside and seafront. Looking to the west along the seawall, there is a row of pastel coloured fishermen's cottages that overlook the beach. The tide is out and the seaweed covered rocks are exposed below the sandy beach.

Turning around, we walk towards the harbour, which is now used mainly as a marina for yachts and pleasure craft. Problems have been experienced with silting up of the harbour entrance, making access difficult for vessels with deeper draughts. We continue along the road above the seawall, unable to gain access down onto the sandy beach until we turn a corner by the beach complex. Down the stone steps we go and at last, onto the beach. Archie cannot wait to be released from his lead and is soon excavating a trench with sand flying up from his rear. Within a few minutes, a large black Newfoundland bitch appears on the scene, five times the size of Archie. After a bit of introductory sniffing, they are playing with each other—a bit of a comical sight with their disproportionate sizes. We spend a bit of time on the beach, enjoying the now blue skies.

It is time to return to catch the bus for the next stage of our journey. After leaving the beach, we pass the medieval cemetery of St. Mary's on Carmelite Street. Opening the wrought iron gates, we enter the old kirkyard. Inside is the old kirk of St Mary's itself, small in size, partly in ruins and no longer used for regular worship. Around the graveyard, there are some very old and interesting tombstones dating from the 1600's and perhaps earlier. Some are mini mausoleums, with one to William Gordon esquire, Rear Admiral of the White Squadron.

Opposite the entrance to the old kirkyard, is High Shore with an attractive group of 18thC buildings, one at the end of the row painted red and a round baronial style turret built into its upper corner.

Back to Low Street to catch our next bus. We have some spare time, so we walk back up Straits Path to the High Street to visit the bakery previously referred to. Panting a bit due to the steep climb (rucksack and all), I purchase two freshly cooked pies for lunch, a macaroni cheese and curried chicken. They smell great.

Back down to the bus stop to wait for the next bus to Elgin. While I am waiting, eating my lunch, a traffic warden patrols up and down the street and is able to place two tickets on vehicles that are supposedly "illegally parked" on a single yellow line. Firstly I am a bit surprised that a relatively small place like Banff needed a traffic warden and secondly, thought it a bit O.T.T. to book vehicles that are not causing any obstruction whatsoever. Still the law is the law, and I suppose that it is good for council revenues. So motorists visiting Banff, beware!

One of the main attractions in Banff, which unfortunately we did not have time to visit, is Duff House, to the south of the Town centre and situated in parkland that forms part of the golf course. Built in the early 18thC for William Duff, the First Earl of Fife, it is classed as one of Scotland's classic houses and is open to the public. Before leaving Banff, it should perhaps be mentioned that Alex Salmon, leader of the SNP and Scotland's First Minister at that time, is the local MP and resident in the Town.

* * * * * * *

Spot on time, the No.305 coach for Elgin arrives at 12.30—another £10.50 single fare. We travel for a short distance along the A98 before making a detour into the villages of Inverboyndie and Whitehills. The countryside is ablaze with the bright yellow of the gorse bushes, also the yellow rapeseed oil crop that I personally consider the scourge of the countryside. Back onto the A96 and then into the fishing village of Portsoy with its 17thC harbour and known for the locally quarried green marble. Further along the coast, we come to the (former) Royal Burgh and attractive little fishing town of **Cullen** (population 1,300) with its sandy beaches, harbour and Mercat Cross standing in the Main Square. The Town is dominated by three disused arched masonry viaducts, which carried the railway line between Banff and Elgin in bygone times. It is perhaps best known for the local speciality dish of "Cullen Skink", a soup with smoked haddock, potatoes, onions and cream as its main ingredients. I am reliably informed that the word "Skink" comes from the Gaelic for essence.

The bus route soon deviates onto the A942 towards the fishing villages of Portknockie and Findockity, each with its own harbour and rows of fishermen's cottages that are constructed from the local stone. The road follows the edge of the coast with some splendid views looking out to sea. We pass the Strathlene Golf Club with splashes of yellow gorse across its lush green course that stand out against the blue skies over the hills to the south. Just before we reach Buckie, there are some excellent examples of geological formations of dipping rock strata that outcrop along the shoreline, with layers of sedimentary rocks upended to approximately 60 degrees.

We then enter the Town of **Buckie** (population 8,000) some 55 minutes after leaving Banff. Buckie, the largest town in Banffshire, is still an active fishing port with its own fleet of fishing boats, RNLI lifeboat and shipyard for their repair and maintenance—used also for the building of new boats. The large fabrication shed of the shipyard dominates the harbour. Constructed in 1877, the harbour is a busy place providing much needed employment for the local population on this stretch of the Moray coast.

We carry on along the coast still on the A942, to the fishing village of Portgordon. Developed in the 18thC by the Duke of Gordon, the harbour these days is used mainly by pleasure craft with a few small inshore fishing boats. Passing through a forest of mainly spruce trees, we are back onto the A98 that soon joins the main A96 Inverness road at Fochabers. Crossing the River Spey and into Morayshire (or Elginshire), we pass Baxter's Food Processing Factory, known principally for their famous soups. A bit further on, there are signs pointing to Garmouth, where a former work colleague and friend of mine now lives. It was with some regret that I did not have the time to stop and visit him—sorry Ian.

We pass through more forests of spruce trees and also by an old yellow painted wooden type AA box—I didn't think any were still is existence these days. It took me back to the days when AA patrolmen on their motorbikes complete with sidecars, used to salute members who displayed their AA membership badges on their car radiator grills—hardly practical in modern times. We are soon back out into the green countryside, before reaching the "Welcome to Elgin" signs.

The bus journey from Banff along the coast and through the many fishing villages, has been most pleasant and interesting, with some great scenery and views both out to sea and inland. Going back in time some 100 plus years, when the herring boom was at its height, it must have been a stirring sight to see the flotillas of fishing boats unloading their catches with their mastheads bobbing about in the many small harbours along this coastline. I think Archie has enjoyed the journey too, spending much of the time looking out of the window at the sea—as previously mentioned, he has a fascination for water. The journey from Banff to Elgin has taken 1 hour 35 minutes, it now being 14.05.

Elgin—Morayshire—26,000 population—former City and Royal Burgh (1153)

The cathedral City of Elgin lost its city status, like Perth, in the 1990's following a governmental review of the definition of a city. It is now begrudgingly referred to as Elgin Town albeit the local football team still keeps the name Elgin City FC. Situated on the River Lossie, Elgin was a popular residence for the early Scottish kings during the 12th and 13th centuries.

Elgin Cathedral, which dates from the 13^{th}C, has had a chequered history and now sadly, stands only as a ruin. Having been rebuilt on at least two occasions, the roof was stripped of its lead after the Reformation which soon resulted in it structural decline. The Cathedral was and still is known as the "Lantern of the North" and in its prime was considered to be "a building of Gothic architecture inferior to few in Europe".

Today, Elgin, with neighbouring Lossiemouth and Forres, is heavily dependent for its economic life on the RAF stations at Lossiemouth and Kinloss. It is also the centre of whisky production with up to 30 distilleries in the local Speyside area. The Glen Moray Distillery is located on the Town's western outskirts and is part of the Malt Whisky Trail that takes in a total of nine distilleries.

From the bus station, we head off along Alexandra Road towards the ruins of the Cathedral. Past the former library building, we enter Cooper Park, a large public park with well-maintained flower gardens, boating lake, bowling greens, etc. Within the Park, there is the imposing Grant Lodge, former residence of the Earls of Seafield and now owned by the Town Council. At the time of my visit, the Town's Information Office and Library are being relocated at the Lodge. Having picked up some literature, we continue in the direction of the Cathedral. The toilets by the bowling greens are the cleanest and best maintained I have seen yet, albeit a small charge is made.

The grounds and ruins of the Cathedral are under the jurisdiction of Historic Scotland, who make a charge for visitors. Fair enough, but we have only limited time so we take a walk around its perimeter. Although a ruin, the west front of the Cathedral is an impressive sight and is dominated by the tall twin towers constructed from the local sandstone. The main entrance between the towers, is through two arched doorways, supported by a central column. Around the corner, is the octagonal Chapter House with its roof still intact and still used for meetings, etc.

Walking on, we cross the twin arched Brewery Bridge, built in 1798 and spanning the River Lossie. It is now for pedestrians only and leads to the Newmill area. Archie wants to be off his lead and into the water, but the flow is too fast. Turning back we walk up to the ruins of the Bishop's Palace, used in the past more as a manse. At the side is the entrance to Elgin's Biblical Garden, said to be the largest of its type in Europe. The Garden, that covers some three acres, incorporates all the 110 plants mentioned in the Bible. There are also a number of sculptures depicting characters and stories from both testaments of the Bible, with a desert area being created to depict Mount Sinai. For those who study the scriptures or for those who just enjoy gardens and gardening, the Biblical Garden is worth a visit and there is no charge!!

We walk back through the gardens of Cooper Park and Archie is given an opportunity to have a romp about on the green parkland chasing his ball. After he has had sufficient exercise, we walk around to the front of Grant Lodge with its elegant façade. Crossing over towards College Street, I look down and see a £2.00 coin lying in the grass. No point in trying to locate who dropped it, so it will go to subsidise in part my seemingly extortionist bus fares in Scotland. Crossing over College Street, we walk towards the top end of the High Street. Here is the arcaded three storey Braco's Banking House with the date 1694 on its front. Across the road is the stone column of the 18^{th}C Little Mercat Cross.

Walking down the High Street towards the Town Centre, we pass the baronial style grey stone building that is now used as the ex servicemen's club. Further down, we pass another 17thC arcaded building and Tower House which is supposed to have originally belonged to the Knights of St. John. The High Street has now broadened out to accommodate St. Giles Church. In front of the church, is the Muckle Cross, an 1888 restoration of the original 17thC Mercat Cross.

Sited in the centre of the High Street, the Church of St. Giles is Elgin's most prominent building, the Cathedral apart. Although there has been a church on the site since the 12thC, the present church was constructed in 1827. The unusual open tower and six fluted columns that form part of the Doric façade, make it an impressive building. In front of the church is a circular three tiered fountain which when operating, must look a fine sight.

Time to move on so we make our way back to the bus station. At the far end of the High Street, there is the grassy mound of Ladyhill that was once the site in the 11thC, of Elgin Castle. On the top now stands a tall column supporting a statue of the 5th Earl of Gordon.

* * * * * * *

Again, I would liked to have stopped a bit longer in Elgin to further explore the Town, but we have a schedule to keep. Next stop Inverness where we shall be staying overnight. Back at the bus station, we catch the No.10 Stagecoach Bluebird bus, leaving at 15.45 for Inverness. For some reason, Archie has taken to sitting on my lap—not his usual place when travelling. He must be wanting something from me.

We leave Elgin town centre passing under Ladyhill and the Earl of Gordon's column, before rejoining the A96. Passing through the Crook of Alves (intriguing name) we see the brown tourist signs pointing to the Benromach Distillery on the outskirts of Forres. The bus takes a detour into the old town of **Forres** (population 9,000), which has been a Royal Burgh since 1140. There are some fine sandstone buildings down the wide High Street including the Tolbooth and the imposing kirk of St Laurence with its tall elegant steeple. The Town's splendid Mercat Cross also stands in the High Street in front of the Tollbooth building.

Back on the A96, we cross over the River Findhorn, leaving Morayshire and entering the former county of Nairnshire, now part of the unitary council area of Highland that reaches as far north as Wick and Thurso. We take another detour into the small village of Brodie, which consists of only a few houses but also the 16thC Brodie Castle, home of the Brodies of Brodie.

We rejoin the A96 through a mixture of farmland and forestry, with hills to the south and blue skies above. The bus then turns off for the village of Auldearn, the site of a battle in 1645 when the Covenanting army was defeated by the Marquess of Montrose. The Moray coastline is again in sight as we cross the River (Strath) Nairn and into Nairn Town itself. The seaside town of **Nairn** (population 8,400) was a popular resort during Victorian times and was once described as "the Brighton of Scotland". It still attracts visitors and with the clean sandy beaches, it enjoys one of the sunniest climates in Scotland. The early 19thC harbour was once the home to a large fishing fleet, but today it is used principally as a marina for pleasure craft. At Fishertown to the south of the harbour, there still stand many of the fishermen's cottages.

Leaving the Town centre, we pass through more forestry and then a housing estate consisting of very plain ordinary cement rendered dwelling houses, which are such a contrast to the sandstone buildings of the surrounding area. I have made this comment previously that I fail to understand why architects and planners cannot produce designs of houses more in keeping with the areas in which they are located—it wouldn't involve such a great extra expense. Maybe had they been built today it would be different.

Continuing along the main road to Inverness, there are new-born lambs in the fields, bouncing up and down as if on a trampoline—the yellow gorse is still prevalent. There are signs for Fort George, which is situated on a peninsula on the narrows of the south bank of the Moray Firth, it serving as an artillery fortress for Government forces during the 1745/46 Jacobite uprising. Passing the airport, there are sign for Culloden and also Culloden Battlefield. The Battle in April 1746, saw the end of the Jacobite Rising as led by Prince Charles Edward Stuart and was the last battle to take place on British soil. As a "Geordie" I best not comment upon the cause of the Jacobite rebellion (reference Part 2 Chapter 8). However, for those visiting the battleground, there is an excellent visitors centre describing the history leading up to the battle and its aftermath.

A bit further along the road, we see in the distance ahead, the Kessock Road Bridge that spans the stretch of water between the Moray and Beauly Firths, which we shall cross tomorrow. We continue on along the A96 and into Inverness, the Capital of the Highlands, arriving at the bus station at 17.05. The skies above are clear and blue.

Inverness—Inverness-shire—70,000 population—City and former Royal Burgh (1214)

Situated at the top of the Great Glen, where the River Ness flows into the Moray Firth, Inverness is Scotland's fifth largest city (city status was granted to the *Town of Inverness* in 2001). The old parts of the City and its Castle, are situated on the south-eastern bank of the River Ness with its six bridges that span the River, connecting both sides. Due to its troubled past, most of the architecture of the City dates from only the 19th century, when expansion took place with the construction of the Caledonian Canal and the arrival of the railway. The present castle that sits high above the River Ness, was constructed during the 19thC. The City is the administration centre for the Highland Region and the base for many business and service industries for the area. The City is also well known for its Highland Games and Piping Competitions.

From the bus station, we make our way to the riverside and walk up Bank Street along the eastern side of the Ness. The water is peaty brown and fast flowing from earlier rains. We are looking for the Old Edinburgh Road where our accommodation has been booked for the night. After receiving directions, we pass the Victorian Town House in Bridge Street and then up Castle Street past the red sandstone Castle, which after a bit of a steep climb, leads to Old Edinburgh Road. Our accommodation is at the Kinkell House Hotel that standing in its own grounds is built from the local sandstone with an attractive exterior—the accommodation inside also proved to be very comfortable. Having booked in and deposited my rucksack, Archie and I set off for a walk around the City, the day still being fine with a few hours of light left.

Off we set back down the hill to the Castle. Built in 1835, the present red sandstone building overlooks the River Ness, with an imposing statue of Flora MacDonald standing at the Castle front. The premises are now used as a Sheriff's court and also as administrative offices. From the grounds, there are excellent views looking down on the River Ness with its six bridges and across to the hills in the west. From the Castle, we head down to the River and along its banks to the war memorial and colourful flower gardens. Crossing the 19thC suspension footbridge over the River Ness, we walk down to the neo-Gothic Episcopal Cathedral of St Andrew's. Built during the 1860's, the Cathedral has an imposing edifice and entrance. Looking across the River, the Castle is standing high above on the opposite bank.

We continue down Ness Walk on the west side of the River before crossing back over the Ness Bridge. From the bridge and looking downstream, the three churches on Bank Street stand out with their tall spires dominating the skyline. The Old High Church that was built in the 1770's, was the original parish church for Inverness and is the oldest building in the City. Back past the Town House in Bridge Street, with the Georgian Tollbooth Steeple opposite (its spire rises to 150 feet), we head along the pedestrianised High Street to Falcon Square, the centrepiece being the tall stone obelisk with a rampant unicorn on the top.

Down Academy Street and opposite the railway station, is the Victorian Market. Built during the late 1800's, the covered arcade houses a variety of unique local shops. At this time of the day, the Market is closed, but I will have need of a visit to the Market before leaving Inverness in the morning. We find a flight of stone steps that leads from the High Street up to Ardconnel Terrace. Getting our breath back after the steep climb, we walk back to Kinkell House where Archie is bedded down for the night. I head off for a pint of Belhaven in the Castle Tavern and a plate of tapas as a starter at La Tortilla Spanish Restaurant, opposite. A fitting end to another enjoyable day.

Chapter 6
Inverness To John O'Groats And Thurso—Day 15.

Thursday 30th April 2009

I am up early, only to find that my watch had stopped during the night; hopefully it's only the battery that needs renewing. After a full Scottish breakfast that included porridge and haggis pudding, we set off from Kinkell House, down the hill past the Castle to the O2 shop in the High Street, to sort out my mobile phone—I had not been able to make any outgoing calls since leaving Berwick due to a bar being placed on my phone by my service provider. With the co-operation of a very helpful assistant, the offending bar is at last lifted, albeit leaving me temporarily £72.69 worse off. When I get home, I will try to have this refunded. At least I am now able to make contact with the outside world—how did we all manage before the advent of mobile phones?

Having made some enquiries, I find that there is a jeweller cum watch shop in the Victorian Market. Here I am able for a very modest sum to have the battery of my watch replaced. Thankfully, that is all it needed. So far so good.

The next stage of our journey is to Dornoch with the bus scheduled to leave Inverness bus station at 09.55. Having got to the bus station in plenty of time, the X25 bus to Dornoch arrives 10 minutes late. It is, nevertheless, a City Link Stagecoach luxury coach that has arrived from Aberdeen and is used for long distance trips. At least we will be travelling in comfort.

We eventually leave Inverness at 10.10 on the A9 past the Tulloch Caledonian Stadium, home of Inverness Caledonian Thistle Football Club. The Club has the dubious distinction of having the longest name for any league football club in Europe. Soon we are crossing over the Kessock Bridge that spans the narrows between the Beauly Firth and Moray Firth. The cable-stayed bridge that was opened in 1982, has a central span of 240 metres and is high enough to allow shipping to pass underneath into the Beauly Firth. Once over the bridge, we are on the Black Isle (not an actual island) in the old county of Cromarty. Continuing along the A9 across mainly farming country, we next reach the multi-span road bridge that spans the Cromarty Firth. Looking up to the west, we can see the market town of Dingwall that is now bypassed by the road bridge over the Firth. Beyond in the distance, there are great views of the heather clad mountains.

Crossing now into Ross-shire, the bus heads on along the north bank of the Firth, before making a detour onto the B817 and into the village of Evanton and then Alness, home of the Dalmore whisky distillery. Soon after, we are entering the town of **Invergordon** (population 4,000), where immediately offshore and looming like giant Colossus' over the Town, there are three oilrigs standing within the Cromarty Firth, undergoing repair and maintenance. Since the North Sea oil boom, Invergordon has become a centre for the construction and repair of oilrigs, with its own fabrication and repair yards. During the 1970's the aluminium smelter in the Town was in full production, but this was later closed in 1981. With the safe anchorages of the Firth, the Town has had a long history as a former naval base during the 19thC and into the mid 20thC. During World War 2, it was a base for Sunderland flying boats. For a town situated in such a remote rural area, it was and still is a hub of activity.

Entering into the Town centre, there are colourful paintings / murals on the brick gable ends to some of the buildings, one depicting various sporting activities and another of firemen fighting a fire at the Royal Hotel. I find it welcoming that the local townsfolk take the initiative to brighten up their town—much, much better than some of the graffiti you see on many buildings in some of our towns and cities. On our bus travels through Invergordon, first making detours around the housing and industrial estates before passing Whyte and Mackay's large grain distillery which produces up to 40 million bottles of blended whisky each year and is a major employer in the area.

After leaving Invergordon, the bus route follows the north bank of the Cromarty Firth with clear views across the waters to the Black Isle on the southern side. As we approach Nigg Bay, we pass Saltburn Pier constructed during the days of the aluminium smelting plant and which stretches out to the deeper waters of the Firth. The fields on the landward side of the road are full of the yellow rapeseed oil crop, which surprises me to find up here in the very north of Scotland. The bus route then heads for the attractive village of Milton, with its handsome stone cottages, village green and market cross. There are road signs to Nigg and to the car ferry that operates a service across the Bay to the small town of Cromarty on the Black Isle.

However, the bus bypasses Nigg and heads inland along the A9 past fields full of yellow gorse bushes towards the historic Royal Burgh of **Tain** (population 4,000). Granted its charter in 1066 by King Malcolm III, Nain is the oldest of all the Scottish Royal Burghs. The Town's history is intertwined with St Duthus, born in Tain in 1,000 AD and to whom is dedicated the Collegiate Church and Chapel. The elegant sandstone buildings of the Town are dominated by the impressive tall tower of the Tolbooth, that was first constructed in 1630. In the Town centre, there is an elaborate Gothic style market cross, resembling a mini-version of the Scott Monument in Edinburgh. Tain also has some fine sandy beaches that overlook the Dornoch Firth to the north. There is a change of bus drivers at Tain, but unfortunately, we do not have the opportunity to leave the bus.

Soon after leaving Tain, we pass the entrance to the Glenmorangie Whisky Distillery, which is located on the banks of the Dornoch Firth. First established in 1738, it is claimed that the range of single malts produced at the distillery are the best selling of all UK malts, with some 10 million bottles produced each year. I do my bit in helping sales. Sadly, the distillery is no longer owned by the local MacDonald family, who ran the distillery for some 90 years. It has recently passed into foreign ownership—French!! *sacre bleu!!* Yet another example of a well-established British company falling under the control of foreign ownership.

Ahead, we can see the multi-span bridge across the Dornoch Firth. Opened in 1991, the new bridge has greatly reduced the distance of travel along the A9 between Inverness and Wick, avoiding the need for a 20 mile trip around the Firth via Bonar Bridge at its head. Previous to the bridge being constructed, there was a ferry that operated across the Forth. However in 1809, nearly 100 passengers and crew of the ferry were drowned, due, it is reported, to the boat being overloaded. On crossing over the bridge and looking up the Firth, there are again some fine views of the hills in the distance.

It is from the head of the Dornoch Firth that it is possible to walk coast to coast across the width of Scotland within a day—that is from the head of the Dornoch Firth on the east coast over the hills and down to the head of Loch Broom, near Ulapool on the west coast, some 33 miles.

Wainwright's Coast to Coast Walk across Northern England is 190 miles long and takes some 12 days to complete.

Once over the bridge, we have entered Sutherland. The restored Skibo Castle, now an exclusive members only country club, is passed on our left. A little further on, the bus takes a right turn onto the A949 towards Dornoch. After two miles, we reach the market place and centre of the historic Town—the time is 11.40. Archie can smell the sea air and after more than an hour and a half on the bus, is ready to get off and do a bit of exploring.

Dornoch—Sutherland—1,200 population—Town and former Royal Burgh (1628)

Although relatively small in population, the Town boasts a cathedral, albeit the smallest in Scotland. Dornoch Cathedral was first constructed in the 13thC and is dedicated to St Gilbert, who as Bishop of Caithness, was responsible for the building of the original cathedral in Dornoch. Following a fire in 1570, it was not until the 19thC that the present Cathedral was rebuilt. In 2000, the Town received some coverage in the national media when the pop star Madonna had her child baptised at the Cathedral.

The bus drops us off virtually in front of the Cathedral. Although an imposing sandstone building, the Cathedral resembles more a large 19thC parish church with its square clock tower and short spire atop. Outside the Cathedral's entrance, there is a painted wrought iron water fountain, complete with canopy and street lamp on top. Immediately opposite the Cathedral is the 15thC Bishop's Palace, now converted to a hotel.

The Cathedral's door is locked, although Archie may not have been welcomed inside. Nevertheless, we take a walk around the Cathedral and its graveyard, which contains the "Plaiden Ell". This is a flat stone slab of fixed length, the "Ell" being used for measuring lengths of plaid or tartan cloth and is one of only three in existence in Scotland. Standing adjacent to the kirkyard wall is the medieval Mercat Cross. Now only a plain square stone column sitting on a stone plinth without any ornamentation, it depicts the site of the fairs and markets held in the Town that would last up to three days, the local alehouses doing a roaring trade during those periods.

Besides its Cathedral, Dornoch is also a popular seaside resort with its clean sandy beaches along the shores of the Dornoch Firth. The golf links at the Royal Dornoch Golf Club are named as the fifth best in the world outside the USA. Archie has had enough of the town and wants to be at the seaside. With map in hand that I had picked up from the Town's Information Office, we set off on a 15 minute walk down Church Street, past the sandstone cottages in Well Street and then along Beach Road to the beach itself. Once over the sand dunes, we are not disappointed when we arrive at the seaside, with the flat expansive golden sands stretching out to the sea. Across the Firth, the coastline of Ross-shire is clearly visible.

Immediately, Archie makes a bee-line for the sea and then starts his usual antics of digging a trench in the sand to bury his ball. We did think that we had the beach to ourselves until a white West Highland terrier appeared on the scene. Archie has found a playmate. Eventually its owner catches up and after a brief chat, is on his way, dog and all. We are on our own again, at least on the ground. Up in the skies, the RAF is at practice with two Tornados disturbing the peace and quiet with their after-burners on full-blast. With the tranquillity and clear blue skies above, I could easily have stopped longer on the beach, but we need to be back into the town to make our next connection.

On our way back to the Town centre, we briefly stopped at the Witch's Stone on River Street. It was at this place in 1727, that Janet Horne, who had been "convicted" of witchcraft, was rolled in tar, placed inside a barrel and burnt alive. It was, thankfully, the last time this form of execution took place in Scotland. A large boulder standing in the private garden of a house with the year 1727 carved into it, commemorates this barbaric event. An information board by the roadside, explains what took place.

* * * * * * *

We are back in the Town centre in time to catch the bus to our next destination, Wick. At 13.30, the X25 Stagecoach bus from Inverness arrives and on we hop. But first, I am asked by the driver if I have booked in advance a place for Archie on the bus. What, I ask, is the need for that, to which I am told that the bus company has a policy of allowing only one dog per bus journey. This is news to me and I am pleased it is near to the end of my trip from Lands End. Had I been aware before now, it would have caused some uncertainty as to whether I would have been able to maintain my schedule. With some further thought on the matter, I can perhaps understand this rule, especially if there are say two aggressive dogs on the bus together. Thankfully, there is no other dog aboard and Archie is well behaved, even though I say so myself. The next "wammie" comes when he asks me for my bus fare—£13.00 single fare for a hour and forty minute journey to Wick—the highest yet!! It must cost the locals a fortune to regular travel by public transport, that is unless you are over 60 and living in Scotland with a free pass.

We leave Dornoch at 13.40—a pretty town, full of interest with a splendid beach and (so I am told) golf course. Soon we are back onto the A9 Inverness / Thurso road. Not far after rejoining the A9, we are held up for nearly 10 minutes due to a stretch of road being under repair and with an escorted convoy system in operation. The bus driver was perhaps expecting this hold-up in the traffic, but he has a schedule to keep.

Eventually we are clear of the road-works and it is soon apparent that the driver intends to make up for time lost. Off we speed along the single carriageway coastal road, around the top of Loch Fleet. The signpost indicates 76 miles to John O'Groats, so not far now to go. The countryside is becoming quite barren, there being few trees and numerous expanses of bare rock.

Next stop will be **Golspie** (population 1,600), a coastal village with its own small harbour, pier and attractive sandstone buildings and cottages. The street names and sign above the post office, are all in Gaelic, the first time that I have noticed its use on my travels so far. It may well be that I have missed previous signs. In the children's play area, there is a redundant full sized road-roller for the kids to enjoy themselves on. What a great idea. However, I cannot see it catching on elsewhere because of the over reaction by local councils to health and safety requirements and possible litigation if someone falls. It is a terrible shame that the children of today do not have the opportunity for adventure and fun that I certainly had when I was younger. How have we got ourselves into this situation? I suspect that I know the answer. (RANT 32)

Immediately to the west of the Village, on the summit of Ben Bhraggie, is a 100 foot high column with the statue of the First Duke of Sutherland atop. During the early 1800's the Duke of Sutherland acquired vast tracts of land in Northern Scotland and was largely responsible for the Highland Clearances. The Clearances resulted in up to 15,000 tenant crofters being forcibly evicted from their homes on the Duke's estates and the land given over to grazing for sheep. The statue of the much despised First Duke dominates Golspie and there have been calls for its removal. However, at the time of my visit, it still remains in place. Nevertheless, I can think that of some "fellas" that would be prepared to do a good job on its demolition.

One mile up the road from Golspie, is the entrance to Dunrobin Castle, the ancestral home to the Dukes and Earls of Sutherland. Although the original castle dates from the 13thC, the present magnificent, baronial fairy tale building, dates from 1840. The designer was Sir Charles Barry, who was also the architect responsible for the design of the Houses of Parliament in London. The formal gardens are said to be based on those at the Palace of Versailles—no expense spared and to h**l with the poor crofters.

Out of Golspie, we are following the railway line alongside the coast with the Moray coastline just visible across the Moray Firth. The sea is to our right, the hills are to our left. The bus travels past by the scattered homesteads and the little village of Doll, and into the small town of **Brora** (population 1,200), once the industrial powerhouse of Sutherland. Up to the 1970's, there was an operating coal mine in Brora, the most northerly in the U.K. Coal had been mined in Brora since the 16thC and had been used in the evaporation of seawater to extract salt, which in turn, was used for the preservation of fish during the herring boom at ports up this northerly section of the east coast. Today, no coal is mined nor salt produced at Brora, although a small fishing fleet still sails from the harbour. One of the main present day employers is the Clynelish Distillery that produces a classic coastal malt whisky. Another is the local quarry, from which white oolitic sandstone rock from the mid Jurassic period is worked. It is reputed that stone from this quarry was used in the construction of John Rennie's 19thC London Bridge, which was replaced in the early 1970's. The original bridge was shipped to Arizona in the USA for $2.5M, where it is said the purchaser thought he was buying the more impressive Tower Bridge. Back in Town centre, there is an interesting tall stone clock tower designed in the Scottish baronial style. The Town also has an excellent golf course and expansive beaches.

Back on our journey north, there is not much traffic on the single carriageway A9 and the bus is bombing along, the driver seemingly trying to make up time lost at the road-works prior to Golspie. The yellow gorse is still prevalent in the treeless open countryside. We pass a small church standing on its own, miles from anywhere, although there are a few scattered dwellings along the way as we travel up the coast. On we travel to Portgower, then Helmsdale with its small harbour, and across the River Helmsdale into Caithness, the most northerly county on the U.K. mainland. The signpost shows it to be another 55 miles to John O'Groats.

Once over the River, the A9 climbs up to the Ord (or Gateway) of Caithness and onto the Berriesdale Braes. The scenery is wild and desolate yet attractive in its own way. Despite recent road improvement works, the road ahead over the Braes is quite tortuous with many twists and turns interspaced with steep descents and climbs. There are gravel traps provided on the downwards descents for vehicles that experience brake failure—thankfully the bus's brakes seem to be OK. The coastline ahead is rugged too, which together with the hilly terrain, caused the railway builders to divert their line to Wick away from the coast at this point and to go inland via the Strath of Kildonan.

On the way to to Berriesdale, we pass a "brown" tourist sign pointing to the "Clearance Village of Badbea" which has been preserved as a historic site. It was in 1793 that 80 people from twelve families were evicted by Sir John Sinclair of Ulbster to give over the land for sheep grazing. The families were moved to the barren coastal strip around Badbea with its steep rugged cliffs, making life very hazardous. Some of the evicted crofters emigrated to New Zealand but many remained, the last inhabitant eventually leaving in 1911. There is a 22 foot high monument to the evicted crofters that was arranged by the Gunn's, one of the crofter families at Badblea.

We reach the small village of Berriesdale, lying below the main road and nestled around its natural harbour at the mouth of Berriesdale Water. On the hills immediately above the village are two crenulated towers known as the "Duke's Matchsticks". Erected by the Duke of Portland, the towers acted as light-houses to guide fishermen into the harbour entrance. The row of white cottages seen from the road is known as Portland Terrace.

Onwards we travel, with the North Sea coast on our right and the hills on our left—the clouds are hovering over the top of Scaraben, 2,053 feet above sea level. The slopes of the hills are covered with conifer trees that have been planted by the Forestry Commission. Seeing these vast tracts of forestry plantations in this remote but beautiful countryside, I have mixed feelings on their contribution to the economy verses their effect on the environment. For sure, they provide timber and local employment but at what cost to the natural wildlife and local flora and fauna. These trees are not part of the natural environment and even the Forestry Commission accept that mistakes have been made in the past on the creation of these artificial plantations. Not least in the border regions of Northumberland where the largest man-made forest in Northern Europe has been created. Today, a more environmental friendly policy has been adopted by the Commission, with the mixed planting of deciduous trees and a reduction in the size of plantations. Also the opening up of many forests for public recreation and the creation of woodland trails has helped. Nevertheless, the change to the countryside in many rural areas has been dramatic with access and views restricted. The presence of these large conifer plantations in areas such as Caithness is certainly not in keeping with the natural environment. However, with the economic benefits, I am not sure what the answer is—any suggestions? (RANT 33). At least the change in land use has not had the same consequences as the Clearances of the early 1800's.

The next village we pass is Dunbeath, which lies beneath the road bridge over Dunbeath Water as it twists and turns to meet the sea. The small harbour, like many along this coast, prospered during the herring boom. Now, there is much less activity. The novelist, Neil Miller Gunn was born in the Village in 1891. He wrote 23 novels based on the Highland communities and landscape he grew up with in his youth. Perhaps the best known is "Highland River", for which there is an effigy in the Village depicting *Kenn and the Salmon*. His autobiography is titled *"The Atm of Light"*.

We head up the treeless yet attractive Caithness coast to Latheron that is the home of the Clan Gunn Heritage Centre. Here the A9 main road heads off due north via Mybster to Thurso, but our bus continues to follow the coast along the A99 to Wick—35 miles now to John O'Groats. A few passengers get on the bus at Latheron and although they seem to be local residents, their English accents suggest that they were not born and brought up in these parts. Although there are many, many Scots living in England, somehow you do not expect to find the English living in the far north of Scotland, but on reflection, why not in these tranquil, beautiful surroundings.

On we travel through Lybster, Ulbster and Thrumster—names traced back to the days of the Norsemen. The treeless fields alongside the road are lined with dry-stone walls. Sheep and some highland cattle have been put out to graze. Some of the fields have crops growing and it appears that the soil in the area is quite rich and fertile. I suppose the temperatures and strong winds in these far northern parts prevent the growing of arable crops on any large scale. One field, in what seemed miles from anywhere, is a cemetery with not a church or chapel in sight.

The driver is making good progress in catching up for time lost earlier. The young couple on the seat in front are in an amorous mood—ahh, young love!! At last, we reach the town of Wick and the bus station, bang on time at 15.10. The driver has done well and I tell him so as we leave the bus. Our stop in Wick is going to be brief as the bus to John O'Groats leaves in 25 minutes. If we miss this bus, we will have no time to spend at our final destination.

Wick—Caithness—7,300 population—Town and former Royal Burgh (1589)

The Town is situated on (surprise, surprise) the River Wick that flows into the North Sea at Wick Bay. The harbour, originally developed by Sir John Sinclair in 1768 and later improved by Thomas Telford, was "the" premier fishing port in Northern Scotland during the time of the herring boom in the 19th century. At its peak, the fishing fleet based at Wick numbered over 1,000 boats. It was Sir William Pulteney, Governor of the British Fisheries Society and MP for Caithness, who engaged Telford to oversee the development of the harbour and new town, Pulteneytown, on the south side of the River. The Old Pulteney whisky distillery founded in 1826 in Pulteneytown is the most northerly distillery in mainland Britain, with the whisky produced having a hint of the sea air. Up to the time of recent local government reorganisations in 1973, Wick was also the county town for Caithness.

As a result of over-fishing during the 1800's and early 1900's, the fish stocks of herring in the North Sea were severely depleted by the mid 20th century and with them, much of the prosperity of Wick. However with the development of North Sea oil, there is once again some activity in the harbour, with vessels servicing the off-shore rigs calling in. The Wick Heritage Museum that focuses on the Town's herring fishing hey-day, has won awards and is worth a visit.

During the last weekend in June of this year, the Wick Harbour Fest 2009 is to be held. The three-day festival is being reintroduced to celebrate the Town's fishing heritage, with the visit of the Scottish Heritage Fishing Fleet, together with the crowning of the Herring Queen (as at Eyemouth). It is hoped that there will be a "home-coming" of many of the exiles of Wick and Caithness who for various reasons, have left the area. Hopefully, its success will encourage the organisers to make it an annual event.

In the Old Town, Ebenezer Place at 6ft 9ins in length and with only one front door, is reputed to be the World's shortest street. Based in the harbour is the RNLI's lifeboat station that is still manned by local volunteers.

Nearby at Altimarlach on the banks of the River Wick, the last battle between the Scottish clans took place in 1680. This was between the local Sinclairs and the Campbells over land rights, in which the Sinclairs suffered a heavy defeat. A memorial cross now marks the site of the battle. To the south of the harbour are the ruins of the Old Castle of Wick, a Norse stronghold standing on the edge of the cliffs and overlooking the sea.

With little time to spend in Wick, we head for the new bus station, off up the High Street and down Bridge Street past the dark sandstone Town House with its domed clock tower, to the old bridge designed by Telford. From the bridge, there is a good view upstream. Above us on the south bank is the railway station, the end of the line from Inverness. Walking back down the High Street, there is a stone plaque commemorating the local novelist, Neil M. Gunn. There is also a good bakers shop where I was able to obtain my lunch. Whilst waiting for our next bus and eating my lunch, a three wheeler motor cycle rides by, unusual insomuch that the two wheels were at the front.

* * * * * * *

Soon it is time for the final stage of our journey from Lands End. At 15.35, the local Rapson's coach arrives to take us up to John O'Groats. Being the time of day, it turns out to be the school bus taking the 12 year old plus children home from secondary school. The bus has five seats across its width with three on one side of the aisle and two on the other and is near full. I guess that being used as a school bus, they try to cram as many passengers aboard as possible. Archie and I manage to find the only vacant double seat, so in we settle amongst all the noise and chatter of the school children, who compared to those from some of the larger towns and cities, are quite well behaved.

Off we go up the A99 to Keiss then onto Nybster. Along this rugged coastline, there are signs of tall stone buildings that could at one time have been fortified houses. The bare coastline with the seas crashing against the cliffs, gives this area an atmosphere of remoteness, yet there are a number of isolated rendered / white-washed farms and cottages that are scattered over the country landscape between the villages. The bus makes a number of stops to let the school children off. Still hardly a tree in sight.

While I am looking out of the bus window admiring the scenery, I fail to notice that Archie had jumped down onto the floor of the bus and is rummaging amongst some papers that have been thrown down under the seat in front. The children in front had been eating chips from wrappers when they got on at Wick and had left their chips partially uneaten on the floor when they had got of the bus. Archie has not yet been fed so he is helping himself to an early dinner of cold greasy chips, which could make him ill. I do manage to pull him back but I know that he has consumed some of the children's left-overs, hopefully not too much. It seems that even up here in the rural areas of the far north, youngsters have little regard for the mess and inconvenience they are creating by the needless throwing away of litter, including on buses. I would have thought that they must be taught about the need to safeguard the environment at school and the damage that is being done by the irresponsible discard of rubbish. Why could they not have taken their wrappers home or put them in a suitable waste bin, rather than give the bus driver the task of clearing up their mess. (RANT 34). At least Archie is showing no signs of any ill affects, although I can tell that he is not too pleased with me.

The bus then leaves the A99 and heads west away from the coast, across heather and gorse moors on a single-track road. The countryside is now really wild and barren with little habitation in sight. I have lost my sense of direction as to which way we are travelling, when suddenly we drop down into the village of Cannisbay, to the west of John O'Groats. We then join the A836 travelling eastwards along the north coast of Scotland overlooking the Pentland Firth for the final few miles to John O'Groats, which we reach at 16.30. The sun is shinning to welcome us at our final destination, having travelled 1,230 miles by bus from Lands End in Cornwall to get here.

John O'Groats—Caithness—300 population—Village

I am not sure why, but in my ignorance, I didn't realise that there is a village with its own harbour at John O'Groats. Perhaps it is because of making a comparison with Lands End where there is only a visitors' centre. However, the bus drops us off at the harbour, having previously discharged the remaining children en-route in the village. I have just over two hours to spend at this northerly point on the British mainland before catching my next bus to Thurso, where I have booked accommodation for the night.

Although often thought to be the most northerly point on the British mainland, that actual distinction goes to Dunnet Head, a little way to the west along the coast of the Pentland Firth towards Thurso. However, John O'Groats is the most northerly settlement on the British mainland and it is from here that many of the long distance walks, cycle rides and some more extreme forms of travel to Lands End begin. The distance shown on the "Journey's End" signpost is 874 miles, presumably "as the crow flies".

John O'Groats came by its name from a Dutchman who was the leader of a small group from Holland who settled in the area and were granted the right in the year 1496, to operate the first regular ferry to the Orkneys. His name was Jan de Groot and at that time, the Orkneys had only recently been transferred through royal marriage from Norway to Scotland. The fare was one groat and it is suggested that de Groot gave his name to the small silver coin, worth four pennies, that ceased to be minted in 1856. However, this story may only be a myth. A ferry still provides a regular service for foot passengers during the summer months from the harbour to the Orkneys, this now operated by the John O'Groats Ferry Company.

Overlooking the harbour there is the John O'Groats House Hotel, built on the site of Jan de Groot's eight-sided house. Built in 1875, the white Gothic building has been a famous landmark for the area, with its eight-sided tower complete with short spire. It is said that de Groot had an octagonal dining table so that each of the eight diners could consider themselves to be at the top of the table. However the building is no longer in use as a hotel and at the time of my visit, appeared to be permanently closed. I understand that there are talks of it being renovated and reopened as a hotel.

Just as I arrive, the ferry from Burwick on the southern tip of South Ronaldsay in the Orkney Isles, has docked just outside the harbour entrance and is discharging its passengers and cargo. However, according to the published timetable, the ferry only operates during the summer months, starting on the 1st May. Today was Thursday 30th April, so it may be a precursor trip in readiness for the following day's first sailing of the season from John O'Groats. Looking out across the harbour and the Pentland Firth, the southern tip of South Ronaldsay on the Orkneys is clearly visible. Eastwards the coastline leads towards Duncansby Head, some two miles away on the very north east point of the mainland.

There are few people about at this time of year and as the time is approaching 17.00, I thought it best to visit the tourist shop before it closes to pick up something to verify that I have actually made it. Whilst I am in the shop, they are delivering cases of Orkney ale that have just been off-loaded from the ferry. Surely a bottle of "Northern Lights Ale", brewed in the Orkney Brewery of Quoyloo would be as good a souvenir as any. So along with a few postcards and nick-knacks, we make our way back to the "Journey's End" signpost where I am able to take a photo of Archie just before they take the signboards down for the evening. To have a professional photo taken in front of the signpost is £12.00 and perhaps with hindsight, I should have stumped up the money to have one taken of us both for posterity, but at this time I am reluctant to part with my money—maybe the Scottish tendencies are rubbing onto me.

On we walk, past "The Last House" shop and museum, towards the coastal footpath that runs eastwards in the direction of Dunansby Head. Time does not allow us to walk the full way to Dunansby Head that is some two miles away. However, with clear skies above and little wind blowing, we enjoy a walk alongside this most northerly coastline with its stretches of silvery sand interspaced with the seaweed covered rock formations that dip gently into the sea. The primroses are out alongside the footpath, which makes a colourful sight. Archie is again in his element playing on the beach and charging into the sea. On a couple of occasions I thought that I had lost him but I should have known better, he always turns up—eventually.

We stop on a pleasant sandy stretch for a while, enjoying the view across the Pentland Firth, when my resistance drops and the bottle of "Northern Lights Ale" is opened. The full bottle is too heavy to carry all the way back home to Lincoln, although I do take the empty bottle back home. In any case, what a pleasant way to celebrate the completion of our bus journey all the way from Lands End, sitting on this remote stretch of beach enjoying the views, peace and quiet. I do manage to find in my rucksack a special treat for Archie. It is very much different to the wild, windy and wet weather we had experienced at Lands End the previous August.

Our two hours in John O'Groats is nearing an end and the weather is beginning to change for the worse. So off we head back along the coastal path to the harbour, where at 18.40, we are due to catch the Rapson bus to Thurso. By now, everywhere is closed and deserted. We are very much on our own. Walking up to the new Craft Village shopping complex which too is deserted, you pass the "Welcome" sign in front of which is a six foot replica of "Eric the Viking" with spear and shield in hand. I have to have a photo of this for my album. It is perhaps a sign of the times that about half of the craft shops in the complex are vacant.

* * * * * * *

The weather is now turning cold and it is starting to rain—such a difference from an hour previous. With no-one else around, I am beginning to feel abandoned, so it is with some relief that I see the Thurso bus drive into the large parking area by the harbour. Apart from the driver, there is no-one else aboard the bus, so we have a choice of seats. It is nice to be in the comfort and warmth of the bus as the temperatures outside are beginning to drop. At 18.40, off we speed along the A836 westwards towards Thurso, the forty-minute ride being the final stage of our bus journey from Lands End.

The first few miles to Huna and Cannisbay look familiar, as we had come along this section of the A836 on our way to John O'Groats earlier in the afternoon, albeit travelling in the opposite direction. The Isle of Stroma is clearly visible on our right. Around Gills Bay we go and on towards Mey. Before we reach the village, there are the tourist signs for Castle and Gardens of Mey, the Caithness home of the late Queen Mother. The 16thC castle was acquired by the Queen Mother in 1952 and it was she who was responsible for its renovation and restoration, including the laying out of the gardens. The Queen Mother, who died in 2002 at the age of 102, spent a lot of time at Mey, enjoying the peace and tranquillity of this most northerly castle on the U.K. mainland. The castle and gardens are now open to visitors.

Next we pass St John's Loch, a relatively small body of water by Scottish standards. Immediately after the Loch, the B885 branches off and leads to Dunnet Head, the true most northerly point on the British mainland at latitude 58 degrees, 40.3 minutes N, some 1.6 minutes further north than John O'Groats. The lighthouse built in 1831 under the direction of Robert Stevenson, stands on the edge of the 300 feet red sandstone cliffs with views across the Pentland Firth to the Orkney Isles. Unfortunately, there are no bus services up to the Head, access being either by foot or by car. We shall have to make do with John O'Groats. From the photographs seen of Dunnet Head, it looks to be a place worthy of a visit with its imposing tall cliffs above the sea.

On we travel around Dunnet Bay with its golden sandy beaches, green fields and bushes growing at 45 degrees as a result of the strong prevailing winds. There are also ice warning signs for drivers. On into Castletown, where two passengers get on the bus, so at least the bus company is going to get more for the trip than the £3.60 that I have had paid for the journey between John O'Groats and Thurso. More passengers get on at Murkle, before we reach the town of Thurso itself. On past the signs for the abbey ruins, over the bridge spanning the River Thurso and into the Town centre, the time being 19.20 and the weather grey, wet and windy.

On getting off the bus, I ask the driver if he knows where the Weigh Inn is in Thurso, the accommodation I have booked for the evening. He thought it to be a little way along the coast towards Scabster, maybe a fifteen minutes walk. Although it is raining, off we set along Traill Street, Oil Rig Street and Smith Terrace in the direction of Scrabster. It seems more like 30 minutes before we arrive at the Weigh Inn, cold, wet and tired. With hindsight, we should have tried to get a taxi.

Having booked in and bedded Archie down for the night (he has had enough exercise for the day and is ready for his bed), I make my way to the bar, looking forward to a few beers and a good meal. Surprisingly for a Thursday night, the bar is very busy, but I am able to find a comfortable seat, order a beer and meal. The beer is McEwen's 70/-, one of my favourite Edinburgh beers although no longer brewed there. The meal that I order is also to my liking, ham and broccoli soup followed by home made fisherman's pie.

It has been a long but most enjoyable day travelling from Inverness across the Black Isle of Cromarty and up the Sutherland / Caithness coastline to Thurso, taking in the five Firths of Moray, Beauly, Cromarty, Dornoch and Pentland. The scenery in this remote part of Scotland has a beauty of its own, with the magnificent sandy beaches, dramatic cliffs and the scattered fishing villages dotted along the coast. The cathedral town of Dornoch was particularly memorable. The countryside inland from the coastline is also different, with the stone walled green fields, bare rock faces and what few trees there are growing at an acute angle due to the strong prevailing winds. The yellow of the gorse bushes at this time of the year give much colour to the land together with the heather-clad hills. All in all, a journey to be remembered and perhaps the most enjoyable section on the whole of my trip. It is a bit sad that my bus journey has now come to an end. Tomorrow, we shall be making our way back home—by train.

Chapter 7
Journey Home—Thurso To Inverness To Lincoln— By Train—Days 16 & 17.

Friday 1ˢᵗ May 2009

After a comfortable night at the Weigh Inn, I am up early to give Archie a short walk before breakfast—the sun is out and the skies are blue. It is the first of the month and "May Day" with all that brings!! Breakfast is in the hotel's conservatory with views out over the bay towards the Orkneys. Breakfast includes "locally landed" kippers (I didn't think that kippers were "landed") and poached egg, all of which is very satisfying.

I cannot help noticing that when a mother and her two children on the table nearby gets up to leave, they have left over half their fried breakfasts. What a waste! Why do people order large fried breakfasts or meals of any kind, if they are going to let more than half go to waste? It would seem that their "eyes are bigger than their bellies" Maybe the wasted food does go for animal feed but the expense in producing and preparing the food served is not small. Perhaps I have strong views on such matters, as I was brought up during the war years of the 1940's when I was taught to eat everything served before me and to leave a clean plate. It is the same with food that is wasted and discarded from supermarkets because their "sell-by dates" have expired by a day or two. We are indeed a very affluent and wasteful society. (RANT 35)

My train from Thurso to Inverness is due to leave at 13.05, so that means I have some three hours to spend in Thurso. Booking out of the hotel at 09.45 we make our way down towards the coast and along a designated cliff top footpath known as Victoria Walk, which leads into Thurso.

Thurso—Caithness—8,700 population—Town and former Burgh of Barony (1633)

As the most northerly town on the British mainland at 59 degrees N latitude, Thurso has as you would expect, a large number of buildings, attractions and other establishments classified as the "most northerly". The railway station is the most northerly station served by Britain's rail network. Also on the same northerly latitude as Thurso, are Juneau in Alaska, Hudson Bay in Canada and Stavanger in Norway.

The Town has historical links going back to the Vikings who first settled in the area during the 900's. The name Thurso is derived from the old Norse word "Torsaa—Thors River". The title of "Burgh of Barony" is defined as where "the title is granted to the tenant-in-chief / the landowner or leading nobleman who held his estates directly from the Crown". I must admit to being not much wiser.

The walk along the top of the cliffs over Thurso Bay is most enjoyable with stunning views across the Bay. To the east are the distant cliffs of Dunnet Head. Looking out to sea, the Isle of Hoy is clearly visible across the Pentland Firth, although it is difficult to make out the rock stack of the Old Man of Hoy. Down below, the gently dipping and folded sandstone rock strata are exposed below high water level. Most of the rocks are covered in seaweed.

To the west is the port and harbour of Scrabster, nestled below Holborn Head, some two miles along the coast from Thurso. The harbour was developed in the 1850's and has become the main port for the area with regular car ferry services to Stromness in the Orkneys. A RNLI off-shore lifeboat is moored within the harbour, waiting to respond to emergencies and I would guess that they will get a number of call-outs during the year on this storm-swept northerly coast of the U.K.

On the landward side of the footpath there is a continuous two-foot high stone wall that runs the full length of the path, the wall being constructed from vertically placed sandstone slabs, looking like a long line of overlapping gravestones. During the 1800's, there was a prosperous industry in the quarrying and preparation of flagstones that was based at Castletown, just to the east of Thurso. At its peak, 35,000 tons of flagstones were being produced each year, these being used to pave the streets of cities around the world, including Paris, Montevideo and Sydney. At this time, over 500 people were employed at the Works.

Inevitably, production ceased in the 1920's although there is a heritage centre at Castletown that preserves the history of the local flagstone industry.

Some eight miles to the west of Thurso, is Dounreay Nuclear Power Station, reported as soon to be decommissioned. The original station was commissioned in 1959 and provided much needed employment for the local population, especially during the period of its construction. My views on nuclear power stations were expressed in Part 1. Hopefully, the local economy will not suffer too much if and when the Station does eventually close.

At a viewpoint half way along the cliff-top path to the Town itself there is a seat built from local stone, with the inscription on the dedication stone "In Memory to Sir William A. Smith, founder of the Boys Brigade". Sir William was born at Pennyland House on the western outskirts of Thurso in 1854 and was responsible for founding the worldwide Christian based movement for youngsters that preceded the Boy Scouts. Today, there are over 500,000 members of the Boys Brigade spread across 60 countries of the World.

The cliff-top walk is popular with dog-walkers and on our morning walk, we meet at least ten other dogs and their owners. Unfortunately, not all have picked up their dog's left-overs despite the provision of "doggie bins". I have already had a Rant about such irresponsibility and the bad name given to all dog owners by an inconsiderate few.

Approaching the Town, there is a circular view-pointer mounted on a stone plinth that has been donated by the local Round Table. Direction lines point to Dunnet Head, Scapa Flow and the Old Man of Hoy although not all are visible. By the view-pointer, there is another stone seat that overlooks the sea but built to an imaginative curved design.

Below us is the sandy beach of Thurso Bay, one of the top international surfing venues—and certainly the coldest—a bit different to Newquay. Regular international surfing championships on the UK tour are now held each year at Thurso. Today, the seas are quite calm, but the powerful waves rolling in from the Pentland Firth obviously create the right conditions for international surfers. Down on the beach, Archie is soon at work digging long trenches in the sand and dashing into the sea chasing his ball.

Up on the promenade on the west bank of the River Thurso, the sandstone ruins of 17thC Thurso Castle stands out on the opposite side of the River. There is a small harbour at the River's estuary, although today

Scrabster provides the main port facilities for the Town. The weather is changing and it is starting to rain. At least we were able to enjoy our cliff-top walk before it started.

Walking up towards the Town centre, we come across the ruins of St Peter's Kirk, dating back to the 13th century and claimed to be one of the finest surviving religious buildings in Northern Scotland. The main window is carved from a single piece of stone, thought to be the largest of its type in the world. The ruins are now under the control of Historic Scotland and at the time of our visit, access is restricted.

On up through the new pedestrianised shopping precinct in Rotterdam Street and back up Traill Street to Sir John's Square where the bus had dropped me off the previous evening—it was raining then too. St John's Kirk stands on the northern edge of the Square with an imposing war memorial in front and colourful flowers gardens leading down to the main road. With plenty of time to spare, we take a short walk down Sir George's Street to the 19thC four arched ashlar bridge that spans the River. The peaty brown fast-flowing waters and the view upstream, make a splendid sight.

The rain is getting heavier, so we (or rather I) decide to make for the railway station, although there is still an hour before our train is due to leave. Up Sinclair Street we head to the Public Library with its columned portico and tall clock tower. At the time the stonework of the building is undergoing renovation work so we are unable to get an unhindered view of this interesting piece of architecture. On we walk up Princess Street to Thurso Railway Station, the most northerly mainline railway station in the U.K.

Inside the station, there is a very pleasant and well-kept waiting area with miniature cactus gardens. Above one of the miniature gardens is a plaque erected by the Thurso Branch of the Royal British Legion in commemoration to "Jellicoe Express" that ran between Euston and Thuro during the years of both World Wars, carrying military personnel on their onward journey to Scarpa Flow in the Orkneys. The station is quite literally "at the end of the line" with the two tracks coming into the station, stopping at the rail buffers.

The rain outside is easing, so I take the opportunity to take Archie for a walk before the long three hour train journey back to Inverness. Down Lovers Lane (how romantic) we go to Camfield Park on the west side of the River and then across the new pedestrian bridge to the open green parkland of Millbank. At least Archie is able to have a run-a-bout off the lead although I have to keep a careful eye on him as he is getting too close to the fast-flowing waters of the River. The old mill building has recently been renovated and is now the Old Mill Theatre. Having been suitably exercised, Archie and I make our way back up Lovers Lane to the railway station. It has started to rain again.

* * * * * * *

After a short wait, the twin coached Scotrail diesel train from Wick draws up at the station platform, spot on time at 13.05. The train started its journey to Inverness from Wick and comes via Loch Watten up to the branch line leading to Thurso, only to reverse back down again in the southerly direction. Although there are a few passengers waiting to get on at Thurso, the train is nearly full. It transpired that there is a party of tourists travelling with Shearings Coaches who are taking in the train trip between Wick and Golspie as one of their sight-seeing daily excursions. I can well understand this excursion, with the train travelling through some remote but beautiful countryside.

I had reserved a seat in advance, but found this to be occupied. There were more of them than just me and Archie (although I know that I can rely on him in such situations), so I do not want to get into a confrontation. Fortunately, the guard is nearby and shows us to a seat in the other carriage. The situation had been defused. Some people seem to be unable to read or maybe they have a total disregard for "reserved" notices and signs. Could have another rant here but with such beautiful scenery surrounding us, I will refrain. However, the situation isn't as bad as I make out, but I am pleased to be settled in a window seat and so to be able to admire the scenery.

Off the train speeds, back down the single track it had just come up, to the rail junction at Georgemas following the valley of the River Thurso. Then off across the wild and remote heather and gorse landscape of the Caithness hinterland that is devoid of any roads or habitation. That is apart from the rail halt that we pass though at Altnabreac, which is spoilt by being surrounded by artificial forestry plantations. Near to the line, a herd of deer are grazing by the side of a lochan, soon to be frightened by the noise of the train and scamper off across the heather moorlands in the opposite direction.

We soon reach the halt at Forsinard, where the train makes a stop by request. The route of the railway at this point joins that of the A897 road that runs across country between Melvich on the north coast and Helmsdale on the east coast. We pass alongside Loch an Ruathair with Ben Griam Beg at 1,936 feet above sea level, to the west. It has stopped raining and the tops of the mountains are clearly visible. Apart from the single tracked "A" road that runs alongside the railway, there are still no signs of any habitation. This is a wild, windswept but beautiful landscape and I can now understand why the coach company Shearings are taking their holiday guests on this particular rail journey. But what must it have been like for those who constructed the railway back in the 1800's when conditions at times must have been quite bleak?

Soon we reach Kinbrace and follow the Strath of Kildonan and the deep tree-lined river valley down towards Helmsdale, on the east coast. As the train winds its way down the steeply sided glen, there are increasingly more signs of civilisation. Nearing Helmsdale, the river valley widens to allow the land to be cultivated. Here the train makes a scheduled stop (the station sign is in the Gaelic Bun Illigh), which is where we passed through the previous day on our bus journey going north to Wick.

The rail line then runs along the edge of the North Sea coast, following the main A9 trunk road, with the Morayshire coastline in the far distance across the Firth. The skies are clear and Archie is taking more of an interest in the sea views, gazing out of the train window. The ever-changing pattern of golden sandy beaches with rocky green headlands to our right and the yellow gorse on the hills to our left, add much colour to the passing landscape. Soon we are arriving at Brora and after a short stop, we travel on across the stone viaduct over Brora Water, continuing down the coast towards Golspie.

It seems that the Shearings passengers have just noticed Archie and all of a sudden, there is a lot of fuss being made over him. "Ahh, what a cutey", "What's his name?", "Can I stroke him", "Does he do tricks?"—give me strength!! Totally unashamed, he is lapping it all up, enjoying every bit of the attention that is being poured out over him. Thinking about it afterwards, if I had had a tin, I could have got him to do some of his turns and taken a collection. It could have gone to subsidising the extortionate bus fares on my journey north. Everyone is really very nice and it is satisfying to see others gaining some pleasure in making a fuss over him. However, it is to be short lived for all the passengers with Shearings Coaches get off the train at Golspie. The train is now virtually empty—peace and quiet.

Soon after Golspie, the route of the railway leaves that of the A9 and diverts inland to Rogart and Lairg. The scenery is getting quite wild again, with flocks of sheep and their newly born lambs nibbling away at the tufted moorland grass. The top of Ben More Assynt at 3,273 ft. ASL can be seen in the far distance to the north west. We are at Lairg, sited at the bottom of Loch Shin. At 17 miles in length, it is one of the longest lochs in Scotland with the water level being raised by some 30 feet in the 1950's by the construction of the Lairg Dam to produce hydro-electric power.

At Lairg, the rail track turns south, past the spectacular Falls of Shin to Invershin, Culrain and then down the side of the Kyle of Sutherland to Ardgay. To get a better view of the scenery and the firths, we move over to the left-hand side of the coach, now that there are plenty of vacant seats. We are now travelling down the south side of the Dornoch Firth towards the road bridge that the bus had crossed yesterday so to avoid the long detour inland via Lairg. The tide is out with the beaches of the Firth exposed.

The train makes a scheduled stop at Tain. The sign on the station platform also informs us that the Gaelic name for the Town is Baile Dubthaitche—I'll stick to calling it Tain. Here the train fills up, including a number of noisy youngsters—peace no longer reigns!! One youngster who I would guess to be about 10 years old and who is with his mother, has his radio blasting out pop music. Now maybe some on the train appreciate this sort of music, but it is certainly not to my taste. Why should I be subjected to this discordant music with such beautiful scenery passing by? Why does his mother not tell him to turn it off or at least turn down the volume a bit? In these days of ipods, why can't he use ear-pieces so as not to inconvenience others with his music? I feel that I really now qualify as a "grumpy old man" but I don't think it unreasonable to complain about my peace being disturbed by this unacceptable noise. (RANT 36). However, not wanting to get into any confrontation with his mother who looks like she is more than capable of handling herself, I say nothing and continue to try to admire at the scenery, trying to block out the sound of her son's music.

The train is more or less following the same route as the A9, leaving the coast at Tain and cutting across to the Cromarty Firth to Invergordon (or Inbhirghordain). As in the Town itself, there are painted murals on the station platform of scenes from the 2nd World War including one depicting soldiers leaving home. Whoever arranged for these paintings to be displayed in public places, needs to be congratulated. They certainly lighten the place up and create an interest. The oilrigs we had passed yesterday are standing like proud sentinels in the Bay, still dominating the landscape.

With the pop music still blaring away, we head down the north bank of the Cromarty Firth, past the road bridge that crosses the Firth, up to the town of Dingwall situated at its head. The historic market town of Dingwall (or Inbhirpheofharain in Gaelic), can trace its origins back to the Norse Vikings and was the administrative centre for the former county of Ross and Cromarty. It is at Dingwall that the rail line branches off to Kyle of Lochalsh and the Isle of Skye, one of the top scenic train journeys in Britain. Also the pop-playing youngster and his mother get off the train—halleluiah!!!

Leaving Dingwall, we are into farming country with ploughed arable fields either side of the track. Crossing the A835 near Maryburgh, there is a long queue of vehicles at the level crossing. I wonder how long they have waited for the train to pass? On through Conon Bridge across the neck of the Black Isle to Muir of Ord, with its whisky distillery, and onto Beauly. Here the line turns east, heading along the south bank of the Firth of Beauly with the Kessock Road bridge that carries the A9 in the distance. Approaching the Bridge, we pass the entrance lock for the Caledonian Canal that runs down the length of the Great Glen towards Fort William.

At 16.50 after a three and three-quarters hour journey, we arrive precisely on-time at Inverness Railway Station. It has been a long journey from Thurso, especially for Archie but he has been very good throughout, sitting for most of the way on the seat looking out and enjoying the views, especially when we were travelling alongside water. It has been one of the most scenic train journeys that I have been on, with constantly changing landscapes and coastal views. The Scotsrail train itself was comfortable and I was certainly not cramped, restless or bored. Well worth the ride and to be recommended.

Having got off the train and out of the Station, Archie leads me towards the nearest lamppost. I guess he must have been sitting crossed-legged on the train. I have reserved a room at the same hotel as we had stopped at on the way up, Kinell House. Having booked in, we go for a walkabout in Inverness, along the sides of the River Ness and across to the cathedral on the opposite bank, finishing up at the Castle Tavern for a pint of Belhaven. Although it is only the first day in May, it is still light at 21.45 (or rather 9.45 pm).

Although we have not travelled by bus today, the train journey from Thurso has been most enjoyable, together with the opportunity to explore Thurso itself. Once settled in my seat on the train at Thurso, at least I didn't have to face the effort and hassle of getting off and on the bus, lumping my kit with Archie tugging away on his lead. The train ride has been much more comfortable compared to being thrown about on the bus. All in all, it has been a much more relaxing day—and the train fare worked out to be 23% of the bus fare between Inverness and Thurso, albeit I did used my senior's rail pass for the train journey.

Saturday 2nd May 2009

It is our last day and the final journey back home to Lincoln.

I am once again up early to give Archie his morning walk to find the weather fine and the skies clear. After a good breakfast at Kinkell House, we set off back down old Edinburgh Road, once again past the Castle into the City centre and onto the railway station. We are due to catch the 09.18 Glasgow train, changing at Perth for Edinburgh. Having bought a newspaper and found the right platform, we clamber aboard the Scotrail train and manage to get a seat with a table. Dropping my rucksack in the open space opposite, we settle down for the next stage of our journey. So far, so good.

Sitting across the table to us is Donald who, it turns out, is an ardent supporter of St Johnston's Football Club in Perth. Today is a big day for St. Johnston's FC who are due to play a league match against Morton Football Club in Scotland's Second Division. If they win today, they will become the league champions and be guaranteed promotion to the Premier Division for next season. Donald has travelled from Brora and is travelling all the way down to Perth to hopefully see his team promoted—a very keen and dedicated supporter. To ease his nervousness, he has a six pack of Scrumpy Jack for the journey to ease his nerves and anxiety.

Spot on time, the train pulls out of Inverness station, southward bound for Perth. On the train travels, climbing up the gradient to Aviemore, the U.K.'s premier skiing resort. In the background, the snow-covered peaks of the Cairngorms are visible. Continuing on up Strath Spey to Kingussie, I notice that my rucksack is no longer in the space opposite where I had put it. Panic sets in, me thinking that someone has taken it, until another passenger says that she had noticed the train conductor move it to the designated luggage rack further along the coach. Looking along the aisle, there it is, correctly placed on the luggage rack. The space where I had left it is for pushchairs and bikes. I do feel a bit foolish for making a fuss. The moral is always put things in their correct place.

Soon we are passing the black and white buildings of the Dalwhinnie Distillery, the highest distillery in Scotland and where they produce the popular Dalwhinnie malt—well worth a visit if you are travelling along the A9 between Inverness and Perth. On up to the summit of the Drumochter Pass, which at 1,480 feet above sea level is the highest point within the U.K. rail network. During the winter months, both the railway and main road are often blocked by snow-drifts.

Having reached the summit of the Pass, the train is now on its way downhill, through Glen Garry running parallel to the A9, then the Pass of Killiecrankie to Pitlochry where the train makes a stop and then continues on down Strath Tay, following the peaty brown river that flows below the line of the tracks. We are nearing Perth, so we get our belongings together to leave the train. Donald promises me to text the result of the match. He never did but St Johnstone did win and gained their promotion to the Premier Division—he was probably too occupied celebrating their win.

At Perth, we have a brief walk outside before catching our connection to Edinburgh. This was the Scotrail 11.59 to Edinburgh Waverley Station that crosses the Kingdom of Fife via Ladybank, Glenrothes and Kirkcaldy. Following the north shore of the Firth of Forth to Inverkeithing, the train crosses the magnificent Forth Rail Bridge with the graceful Forth Road Bridge spanning the estuary to our right.

On our train journey, two gentlemen are sitting opposite us across the table. One would seem to be in his sixties, the other perhaps his eighties, although both looked fit and well. It transpired that both are close friends and keen golfers. The older of the two had apparently played to a high standard all over the world, including the USA and Australia. He still plays regularly but the cold winds don't do his arthritis any good. The younger of the two has just retired and spends much of his time on the golf course. Having asked me what I have been up to with Archie, he tells me that he too is planning something similar and that is to play on the most northerly, southerly, easterly and westerly golf courses on the U.K. mainland. These will be at Thurso, Mullion (Cornwall), Yarmouth and Ardnamurchan (NW Scotland) respectively. To make it a bit more of a challenge, he will be travelling by public transport between the courses. He then asks me if I have another "project" planned to which I say that I intend writing a book of my travels. He replies by saying what he really means is do I have another trip planned. Well I hadn't really thought much about that, but it is he that suggests that having gone from south to north on the bus with Archie, why not plan a trip east to west. What a great idea!!! I had not considered it. Watch this space!!!

We pull into Edinburgh Waverley on time. Compared to what I had been used to further north, the station and streets outside are crowded with people. Having to fight our way out of the station and through the crowds, we make for the gardens of Princess Street. The sun is shining so an ice cream was appropriate—I always get an extra cornet as Archie too likes his ice cream albeit only a very small portion on mine. Sitting on the seat enjoying the sunshine and ice cream, Archie is giving his forlorn look from the ground asking for more. At least five passers-by give the "Ahh—isn't he cute" words and bend down to stroke him. He sits there totally unashamed, lapping it all up.

Time to get back to the station for our next connection, this time changing at Newcastle. We make our way onto the platform and board one of the coaches. It is empty and has not been cleaned out from its previous journey. A guard then asks me where I am bound for and then tells me that I should be boarding the train on the opposite side of the platform. Why do I not read the signs!!! There is plenty of room in the train carriages, so we have our pick of seats (except of course for the few that have been reserved). We find a good window seat on the left hand (scenic) side of the carriage next to the buffet bar—very handy.

Despite the general criticism, I have found that most trains do run on schedule. Ours pulls out of Edinburgh Waverley on time, passing under Arthur's Seat and heading along the south side of the Firth of Forth to Dunbar and then along the top of the cliffs overlooking the North Sea towards Berwick. As we speed by with some great views out to sea, the golfers are out on the cliff-top links. I guess that you need to be fairly accurate with your drive as any stray golf balls going over the cliffs will be given up as lost. Soon we have crossed the border and are back into England. Soon we are pulling into Berwick Station, where we had started our Scottish trip some seven days previous.

On leaving Berwick, the train crosses the high level masonry arched bridge over the River Tweed with the Town behind us and the other two bridges down on our left—what a great view. On we travel down the Northumberland coast, passing Holy Island, Bamburgh Castle and Alnmouth on our left, on towards Morpeth. The area we are now passing through, had at one time been awash with colliery villages, each dominated by their winding equipment and slag heaps. Now, everything has gone, even most of the miners' houses. In our carriage, there is a "bossy" woman trying to organise the person she is speaking to at the other end of her mobile phone. It sounds as if some poor soul is in trouble. At 15.30, the train pulls into Newcastle Central Station.

We have approximately 60 minutes in Newcastle, time enough to give Archie some exercise. We walk up Grainger Street that I had known so well in my youth but now hardly recognised. Being a Saturday it is very busy, but that is no excuse for the amount of litter and discarded food scattered over the pavements. I have a problem keeping Archie from picking up the half-eaten burgers. Looking down on us from his high pedestal at the top of Grainger Street, is Earl Grey, the column known as Grey's Monument. At nearby Eldon Square, I have difficulty in finding anywhere to sit because of the number of folk about. I have already had a Rant about the destruction that the planners inflicted upon Eldon Square with the destruction its former elegant Regency buildings, so I'll not start again on that issue. It is all bit of a sad experience and perhaps with hindsight I should have gone somewhere else rather than up to Eldon Square. Memories of bygone years are hard to erase.

Newcastle United are playing at home later in the afternoon. Struggling to keep their place in the Premier Division, they are fighting against relegation down to the Championship (the old Division 2). Subsequent events and results show that they were not successful and down they went with Middlesborough and West Brom. It was indeed a black day for the United fans along with those of Boro' and I guess West Brom too. Hopefully they will bounce straight back the following season (in fact they do as champions of the Championship).

Back down to the Central Station for our next train. This will be the London Kings Cross train stopping at Doncaster that is due to leave at 16.29. The train also stops at Newark that is nearer Lincoln and may have been a better option than getting off at Doncaster. The train pulls out of the station and immediately we cross over the River Tyne with the High Level, Swing and New Tyne Bridges all to our left and the waters of the Tyne glittering in the sunshine below. Soon we have gathered up speed passing through Gateshead with the Angel of the North standing on the high ground to our left. At Durham, the Cathedral and Castle stand out proud against the skyline across the valley of the River Wear. Stopping at Darlington and York, we arrive at Doncaster at 17.55.

The original plan was to catch another main-line train that stopped at Retford, from where we would get the local train from Sheffield to Lincoln. However, this would mean an hour's wait at Retford, which was not to be looked forward to. Nevertheless, on getting off the train at Doncaster, the Arrivals / Departures monitor shows that a train for Lincoln would be leaving in five minutes time at 18.02. Having checked that the train did actually go to Lincoln, we get on board. It transpires that it is the same train that I would have caught at Retford on my original itinerary. Rather than the 60 minute wait on Retford station platform, we have the delights of travelling around South Yorkshire, stopping at Mexborough, Rotherham, Meadowhall, Sheffield, Woodhouses, Worksop before we eventually arrive at East Retford. At least we are sitting in relative comfort. On the train rattles over the River Trent and into Gainsborough, which I had passed through on our bus journey during August last year. We are on the final stretch before reaching home, arriving tired and weary in Lincoln at 20.10. My wife Florence, is waiting at the station with the car to take us home.

And so the end of a most memorable and enjoyable journey, but pleased to be home. We have been to places that we would otherwise never have visited, met up with some interesting characters, and seen some magnificent scenery. I hope that Archie has enjoyed himself too although he can hardly tell me so if he didn't. He did at least enjoy romping about and digging in the sand on the many different beaches we visited on our travels and being petted by many of the passers-by.

Now to get down to writing the book!

PART 4

SUMMARY AND FINAL THOUGHTS

Chapter 1
Travels Up Through England

We really do live in a beautiful Country with a wide variety of country landscapes and coastline. The villages, towns and cities of our homeland provide a wealth of historic and cultural interest with designs of buildings and architecture changing as you travel across the Regions. It is perhaps only when you visit other countries overseas, either when working or on holiday, that you appreciate the real beauty of our countryside together with the diversity of our towns and villages. When flying back home across the Channel or North Sea and I see laid out beneath me, the green fields with their hedgerows, the scattered copses of trees, the orderly villages centred around their parish churches, I am glad to be living in England. As attractive places are like France, Spain, Italy and beyond, there is still no place like home. I personally have no wish to live elsewhere, despite some of the social problems that we seem to be experiencing. As an island nation, we do have our own traditions and identity, and no edict from the European Union will ever change that—must try to not embark on another ranting.

Travelling up and across the Country by bus, taking time to stop off and visit places of interest, is an excellent way to experience the splendours of our countryside and towns, also our vast heritage of castles, cathedrals and other historic buildings. It was a great (and cheap) way of visiting places I had not previously been to and also in meeting a wide cross-section of people en-route.

For a relatively small country, we have a wide variety of cultural traditions across the Regions, not least the various local dialects and accents. Although I have no difficulty with the Geordie dialect of Tyneside despite having lived away for so many years, it is like a foreign language to many. Contrast that to the West Country burr of the Cornish accent or the rhyming slang of the Cockney accent. Even the Brummy accent of the West Midlands has its own distinct twang. It is perhaps no wonder that when visitors from overseas come to England (and indeed the U.K.), they become very confused as to what is being said, especially with some words having different meanings and interpretations from Region to Region. The subject of accents and dialects can (and has) filled a book, but I raise it here just to refer to the variations in speech that I experienced as I travelled up through England, not to mention Scotland.

Not having visited Lands End previously, it was a pity that I, or rather we, saw it during a period of exceptional bad weather, especially for that time of year, August. With rain and a nearly force eight gale blowing in off the sea, the conditions could have been better. At least there were not too many people about. It was a pity, as I should have liked to been able to walk further along the footpath that follows the rugged cliff edges that forms part of the long-distance Coastal Footpath. I suppose that this highlights the extreme vagaries of our British climate, which are not always predicted by the season, nor indeed the weather forecasters. I sometimes think that it must be boring to live in a country when you know that each day it is going to be hot and sunny—some, perhaps most, would disagree. Perhaps it is why that in England, the weather is always the centre of conversation.

One of the many enjoyable aspects of our bus journey was to pick up relatively unknown gems of information of our Country's past. One such gem was at the small village of Porthcurno on the bus route to Lands End. At this remote spot on the southwest coast of Cornwall, most of the submarine cables that linked Britain with the countries of its former Empire, came ashore. This made Portcurno, with its transmitting station, a focal point in the administration and governance of the British Empire during the late 19th and early 20th centuries. Not many people are aware of this, except for locals and visitors to the area.

The winding narrow country lanes of Cornwall and indeed the South West are difficult to negotiate especially if driving a bus. During the holiday periods especially, there is a mass influx of caravans, most of which follow the main roads direct to their holiday destinations. Nevertheless, some still do stray onto these narrow country lanes, with resulting blockages and congestion. Thankfully, our bus from and to Penzance did not experience such encounters, although a number of private cars did have to give way and back up to the nearest passing place. I would certainly not want to have to back a caravan up these narrow lanes with the possibility of scrapping the sides along the high stonewalls. Driving can be a bit stressful and sitting on a bus is much more relaxing, for the passengers at least. As a bonus, you are able to view over the tops of the stonewalls that line these leafy country lanes, something that is not possible when travelling by car.

Travelling through the Cornish towns of Camborne and Redruth, there were many reminders of the past glory days of tin and copper mining. The abandoned engine houses with their tall chimney stacks, identified the locations of some of the deep mine shafts that lead to the underground mineral seams which were worked by the local Cornish miners. It perhaps brought it home as to how rich a country England was during the 18th and 19th centuries in respect of its available minerals deposits, a good proportion of which were exported overseas. Also to the working and living conditions for these miners and their families, who did not see much financial benefit from their hard labours. It was inevitable that eventually the accessible mineral reserves were going to be worked out and the mines would become unprofitable, especially with the import of minerals from abroad. To send men deep down into the bowls of the Earth working in such hazardous conditions cannot be a good thing in today's modern society. Whilst no doubt the local people now live and work in a much healthier environment, the levels of unemployment are high. Nevertheless, the tin mining of Cornwall is part of our industrial heritage and it is good that some buildings and machinery have been preserved for future generations to view and experience, not least some of the original steam pumping engines. It was a pity that I did not have more time to explore some of theses old mine workings together with the local mining museums.

In many of the towns and cities we travelled through, there were statues erected to people of past years, well known both locally and nationally. To be reminded of the tremendous contribution that many of these men and women made that has been of benefit to mankind throughout the World, should be a matter of national pride to all Britons. In Penzance, there is a statue to Humphry Davy, inventor of the miner's safety lamp among other things. In Cambourne, a statue stands in the Town centre to Richard Trevthick, who perfected the steam driven beam engine used for pumping water from the deep mine workings in Cornwall. We would come across many more statues to famous people on our travels, not least that to my illustrious ancestor, Issac Newton in Grantham.

At many of the places where we stopped to change buses, we were able to have time to wander about exploring places and buildings of interest. In particular, I had planned our route to take in as many cathedral cities as possible, the first being at Truro. A number of ancient monuments and castles, most now in ruins, were also passed with the mind going back, trying to envisage life in those troubled far-off days and the conflicts that took place. At least these days we live in relative peace, despite the threat of terrorist activity.

Archie likes the seaside, especially where there are sandy beaches. On reaching Newquay and sniffing the sea air, he went wild with excitement. Although some parts of beaches are out of bounds to dogs during the holiday season (and rightly so), he does enjoy his romp on the sands, investigating the rock pools and splashing about in the sea. After being cooped-up on the bus for such long periods, he deserved his seaside romp. After leaving Newquay on the southwest coast, it would be some time before we reach the seaside again, this being at Bridlington on the northeast coast of Yorkshire.

The bus journey from Newquay to Exeter was the longest on our whole trip. Ideally, we should have broken our journey at Launceston or Okehampton but with only three buses a day, this would have resulted in a major disruption to our travel plans and itinerary. It was indeed on this bus route, that I had to pay the fare for the first part of my journey, rather than travel free using my bus pass. Being the only way out of Cornwall using service buses and with only three buses a day, I had little option but catching the No.510 bus to Exeter leaving Newquay at 9.15am. At least the helpful lady bus-driver only charged me for the first fifteen minutes of travel, thereafter I travelled for free. It did go slightly against the principles of my bus trip in travelling across and up England without the need to pay, but at least this was the only occasion on my whole trip. I suspect that others undertaking this journey have also come across the same situation. Nevertheless, it was a memorable bus ride, sitting on the top deck and taking in the views firstly along the Atlantic Highway of the Cornish coast and then across the wild open moorlands of Bodmin and Dartmoor.

Crossing over the county boundary from Cornwall to Devon, we had the opportunity to get off the bus for five minutes at Okehampton. Unable to buy a Cornish pasty at the local bakery, I had to settle for a "traditional pasty", being outside the county of Cornwall. The same protected areas apply to pork pies from Melton Mowbray and maybe soon, sausages from Lincolnshire and kippers from Craster. What are Scotch eggs to be called if made and sold in England, or Lancashire hotpot in Yorkshire? It is best that I don't get too involved in this discussion.

I had never been to or visited Exeter previously. Situated at the other end of the Foss Way to my home city of Lincoln, I was most impressed by the modern centre-of-town shopping developments and pedestrianised areas. Also of course with the historic area and precincts around the Norman cathedral. I did not have time to visit the castle nor the riverside area, but like many other towns and cities I visited, it gave me a taste of what there is to see and a desire to return at a later date to explore the City in more depth.

Travelling through the green pastures of North Somerset, there were plenty of reminders of the English Civil War of the 1640's and the later Monmouth Rebellion of 1680's. During these times of civil strife when families were split and fighting each other, the whole countryside must have been in turmoil with severe punishments handed out. At least these days, family feuds are hopefully not so violent.

Glastonbury is somewhere I had not been to previously, being of an age too old to have enjoyed its annual Pop Festivals. It was interesting to learn of Glastonbury's ancient history that is linked around Joseph of Arimathea and the Arthurian Legends. There is a great richness and depth of English history, a subject that I personally find of great interest. I therefore find it regrettable that the subject seems to have been downgraded in the school syllabus these days. I have always maintained that there is so much we can learn from history so as to avoid the mistakes made in the past. Sadly, this is not always the case with the same errors being repeated at the expense of communities and populations throughout the World.

Calling in at the cathedral city of Wells on the way to Bath was a delightful experience, with its magnificent cathedral and other historic buildings. So too at the beautiful city of Bath, with its Roman hot-water spas and Georgian terraces. No wonder it is one of the top tourist destinations of England. Its rugby team is not bad either. I was pleased that we made time to be able to wander about the City centre to take in some of its splendid buildings and places of interest. Until reading about its history on Wikipedia, I had never previously heard of the Baedecker Blitz that was carried out by enemy aircraft during the Second World War and in which Bath suffered. I suppose that such action illustrates the futility of war together with the damage and unnecessary destruction caused for virtually no benefit. Unfortunately, such actions still take place in other parts of the World this day, so we cannot say that such pointless destruction is a thing of the past.

Passing through Calne brought to mind our Neolithic past, where there is no written history. There is much speculation as to how these past civilisations lived together with the purposes for which many of the standing monoliths were intended at that time. The Stone Circle at Avebury, the Long Barrow at West Kennet, the significance of Silbury Hill are all shrouded in mystery. It is also interesting to speculate how these monoliths and earthworks were constructed with the resources available at that time. For such, these people that inhabited the English countryside some 3,000 to 4,000 years ago processed skills and intelligence that seem to have become lost during subsequent years.

Travelling across the county boundaries into Wiltshire, we passed by RAF Lyneham and onto the small town of Wootton Bassett. Both have appeared on our televisions much too often in past months, where the flag draped coffins containing the bodies of our soldiers killed in action in Afghanistan and elsewhere are brought home to rest. Seeing the slow moving hearses passing through Wootton Bassett with the local people standing in silence and flags dipped, is very moving. It is a meaningful farewell to our servicemen killed in action overseas and it is a credit to the folk of this small Wiltshire town to provide this final tribute. My thoughts were with the families of these soldiers killed in the service of our Country as we passed through Wootton Bassett.

So onto Swindon, a former railway town and the hub of Brunel's Great Western Railway system. Like many other towns and cities in the Country, Swindon has suffered much with the demise of the heavy engineering industry. Whilst still preserving parts of their past industrial heritage for future generations to enjoy, Swindon has moved on with new industries being set up in car manufacturing and in the hi-tech sector. As a result, unemployment is lower than elsewhere in the Country. It is a lesson that needs to be implemented elsewhere in that we should not bemoan the passing of our industrial past of heavy engineering and shipbuilding, but to look forward and to invest in new hi-tech industries and research at which this country excels.

Our next port-of-call was Oxford, the "City of Dreaming Spires". Although I had often driven around the City via the bypass, I had never previously been into the City proper and to walk around its streets, footpaths and parks. What a delight, and I was pleased that I had allowed plenty of time to take in some of the beautiful sights the City has to offer. I had previously seen pictures of the many famous buildings in books, magazines and on the television, but to see them up front puts them in an entirely new perspective. My camera was in constant use and I was pleased that I decided to view the City sights in the first instance, from the top deck of an open-top tourist bus. My short stay in Oxford was very pleasurable but in addition to the historic buildings and colleges that adorn the City centre, perhaps most memorable, was the visit to St John's College and to be able to walk around its tranquil grounds and gardens. I don't suppose that it will ever be possible to assess just how much the University of Oxford and those who have graduated from its numerous colleges, have contributed to the scientific and literary world over the centuries. For sure, without such a place with all its facilities for learning and research, the World would have been a poorer place. The rivalry with Cambridge is healthy and it must be the envy of many countries overseas that we in Britain have two such prestigious institutions of learning.

Moving out of Oxfordshire and into Northamptonshire and the East Midlands, the bus passed through the villages of Brackley and Silverstone, both places renown in the sport of Formula One motor racing. The year 2009 was particularly exciting for British motor racing enthusiasts with the newly formed Brawn GP team in the lead with the World Constructors' Championship and its driver, Jenson Button leading in the Drivers' Championship. It turned out to be a close finish, but at the end of the racing season, both Brawn GP and Jenson Button were victorious. Another great British achievement and a proud moment for all involved.

Then to the "town" of Northampton itself. With its long history and sizable population, it seems strange that it has not yet achieved city status. I must confess to being a bit disappointed with Northampton and its town centre. Apart from the 17th century All Saints Church with its magnificent portico and the 19th century Guildhall, I did think that there was little of interest in the way of historic buildings and architecture for such a large town that first obtained its Charter in 1189. It would seem that much has been demolished and pulled down over the centuries, which is a great shame. No doubt, it is a great mecca for the shopaholics and for the followers of sport. However, my comments are based on my first impressions of the town centre, which may have been influenced by the wet weather. At least I thought that the large brick-clad structure that houses the bus station at Greyfriars was not the "behemoth" (not my words) that it has been labelled by the locals.

Despite my comments on the Town itself, Northamptonshire as a County must be one of the most pleasant of the rural shires of central England, possessing many beautiful buildings constructed in the locally quarried Northamptonshire sandstone. There are many attractive villages situated within the rolling countryside, each with their own parish church and local pub. Also a number of country estates scattered across the

County, with their stately halls and mansions. Two we passed on our bus journey after leaving Northampton on the road to Leicester, these being Lamport Hall and Kelmarsh Hall. Both are now open to the public and available for special functions, due no doubt to the pressures from the costs of upkeep and maintenance. However, it must be a good thing that such stately buildings, their treasures and their grounds should be open to the general public and the enjoyment of their beauty not be confined to only just a few.

We were again reminded of the English Civil War of the 17th century when passing nearby the site of the Battle of Naseby in 1645. The outcome was in favour of Cromwell's forces and was a turning point in the Civil War that lead to the abolition of the monarchy, albeit temporarily, with the transfer of greater powers to Parliament. Whilst there were many wrongs committed during the period of the Commonwealth under the governance of Oliver Cromwell, it did provide the foundation for true democracy in Britain that has been used as an example throughout the World. I make it clear that I am a supporter of the present monarchy together with the Parliamentary system that has been inherited from the time of Cromwell. I realise that many want to see the monarchy abolished and to be replaced by a Presidency. I suggest we should learn from the history of past years and be grateful for the traditions and pageant associated with our monarchy, which are the envy of the rest of the World. I could go on at length but will conclude by saying that the newspapers and magazines would be bereft of material should the British monarchy ever come to an end. This discussion was started from the Battle of Naseby, which perhaps illustrates the importance of its outcome.

After Market Harbrough, the bus route passed nearby to Foxton Locks. The original inclined boatlift on the Grand Union Canal at Foxton, formed part of the vast inland waterway system across England and Wales. The inland waterways have been used for the transport of goods since Roman times with the canal systems being expanded during the 18th and 19th centuries only to be surpassed by the railways of the late 19th century. The canal engineers and the navvies of this period were responsible for some magnificent structures, including the imposing stone aqueducts that now are part of our industrial heritage. The ingenious designs of the boatlifts and lock systems all add to this heritage. It is because of the excellence of the engineering design and construction of this period, that many of these canals and structures are still standing and available for use these days, by mainly pleasure craft.

Outside London, the City of Leicester must be one of the most cosmopolitan places in the Country. With nearly fifty percent of the resident population having roots to the sub-Asian continent, most people seem to live in harmony with each other. There may well be some undercurrents of prejudice, but being reasonable familiar with Leicester, it is a fairly safe place to be, compared to other parts of the Country. No doubt much hard work has been done over the years by the City Council and the various ethnic organisations to achieve this harmonious situation across the various cultures living within the City. The wealth and prosperity of the City is much dependant upon the labours of people of non Anglo Saxon origin without which the services and economy of the City would suffer. Maybe if I actually lived in Leicester I might have slightly different views but I feel it does add to the City's vibrancy and culture, especially when travelling down Belgrave Road in the heart of the City's Asian community.

On leaving Leicester, we were soon back out into the green rolling landscapes of rural England, travelling towards Melton Mowbray, famous for its pork pies and Stilton cheese. I sometimes fail to understand as to why we as a nation, do not make more of the wide variety of excellent cheeses that are produced within our Country. We seem to import a lot of French cheese but do they in turn import much of ours? Somehow I doubt it. I personally never thought that wine and cheese went together, much better a slice of Stilton or Cheshire with a pint of bitter. Maybe the cheese promoting organisations and societies should work on this with the hoteliers and pub landlords across the Country.

Soon we were again crossing the county boundary into Lincolnshire, the historic County covering an area of approximately 2,000 square miles from the Humber to the Wash and from the River Trent to the North Sea coast. For those unfamiliar with the Lincolnshire countryside, it is not all flat open fenlands. The unspoilt rolling landscapes of the Lincolnshire Wolds and Heathlands cover most of the centre and west of the County, with many picturesque market towns and villages made all the more attractive by their traditional stone cottages and buildings.

Our first stop-over was Grantham, whose most famous son was undoubtedly Sir Issac Newton. Born nearby, he received his early education in Grantham, his statue standing proudly in the Town centre in front of the Town Hall. I have previously mentioned that my son traced our ancestry back to Sir Issac, albeit taking a rather tenuous route, but in my opinion, he was the greatest Briton that ever lived. In the BBC TV poll that took place in 2002 for the top 100 Great Britons, he came sixth. The reason that he did not come top I put down to blatant prejudice. Maybe too it is the fact that this Country has produced so many great men and women who have had such a major influence on the World stage, that five more people were considered ahead of the greatest mathematician and scientist of all time. I know that I am biased. Grantham's most famous daughter, is undoubtedly Lady Margaret Thatcher, although her statue has yet to be erected, no doubt because in 2010, she is still with us.

Approaching Lincoln, we passed by RAF Waddington, one of the largest operational stations in the Country. Despite the stringent cuts in defence and reductions in our armed forces in recent years, this Country is still a force to be reckoned with. I remember well the massive Vulcan bombers that were based at Waddington during the period of the Cold War with their role in the Falklands conflict. It may be that we are no longer the World power that we once were and perhaps we should accept that our role on the World stage has declined. Nevertheless, there is much respect for the British forces overseas and as a nation, we should be proud and grateful for what they achieve in the defence of this Country. Hopefully, at the end of the current (2010) Government review and spending cuts, we will still be left with an operable and efficient army, navy and air force that are still capable of defending the realm both at home and overseas.

So to my home city of Lincoln. The extra few nights in my own bed at home was a welcome interlude midway through our bus journey up England. Archie certainly settled back in quickly. Like Exeter and Bath, Lincoln's origins go back to the Roman times and there is still evidence of their presence today in the historic area of the City, not least in the only complete archway in the Country under which traffic still passes. Having taken an interest in the Romans together with their civilisation and infrastructure, I am full of admiration for their achievements, especially their engineering skills. Even today, there is still uncertainty as to how they managed to build some of their structures together with the techniques they employed, taking into account the equipment and resources that they had at their disposal at that time. I often question where we might have been today had it not been for the decades of the Dark Ages that followed the departure of the Romans from these shores and if the learning and skills of the Romans had been allowed to progress unhindered? Just think how much we have achieved over the past one hundred years and where we might be in say four hundred years time, a similar period lost due to the Dark Ages? I am not too sure if I really want to speculate what life will be like so far ahead, as it may not be what we would want. For sure outer space will be much explored and it may well be that we will be inhabiting other planets within our own Solar System and even beyond.

Back to Earth and to our bus journey up England. Travelling up through Lincolnshire and Yorkshire, there are numerous towns and villages with place-names ending in *thorpe, holme* and *by*, for example Scunthorpe Killingholme and Grimsby. These are reminders of the invasion and occupation of these areas on the eastern side of the Country by the Danish Vikings during the 9th and 10th centuries and the imposition of Danelaw. A Danish visitor to this area of England once remarked that when touring around, he could not help but notice that we English had pinched many of their own place names back in Denmark. Of course, many of these Viking raiders settled in England and turned to farming the land, having abandoned all their past activities of plundering, pillaging and raping. Maybe there is some Viking blood in many of us today that may contribute to the British fighting spirit that used to instil fear in many of our opponents and enemies.

Crossing the Humber Estuary over the impressive Humber Suspension Bridge, was a memorable part of our journey. Linking Lincolnshire and Yorkshire, this magnificent triumph of British civil engineering was at the time of its construction in the late 1970's, the longest single span structure in the World. Much to the dismay of my children, we often visited the Bridge during the course of its construction, of which they still often remind me. Another first for Britain although there have been a number of bridges build since that have superseded its 4,626 feet span. Nevertheless, the slender high concrete towers on each bank with the catenaries of the suspension cables hung between, are a magnificent sight, especially when viewed from upstream.

The City of Kingston upon Hull was next. Much has changed from its former glory days as one of the World's premier fishing ports. Very little is now left of the fishing industry in Hull. So too the chemical industry that once lined the north bank of the Humber. Sadly, alternative forms of industrial enterprise have been slow to come to Hull, despite the efforts of the local politicians and others, leading to unacceptable high levels of unemployment and the associated social problems. Government and national agencies do their best, but many factors come into play when trying to attract new industries, especially when competing with other locations around the World. Retraining is fine but there must be the work opportunities at the end. It is indeed tough on some families when long-term traditional industries go into decline and there is little to be found in the way of alternative employment. Nevertheless, being at the "Gateway to Europe", and close to the designated areas of the vast wind farms that are proposed for the North Sea, new industries will hopefully be established and the City's prosperity be returned.

Yorkshire has a varied and attractive coastline. From the towering cliffs of Flamborough Head, to the sandy beaches of Bridlington and Scarborough, to the coves of Robin Hood's Bay and Staithes, there is plenty for the visitor to do and enjoy. For those who are more energetic, there is the long distance Cleveland Way Coastal Footpath that follows the coastline south as far as Filey. The focal point for most people is of course Scarborough, one of the Country's top seaside resorts. As a family, we have spent many happy days at Scarborough, which provides something for everyone, whether young, middle aged or elderly. There are some excellent beaches, parks and gardens with a variety of entertainment and nightlife to please everyone. The bus journey up the Yorkshire coast was interesting and enjoyable, travelling across open moorland and calling in at Robin Hoods Bay, Whitby and Staithes. This part of the coast is of particular interest to geologists with traces of jet still to be seen in the cliff faces at Whitby.

Next to Teesside and Middlesbrough. Once a power-house of the nation's heavy engineering industry, much has changed. The recent closure of the steelworks was a great blow to the local economy, though hopefully it may be reopened in the not too distant future. In some respects, the story at Middlesbrough is similar to that at Hull, albeit different industries were involved. At least, the large chemical complexes on Teesside are still functioning, albeit at reduced outputs. I remember Teesside from the 1950's when a red cloud hung constantly over the valley created by the steelworks and industry. At least that has now gone.

Travelling up through County Durham was a bit nostalgic and to some degree, sad. From my youth, I remember all the pit villages and mining towns that were spread across the County, each with their own close-knit community, churches, pubs and brass bands. Also the winding gear towering above the pit shafts that lead down to the rich coal seams below. Adjacent were the high pyramidal shaped slag-heaps of spoil material that gave the Durham landscape a strange hilly appearance. Since the closure of the coalmines, virtually all of the evidence of the former mining industry has disappeared, including in some cases, the pit villages themselves. All have fallen to the demolition ball and are now just a past memory. Hopefully, there will be plenty of photographs and drawings for posterity, so to allow historians to research their past. As I made the point in the main text of this book, my views over the closure of the coalmines, especially in the North East, is a bit mixed. Whilst there is some sadness to see the break-up of these closely-knit communities and the employment opportunities created by the coalmines, sending men deep down into the bowels of the Earth to work in dark, hazardous, unhealthy conditions, cannot be considered acceptable in today's modern world. I guess that we should also consider the present views on the burning of fossil fuels and CO_2 emissions. The World moves on and we must keep up with all its new developments.

Durham City is a gem with its Norman Cathedral and Castle sitting on the high ground above the tight bend of the River Wear. Once the home of the Prince Bishops, this university city is steeped in history with many interesting old buildings and some beautiful walks along the banks of the River. At any time of the year, rowing crews and scullers can be seen on the River, pulling on their oars as they prepare for the countrywide rowing regattas, including that held at Durham itself. It was good also to meet up with my brother Ken who I had not seen for some time.

It was a pleasant surprise when the bus passed close by to *the Angel of the North*. I had not been so close up to this now iconic figure that symbolises the North-East of England before and I resolved to visit the site on which *the Angel* stands when I am next in the area. (This I have since done on a fine sunny day—it is indeed an impressive structure close to.)

Being born and bred on Tyneside and having lived away in Lincolnshire for the past forty plus years, it is always an emotional moment when crossing over one of the bridges that span the River Tyne into my home City of Newcastle. I was pleased that I had allowed some time to explore at least, some parts of the City before catching our next bus. Much had changed since my days, some for the better, some for the worse, included the demolition of some of the City's fine Georgian buildings. I have said enough in my ranting on this issue in the main text, so I will not repeat that already said. However much has remained as I remembered and it was an enjoyable nostalgic visit.

Calling in first at the attractive market town of Morpeth, our next destination was the old County Town of Alnwick, home to the Duke of Northumberland and who still resides in the Castle. Alnwick is an attractive market town, centrally situated in the heart of the beautiful County of Northumberland and is an excellent centre for exploring the County and its coastline. Our overnight accommodation at The Oaks was perhaps the best on our journey from Lands End, that is apart from that in Lincoln.

The next and final stage of our bus journey up England was the most enjoyable of the whole trip. The "Coast and Castles" double-decker bus from Alnwick to Berwick-upon-Tweed, initially travelled eastwards before turning northwards to follow the beautiful coastline of north Northumberland. Passing through the picture-postcard fishing villages of Craster, Newton-by-the-Sea, Beadnell and Seahouses was a delight, bringing back memories when in my youth, I used to go out for the day on my bike and cycle around these parts. Perhaps the highlight was seeing the Farne Islands just off-shore across the sandy dunes, soon to be followed by passing underneath the high basalt crags at Bamburgh on top of which stands its ancient Castle. This impregnable fortress dominates the surrounding area and has been the scene for many paintings, TV documentaries and films. The golden sandy beaches along this coast are virtually empty albeit the temperatures of the seawater are not too high. This part of Northumberland is unspoilt and up to fairly recently, unknown except to the locals. Slowly however, it is becoming more popular to holidaymakers outside the North-East of England, who are beginning to appreciate the beauty and splendour of these parts.

Crossing the Royal Tweed Road Bridge into Berwick-upon-Tweed signalled the end of our journey up England. The historic border town of Berwick was an appropriate place to break our journey north to John O'Groats. Its Elizabethan town ramparts and the backdrop of the three bridges that span the River Tweed, make a visit well worthwhile. Certainly, J.S. Lowry thought so. Perhaps more important for us, was that fact that Berwick is situated on the main-line East Coast railway line, making our journey back home that much easier.

I have made mention that when undertaking our bus journey up through England, I was studying for an Open University course, the exam being only some two months away. I had thought that I might be able to undertake some study work whilst travelling on the buses and also at night before turning in. This turned out to be a serious mistake. If I only had thought about it previously, I would have realised that trying to concentrate on my studies whilst passing through the varied and beautiful countryside of England and making notes for this book, would have been a near impossible task. I soon had to abandon any hope of studying whilst travelling and to catch up with my work when I finished my journey and returned home. I could have lightened my load by not having to carry my coursework text books.

Only in Cornwall and Lincolnshire did I have to pay a bus fare for Archie. Whilst the charge was by no means excessive, it did seem strange that the same bus companies operating in other parts of the Country, made no charge for dogs travelling on their buses. Perhaps I should not make too much of this as they may review their policies and make a charge for dogs on all bus routes throughout. I did however find it amusing that I was able to obtain a day pass for Archie to travel on the buses in Cornwall. However, with a dog-year being the equivalent to seven man-years, I did wonder if when Archie was nine years old, he too would qualify for a bus-pass. If so he has not long to go to qualify. I must therefore sort out a photo of him for encapsulation on his bus-pass.

In conclusion, our bus trip across and up England was a great and enjoyable experience, albeit not the most comfortable, with much more of the countryside being seen from the bus than from the car. The only downside was having to carry my rucksack about with me all of the time, including when exploring the cities and towns at our stop-off points. Nevertheless, not having to drive was a bonus although it did mean that I could not stop at places I might otherwise have wanted to without having to catch the next bus. I think Archie enjoyed the trip especially when at the seaside, although he was hardly able to say otherwise. And so to the next stage of our journey, up Scotland to John O'Groats.

Chapter 2
Travels Up Scotland To The Top

My bus-pass was only eligible for use in England, so I had to pay for each of my bus journeys up through Scotland to John O'Groats. It went a bit against the objective of my bus trip and maybe for this section, I should have re-titled my book to exclude the "Bus Pass". With the fares for four of the journeys costing £10.00 and more, bus travel was not as cheap as I would have expected, working out to be nearly 30 pence per mile. At least Archie went free. I must say that I was a little disappointed in not being able to use my bus-pass for the first few miles north of Berwick when travelling up to the Scottish border whilst still in England. It is perhaps worth mentioning that it was cheaper travelling back by train from Thurso.

Nevertheless, our bus trip up the east coast of Scotland was a holiday in itself. Calling in at Edinburgh, Perth, Dundee, Aberdeen, Inverness and Wick, we passed through some wonderful countryside and alongside some lovely stretches of coastline. Perhaps the best was the penultimate section of our trip from Dornoch to Wick. It was also the most costly. There were also many open sandy beaches for Archie to run around on, chasing his ball and burrowing into the sand, so he was kept happy.

We picked up our trail again at Berwick after a gap of eight months and a replacement knee. After an overnight stop there, we resumed our bus travels north towards Edinburgh. The rugged coastline of North Berwickshire along which are situated the fishing ports of Eyemouth, St Abbs and Dunbar, is a stretch of fascinating coast to visit, especially for ornithologists. The fresh green of the countryside and bright yellow flowers of the gorse bushes provided plenty of colour. Seeing the Bass Rock off the coast from Dunbar made me realise what a sinister and formidable place this must have been for any prisoners and how difficult it must be to land a boat there, especially in rough seas. No wonder the author Robert Louis Stevenson used it for the location for one of his novels.

On passing through Haddington, birthplace of the Protestant Reformer John Knox, I was reminded of the religious reforms and upheaval that took place during this period of the 16th century in both

Scotland and England. Also what otherwise might have resulted had Knox not started his reformation that lead to the establishment of the Presbyterian Church in Scotland and elsewhere. The subsequent violent disputes and feuds between Protestants and Catholics are a little difficult to understand in these days of Christian ecumenicalism, although sadly in certain parts of the Kingdom, they still take place, albeit not quite as violent. There is only one God and all Christians follow the teaching of Jesus, with each denomination entitled to its own forms of worship and traditions. To some degree, it is perhaps understandable that many people become disenchanted with religion, resulting in our nation becoming more and more a secular society. Over recent years, greater tolerance between the denominations has been in evidence and as a Christian, I welcome this. If the Church is to survive and grow which I am sure it will, unity and flexibility are essential, a fact on which most would agree. Acceptance for change will also be necessary, in some respects similar to the challenges faced by Knox in Scotland during the 16th century and by Wesley in England during the 18th century.

Words fail to describe the splendour and beauty of Edinburgh, dominated by its Castle and sometimes referred to as "The Athens of the North". I had been to Edinburgh many times in the past so many of its sights and attractions were familiar to me. The views from the top of Carlton Hill on a fine clear day, such as we experienced in April, are spectacular. What did take me by surprise was the complete closure of Princes Street to traffic and the disruption in the City centre caused by the construction of the new tramway system from Leith to the Airport. It seemed apparent that the project was very controversial with the original estimate of nearly four hundred million pounds likely to be exceeded by some fifty percent. Contractual disputes and projected delays of up to two years have resulted in possible cuts to the original proposals. In these days of austerity, we need to seriously consider the cost benefits of such infrastructure projects to ensure that they are both economically and environmentally viable, although far be it for me to suggest that this is not the case with the new Edinburgh Tramway System.

Crossing the Forth Road Bridge with the landmark Forth Railway Bridge immediately downstream, was another highlight of our bus trip. The three great trapezoidal open lattice steel towers of the Railway Bridge stand out against the clear skies above the Firth and is a sight that has been reproduced by painters and photographers since the bridge was built over one hundred years ago. It is another triumph of Victorian engineering and a vista that is recognised all over the World. Following recent refurbishment work, it is said that the Railway Bridge will last at least another hundred years. Sadly, with the corroding suspension cables of the much newer Road Bridge, the same cannot be said.

Our stop-over in Dunfermline in the Kingdom of Fife, was an unexpected surprise. I had not previously appreciated the historic treasures possessed by this ancient Royal Burgh, once the capital of Scotland. Its abbey church that contains the tomb of Robert the Bruce and royal palace where King Charles I was born, are all worth a visit. So too are the gardens and grounds of the extensive Pittencrief Park, a legacy of Andrew Carnegie, the US steel baron and philanthropist who was born in Dunfermline and who never forgot his Scottish roots.

Although there are many pretty towns and villages in Fife, Glenrothes, like many other new towns, lacks character and a soul. It was raining when we passed through but perhaps it is not too surprising that it did receive the "Carbuncle Award" for 2009.

A little further on is Falkland, another historic and interesting town with its old Royal Palace and nestling under the grassy slopes of the Lomond Hills. The bus route did not pass through the centre of the Town itself, which was a pity. Next was Auchtermuchty, well known to many as Tannochbrae in *"Dr Finlay's Casebook"*. I am still reminded of Rich Hall's joke when the name "Auchtermuchty" is mentioned.

Perth was a city that disappointed me a little, maybe I was expecting more. Don't misunderstand me, the *"Fair City"* is an attractive place but with its strategic position on the River Tay and its long history, I had expected there to be more to see in the way of old historic buildings and fortifications. It is a fact that much was destroyed and demolished over recent centuries and there are indeed some interesting houses and churches with their tall spires dominate the City, albeit most dating only from the 18th and 19th centuries. The North and South Inchs with the fast flowing River Tay running alongside, do provide two large expanses of parkland that add to the beauty of Perth. I do hope that Perth soon gains its City status back.

Our overnight stop at the old coaching inn at Longforgan on the shores of the Firth of Tay, was a good choice and the hostelry is recommended for its accommodation, food and hospitality. The next day, we were in Dundee. Much had changed since my Uncle had lived and worked there in the 1950's, much for the better although many of the traditional industries have since been closed down. Nevertheless, it was fun to see the bronze figures of *Desperate Dan, his Dawg and Beryl the Peril* in the main pedestrian area of the City centre. This brought back happy memories of reading the Beano and Dandy in my youth. Also to see Scott's ship, the *RSS Discovery* restored and preserved in the permanent drydock down on the waterfront of the Firth. I realise that I am repeating myself but I do consider it necessary that we should spend time and money (within reason) in preserving our heritage of past years. Scott's ship is looking in pristine condition and it would have been interesting to have gone aboard. Across the Firth of Tay span the new road and rail bridges, with the stumps of the ill-fated railway bridge of the 1880's still visible above the waters of the Firth. Perhaps this is a reminder that not all Victorian engineering was to a high standard of design and construction.

The ancient burgh of Arbroath, a little further along the coast, was another interesting stop-over. In addition to its 13th century abbey, harbour and beaches, what was most memorable for myself was being invited inside one on the smokehouses that prepare the famous "Arbroath Smokies". The smell from the smoked haddock fillets remained with me for sometime. Travelling further along the Angus Coastal Road is Montrose. I remember Montrose best for the long walk from the Town centre to the seafront only to be greeted by an icy cold wind coming off the sea and thinking to myself that I could have better spent our time exploring other parts of the Town, such as the gardens of the Mid Links and the area of the tidal Basin.

Calling in at the fishing villages of Johnshaven, Gourdon and Inverbervie as we followed the Angus coast towards Aberdeen, reminded me of our travels along the Northumbrian coast. I still regret not making time to look around Stonehaven where my Mother-in-Law once lived. The old parts of the Town are well worth a visit and it would have been nice to have re-visited the harbour area especially.

The City of Aberdeen is a prosperous and busy place. The grey granite buildings of the City centre initially seemed a little foreboding, but when looking at them in more detail, there are some architectural delights. An unexpected surprise was to walk part of the expansive sandy beaches that are so close to the City centre and that stretch along the coastline of the North Sea. It was also good to meet up with my brother-in-law Mike and to join him in one of the best fish dinners I have ever had, courtesy of the Ashvale. However, I have subsequently taken some "flack" from Mike for not bringing him some "smokies" from Arbroath, even though I have explained to him the circumstances of the overly hot back seat on the bus to Aberdeen and the smell that might have resulted.

Aberdeen's recent industrial growth and prosperity is due to North Sea oil. The immensity of the oil industry and the vast sums of money spent on the exploitation of oil is staggering. Maybe one day the World might find an alternative to burning oil as a fuel. However, with all the financial investment in the oil industry worldwide and me being a bit of a sceptic, I do wonder if there are commercial pressures to slow down such research and the development of an alternative fuel.

I had never before travelled along the coast of the Moray Firth between Banff and Inverness. I am not quite sure as to what I had expected, but I was surprised to see the number of towns and villages that are spread out along this coastline, together with the shipyards and engineering works at Macduff and Buckie. Much of its past wealth was based on fishing, especially during the period of the herring boom. Although few, there are still some fishing boats about despite EU quotas. Elgin is another gem, with its 13th century Cathedral, Biblical Garden and historic High Street. This area is renowned for the number of whisky distilleries, many of them being located in nearby Speyside. There are also some excellent beaches that are popular with the local Scots, Nairn being a favourite resort. It is indeed an area where you could spend an enjoyable holiday that could include visits to the distilleries and the sampling of their malt whiskies.

Inverness is an attractive place and turned out to be a good location for overnight stops both on the way to John O'Groats and on the way back. The view from the Castle over the River Ness and beyond, is worth the climb.

The next stage of our journey, from Inverness to Wick, was without doubt, the most scenic and pleasurable—also the most expensive. The first part involved crossing over the bridges of the four firths (say it quickly), passing through Invergordon with the towering oilrigs standing within the Firth just off-shore, before arriving at the historic cathedral town of Dornoch. The original 13th century Cathedral was rebuilt following a fire, with the present 19th century church dedicated to St Gilbert. There is plenty of interest to see in this small Town, not least the "Plaiden Ell", a flat stone of a fixed length used for measuring tartan cloth. It is a popular place for golfers, the golf links of the Royal Dornoch Golf Club being listed as the fifth best in the World outside the USA. Perhaps most memorable for Archie were the vast empty sandy beaches where he had a field day. I still feel uncomfortable over the tarring and burning alive of poor Janet Horne for witchcraft in 1727. Even for the 18th century, it was a most barbarous act, especially when the poor woman was probably innocent of any serious misdemeanours.

The next stage of our bus journey closely followed the coastline, passing through a number of small towns and villages enroute. The countryside was ablaze with colour from the yellow of the gorse and the purple of the heather. To the east, were the grey waters of the North Sea and its rugged coastline. Passing through Golspie, there were the first signs of the Gaelic language on the street name-plates, reminding us that languages other than English are spoken in the British Isles. A little further on, we came to the small town of Brora, where up to as recently as the 1970's, coal was mined. I had not realised that there were coal deposits this far north. Something else new I had learnt from our bus trip.

Near Berriesdale, was the now abandoned village of Badbea, a reminder of the Highland Clearances of the late 1700's carried out by landowners to make space available for sheep grazing. To move whole families and communities to such barren places as at Badbea situated on the cliff edges to make way for sheep, was a despicable act. It is hardly surprising that many did emigrate to lands overseas where conditions were better and the land more productive. The First Duke of Sutherland was not a popular man.

Approaching Wick, we passed through the villages of Lyster, Ulbster and Thrumster, the names a reminder of the days when the Norsemen inhabited this area of Northern Scotland. With Norway being due east, this coastline would have been their first port of call when carrying out their raids on the British Isles and like the Danish Vikings further south, they no doubt used this area as a base and settled. During our travels in late April, the sea was relatively calm, but I can imagine what it must look like under stormy conditions, which must surely have been experienced by the Norsemen in their longboats.

We had little time to spend in Wick, which was a pity. I would have liked to explore Telford's "new" harbour that was constructed in the 19th century to handle the vast catches of fish during the period of the herring boom. At this time, Wick must have been a bustling place and it was nice to learn that still today, the old traditions are preserved at the Wick Harbour Festival and the crowning of the Herring Queen. Maybe one day, the fish stocks might return to these waters of the North Sea in sufficient quantities for the fishing industry in these parts to be revived. However, this maybe wishful thinking with the controversial quotas imposed by the EU for fishing and the distribution of these quotas to other fishing fleets within the EU. I am trying very hard not to have another Rant concerning my dissatisfaction of the workings of the European Union and its commissioners.

After a too brief a stop at Wick, we caught the school bus up to John O'Groats on the final stage of our journey north. With hardly a tree in sight, the bus made its way north across some wild open landscapes, stopping at small villages and remote farmhouses, until we were there, John O'Groats. Having taken the equivalent of thirteen days to travel the 1,230 miles from Lands End by service bus, we had at last arrived. It was mid-afternoon and the sun was out to greet us. The ferry from the Orkney Isles had just docked, this the first ferry of the summer season, bringing with it a few packs of the local Orkney beer. I bought a bottle of Northern Lights Ale to celebrate our arrival at our final destination. Sitting on the sand dunes looking out to the Orkneys across the Pentland Firth and enjoying my ale, was a fitting way to conclude "The Trip". I still have the empty bottle as a memento. It is of course a fact that John O'Groats is not the most northerly point on the British mainland, this being at Dunnet Head a few miles further west. John O'Groats is however, the most northerly settlement.

After having taken the obligatory photographs, including the landmark direction post with Lands End shown to be 874 miles to the south, and also of Eric the Viking, we caught our final bus westwards to Thurso where I had booked accommodation for the night. When we arrived, it was cold and raining with a long walk to our hotel. However, in the morning, there were clear skies and the views across the Pentland Firth were stunning. The walk back to the Town centre following the coastal footpath was most enjoyable and also of interest. The unique design of the seaward-facing seats along the cliff edge made from locally quarried stones, were most unusual, with one dedicated to Sir William Smith, founder of the Boys Brigade. Sir William was born in Thurso and the youth movement he founded, has been to the benefit and enjoyment of many thousands of youngsters worldwide.

Our journey back by train from Thurso, the most northerly railway station in the U.K. was also an experience. The scenic train ride back to Inverness, especially the first section, is a journey popular with tourists and to be remembered. First crossing the remote open moors and highlands, then down the tree-lined glens to the North Sea, the railway line followed the scenic coastal route the bus had taken the previous day. Continuing south from Inverness, the railway passes over the high ground of Drumochter Pass between the snow-capped peaks of the Cairngorms, before dropping down through Glen Garry and Strath Tay, past Pitlochry to Perth. This is another of Britain's great train rides. Finally, crossing between the riveted steel latticework of the Forth Rail Bridge with the much newer Road Bridge immediately up river, is always an enjoyable experience.

It was in fact whilst crossing over the Rail Bridge, that one of our travelling companions put it to me that now that I had competed our bus journey from the south to the north of mainland Britain, why not take up the next challenge of travelling from the east coast across to the west coast of the Mainland? This sounded like a good idea and by the time I had reached home later in that day, outline plans had already been prepared.

Chapter 3
Some Comments On The Buses And Bus Stations

For our 1,230 mile bus journey between the most south-westerly and north-easterly points of mainland Britain, we travelled on a variety of different types of buses, some luxurious and comfortable, others noisy and not too comfortable. We also experienced varying standards of bus stations, some well laid-out, safe and accommodating for passengers, others dim, poorly designed and unwelcoming. Some towns did not possess bus stations at all, where passengers waited at designated stops on the main streets of the town centre for their buses to arrive.

There was a wide variation in the types of bus vehicles we travelled in, from luxury coaches, to double-deckers, to single-deckers, to a school bus and to runabouts. It all contributed to the experience. It would have been great to have been on the upper deck of the open-top double-decker bus from Penzance to Lands End and enjoyed the views. Unfortunately, the weather conditions prevented this and we had to make do with travelling on the lower deck in shelter from the rain. It was a surprise to have the double-decker bus transporting us on the three hour journey from Newquay to Exeter although the views from the top deck across the open landscapes of Bodmin Moor and Dartmoor were most enjoyable. So too, were the views from the top deck of the "Coast and Castles" special from Alnwick to Berwick in North Northumberland.

For most of our journeys, we travelled in normal single-decker public transport buses. Most were fairly new, clean but suitable for only relatively short trips. I suppose that it is a credit to the bus companies that their fleet of buses are well maintained, kept clean and regularly replaced with new vehicles. The days of the old bone-shakers that used to belch out clouds of black exhaust fumes, have long gone, partly as a result of government legislation for public transport. The only memorable ride as far as discomfort was concerned was that on the No.6 bus between Dunbar and Edinburgh. The bus suspension was suspect, the engine noisy and the seats and upholstery worn and dirty. This vehicle certainly had seen better days, but it should be said that this was a one-off. Another uncomfortable journey was that from Montrose to Aberdeen when we were sitting on the back seat of the No. 107 double-decker bus. The engine on this bus was at the rear, more or less under the back seat. For the three hour journey, the back seat got very warm and a bit uncomfortable but it was my own fault in that I could have moved seats.

On the more positive side, we travelled in luxury to Dunfermline on the next stage of our journey from Edinburgh. The X54 which was travelling on to Dundee, was a long-distance coach fitted with all the comforts for such travel. The reclining seats with their headrests were a pleasant change from the previous day's travel from Dunbar. It was a pity that we were only travelling as far as Dunfermline. So too was the long-distance No.X25 City Link coach from Inverness to Dornoch that was going onto Wick. Perhaps it was no wonder that the fares were so expensive.

Our final journey to John O'Groats was in the specially adapted Rapson's bus used for transporting school children. The seats were a bit narrow so to be able to accommodate more school children, but nevertheless, it got us to our final destination in reasonable comfort.

I must make mention of the drivers. The majority were courteous, helpful and well dressed. Maybe I am a bit old fashioned, but I do like to see the drivers and conductors of public transport to be properly attired, preferable in company uniform. I am especially reminded of the lady driver on the Western Greyhound No. 510 from Newquay being very apologetic about having to charge for the first fifteen minutes of my journey prior to 9.30 am. The No. 6 bus from Dunbar again proved a bad experience with the driver not telling me in advance about there being no change given in payment of fares.

If I had been a real "bus geek", I could have gone on at some length about the manufactures, year and models, seating capacities, engine capacities, etc, etc, of our various modes of transport. You will probably be pleased to know that I have no such intention. I did not in any case take down such details as we travelled on our journey.

What I did find, however, was that many of the old, well-known, local bus companies had been acquired by one of the more recently established large national bus companies that between them, seem to have a monopoly on public road transport across Britain. Maybe I am a traditionalist, but I did find it a little sad that such names as Midland Red, Southdown, Lincolnshire Road Car, United Counties, etc, etc, have all but disappeared to be replaced by Stagecoach, First and to a lesser extent Arriva. We did travel on some buses owned and operated by small privately owned companies, but even these are fast disappearing with Rapsons in the north of Scotland having recently been acquired by Stagecoach, who now operate across the whole of the Country. Such an apparent monopoly cannot be healthy although I would assume that bus fares are monitored and regulated across the country by some independent body. On the plus side, we do seem to be getting fleets of new buses to replace those of twenty-plus years old and that were still in operation prior to de-regulation.

As a final comment on the buses, I still find it amusing to recall the day bus-pass that I had to purchase for Archie whilst travelling in Cornwall. Thankfully, this was not policy in other parts of the Country. That is except in Lincolnshire, where I had to pay 50 pence per trip. I am also still a bit miffed about having to pay for the first few miles of our bus journey north up to the Scottish border from Berwick whilst still travelling in England.

Turning now to the bus stations that we encountered on our journey. There was quite a variation, with star ratings not necessarily dependant upon the size of population of the town or city. Having called in at a total of 39 bus terminals from Penzance to Wick (Lands End and John O'Groats don't count), each one was different and there appeared to be no standard design although there were many common features. To comment on each individual bus terminal would be lengthy and boring. At many of the larger towns and cities, there was more than one bus station that resulted in some confusion on my part and a dash from one to the other, such as at Leicester, Newcastle and Dundee.

Some bus stations had been incorporated into shopping malls and commercial office complexes, which made much sense. Northampton in particular was an example of this and despite the building being called a "behemoth", I did find the bus station itself passenger friendly with easy safe access to and from the points of bus departure. In particular, I liked the sliding glass doors at the bus stands that prevented exhaust fumes from the buses being pumped out onto waiting passengers. The main bus stations at Leicester and Edinburgh were also under cover and had these sliding glass doors installed. As at Northampton, both have shops, cafes, toilets and the services within the station itself that one would normally expect at major public transport hubs.

The Paragon Interchange at Hull is interesting in that it encompasses both the existing railway station with the main bus and coach station under one roof. As such, passengers may move between the train platforms and bus stands under cover from the weather. Opened in 2007, it provides a modern central transport hub for the City of Hull with shops, cafes, toilets and all the other passenger services that are expected.

Most of the bus stations we encountered were typically open area bus terminals with covered service areas and access for the passengers, most of which included the usual services and facilities. Exeter, Swindon, Durham, Dunfermline, Dundee and Aberdeen were all typical with large open areas to enable buses to manoeuvre and park at the designated bus stands located under shelter. Glenrothes, where we had to wait for thirty minutes sheltering from the rain, was simply a series of glass shelters alongside which the buses drew up.

It is surprising that towns such as Scarborough, Berwick, Montrose and Banff did not have centrally established designated bus stations. At Scarborough and Berwick, open bus stands were located alongside the railway stations and elsewhere, their whereabouts known only to the locals. At Montrose, the stands were on the pavement of the main High Street in the Town centre which caused some congestion. Similarly at Banff, the stop was outside the Town House on the main road through the Town.

I have left until last my comments about the bus station at Lincoln, my home City. Scoring from one to ten, I reckon it would score between two and three. Constructed in concrete in the 1970's, undercover with an open car park above, it is scheduled for demolition. Being undercover, it is permanently dim with poor artificial lighting, noisy with the sound of the bus engines reverberating from the underside of the concrete roof, smelly from the bus exhaust fumes and dank. There is congestion when queuing at the stands, due in part to the large rectangular concrete columns that partially block access. Moving from stand to stand is hazardous with buses motoring and manoeuvring between the standing areas. I could go on but for me, the sooner the complete structure is demolished for something newer, safer and more passenger-friendly, the better.

Chapter 4

Some Comments On My "Rants"

In total, I have made 36 rantings whilst trundling along on our bus journey, these being summarised at the end of this book. These vary from what might seem to be small irritants to semi-political issues upon which opinions will differ. I perhaps need to state that the issues raised and opinions given are those of myself. Everyone is entitled to his or her own views and it would be a boring world if we all agreed on matters affecting our everyday lives. In fact it is often beneficial to be able to have a debate so long as this can be done rationally and without violence.

I have already labelled myself as a "grumpy old man". I would guess that if we are honest, we all have pet issues that cause us a degree of irritation. Maybe I have more than most people. Nevertheless, my rantings are a way of "letting off steam" on issues that annoy me together with policies that I disagree with. Please be patient with me.

On my 36 rantings together with the comments that I have made, I have tried to keep within the limits of political correctness (PC). This could be another subject for a Rant, but I had best not go down that road. Whilst many will disagree with some, or maybe all of my rantings, I do hope that I have kept within the PC guidelines and that I have not offended anyone. I will just say that we seem to have got ourselves into a situation in this Country where a frank expression of opinion on certain issues, is taboo. There seem to be many groups representing the rights of what are called underprivileged minorities that seem to have dictated to our PC society regarding what is said and done. Most I have no problems with but as an English hetrosexual white male, I feel left out with no group representing my rights.

A number of my rantings, such as use of mobile phones, creating litter, dog owners not "picking up", inconsideration to other passengers, etc, I would hope that most people would go along with. If we are to live in a tolerant and civilised society, respect for others is a prerequisite. However, the very fact that these matters have been raised does indicate that there is a minority (hopefully) that do disregard some of the basic rules of the behaviour required in a civilised society. Maybe they are unaware of their actions, probably it is down to laziness and a "couldn't care less" attitude. For whatever reason, some sort of education and if necessary, discipline with means of enforcement should be introduced, perhaps more that that in place at present. I remember the "Keep Britain Tidy" campaign that was introduced in the 1960's in schools especially. If we are to protect our countryside and roadsides from becoming one big rubbish tip, then some sort of similar campaign is again required.

A few of my personal rantings were not meant to be taken too seriously and were only included to perhaps raise a smile as do similar thoughts that go through our minds. "Leave me alone, I don't want to talk to you", is I would admit down to me being unsociable and not wanting to get involved. Also the issue of having to pay for Archie on buses in Cornwall and Lincolnshire is a bit unreasonable of me, especially as I travelled free. The term "free loading old wrinklies" rather than "senior citizens" I found amusing and maybe appropriate. I am still amused at not being able to buy a "Cornish" pasty just over the border in Devon although I would accept the need to protect the names of locally made produce. However I still stand by my distaste of the tattooed bare-chested kilted street-performer doing his act outside St Giles Cathedral in Edinburgh on a Sunday. Maybe I have old-fashioned morals.

A few of my rantings relate to policies and happenings of past years, such as the demise and take-over of British industry, the loss of our engineering skills, etc. Whilst there is a need to preserve our heritage, especially our industrial heritage, the days when Britain was the "Workshop of the World" will never return. Hopefully, the reintroduction of apprenticeship training schemes with the establishment of more high-tech industries may see some return to Britain's manufacturing base and prestige in the world of industrial production. However we have a lot of catching up to do against the likes of Germany who saw the need for long-term investment and not just for quick profit investments as has been the case in the U.K. As a Country, we seem to be far too reliant upon the banking and services sectors to drive our economy and less on the manufacturing of goods and equipment. Perhaps I am influenced in my views because of my own profession as a civil engineer.

Under this heading should be included the urban vandalism as at Eldon Square in Newcastle and the dreadful architecture and planning of the 1950's. Hindsight is a great thing and perhaps at that time when views and priorities were different, it may have been the correct path to follow. However, times do change, leaving today's and future generations left with these eyesores.

I guess computers and IT are always going to get blamed when things go wrong. However as I wrote in the main text, it is the people operating the computers that get things wrong, not the computers themselves. Sometimes we are too ready to blame others or other things for our own failings.

One of my rantings concerning the destruction of the English countryside may come back and "bite me". Living in Lincolnshire and previously working across the County, I have a number of friends and acquaintances who are farmers and who are unlikely to share my views, especially on the grubbing-up of hedgerows. To them, I say "tough!!", these are my views and I stand by them. It may be that I will have to buy my own beer when in the pub in the future.

Major political issues concerning energy supplies, CO2 emissions, Health and Safety and especially the EU are totally out of our control, despite going through the so-called democratic electoral processes. Once elected, pledges are broken and it is another five years before any rectification can be done. Even if a new government is elected, the process repeats itself. The decisions to go into war in Iraq and Afghanistan were not discussed and debated properly with a general consensus of opinion nationwide obtained. I am still not too sure as to what we are trying to achieve in Afghanistan, with the tragic loss of so many young British lives together with the maiming of so many servicemen. As for the democracy in the EU !!!

There are still a few of my 36 rantings that I have not covered, but I think enough is enough. In truth, I could have included many more rantings on my dissatisfactions with our present way of life and standards that seem to have been lowered. I will not go into my views on such matters as EU legislation, immigration, punishment for offenders, etc, although I will say that I am strongly against the death sentence, no matter what the crime. As I have previously admitted, I am a "grumpy old man" and feel that I would qualify for an appearance on the popular BBC TV half-hour series of shows. However, to avoid too much controversy and possible court action, I will refrain and stop here.

Chapter 5

Final Thoughts

Travel broadens the mind, or so they say. I believe it is a fact and that any form of travel, whether it be for only a short distance, can be an adventure. For most of us, there is an inner desire to explore territories that we are not familiar with. It may have been this desire to explore that drove the early British explorers to foreign unknown lands, during the 17th and 18th centuries. Maybe it is a British trait to travel and explore, but as a nation we do seem to look for adventure and new places to visit no matter how far away and difficult to reach.

Our bus journey from Lands End to John O'Groats can hardly come within the category of "an adventure of exploration". Maybe a thousand or more years ago when the Celts were inhabiting Cornwall and the Picts in the north of Scotland. Fortunately, things have improved since those days with transport over the land, in the air and on the sea being much faster and more comfortable. Nevertheless, many of the places we passed through I had not been to previously, especially in the far northeast of Scotland, and to visit such places was in itself for me, an adventure of exploration.

Although I have driven around Oxford many times in the past, I had never taken the opportunity to explore the City's heritage and architectural delights. Exeter and Wells with their beautiful ancient cathedrals were both new to me. So too was the cathedral town and Royal burgh of Dornoch up in Sutherland. Although I have travelled to many parts of the World, there is still much of Britain that I have not yet visited and travelling by bus is a good means of exploring such places.

It was perhaps appropriate that we passed through Market Harborough, the home town of Thomas Cook and who in the mid 1800's, organised his first group excursion from Leicester to Loughborough. How organised travel has progressed since that time. Also on television, there have been a number of excellent programmes that have explored the British Isles. These included Michael Portillo's BBC TV series "Great British Rail Journeys" shown during January and February in 2011 where he followed the train journeys of the mid 19th century undertaken by George Bradshaw, referring to the guidebook he prepared at that time as he journeyed across the various parts of the Country. Another excellent programme has been the BBC TV series "Coast", that has travelled around the coastlines of the British Isles, exploring its history, landscapes, geology together with its flora and fauna. Watching these TV series, brought back some memories of our trip across and up England and Scotland.

Accordingly, we attempted to cram in as much sightseeing as possible. A good way of achieving this was as at Oxford, where we climbed aboard the open-topped City tourist bus for a round trip of the City sights. As I have already mentioned, one of the downsides of our trip was to have to carry my rucksack virtually everywhere I went on foot. On reaching Aberdeen, it was better still in that we were chauffeur-driven by my brother-in-law Mike around the City.

The introduction for free bus passes, albeit for travel only within England and with certain conditions applying, has been a great benefit given to pensioners, or rather "the free-loading old wrinklies". Thanks Gordon! I know that I am far from being the first to travel from Lands End to John O'Groats with my bus pass, but I do believe, unless informed otherwise, that I am the first to travel with a dog.

In writing the narrative of our journey, I have tried to make it more than just an account of our journey from A to B and from B to C. Hopefully some of the historical details and factual information included of the towns and cities visited and passed through, will be of interest. Much of this information I gleaned from the relevant Wikipedia websites via the internet, for which I am most grateful. As to my rantings, it was a friend of mine who termed the word "Rant". How else could I have expressed my observations, thoughts and displeasures on certain issues as we travelled along the road.

All in all, it was a most enjoyable experience, albeit a bit uncomfortable and back-breaking at times. On looking back, these discomforts are soon forgotten and only the more pleasant memories remain. Even the cold and wet conditions we experienced at Lands End now seem to have been surpassed by sunshine. I have mentioned that on our way back on the train from Thurso, via Perth and Edinburgh, I got into conversion with two gentlemen sitting opposite. On enquiring where we had been travelling and our purpose, he suggested that now we have completed our bus journey from "south to north", then perhaps we should consider the challenge of travelling by bus for "east to west". It sounded like a good idea so "watch this space"!

Footnote.

Our bus trips were undertaken during August 2008 and April 2009 over two periods separated by eight months. Writing this book and getting it published has taken much longer than I originally expected, partially due to my Open University studies. I am ashamed to admit that I eventually completed the writing in February 2011, nearly two years after we had completed our trip. Over the two years and allowing the extra time for printing and publishing, changes have and will be taking place (not least the relegation of Lincoln City FC from Division Two of the Football League) and are likely to have affected some observations and views expressed in the narrative of our bus journey. I would therefore ask the reader to bear this in mind when reading my book, although by the time you reach this final section, you will hopefully have completed your reading. As to our future project, I can tell you that Archie and myself did undertake the journey by service bus between Lowestoft in the east and St David's in the west during April in 2010, taking six days to complete the 400 mile bus journey. Again we passed through a number of cathedral cities including Norwich, Peterborough, Coventry, Worcester, Hereford, Brecon and finally St David's itself. The crossing point with our trip from Lands End was at Northampton where we again stayed overnight.

Having completed a bus journey from Lands End in the southwest of England to Berwick-upon-Tweed in the northeast, and from Lowestoft in the east to St David's in the west, there is one last journey to make. To complete a six-pointed star across England, we need to undertake the journey from the most south-easterly point to the most north-westerly point of England, that is from Dover to Gretna Green, just over the Scottish border. To complete the "star", our crossing point shall again be Northampton and again we shall endeavour to pass through as many cathedral cities as is possible. As I write this footnote and assuming that the Government does not take away our bus passes beforehand, I am planning to undertake this journey during 2011, although I have yet to tell Archie!

LIST OF RANTS

RANT 1.— "Just leave me alone, I don't want to enter into a conversation with you"—on the bus from Newquay to Wadebridge.

RANT 2.— Why can't politicians make important decisions such as where our future energy supplies are to come from?—passing wind-farm on Bodmin Moor

RANT 3.— Why do we seem to be ruled by minority groups?—on bus passing by Roadford Reservoir in Devon

RANT 4.— Is there really a problem in calling pasties "Cornish pasties" throughout the land?—bus stop at Okehampton, Devon

RANT 5.— With the need to reduce our CO2 emissions, what is so bad about nuclear generated power?—Hinckley Power Station, Stolford, Somerset

RANT 6.— Introduction of cost-cutting measures that affect service to customer—no conductors on buses any more—bus leaving Bath

RANT 7.— Futility of war with unnecessary sacrifice of life—where are some of the other NATO countries in Afghanistan?—RAF Lyneham

RANT 8.— U.K. industry being seemingly uncompetitive against foreign companies—car industry in Oxford

RANT 9.— In-breeding of dog breeds to satisfy show judges so to win shows—after recent media publicity on issue—Oxford

RANT 10.— The power of the supermarkets to the detriment of suppliers and local / high street shops—Tesco, Northampton

RANT 11.— The inconsideration of the comforts to other passengers—opening of the bus window on the bus between Northampton and Leicester

RANT 12.— Bring back our local bus companies!—all the traditional names have disappeared following the wholesale take-over of local buses by the Big 3—at least a few survive as at Melton Mowbray

RANT 13.— Stewardship of the countryside and the destruction of hedgerows by farmers—travelling between Grantham and Lincoln in Lincolnshire

RANT 14.— The charge for dogs to travel on the buses in Lincolnshire only—why can't a national company like Stagecoach have a universal policy

RANT 15.— Preservation of our heritage, such as the old type red BT telephone boxes, as at Blyton, Lincolnshire—also the blue police boxes

RANT 16.— Politicians not listening to local opinion—re the creation of new counties and authorities not popular and subsequently changed—as in Humberside.

RANT 17.— Reference to those over 60 as "senior citizens"—rather use the term "free-loading wrinklies" as used by the Stagecoach Bus Company in Scarborough

RANT 18.— The use of mobile phones on buses—users seem unable to speak in normal tones and to keep their conversations brief and to the point—bus from Hull

RANT 19.— Wholesale take-over of British industries and business by foreign companies—as with ICI on Tesside

RANT 20.— The discarding of newspapers and littering of the floor of buses with mess caused that will have to be cleared up by driver—bus from Durham

RANT 21.— The loss of engineering skills and experience because of lack of investment and training brought about by financial pressures—on Tyneside

RANT 22.— Urban development vandalism brought about by the lure of money / profit at the expenses of preserving our urban heritage—Eldon Square, Newcastle

RANT 23.— Irresponsible dog owners not "picking up" after their dogs leaving pavements a hazard to other users—should not own a dog—Alnwick

RANT 24.— Chewers of gum spitting out their gum onto the floors of buses and pavements and not wrapping in paper—should be a ban on gum—Berwick

RANT 25.— The amount of litter that is scattered on our streets and pavements—should start another "Keep Britain Tidy" campaign—Newcastle—Stage 2 of trip

RANT 26.— We are too reliant on computers that get blamed for anything that goes wrong—usually a human error—bar on mobile phone in Berwick

RANT 27.— Unhelpful, (perhaps anti-English) attitude of the bus driver—ref coins in slot for fares—at Dunbar

RANT 28.— Preservation of our industrial heritage—when Britain was the Workshop of the World—steam train between Haddington and Edinburgh

RANT 29.— Inconsideration to other bus passengers with youngster parking his dirty trainers on bus seat across from him—Musselburgh

RANT 30.— Unattractive design and layout of houses and housing estates built during 1950's—lack of imagination—Musselburgh

RANT 31.— Abuse of moral standards for Sundays—tattooed street performer outside St. Giles Cathedral in Edinburgh

RANT 32.— Over-reaction to the requirements of Health and Safety—taking a lot of fun and adventure out of life—old steam-roller in children's play area—Golspie

RANT 33.— Planting of artificial forests of conifers by Forestry Commission—un-natural surroundings—argument of timber / work versus environment—NW Scotland

RANT 34.— Litter and food being left on the floors of buses, especially by school children—chips and papers on bus from Wick to John O'Groats

RANT 35.— Living in an apparent very affluent and wasteful society with sell-by / used-by dates on produce—family leaving half the breakfast at Thurso

RANT 36.— Portable radios playing loud pop music on trains—lack of consideration to others, especially if music is not their taste—train from Thurso to Inverness

BUS JOURNEYS, TIMES AND MILEAGES

ENGLAND—*LANDS END to BERWICK-UPON-TWEED*—*8 DAYS*

		times	mileages	
			journey	day
1.	Lands End to **Penzance** (Cornwall)			
	First 300 via Sheffield, St Buryan, Porthcurno	55mins	12	12
2.	Penzance to Truro (Cornwall)			
	First 18 via Cambourne, Redruth	1hr 37mins	30	
3.	Truro to **Newquay** (Cornwall)			
	First 89 via Trispen, Mitchell	48mins	15	45
4.	Newquay to Exeter (Cornwall and Devon)			
	Western Greyhound 510 via Launceston, Oakhampton	3hr 30mins	90	
5.	Exeter to **Taunton** (Devon and Somerset)			
	First 92 via Cullompton, Wellington	1hr 18mins	34	124
6.	Taunton to Wells (Somerset)			
	First 29 via Othery, Street, Glanstonbury	1hr 19mins	30	
7.	Wells to Bath (Somerset)			
	First 173 via Gurney Slade, Midsomer Norton	1hr 17mins	22	
8.	Bath to Chippenham			
	Pickford X31 via Box, Corsham	45mins	15	
9.	Chippenham to **Swindon**			
	Stagecoach 55 via Calne, Lyneham, Woorton Bassett	58mins	24	95
10.	Swindon to Oxford			
	Stagecoach 66 via Shrivenham, Faringdon	1hr 15mins	32	

11.	Oxford to **Northampton**			
	United Counties X88 via Bicester, Silverstone, Towcester	1hr 50mins	48	80
12.	Northampton to Leicester			
	Stagecoach X7 via Brixworth, Mkt Harborough, Oadby	1hr 20mins	34	
13.	Leicester to Melton Mowbray			
	Arriva 5A via Syston, Ashfordby	50mins	18	
14.	Melton Mowbray to Grantham (Leicestershire and Lincolnshire)			
	James (O'Brian) 8 via Waltham, Harlaxton	35mins	15	
15.	Grantham to **Lincoln** (Lincolnshire)			
	Stagecoach 1 via Leadenham, Navenby	1hr 20mins		94
16.	Lincoln to Scunthorpe (Lincolnshire)			
	Stagecoach 100 via Stow, Gainsborough, Blyton	1hr 50mins	36	
17.	Scunthorpe to Hull			
	East Yorkshire 350 via Winterton, Barton, Humber Bridge	1hr 8mins	24	
18.	Hull to Bridlington (East Yorkshire)			
	East Yorkshire 121 via Beverley, Driffield	1hr 45mins	35	
19.	Bridlington to **Scarborough** (East and North Yorkshire)			
	East Yorkshire 121 via Primrose Valley, Filey	1hr 25mins	20	115
20.	Scarborough to Middlesborough (North Yorkshire and Cleveland)			
	Arriva X56 via Whitby, Loftus, Guisborough	2hr 10mins	50	

21.	Middlesborough to Durham (Cleveland and Durham)			
	Arriva X1 via Stockton, Sedgefield, Coxhoe	1hr 5mins	26	
22.	Durham to Newcastle			
	Arriva X1 via Chester-le-Street, Gateshead	55mins	18	
23.	Newcastle to **Alnwick**			
	Arriva 505 via Morpeth, Felton	1hr 15mins	46	140
24.	Alnwick to Berwick (Northumberland)			
	Arriva 501 via Craster, Bamborough, Belford	2hr 10mins	35	35
	Totals (England)	**33hrs 20mins**		**740**

SCOTLAND—*BERWICK-UPON-TWEED to JOHN O'GROATS*—*5 DAYS*

		times	mileages	
			journey	day
1.	Berwick-upon-Tweed to Dunbar (Berwickshire and East Lothian)			
	Perrymans 253 via Eyemouth, Cockburnspath, Inverwick	1hr 13mins	35	
2.	Dunbar to **Edinburgh** (East Lothian)			
	First 6 via East Linton, Haddington, Musselbourgh	1hr 22mins	28	53
3.	Edinburgh to Dunfermline (East Lothian and Fife)			
	Stagecoach X54 via Forth Road Bridge, Rothsyth	49mins	18	
4.	Dunfermline to Glenrothes (Fife)			
	Stagecoach X54 via Cowdenbeath	37mins	18	
5.	Glenrothes to Perth (Fife and Perth & Kinross)			
	Stagecoach 36 via Falkland, Auchtermuchty, Newburgh,	1hr 15mins	30	
6.	Perth to **Longforgan** (Perth & Kinross)			
	Stagecoach 16 via Glencarse, Errol, Inchture	45mins	18	84
7.	Longforgan to Dundee			
	Stagecoach 16 via Invergowerie,	40mins	7	
8.	Dundee to Arbroath			
	Stagecoach 39 via Broughty Ferry, Muirdrum	50mins	18	
9.	Arbroath to Montrose			
	Stagecoach 39 via Inverkeilor	30mins	15	
10.	Montrose to **Aberdeen**			
	Stagecoach 107 via Johnshaven, Inverbervie Stonehaven	3hr 10mins	40	80

11.	Aberdeen to Banff			
	Stagecoach 305 via Meldrum, Fyvie, Turrif, Macduff	55mins	48	
12.	Banff to Elgin			
	Stagecoach 305 via Portsoy, Cullen, Buckie, Fochabers	1hr 35mins	40	
13.	Elgin to **Inverness**			
	Stagecoach 305 via Forres, Nairn, Tornagrain	1hr 20mins	40	128
14.	Inverness to Dornoch (Easter Ross and Sutherland)			
	City Link 25X via Tore, Invergordon, Milton, Tain	1hr 45mins	45	
15.	Dornoch to Wick (Sutherland and Caithness)			
	Stagecoach 25X via Brora, Helmsdale, Berriedale, Lybster	1hr 39mins	60	
16.	Wick to John O'Groats (Caithness)			
	Rapsons 77 via Reiss, Keiss, Nybster, Canisbay	55mins	20	
17.	John O'Groats to **Thurso** (Caithness)			
	Rapson 80 via Canisbay, Mey, Dunnet, Castletown	40mins	20	
	Totals (Scotland)	**20hrs 00mins**		**490**
	Overall Totals	**53hrs 20mins**		**1,230**

Overnight stops shown in "**bold**" type

Index of Places Visited

Town / City	County	Part and Chapter
Aberdeen *	Aberdeenshire	Pt 3 Ch 4
Alnwick *	Northumberland	Pt 2 Ch 9
Arbroath *	Angus	Pt 3 Ch 4
Auchtermuchty	Fifeshire	Pt 3 Ch 3
Bamburgh	Northumberland	Pt 2 Ch 9
Banff *	Banffshire	Pt 3 Ch 5
Barton-upon-Humber	N. Lincolnshire	Pt 2 Ch 7
Bass Rock	East Lothian	Pt 3 Ch 2
Bath *	Somerset	Pt 2 Ch 4
Beadnell	Northumberland	Pt 2 Ch 9
Belford	Northumberland	Pt 2 Ch 9
Berwick-upon-Tweed *	Northumberland	Pt 2 Ch 9
		Pt 3 Ch 1
Beverley	E. Yorkshire	Pt 2 Ch 7
Bicester	Oxfordshire	Pt 2 Ch 5
Bilsworth	Northants	Pt 2 Ch 5
Birtley	Tyne and Wear	Pt 2 Ch 8
Boulmer RAF	Northumberland	Pt 2 Ch 9
Box	Wiltshire	Pt 2 Ch 4
Brackley	Northants	Pt 2 Ch 5
Bridlington *	E. Yorkshire	Pt 2 Ch 7
Brora	Sutherland	Pt 3 Ch 6
Buckie	Banffshire	Pt 3 Ch 5
Burton Agnes	E. Yorkshire	Pt 2 Ch 7
Calne	Wiltshire	Pt 2 Ch 4
Cambourne	Cornwall	Pt 2 Ch 2
Camelford	Cornwall	Pt 2 Ch 3
Caythorpe	Lincolnshire	Pt 2 Ch 6
Chester-le-Street	Co. Durham	Pt 2 Ch 8
Chippenham *	Wiltshire	Pt 2 Ch 4
Corsham	Wiltshire	Pt 2 Ch 4
Craster	Northumberland	Pt 2 Ch 9
Croughton RAF	Northants	Pt 2 Ch 5

Cullen	Banffshire	Pt 3 Ch 5
Dornoch *	Sutherland	Pt 3 Ch 6
Driffield	E. Yorkshire	Pt 2 Ch 7
Dunbar *	East Lothian	Pt 3 Ch 2
Dundee *	Tayside	Pt 3 Ch 4
Dunfermline *	Fifeshire	Pt 3 Ch 3
Durham City *	Co. Durham	Pt 2 Ch 8
Edinburgh *	East Lothian	Pt 3 Ch 2
Elgin *	Morayshire	Pt 3 Ch 5
Exeter *	Devon	Pt 2 Ch 3
Eyemouth	Berwickshire	Pt 3 Ch 2
Falkland	Fifeshire	Pt 3 Ch 3
Faringdon	Oxfordshire	Pt 2 Ch 5
Farne Islands	Northumberland	Pt 2 Ch 9
Felton	Northumberland	Pt 2 Ch 9
Filey	N. Yorkshire	Pt 2 Ch 7
Forres	Morayshire	Pt 3 Ch 5
Forth Railway Bridge	E. Lothian / Fife	Pt 3 Ch 3
Forth Road Bridge	E. Lothian / Fife	Pt 3 Ch 3
Foxton	Leicestershire	Pt 2 Ch 6
Fulbeck	Lincolnshire	Pt 2 Ch 6
Gainsborough	Lincolnshire	Pt 2 Ch 7
Gateshead	Tyne and Wear	Pt 2 Ch 8
Gladstonbury	Somerset	Pt 2 Ch 4
Glenrothes *	Fifeshire	Pt 3 Ch 3
Golspie	Sutherland	Pt 3 Ch 6
Grantham *	Lincolnshire	Pt 2 Ch 6
Guisborough	N. Yorkshire	Pt 2 Ch 8
Haddington	East Lothian	Pt 3 Ch 2
Haggerston	Northumberland	Pt 2 Ch 9
Harlaxton	Lincolnshire	Pt 2 Ch 6
Hayle	Cornwall	Pt 2 Ch 2
Hessle	E. Yorkshire	Pt 2 Ch 7
Hull (Kingston) *	E. Yorkshire	Pt 2 Ch 7
Humber Bridge	Lincs / Yorks	Pt 2 Ch 7
Invergordon	Ross-shire	Pt 3 Ch 6
Inverness *	Inverness-shire	Pt 3 Ch 5
John O'Groats	Caithness	Pt 2 Ch 6
Lands End *	Cornwall	Pt 2 Ch 1

Launceston	Cornwall	Pt 2 Ch 3
Leadenham	Lincolnshire	Pt 2 Ch 6
Leconfield RAF	E. Yorkshire	Pt 2 Ch 7
Leicester *	Leicestershire	Pt 2 Ch 6
Lincoln *	Lincolnshire	Pt 2 Ch 6
Lindisfarne	Northumberland	Pt 2 Ch 9
Longforgan	Perth and Kinross	Pt 3 Ch 3
Lyneham RAF	Wiltshire	Pt 2 Ch 4
Macduff	Banffshire	Pt 3 Ch 5
Market Harborough	Leicestershire	Pt 2 Ch 6
Middlesbrough *	N. Yorkshire	Pt 2 Ch 8
Montrose *	Angus	Pt 3 Ch 4
Morpeth	Northumberland	Pt 2 Ch 8
Musselburgh	East Lothian	Pt 3 Ch 2
Nairn	Nairnshire	Pt 3 Ch 5
Newcastle upon Tyne *	Tyne and Wear	Pt 2 Ch 8
		Pt 3 Ch 1
Newquay *	Cornwall	Pt 2 Ch 2
Newton-by-the-Sea	Northumberland	Pt 2 Ch 9
Northampton *	Northants	Pt 2 Ch 5
Okehampton	Devon	Pt 2 Ch 3
Oxford *	Oxfordshire	Pt 2 Ch 5
Penzance *	Cornwall	Pt 2 Ch 2
Perth *	Perth and Kinross	Pt 3 Ch 3
Pitsford Reservoir	Northants	Pt 2 Ch 6
Porthcurno	Cornwall	Pt 2 Ch 1
Radstock	Somerset	Pt 2 Ch 4
Redruth	Cornwall	Pt 2 Ch 2
Roadford Reservoir	Devon	Pt 2 Ch 2
Robin Hood's Bay	N. Yorkshire	Pt 2 Ch 8
Rosyth	Fifeshire	Pt 3 Ch 3
Saxilby	Lincolnshire	Pt 2 Ch 7
Scarborough *	N. Yorkshire	Pt 2 Ch 7
Scremerston	Northumberland	Pt 2 Ch 9
Scunthorpe *	N. Lincolnshire	Pt 2 Ch 7
Seahouses	Northumberland	Pt 2 Ch 9
Sedgefield	Co. Durham	Pt 2 Ch 8
Shillbottle	Northumberland	Pt 2 Ch 8
Shrivenham	Oxfordshire	Pt 2 Ch 5

Silverstone	Northants	Pt 2 Ch 5
South Ferriby	N. Lincolnshire	Pt 2 Ch 7
St Abbs	Berwickshire	Pt 3 Ch 2
St Michael's Mount	Cornwall	Pt 2 Ch 2
Staithes	N. Yorkshire	Pt 2 Ch 8
Stockton-on-Tees	Co. Durham	Pt 2 Ch 8
Stolford	Somerset	Pt 2 Ch 3
Stonehaven	Aberdeenshire	Pt 3 Ch 4
Stow	Lincolnshire	Pt 2 Ch 7
Street	Somerset	Pt 2 Ch 4
Swindon *	Wiltshire	Pt 2 Ch 5
Tain	Ross-shire	Pt 3 Ch 6
Taunton *	Somerset	Pt 2 Ch 3
Tay Railway Bridge	Tayside / Fife	Pt 3 Ch 4
Tay Road Bridge	Tayside / Fife	Pt 3 Ch 4
Thurso *	Caithness	Pt 3 Ch 7
Towcester	Northants	Pt 2 Ch 5
Truro *	Cornwall	Pt 2 Ch 2
Turriff	Aberdeenshire	Pt 3 Ch 5
Tweedmouth	Northumberland	Pt 2 Ch 9
Waddington RAF	Lincolnshire	Pt 2 Ch 6
Wadebridge	Cornwall	Pt 2 Ch 3
Waltham-on-Wolds	Leicestershire	Pt 2 Ch 6
Wellington	Somerset	Pt 2 Ch 3
Wells *	Somerset	Pt 2 Ch 4
Whitby	N. Yorkshire	Pt 2 Ch 8
Wick *	Caithness	Pt 3 Ch 6
Winteringham	N. Lincolnshire	Pt 2 Ch 7
Winterton	N. Lincolnshire	Pt 2 Ch 7
Wootton Bassett	Wiltshire	Pt 2 Ch 4

An asterisk * after a city or town's name indicates places visited between bus journeys